SCATTERED MUSICS

SCATTERED MUSICS

Edited by Martha I. Chew Sánchez
and David Henderson

University Press of Mississippi • Jackson

The University Press of Mississippi is the scholarly publishing agency of
the Mississippi Institutions of Higher Learning: Alcorn State University,
Delta State University, Jackson State University, Mississippi State University,
Mississippi University for Women, Mississippi Valley State University,
University of Mississippi, and University of Southern Mississippi.

www.upress.state.ms.us

Designed by Peter D. Halverson

The University Press of Mississippi is a member
of the Association of University Presses.

Copyright © 2021 by University Press of Mississippi

All rights reserved

First printing 2021

∞

Library of Congress Cataloging-in-Publication Data

Names: Chew Sánchez, Martha I., 1969– editor. | Henderson, David, 1968– editor.
Title: Scattered musics / Martha I. Chew Sánchez, David Henderson.
Description: Jackson: University Press of Mississippi, 2021. | Includes bibliographical references and index.
Identifiers: LCCN 2020034662 (print) | LCCN 2020034663 (ebook) | ISBN 978-1-4968-3236-8 (hardback) | ISBN 978-1-4968-3235-1 (trade paperback) | ISBN 978-1-4968-3237-5 (epub) | ISBN 978-1-4968-3238-2 (epub) | ISBN 978-1-4968-3239-9 (pdf) | ISBN 978-1-4968-3240-5 (pdf)
Subjects: LCSH: Music—Social aspects. | Music—History and criticism. | Immigrants—Music—History and criticism. | Emigration and immigration—Songs and music—History and criticism.
Classification: LCC ML3916 .S47 2021 (print) | LCC ML3916 (ebook) | DDC 780.9—dc23
LC record available at https://lccn.loc.gov/2020034662
LC ebook record available at https://lccn.loc.gov/2020034663

British Library Cataloging-in-Publication Data available

CONTENTS

VII   Introduction
        DAVID HENDERSON

3   Chapter 1: "An Ireland over There"?
      Dance Halls and Traditional Music in the Irish Diaspora, 1945–70
      SARA S. GOEK

24   Chapter 2: *Cumbias y Rebajadas*:
       Aurality, Race, and Class in Monterrey's "Colombia" Culture
       JUAN DAVID RUBIO RESTREPO

57   Chapter 3: Cubatón's Transnational Creolizations
       WILLIAM GARCÍA-MEDINA

73   Chapter 4: Letter to Gautam Gupta
       EYVIND KANG

90   Chapter 5: Connecting Identity:
       The Rasta Reggae Diaspora in Columbus, Ohio
       IVY CHEVERS

109   Chapter 6: Michie Mee:
       Rap Music, Cultural Representations, Identity, and the
       Caribbean Diaspora in Toronto
       ATHENA ELAFROS

131   Chapter 7: *Journey to Jah*:
       The Discourse of Internationalization in German
       Reggae and Dancehall Media
       BENJAMIN BURKHART

149   Chapter 8: "We're Called Neck, and We Play
       Psycho-Ceilídh—It Goes Something Like This..."
       GARETH DYLAN SMITH

166 Chapter 9: Reworking the *Brasilidade* Narrative: *Dekassegui, Música Sertaneja,* and the Performance of Identity in the Japanese Brazilian Expatriate Community
JUNKO OBA

189 Chapter 10: *La Música Ranchera* in the Reconfiguration of *Hispanismo* and *Mexicanidad* in Musical Exchanges between Spain and Mexico
MARTHA I. CHEW SÁNCHEZ

218 Chapter 11: British Asian Culture and Its Margins in East London
NILANJANA BHATTACHARJYA

237 About the Authors

240 Index

INTRODUCTION

DAVID HENDERSON

This book is about the musics that migrant and diaspora populations are inspired to make. Its title is meant to restore to our word *diaspora* more of the meaning of the Greek word, διασπορά, which expresses the action of vigorously scattering apart. What remains when people have been scattered apart is a strong urge to gather together, to collect. In this volume, we show how people use sound to pull themselves across long distances to the places they've left behind. But also evident throughout is how people use sound to anchor themselves in the places they are now. And, frequently, people use sound to draw in other places as well—places they've been to, places they've heard of, places they've only imagined.

Sound can be a powerful index of place. Think of the sound of Merle Haggard's voice, and how it takes us somewhere. Listen to the steel drum in Blondie's 1980 reggae cover "The Tide Is High," and how a bit of tropical moisture blows through the track at that moment. Hear how mariachi singer Nydia Rojas's 1996 version of that song, "La número uno," takes us someplace else entirely. And it is not just the sound of music, of course: the sound of gentle waves invites us to imagine relaxing on a beach, while the sound of rush-hour traffic might make us wish we could be relaxing on a beach. There is often an element of time travel involved as well: the sound of a 78 rpm record reminds us of the time from which it came, and the sound of an Arp synthesizer might transport us across memory to when we first heard such a sound. So it should be no surprise that for people who feel the pull of multiple places, music would be one of the most powerful ways of connecting, reconnecting, and even disconnecting when necessary.

One of the surprises that emerged in working on this book is how frequently displacement itself becomes a form of pleasure, a means of converting loss into gain. The news of recent years is packed with images and sounds of loss, separation, suffering, death: rickety boats capsizing in the Mediterranean, Kurds being kept out of Australia and held in detention in Papua New Guinea, barbed-wire fences being erected in Hungary to discourage refugees, Rohingya fleeing across the border into Bangladesh, parents being separated from their children as they attempt to cross into the United States from Mexico. Our experience of the suffering of migrants is so extensive that sometimes it is hard even to imagine that there is any room for pleasure, for comfort, for joy in exile. Yet there it is: Irish immigrants meeting and falling in love at the Dudley Street Opera House in Boston, a Gambian reggae enthusiast sharing his love of the music with customers at Roots Records in Columbus, *Nikkey* Brazilians dancing in each other's arms to *música sertaneja* in Tokyo.

But this is rarely an undiluted pleasure. Both Junko Oba, in her chapter focusing on *música sertaneja* singer Joe Hirata, and Gareth Dylan Smith, in his chapter focusing on psycho-ceilídh singer Leeson O'Keeffe, describe the bittersweet experience of being never fully home, never fully away. And Sara Goek, writing about Irish dance halls in the diaspora in the middle of the twentieth century, and Nilanjana Bhattacharjya, writing about British spaces for Bangladeshi performance in the late 1990s, make clear that while these spaces provided opportunities of different sorts, they were also fraught with tensions.

In writing about the musics of different diasporas, the contributors to this volume have worked to find words that open themselves up to the experience of being in two or more places at once. The power of "elsewhere" to infect and inflect the here and now is evident especially in the chapters by Athena Elafros on rap music in Toronto and Juan David Rubio Restrepo on *cumbia* in Monterrey. Bridges do literal and figurative duty connecting places: the Puente de Papa bridge of Rubio's chapter looks very different from the one in Ivy Chevers's chapter as she "examines the historical events and people that bridge the African diaspora in Ohio, Jamaica, and Ethiopia" (91). Not surprisingly, the prefix *trans-* (meaning across, over, beyond, or through, and suggesting a movement from one place to another) figures prominently, a kind of perpetual shuttle service between both real and imagined locations. "Transnational": William García-Medina explores the term extensively in his chapter on *cubatón*, and Martha Chew Sánchez uses the term as well to help understand how *música ranchera*, one of the most Mexican of Mexican musics, was shaped by transnational voices. "Transculturality": in his chapter on reggae and dancehall in Germany, Benjamin Burkhart elaborates on how one must start from the observation that, as he puts it, "modern cultures should be conceived of as deeply interwoven" (133). And composer Eyvind Kang, writing about jazz musician Ornette Coleman's Harmolodics, brings the transmodern into conversation with more localized actions like transduction, translation, and transposition.

We invite you to read the chapters in the order presented. We've thought carefully about the order of performance, about how both similarities of approach and contrasts of style from chapter to chapter would work on an audience. Rather than group the chapters into sections, we've kept them as a more fluid whole, with themes sounded in early chapters echoed later in the book. But each chapter also stands on its own, and they could be read in whatever order desired. We've made a point to gather together scholars who would bring different perspectives to the study of diasporic musics: collected here is the work of ethnomusicologists, sociologists, historians, and artists.

While place serves as essential background throughout this book, motivating and shaping musical activity, Sara Goek puts place in the foreground in our first chapter, focusing on the Irish dance halls of Boston, New York City, and London following World War II. Oral histories animate her work, and her interviews with musicians in Ireland, and those in the UK and the United States, show that dance halls emerged not just in the context of growing immigrant populations but in the midst of larger patterns of musical and social change. A compelling insight here is that dance halls functioned as both centers and margins, so to speak—as both hubs for their Irish communities and as liminal spaces in which a gradual shift from one form of identity (Irish) to another (Irish British, Irish American) was only to be expected. Unlike the notion of a liminal phase developed in anthropology by van Gennep and Turner, however, it is almost as though dance halls existed in permanent limbo. Though they were predominantly commercial enterprises, they were also ongoing spaces for the construction and negotiation of Irishness (as well as for simply seeking work opportunities, having a little fun, and making new friends) beyond Ireland's borders—at least until they closed in the face of ongoing musical, social, and economic shifts.

In chapter 2 Juan David Rubio Restrepo reads our title literally, looking at musics rather than musicians that have been scattered. He spins a record of *cumbia* in Monterrey, Mexico. The groove he explores most is that of *cumbia rebajada*, recordings of Colombian cumbia that *sonideros* in Monterrey's *colombia* culture have deliberately slowed down. Rubio narrates a passage by accordionist Alfredo Gutiérrez that has been "watered down" by local sonidero Gabriel Dueñez: "the passing notes he uses so often to beautifully anticipate a good destination, but that in its rebajada guise seem to last for ages, creating a shocking and beautiful dissonance unheard of in this music" (48). While this chapter revolves around sound, Rubio painstakingly maps out a sense of place as well, starting with a drive up the hillside of Loma Larga to meet Dueñez, and proceeding to lay out how different margins and centers continually pull against one another. He sets these tensions atop what some have called *el giro decolonial*, the decolonial turn, showing how the colonial past continues to resonate in the sounds of the present. Or, put the other way, as Rubio does, "The aural opens the door of a silenced past and voices the marginalized" (149).

In "Cubatón's Transnational Creolizations," William García-Medina emphasizes the complexity of the Caribbean, seeing it as a space of multiple points of encounter and multiple historical linkages, and working toward understanding the fluid, overlapping identities of the Hispanic Caribbean. His writing wires *cubatón* into a vast circuit board of economics and embodiment, politics and pleasure, culture and capitalism. Particularly compelling about his approach is his refusal to separate the debates between hip hop and *cubatón* artists in Cuba from wider debates, including those among popular music scholars. He hears, instead, one big messy conversation, and, importantly, helps us find a way to listen both critically and openly.

Eyvind Kang's "Letter to Gautam Gupta" is perhaps more performance than letter, perhaps more philosophical treatise than performance. In writing to a friend about Ornette Coleman's Harmolodics—read in part through the lens of North Indian music theory—Kang effectively performs the way any musician of any diaspora might perform: taking familiarities and unfamiliarities, compatibilities and discrepancies, and pulling them together into a new composite, a composite perfectly suited to one's own distinctive path through the world. Yet it is not only ways of thinking about and creating music that are under scrutiny, but also ways of being in the world; and, in the best philosophical tradition, Kang takes seemingly diverse points of view and strives to find coherence, even unity, within them.

Sitting at the center of this volume is a triptych of chapters on reggae, dancehall, rap, and hip hop—in Canada, the United States, and Germany. All emphasize how both musicians and listeners experience a doubled, or even tripled, sense of place through sound. Even as High Street in Columbus, Ohio, for example, is important in shaping the reggae scene there, Jamaica stands as a beacon, shining through the music as well as through what people have to say about the music. In chapter 5 Ivy Chevers relies primarily on her own interviews in exploring the reggae scene in central Ohio. Having lived in both Jamaica and Ohio, she gives her chapter a personal touch while also grounding it in both historical and ethnographic perspectives on Rasta and reggae in the United States. Athena Elafros, in chapter 6, points to the importance of the interconnections between Canada, the United States, and the Caribbean in the emergence of rap and hip hop in Toronto. Using a wide range of sources, from demographic reports to transcripts of her own interviews, she plots out an intersubjective perspective on how music and identity intertwine, focusing especially on "The First Lady of Toronto Hip Hop," Michie Mee. Elafros's work highlights the important role that diasporic and/or transnational networks of production play within all cultural fields. And in chapter 7, Benjamin Burkhart gives two takes on the reggae and dancehall scene in Germany: one from the pages of *Riddim* magazine, a German publication in circulation since 2001; and the other from a 2014 film, *Journey to Jah*, which featured reggae artists Gentleman (from Germany) and Alborosie (from Italy). This end of the triptych hits upon a point that echoes through all of the chapters in this volume: that some musics bear a strong imprint of their origins, no matter how far they travel, whereas others seem to shake free of their roots as they move across the globe.

Gareth Dylan Smith played drums with Neck, which he describes as a "London Irish punk 'psycho-ceilídh' band" (149). from 2002 to 2016. His chapter on the band draws extensively from his interview with British-born Irish frontman Leeson O'Keeffe in 2012. O'Keeffe comes through loud and clear as a charismatic individual who has thought extensively about the Irish diaspora, his own sense of Ireland as home, and his feelings of belonging and not belonging in London. O'Keeffe's thinking about the Irish diaspora infuses the songs he writes and performs with Neck, and throughout this chapter Smith skillfully balances O'Keeffe's spoken words with his sung lyrics. A particularly powerful point emerges from Smith's countless observations of different audiences from his vantage point behind the drum kit, at the back of the stage: a band like Neck has to appeal to its varied audiences on different levels. Regardless of how overt a band's engagement with questions of diaspora and identity, it still needs to appeal to people who are not part of the diaspora it imagines and creates through song. But music does not often exclude. Indeed, part of music's power is its ability to pull an audience—or at least everyone willing to be pulled—toward a collective sense of shared (e)motion.

Junko Oba's chapter delves further into the fact that, in many diasporic communities, a double displacement is also a double emplacement. In the 1990s, a large number of *Nikkey* Brazilians (Brazilians of Japanese descent) travelled to Japan to become *dekassegui* ("working away from home for money") workers. Oba recounts in particular the story (or, rather, stories) of Joe Akio Hirata, who has had a successful career as a performer of *música sertaneja* (Brazilian country music). To sing *música sertaneja* is to dwell in a characteristically Brazilian sense of loss and displacement, but *Nikkey* Brazilians of course sing about and around their own particular experiences, feeling both out of place and at home in both Brazil and Japan. For singers like Hirata and their audiences, music is a vehicle for shuttling between displacement and emplacement, a medium for thinking about, performing, and living with both.

My coeditor, Martha Chew Sánchez, reminds us in her chapter that notions like *hispanismo* and *mexicanidad*, like other notions of identity, are both "fluid and not so fluid" (189), and she zigzags back and forth between Spain and Mexico in exploring how these terms flowed across and through cultural, political, and economic formations of the twentieth century. Always in the foreground is the *música ranchera*, while she painstakingly fills in the background upon which it emerged and thrived. Chew Sánchez observes that the historical development of *hispanismo* "is far from linear and homogenous, due in part to international asymmetric interdependency, complex circular relationships between the local, national, and global, and the reinvention and reconnection of cultural industries to different markets" (199). Paralleling this powerful observation, she refuses to write in a linear and homogenous fashion; she chooses to explore complex circular relationships by writing in a complex circular way, allowing those relationships to accumulate and gather force over the span of her chapter. To do otherwise would risk oversimplifying, and Chew Sánchez, in her approach, affirms our obligation as scholars and writers not to do so.

In our final chapter, "British Asian Culture and Its Margins in East London," Nilanjana Bhattacharjya opens up questions of how institutions and media create complicated spaces for the presentation and interpretation of difference. Bhattacharjya explores two separate but partially overlapping events from 1999: Arts Worldwide's Bangladesh Festival and the Whitechapel Gallery exhibit *ooo: British Asian Cultural Provocation*. Both provided welcome opportunities for British Bangladeshi musicians to perform, but their music also took on a variety of hues not of their own making. Celebrated under the slogan "Brown is the new Black," their work could alternately be seen as expressions of Bangladeshi, British Bangladeshi, British Asian, British Black, or British identity. Musicians such as State of Bengal and Asian Dub Foundation had to negotiate their way through other people's desires in how to present them, and Bhattacharjya deftly traces her way through a maze of marketing and reporting from the two events.

Scattered Musics joins a growing literature on music and migration. There is rich ethnomusicological work on particular diaspora and migrant populations: for example, Tom Turino's work on the music of the Peruvian Altiplano (1993), Jane Sugarman's work with Prespa Albanians (1997), Kay Kaufman Shelemay's work with Syrian Jews (1998), Carol Silverman's work on Romani music (2012), and Adriana Helbig's *Hip Hop Ukraine* (2014). And historians, sociologists, anthropologists, and others interested in diaspora and migrant populations have also taken music as their focus: for example, Martha Chew Sánchez's own work on corridos (2006), María Elena Cepeda's exploration of US-Colombian identity (2010), Michelle Bigenho's study of Andean music in Japan (2012), Shana Redmond's *Anthem: Social Movements and the Sound of Solidarity in the African Diaspora* (2014), and Alex E. Chávez's *Sounds of Crossing: Music, Migration, and the Aural Poetics of Huapango Arribeño* (2017).

This book is built on the premise that by reading across borders, across disciplines, we begin to see diaspora and migration as the warp to the weft of culture and identity. Diaspora and migrant populations have transformed the musical expressions of their home countries as well as those in their host communities, and the studies collected here show how these transformations are ways of grappling with ever-changing patterns of movement. "Home" and "away" are forever linked, with those who are "away" not just hanging on for dear life to "home," but home being constantly transformed by what (and who) comes back to it from away. Different diasporas, too, hold their homelands in different regards: some communities try to recreate home away from home in musical performances, while some use music to critique and refine their senses of home. Through music, people seek to reconstruct and redefine collective memory and a collective sense of place. Through music, people find a space for play in seeking to understand (diasporic) identity not as a fixed entity, but as an ever-changing relation (to the world around oneself).

BIBLIOGRAPHY

Bigenho, Michelle. 2012. *Intimate Distance: Andean Music in Japan.* Durham, NC: Duke University Press.

Cepeda, María Elena. 2010. *Musical ImagiNation: U.S.-Colombian Identity and the Latin Music Boom.* New York: New York University Press.

Chávez, Alex E. 2017. *Sounds of Crossing: Music, Migration, and the Aural Poetics of Huapango Arribeño.* Durham, NC, and London: Duke University Press.

Chew Sánchez, Martha I. 2006. *Corridos in Migrant Memory.* Albuquerque: University of New Mexico Press.

Helbig, Adriana N. 2014. *Hip Hop Ukraine: Music, Race, and African Migration*. Bloomington and Indianapolis: Indiana University Press.

Redmond, Shana L. 2014. *Anthem: Social Movements and the Sound of Solidarity in the African Diaspora*. New York: New York University Press.

Shelemay, Kay Kaufman. 1998. *Let Jasmine Rain Down: Song and Remembrance among Syrian Jews*. Chicago: University of Chicago Press.

Silverman, Carol. 2012. *Romani Routes: Cultural Politics and Balkan Music in Diaspora*. New York: Oxford University Press.

Sugarman, Jane C. 1997. *Engendering Song: Singing and Subjectivity at Prespa Albanian Weddings*. Chicago: University of Chicago Press.

Turino, Thomas. 1993. *Moving Away from Silence: Music of the Peruvian Altiplano and the Experience of Urban Migration*. Chicago: University of Chicago Press.

SCATTERED MUSICS

1

"AN IRELAND OVER THERE"?

Dance Halls and Traditional Music in the Irish Diaspora, 1945–70

SARA S. GOEK

Over many generations migrants have carried Ireland's traditional music to all corners of the globe, adapting themselves and it to new contexts. Among the Irish populations in British and American cities after World War II, dance halls took primacy as social venues that featured the historically rural music alongside more modern, urban forms. Fiddler Kevin Burke grew up in London's Irish community and reflects:

> There was great music and great dancing, but it wasn't couched in terms of culture, it was a commercial venture—some Irish guy opened a dance hall, put Irish bands in there, attracted an Irish audience, and they were just by definition fostering Irish music and culture. But that wasn't their intention. They wanted to make some money and this was the best way they knew of how to do it—open a dance hall, get some Irish music in there, and it'll attract a bunch of Irish people and they'll pay to get in and I'll make some money. And of course, like anywhere else, the better the music you have or the better setup you have, the more people want to come, so the more people come and the more money made. So a lot of the places that had a great effect in that line of fostering Irish culture didn't have that as their intention. But it happened anyway, I think.[1]

Despite their commercial function, dance halls became informal community centers that figured prominently in migrants' lives. The fact that so many ethnic venues thrived in the postwar era reflected the recognition that participation in Irish cultural practice—in this case, music and dance—served as a mechanism of adjustment in an unfamiliar milieu. By dancing to Irish music while surrounded by familiar Irish voices and faces, migrants enacted a connection to "home" (Collins 2010; Morrison 2001). It helped them displace feelings of marginalization, while the adapted settings, style, and format of the music also evinced their new situation and needs.

This chapter draws on original and archival oral histories collected from traditional musicians who left Ireland for the United States and Great Britain between 1945 and 1970. They were part of a postwar exodus of over 665,000 people, 22.5 percent of the Irish population in 1945 (CSO 2007; NESC 1991, 55).[2] The majority were young and from rural areas, particularly from Ireland's western counties where traditional culture remained strongest. As immigrants they tended to settle in ethnic enclaves in urban areas. As the public face of their culture, musicians and performers found themselves at the front lines of the conflict between varying conceptions of Irishness across the diaspora. Their narratives reflect how they negotiated the disparities. However, the process was not uniform, and comparative historical analysis of Irish music in three cities—London, New York, and Boston—shows that while similarities existed in the nature of musical performances, local trends resulted in different experiences over time. Comparison mitigates the otherwise homogenizing effects of diaspora studies (Kenny 2003). Historical and cultural analysis of Irish music in dance halls serves as a case study that highlights the symbiotic relationship between place and diasporic identities. This chapter argues that the apparent tension between old roots and new in musical practices reveals how Irish identity was negotiated and contested, interpreted and performed. Both cohesion and diversity emerged from the mix.

IRISH TRADITIONS

The background of the postwar migrant generation—the society they left and the cultural traditions they took with them—is crucial to understanding their experiences in the diaspora. They came of age in Ireland between 1930 and 1960, an era of economic stagnation. Singer Liam Clancy recalls, "my memories of those years are the sizzling of wet turf, wet logs, constant rain, depression, everybody leaving, no work, ration books, the slow reemergence."[3] While historians have argued against this dreary characterization, asserting instead that the era laid the foundation for changes to come (Fallon 1998; Kennedy 1989), any economic merit it possessed failed to stem the flow of the nation's children overseas.

Despite the harsh environment, oral histories and memoirs also emphasize positive values associated with strong social networks and culture. In rural Ireland, social gatherings with music, dance, song, and storytelling took place for any and all occasions: christenings, weddings, harvests, charitable benefits, religious holidays, or simply social evenings during long winter nights. Friends, relatives, and neighbors would gather in a house with space for dancing on the kitchen flagstones or at a barn or crossroads. Fiddle player Junior Crehan from County Clare recalls, "The country house was the center of all social activity in those days. It was not only a place of entertainment, it was also a school where the traditions of music-making, story-telling and dancing were passed on from one generation to the next" (1977, 72). Though the interviewees in this study come from all parts of Ireland, those from rural areas describe similar patterns of socializing (Goek 2015, 68–71). Fiddle player Connie O'Connell recalls attending house dances with his mother, who played melodeon:

> In where I come from, Cill na Martra [near Ballyvourney, Co. Cork], there was a tradition of house dances when I was young, when I was very young, and my mother used to play for these house dances. You'd go into the kitchen and you'd sit down and you'd play for sets. Probably there'd be only room for one set on the floor, just barely on the floor of a kitchen; farmhouses were bigger. They danced sets and I was listening to this music and watching them dance sets as well, as just a kid sitting in the corner until a certain hour of the night, then probably be taken home or whatever. I'd say the dancing went on much later. They used to have occasions such as threshings, things like that, and weddings of course. Weddings were in the houses at that time as well, not in hotels like they are nowadays. They'd be dancing mainly sets and the music for those. I was listening to it as a kid so I think it is from there it grew in me that I started playing music.[4]

Like Crehan, he refers to the importance of these gatherings for musical transmission across generations, repeatedly referencing his vantage point "as just a kid sitting in the corner." Through house dances, along with other types of informal music making, musicians learned their trade—the tunes and local inflections that define their repertoire. This supports Crehan's statement that the country house served not only as a social venue but also as a "school" of the tradition.

However, these events somewhat inadvertently fell under scrutiny in the early years of the Irish Free State (established 1922). A fear of "jazz" (a catchall term used for all modern dancing) and its perceived immoralities resulted in a movement to regulate dancing (Duffy 2009; Finnane 2001; Ó hAllmhuráin 2016, 108–9; Smyth 1993). In response, the government established the Carrigan Committee in 1930–31 to inquire into the moral state of the country. The subsequent Public Dance Halls Act of 1935 stipulated that all public dances must have a license, which only a person of "good character" could obtain from a district justice. Failure to comply could result in prosecution. Though intended to apply to unlicensed dance halls rather than house dances, many parish priests (often colluding with the local police) took matters into their own hands and "misapplied" it in an inconsistent fashion (Ó hAllmhuráin 2005, 11–13). Flute player Kevin Henry recalls being pulled by the ear out of an "illegal" dance at the age of eight (ca. 1937) and the detrimental effect such measures had on informal charitable fundraisers in his community.[5] The clergy also realized that holding dances in parish halls would enable them to both collect an entry fee and supervise the proceedings. Consequently, in the late 1930s a dance hall "building boom" took place (Ó hAllmhuráin 2005, 17).

This development is relevant to music in the diaspora because it signaled a parallel shift from private to public spaces occurring on both sides of the Atlantic. That shift affected styles of music and dancing. Country house dances had featured set dancing, often to the tune of a single musician. In the parish halls the clergy promoted what became known as céilí dances and, to suit the larger venues, céilí bands. Set dancing varies across Ireland, but it is characterized by loose body posture and footwork, with between one and four couples dancing a series of figures. In céilí dancing, by contrast, dancers hold their bodies more rigidly and the dances are usually done in bigger groups. The céilí itself is a product of the diaspora: the Gaelic League developed the standardized and formalized dances to suit large crowds and venues in London in the 1890s (Cullinane 1994, 197). Parish dances in the 1950s featured céilí standards such as the "Siege of Ennis" as well as waltzes, polkas, quicksteps, and foxtrots.[6] Céilí bands—a designation also first used in London—consist of five to ten musicians, with melody instruments playing in unison accompanied by piano and drums (Ó hAllmhuráin 2016, 166). The format was also subject to standardization: *Comhaltas Ceoltóirí Éireann* [Irish Musicians' Association], founded in 1951, started an annual traditional music competition, the All-Ireland *Fleadh Cheoil*, which from its inception had a category for céilí bands.[7] The change in musical forms that emerged with dance halls thus resulted from the intersection of political, religious, and cultural structures. While country house dances continued to take place, these external factors shaped traditional music and the perceptions of it that migrants took with them when they left Ireland.

DANCING IN THE DIASPORA

In the United States and Great Britain, dance halls had established themselves as popular commercial leisure venues in the first decades of the twentieth century, furthered by the introduction of radio, records, and jazz. Ethnic dance halls grew with them (McBee 2000; Moloney 1992, 1998). After World War II they continued to function as one of the most important social institutions in the Irish migrant community in both Britain and America: you were sure to meet someone you knew from home, someone who knew where you could get a job, someone who could find you lodgings, or even a nice young man or woman to court (Delaney 2007, 170–71; Goek 2015, 124–35, 182–89). Away from the watchful eyes of parents or parish priests, the widespread adoption of this form of leisure highlights ways women in particular experienced "greater economic independence and personal freedom" outside Ireland (Sheridan 2012, 96). As one woman recalled, "Dance Halls [sic] were the main way of meeting people, and most Irish people met their future husband or wife there, and made many friends too."[8] A scattered population drew together in these ethnic venues. Music, adapted to a modern urban setting, served as a "bonding mechanism," but one with a "wider social and cultural role" (Lee and Casey 2006, 29; Ní Fhuartháin 1993, 132). As the backdrop for these functions, dance halls featured a hybrid mix of music styles, something between the old world and the new. They became both cultural centers and liminal spaces. While they served to cement the Irish community, they simultaneously separated it from the wider society, occupying a position between the two.

Within the dance halls, patrons were predominantly (though not exclusively) Irish-born or second-generation. The halls were often located in Irish-dominated neighborhoods. In Boston all five main dance halls in the 1950s were situated in Dudley Square in Roxbury, an Irish area, and also near the terminus for the city's tram lines, so anyone living or working anywhere in the city could get there. In London and New York the halls had a wider geographical spread, as did those cities' Irish populations. In London at least twenty may have existed at any one time in the postwar era (more than twice as many as in Boston or New York).[9] Most dance halls did not serve alcohol until at least the midsixties, but a pub was never far away, and many men stopped there before the dance. Migrants would hardly have expected a replica of what they knew at home, but the halls offered enough of the familiar (in music, dancing, and patrons) to make them feel comfortable, and enough that differed (a cosmopolitan aura and selection of popular British and American music and dances) for them to feel part of the lifestyle of the urban centers. Music and dancing gave migrants a way to connect to their origins while adopting new identities, neither wholly Irish nor American or British, but emerging out of both.

Commercial Irish dance halls in both Britain and America usually offered some combination of "modern" (popular) music and traditional music.[10] This took one of three forms. In the first, a mixed or hybrid group of musicians (saxophones, brass, fiddles, accordions, etc.) needed to play both genres. The traditional musicians who could read music or learned to play popular modern dances would alternate and the musicians from the "modern" side of things would often play the Irish tunes from written notation. These groups often bore the name of "orchestras" and were more common from the 1920s through World War II.

The early 1950s witnessed the separation of musical performance into modern and céilí genres as the influx of new migrants from rural Ireland brought associated attitudes and preferences, influencing prevailing practices. In the second form, two separate bands took turns on stage, with perhaps forty minutes of modern music, and then twenty minutes of traditional music provided by a smaller group, usually headed by an accordion player, while the modern band took a break. Jerry Lynch describes playing accordion in the Red Mill dance hall in New York under this setup in the early sixties: "it was going for three and four nights a week and it turned out that I played in that, just the traditional music. There was a jazz band playing there and every half an hour or three-quarters of an hour they took a break and I played for twenty minutes, three of us, piano accordion, myself, and a drum."[11] Union regulations may also have influenced the adoption of this format in the United States (Goek 2015, 125–26).

In the third form, the larger halls had separate rooms, with one featuring predominantly modern music and the other featuring Irish music and céilí dancing. Customers paid one entry fee and could then choose their preferred style or alternate between them. The two latter practices predominated in the postwar era; the one adopted in a particular venue often depended on its size. In this way, the owners or managers attempted to offer something for everyone. Their methods seem to have worked, as the dance halls feature prominently in the memories of many migrants in this period.

Traditional musicians who played in the dance halls, even those who had played with céilí bands in Ireland, found the adjustment from small parish halls and rural farmhouse kitchens challenging.[12] Fiddle player Larry Reynolds recalls that he first went to one of the Irish dance halls in Boston's

Dudley Square on the night he arrived from Ahascragh, Co. Galway, in 1953. However, he found the sound of the music different from what he was accustomed to and says, "I didn't care for it, to be honest with you, when I came here. It took me a while to acquire a taste for it. It was different than what we had listened to at home, you know."[13] Similarly, Jerry Lynch says that on his arrival in New York in 1959, "we played a lot of music and I enjoyed it but it was different altogether, a different scene in New York, the dance halls. It was a different feeling when you were over there first but then you got used to it, you acclimatized."[14] This "acclimatizing" forms the essence of the adoption or modification of a new identity.

Reynolds and Lynch's views also reflect the general feelings toward emigration. Most Irish migrants came from rural areas and had traveled little prior to their departure, so many shared stories of adjustment to all the aspects of their new lives, from understanding the differences in the English spoken to navigating the subway and working by the clock. Despite their reservations about the differences, those musicians who did find opportunities to play expressed gratitude for that and managed to adapt to the new urban feel and setting.

The social networks of friendship, kinship, and employment that sustained Irish migrants developed around these music venues and played an important, if unintentional role, in sustaining ethnic culture. Commercial dance halls intended to provide entertainment and leisure, but among the Irish they filled a multitude of additional roles, aiding adjustment to life abroad. Their owners did not necessarily set out with this purpose in mind, but in the context of large-scale postwar migration they found themselves running venues that inadvertently contributed to the development of an Irish community and identity.

DIASPORIC DIVERSITY

Despite the similarities in function and form among Irish dance halls in Britain and the United States, significant differences existed in how they evolved over time, reflecting the communities they served. While America had been the preferred destination of Irish migrants from the nineteenth century, immigration restrictions and the cost of travel meant that fewer young, postwar migrants went there and the Irish-born US population steadily aged and declined (Kenny 2000, 225–28). Those who did enter the United States continued to favor urban centers, particularly in the Northeast, as they had in the nineteenth century. By the 1930s the migrant flow shifted more toward Britain, and by the 1950s it became the destination for approximately 80 percent of Irish migrants (Delaney 2002, 10). The ease of travel and the burgeoning postwar economy attracted these new arrivals, though they would also encounter housing shortages and discrimination. Most settled in the southeast of England, particularly in London. These demographic patterns shaped the nature of the music scenes in London, New York, and Boston.

London

The large number of Irish migrants and the entrepreneurship of the pub and dance hall owners combined to make London a mecca for Irish music and musicians. Jimmy Ó Ceannabháin recalls that by the time he lived there in the late 1960s, "London was the place for the music. There was dance halls there of the best that time and fine young women. And the pubs were good . . . music coming out every door and I'm talking now music that you'd listen to seven days a week, twenty-four hours a day." While highlighting the lively atmosphere and excellent quality of the music, he also acknowledges that the conditions in Britain pushed the music into these public spaces: "when you were living in England they were small places and you couldn't play music [at home]."[15] Bomb damage from World War II and a population boom following demobilization created a housing crisis (Stevenson 1991, 97–98). With council houses in short supply and English-born people given preferential treatment, migrants found themselves forced to turn to the private sector, where they faced dilapidated and overcrowded conditions and extortionist landlords in a market that favored owners over tenants. While much socializing and music making in Ireland had taken place in private homes, in England 74 percent of the Irish lived in private rented accommodation (Corbally 2009, 113) and its poor quality led them to seek alternate spaces for leisure.

The largest and most famous of the Irish dance halls in postwar England was the Galtymore in Cricklewood, London, which opened in 1952 and had a record attendance of nearly 7,000 paying customers one night in the 1960s (McGreevy 2008). Packie Browne, a singer from Ballyduff, Co. Kerry, who lived in England for eighteen years, emphasizes how it was a normal part of life of the Irish population in the city when he says, "I went to the Galtymore on Saturday nights. I done [sic] the usual things that most Irish people do."[16] At its height all the major Irish showbands, céilí bands, and great individual musicians and singers played there. It had the added attraction of a setup that offered a mix of styles of music, with customers paying a single-entry fee for

Paddy Fahey, Cork Association New Year's Eve celebration at the Galtymore, London, ca. 1964. © Brent Museum and Archives.

two separate dance floors, one featuring modern music and the other with a resident céilí band. In the former, showbands played covers of hits and popular Irish singers such as Bridie Gallagher and Delia Murphy offered more sentimental fare. Nothing too modern, though: it prominently displayed a sign reading "jiving strictly prohibited"![17] Kevin McDermott (n.d.) writes, "in many of the Irish halls in the fifties, jiving or jitterbugging was not allowed and there were notices to that effect stuck on the walls. Rock and Roll was gaining popularity at the time but many of the Irish halls stuck to the 'no jiving rules' with a certain amount of rigidity." This illustrates tensions between international popular culture and Irishness, with the Galtymore seeking to promote a "respectable" and moral image, evident in the selection of music as well as the dress and behavior of the musicians and patrons.

While catering to different tastes under the unifying banner of ethnicity, this setup also reflected divisions within the Irish population. Reg Hall, a longtime participant in the London Irish music scene and later its historian, observes:

> One [side] was céilí, which obviously was a Gaelic League repertory but it was West-of-Ireland-ized.... So there would be the dance hall, which would be the céilí dance hall, and of course as more West-of-Ireland fellows came over and girls came over, it became much more the old rural way of dancing. In the other hall was the modern dancing where you'd do the quickstep, foxtrot, perhaps even the tango or the samba or something like that.... These divisions.[18]

The "West-of-Ireland fellows" faced the intra-ethnic stereotype of "being a bit 'culchie,' a bit uncouth," of a lower social stratum. As one woman said, "we may have been totally wrong, but we were looking for something a little bit more refined" (quoted in Dunne 2003, 37–38). She and her compatriots chose where they danced based on that perception. The Galtymore, by virtue of its commercial focus, size, and popularity, could accommodate "these divisions" under one roof. In other circumstances, differences between venues mirrored the same divide. Where the migrants danced or which side of the wall they danced on illustrates the persistent class distinctions in interpretations of Irish identity.

New York City

By the postwar era, New York City's "golden age" of Irish music—fueled by record companies and the popularity of Tin Pan Alley songs between 1900 and 1940—had passed. Beginning in the 1940s record companies went increasingly mainstream, catering to mass audiences rather than niche markets, while Irish immigration to the United States also declined. New York City's Irish-born population, while comparable to London's in numerical terms in the 1950s, differed in character, being older and more dispersed. East Galway flute player Mike Rafferty recalls, on arriving in New York in 1949:

> Music was slack. I thought everything was gone. Music was slack at that time, yeah. There was nobody to play with. There was one fellow, he came over two months ahead of me, but he was living in the city and I was living actually in Purchase, New York. And then, of course, I moved to New Jersey

and he was living in New York and transportation was rough at that time . . . and then I got married in 1953 and then you're raising a family and you had to concentrate on work and music, I hadn't played for a long time."[19]

Another East Galway flute player, Jack Coen, arrived in the Bronx the same year and corroborates this view on the difficulty of finding music or other musicians: "I never could seem to get in touch with any musicians, good or bad. Then I went to work out in Jersey for a year, a year and a half, and there was no Irish music out there at all, actually, good or bad. Then I moved back into the Bronx again, and there was a good five or six years that I hardly played at all, good or bad."[20] Unlike the positive views of the vibrant Irish music scene in London, he points to a perceived lack of traditional music of any quality.

Coen also suggests that, although in retrospect many excellent musicians lived around the city, perhaps most music was played in private homes as opposed to public venues. Kerry singer and publican Jimmy O'Brien, who lived in New York between 1956 and 1961, supports that conclusion: "House parties were great. There'd be fellows after arriving out, a new recruit, and they'd be trying to boost you up a bit. Then there'd be fellows leaving and coming home. . . . 'Twas like the house parties I told you about would be in the wintertime in the country places like Sliabh Luachra and all over, it wasn't any different."[21] The preference for private socializing may have reflected the existence of an established Irish and Irish American homeowning population. No doubt the property market, less crunched than its equivalent in London, partly enabled and influenced this trend. Jimmy's direct comparison between house parties in Kerry and New York also highlights a sense of continuity in the musical tradition despite the rural to urban shift.

By the end of the 1950s, more Irish dance halls had opened, and by the early 1960s "you had about nine dance halls that were going full-swing, bands and céilí units in every one of them."[22] These included the Jaeger House on the Upper East Side and the City Center Ballroom on the West Side, both featuring a mixture of musical genres (Miller 1996, 492–94; Ó hAllmhuráin 2009, 15). In these venues audience preferences determined the privileging of American popular music over Irish traditional. Accordion player Joe Madden arrived in New York from east Galway in 1959; he suggests that, in the interests of commercial viability, he let the audience dictate the style he played: "What we tried to do was we had gigs going down in the hotels in the city now, we'll say, where you had half Americans [and] half Irish, there was no way in hell that you could go in and play traditional music all night, you had to play the Irish American music too, otherwise they didn't want you."[23] He implies that Irish Americans showed a marked preference for American music, but in dance halls where the Irish-born predominated, modern music also took precedence, suggesting it had less to do with place of upbringing than associations. Louis Quinn, who had lived in New York since the 1930s, felt that the postwar generation cared little for traditional music: "the majority of the Irish emigrants coming out here, you know, wanted no part of it, they didn't want to hear traditional music. It was bog music, it was coming from the mountains, who wanted to associate themselves with that, you know? A lot of the Irish lads were ashamed to be associated with either the playing of traditional music or listening to it or dancing to it."[24] As in Britain, traditional music carried negative associations because of its origins among Ireland's rural working classes, a background that upwardly mobile migrants wanted to move beyond (Miller 1996, 498). A combination of these factors produced a markedly different sound in dance halls in the United States compared to their counterparts in Ireland.

Boston

While New York seemed to have passed its heyday by the 1950s, the Boston Irish music scene reached its apogee. Though in absolute numbers the city and its Irish community were much smaller, in 1960 nearly 10 percent of the total population of Boston was Irish-born.[25] Social life centered on a geographical focal point: "Dudley Street was a mecca of music and it was a place where there was at least 2,000 people any given night, anywhere from 1,500 to 2,000 people at the various dance halls and of course they were coming together meeting and marrying and all this stuff. It was a mecca for music and entertainment and also camaraderie."[26] This highlights the theme of community: not only did the halls provide entertainment and social life, but through them people made connections to others across the city. Also nearby was the O'Byrne DeWitt House of Irish Music, a music shop and travel agency opened in 1926 by Justus O'Byrne DeWitt, the son of Leitrim native Ellen O'Byrne DeWitt, who had run a similar operation in New York City (Gedutis 2004, 149–58; Moloney 1982, 90; Ní Fhuartháin 1993).

As elsewhere, the dance halls in Boston provided a mixture of musical styles. Sometimes musicians accustomed to different genres played together in a mixed group and sometimes in different rooms in the same building. Accordion player Jack Conroy says of one of the halls: "The Hibernian building had three floors: you had the grand ballroom up on the top floor, the

Johnny Bresnahan accompanied by J. Maloney on banjo with unidentified woman on piano, Hibernian Hall, 1955. Contributed by Roger Bresnahan. Courtesy of the University Archives and Special Collections Department, Joseph P. Healey Library, University of Massachusetts Boston, MA. Memories Road Show collection.

second floor had a range of smaller halls, and they had very small halls down on the first floor," and bands playing different musical styles and selections would be on each floor.[27] In addition to these internal distinctions, each hall tended to have a following from a certain area: for example, the Dudley Street Opera House drew a Kerry crowd; the Winslow Hall had a following from Connaught; and the Rose Croix drew in a lot of Scots and Canadians as well as Irish.[28] As in the other cities, the music, geography, and structure of these venues illustrates the process of adaptation of the migrants, the traditions they brought with them, and the urban environment, as the modern-style dance hall became the center of Irish cultural and social life.

DECLINE

All golden ages come to an end, and over time the dance halls gradually lost their allure and their audience. In Boston, many factors influenced the decline of dancing in Dudley Square. They were in part commercial: the New State Ballroom opened on the other side of the city and more pubs introduced music and dancing. Demographic aspects perhaps had greater significance: immigration from Ireland slowed; the postwar generation married and started having families, spending less time out dancing; and the Irish moved out to the suburbs, while the neighborhood of Roxbury developed an African American majority. Despite the gradual nature of these trends, the end seemed to take the Irish community by surprise. During unrest in the area related to the racial tensions in 1968, Mickey Connolly was playing in the Intercolonial when an armed man entered and told them to get out. He said that afterward, "we never went back to Dudley Street. A week after, there were bars on the doors. That was the end of Roxbury. The night they rioted there, that was the last night we played there" (quoted in Gedutis 2004, 197). Some performers whose musical lives centered on the dance halls felt abandoned by these changes. In the most extreme case, accordion prodigy Joe Derrane gave up Irish music almost entirely until his "rediscovery" in the 1990s (Alarik 2000).

In New York the decline has a less dramatic status in collective memory; the halls simply "started to fade."[29] A number of musicians attributed this to the reduction in levels of Irish immigration by the 1960s.[30] The decade also witnessed a transformation in musical tastes, with decreasing popularity of ballroom dances and the rise of the Beatles. In American cities the dance halls "fizzled out," forcing musicians to find alternative outlets for their energies.[31]

In London, too, the number of Irish dance halls gradually declined, but the most tenacious, the Galtymore, held on until 2008, attesting to the larger size and strength of the postwar migrant generation there. Its closure marked the end of an era. The remnants of the postwar cohort could no longer sustain such a commercial venue, while their younger counterparts found other social outlets.

Historian Kathleen Neils Conzen argues that "the basis for ethnic identity itself may change over time, with ethnicity becoming 'desocialized' as the ethnic group loses its structural foundations—its neighborhoods and organizational networks—and becomes transmuted into something more cultural and symbolic" (1979, 612). For communities in the Irish diaspora, this can help explain the changes of the postwar era: over time, expressions of Irish ethnic identity diversified and evolved in tandem with the historical forces that shaped them.

Examining Irish music and dancing in a comparative context highlights not only similarities but also many differences resulting from specific local, geographical, and demographic circumstances and the "complementary tensions of tradition and accommodation" (Rogers and O'Brien 2009, 6). While in all three cities dance halls acted as liminal spaces where migrants adjusted to their new lives and negotiated new identities, the nature of both the ethnic and host communities shaped their experiences.

CONCLUSION

Not all migrants found what they imagined and none adapted perfectly. There was no single typical experience, and some even chose to reject their Irish identity. Liam Clancy, though associated with the Irish folk song tradition, consciously distinguished himself from his contemporaries. He arrived in New York in January 1956, and later reflected:

> Of course my arrival here was so totally different even from the people who arrived in their droves from Ireland at the time.... They would've gone to one of the Irish ghettos—Yonkers or the Bronx or far Rockaway or whatever. And they would never have moved out of those areas. You wouldn't hear anything but an Irish accent. They had their dance halls. They tried to meet someone, preferably from their hometown, if not from their home county, marry them, and continue that blinkered ghetto mentality. I was brought here by a Guggenheim, brought up to see her uncle's museum.... It was very different, we were a very different type of immigrant from the people who joined the mass exodus.[32]

"Blinkered ghetto mentality" is hardly a complimentary phrase. He associates "*their* dance halls" with the mono-ethnic "ghetto" that he avoided in favor of the bohemian folk clubs of Greenwich Village. While the songs he and his brothers sang came from their rural Irish roots, the arrangements and choreography of their performances owe much more to the urban folk revival.

For those who did patronize the dance halls in Britain and America, they found there a means of alleviating the initial culture shock and sense of dislocation resulting from migration. Teresa McMahon, who plays accordion, piano, and sings, and spent fifty years living in London, says of the Irish in the city, "we formed our own community there. We had our own little Ireland. We had an Ireland over there.... We had a fantastic Ireland. We had probably a better Ireland than the one here."[33] She and her contemporaries created a home that felt more like what "home" (in its ideal, imagined sense) should be than it was in reality. Rather than seeing the Irish community as an isolating factor, Teresa and her husband Martin used it to establish strong social networks that mirrored what they had known in rural Ireland. In the postwar era, cities like London, Boston, and New York also provided what Ireland could not: jobs. For migrants who spent their days working on urban building sites, factory floors, or hospital wards, evenings spent in Irish dance halls helped them acclimatize. Though physically distant from their homeland, in closing their eyes and hearing the familiar sounds of Irish music and voices they could imagine themselves closer to home.

The featuring of traditional music alongside more modern forms in dance halls underscores the cultural dimension of Irish identity. Cultural practices serve as a marker of identity, because, as Joane Nagel argues, "culture provides the content and meaning of ethnicity" and it is constructed in much the same way (1994, 162). It is not static but exists through words and actions, subject to change over time. Rather than existing outside of history, the process of migration itself could bring about an awareness of ethnicity. For some musicians and audiences, this may have been the first real consideration they gave to what it meant to be Irish. At home, the identification of themselves and their music as Irish never came into question, but suddenly in another country that was no longer the default. Larry Reynolds said, "I believe that I became more of an Irishman than I was, because you never thought of it when you were home"; but if it was ever in doubt he said, "I was always very quick since I came here, to let someone know, if I met them, that I was Irish. And proud of it. A lot of people felt that way" (quoted in Gedutis 2004, 77).

By choosing to go to dance halls and pubs run by Irish businessmen, marketed to an Irish audience, and featuring Irish music and dances, migrants ascribed to themselves a certain sense of "Irishness," whether or not they did so in other areas of their lives. Of course, not all made that choice, and multiple identities are always possible: many also adopted aspects of Americanness or Britishness. The dance halls in Britain and the United States provided liminal spaces for the negotiation of ethnic identity, while the music played within them and memories that music evoked point to the fluid nature of that identity. These venues became community centers even if, for a time, those communities existed on the margins in relation to both the home and host countries. Not all migrants found in London, New York, or Boston exactly what they went looking for, but they acclimatized. In the process they created, if not quite another Ireland, then something that sounded a lot like one.

BIBLIOGRAPHY

Author's interviews

Browne, Packie. November 6, 2010. Ballyduff, Co. Kerry.
Burke, Kevin. May 12, 2012. Baltimore, Co. Cork.
Conroy, Jack. December 8, 2009. Boston.
Henry, Kevin. April 19, 2013. Chicago.
Lynch, Jerry. November 20, 2010. Corofin, Co. Clare.
McDermott, Kevin. December 10, 2011. Wexford, Co. Wexford.
McMahon, Martin and Teresa. December 6, 2010. Shannon, Co. Clare.
O'Brien, Jimmy. April 11, 2012. Killarney, Co. Kerry.
Ó Ceannabháin, Jimmy. January 8, 2011. Spiddal, Co. Galway.
O'Connell, Connie. November 11, 2008. Cork, Co. Cork.
Reynolds, Larry. October 29, 2009. Boston.

Archives of Irish America, New York University

Clancy, Liam. Interview with Miriam Nyhan. March 29, 2009. Ireland House Oral History Collection.
Coen, Jack. Interview with Mick Moloney. February 28, 1976. Mick Moloney Irish-American Music and Popular Culture Collection, Part II: Field Recordings.
Connolly, Mattie. Interview with Mick Moloney (n.d.). Mick Moloney Irish-American Music and Popular Culture Collection, Part II: Field Recordings.
Cudahy, Dorothy Hayden, and John Cudahy. Interview with Mick Moloney. December 31, 1982. Mick Moloney Irish-American Music and Popular Culture Collection, Part II: Field Recordings.
Madden, Joe. Interview with Mick Moloney, August 13, 1985. Mick Moloney Irish-American Music and Popular Culture Collection, Part II: Field Recordings.
Mulhaire, Martin. Interview with Mick Moloney. December 5, 1981. Mick Moloney Irish-American Music and Popular Culture Collection, Part II: Field Recordings.
Quinn, Louis. Interview with Mick Moloney. May 17, 1977. Mick Moloney Irish-American Music and Popular Culture Collection, Part II: Field Recordings.

Other archival sources

Derrane, Joe. Interview with Brian Lawler. April 25, 2002. Irish Music Center, John J. Burns Library, Boston College.
Murray, Mary Anne. 2004. "Irish Dance Halls." Reminiscences Collection, Archive of the Irish in Britain, London Metropolitan University.

Books and articles

Alarik, Scott. 2000. "To His Surprise, He's an Irish Music Legend." *Boston Globe*, March 12.

Almeida, Linda Dowling. 2006. "Irish America, 1940–2000." In *Making the Irish American: History and Heritage of the Irish in the United States*, edited by J. J. Lee and Marion Casey, 548–73. New York: New York University Press.

Collins, Tim. 2010. "'Tis Like They Never Left: Locating 'Home' in the Music of Sliabh Aughty's Diaspora." *Journal of the Society for American Music* 4: 491–507.

Conzen, Kathleen Neils. 1979. "Immigrant Neighborhoods and Ethnic Identity: Historical Issues." *Journal of American History* 66: 603–15.

Corbally, John. 2009. "Shades of Difference: Irish, Caribbean, and South Asian Immigration to the Heart of Empire, 1948–1971." PhD diss., University of California, Davis.

Crehan, Junior. 1977. "Junior Crehan Remembers." *Dal gCais* 3: 72–85.

Cullinane, John P. 1994. "Irish Dance World-Wide: Irish Migrants and the Shaping of Traditional Irish Dance." In *The Irish World Wide: History, Heritage, Identity*, vol. 3, *The Creative Migrant*, edited by Patrick O'Sullivan, 192–220. London: Leicester University Press.

Delaney, Enda. 2002. *Irish Emigration since 1921*. Dublin: Economic and Social History Society of Ireland.

Delaney, Enda. 2007. *The Irish in Post-War Britain*. Oxford: Oxford University Press.

Duffy, Johannah. 2009. "Jazz, Identity and Sexuality in Ireland during the Interwar Years." *Irish Journal of American Studies Online* 1.

Dunne, Catherine. 2003. *An Unconsidered People: The Irish in London*. Dublin: New Island.

Fallon, Brian. 1998. *An Age of Innocence: Irish Culture, 1930–1960*. Dublin: Gill & Macmillan.

Finnane, Mark. 2001. "The Carrigan Committee of 1930–31 and the 'Moral Condition of the Saorstát.'" *Irish Historical Studies* 32: 519–36.

Gedutis, Susan. 2004. *See You at the Hall: Boston's Golden Era of Irish Music and Dance*. Boston: Northeastern University Press.

Goek, Sara. 2013. "'I Never Would Return Again to Plough the Rocks of Bawn': Irishmen in Post-War Britain." In *Locked Out: A Century of Irish Working-Class Life*, edited by David Convery, 157–72. Dublin: Irish Academic Press.

Goek, Sara. 2015. "Farewell to Erin: Oral Histories of Post-War Irish Music & Migration." PhD diss., University College Cork.

Hall, Reg. 1994. "Irish Music and Dance in London, 1890–1970: A Socio-Cultural History." PhD diss., University of Sussex.

Henigan, Julie Ann. 1989 [revised 1994]. "Sean-nós in America: A Study of Two Singers." MA thesis, University of North Carolina at Chapel Hill.

Kennedy, Liam. 1989. *The Modern Industrialization of Ireland, 1940–1988*. Dundalk: Dundalgan Press.

Kenny, Kevin. 2000. *The American Irish: A History*. Harlow and New York: Longman.

Kenny, Kevin. 2003. "Diaspora and Comparison: The Global Irish as a Case Study." *Journal of American History* 90: 134–62.

Lee, J. J., and Marion Casey, eds. 2006. *Making the Irish American: History and Heritage of the Irish in the United States*. New York: New York University Press.

McBee, Randy. 2000. *Dance Hall Days: Intimacy and Leisure among Working-Class Immigrants in the United States.* New York and London: New York University Press.

McDermott, Kevin. n.d. "London's Irish Dance Halls." In *Ireland's Own* (copy provided to the author).

McGreevy, Ronan. 2008. "End of an Era for Irish in London as Iconic Galtymore Dance Hall to Close Its Doors." *Irish Times*, April 28.

Miller, Rebecca. 1996. "Irish Traditional and Popular Music in New York City: Identity and Social Change, 1930–1975." In *The New York Irish*, edited by Ronald H. Bayor and Timothy J. Meagher, 481–507. Baltimore and London: Johns Hopkins University Press.

Moloney, Mick. 1982. "Irish Ethnic Recordings and the Irish-American Imagination." In *Ethnic Recordings in America: A Neglected Heritage*, 84–101. Washington, DC: American Folklife Center, Library of Congress.

Moloney, Mick. 1992. "Irish Music in America: Continuity and Change." PhD diss., University of Pennsylvania.

Moloney, Mick. 1998. "Irish Dance Bands in America." *New Hibernia Review/Iris Éireannach Nua* 2: 127–37.

Morrison, J'aime. 2001. "Dancing between Decks: Choreographies of Transition during Irish Migrations to America." *Éire-Ireland* 36: 82–97.

Nagel, Joane. 1994. "Constructing Ethnicity: Creating and Recreating Ethnic Identity and Culture." *Social Problems* 41 (Special Issue on Immigration, Race, and Ethnicity in America): 152–76.

National Economic and Social Council. 1991. *The Economic and Social Implications of Emigration.* Dublin: NESC.

Ní Fhuatháin, Méabh. 1993. "O'Byrne De Witt and Copley Records: A Window on Irish Music Recording in the USA 1900–1965." MA thesis, University College Cork.

Ó hAllmhuráin, Gearóid. 2005. "Dancing on the Hobs of Hell: Rural Communities in Clare and the Dance Halls Act of 1935." *New Hibernia Review/Iris Éireannach Nua* 9: 9–18.

Ó hAllmhuráin, Gearóid. 2009. "Dance Halls of Romance and Culchies in Tuxedos: Irish Traditional Music in America in the 1950s." In *After the Flood: Irish America, 1945–1960*, edited by James Silas Rogers and Matthew J. O'Brien, 9–23. Dublin and Portland: Irish Academic Press.

Ó hAllmhuráin, Gearóid. 2016. *Flowing Tides: History and Memory in an Irish Soundscape.* New York: Oxford University Press.

Rogers, James Silas, and Matthew J. O'Brien. 2009. *After the Flood: Irish America, 1945–1960.* Dublin and Portland: Irish Academic Press.

Sheridan, Louise. 2012. "More than One Story to Tell: Exploring Twentieth-Century Migration to Northampton, England in Memoir and Oral Narratives." *Irish Review* 44: 89–103.

Smyth, Jim. 1993. "Dancing, Depravity and All That Jazz: The Public Dance Halls Act of 1935." *History Ireland* 1: 51–54.

Stevenson, John. 1991. "The Jerusalem That Failed? The Rebuilding of Post-War Britain." In *Britain since 1945*, edited by Terry Gourvish and Alan O'Day, 89–110. Basingstoke: Macmillan Press.

Other sources

Central Statistics Office. 2007. Census of Population of Ireland, 2006, vol.4, Usual Residence, Migration, Birthplaces and Nationalities. Dublin: Stationary Office.

Rafferty, Mike. 2010. "A Conversation with Irish Flute Player and National Heritage Fellow Mike Rafferty." National Endowment for the Arts. Audio podcast. Accessed June 2016. https://www.arts.gov/audio/mike-rafferty.

Quinn, Bob. 2002. Damhsa an Deoraí [The Immigrant Dance]. Video. Ireland: Gael Media/TG4.

NOTES

1. Kevin Burke, interview with the author, May 12, 2012, Baltimore, Co. Cork.

2. This figure is the estimated total net migration, 1945–1971. Gross estimates would be much higher.

3. Liam Clancy, interview with Miriam Nyhan, March 29, 2009, Ireland House Oral History Collection, Archives of Irish America, New York University.

4. Connie O'Connell, interview with the author, November 11, 2008, Cork, Co. Cork. Threshings were occasions when locals got together to thresh hay, and they would often celebrate when the task was complete.

5. Kevin Henry, interview with the author, April 19, 2013, Chicago.

6. Jerry Lynch, interview with the author, November 20, 2010, Corofin, Co. Clare; Kevin McDermott, interview with the author, December 10, 2011, Wexford, Co. Wexford.

7. The first céilí band competition took place in 1946 (Ó hAllmhuráin 2016, 169–70).

8. Mary Anne Murray, "Irish Dance Halls," December 2004, Reminiscences Collection, Archive of the Irish in Britain, London Metropolitan University.

9. Kevin McDermott names twenty-eight and Reg Hall names forty-four, but in some cases the same venue changed name or ownership and in others owners/managers moved their hall from one location to another (Hall 1994, 536–38; McDermott n.d.).

10. Irish traditional musicians are imprecise in the terms they use to describe the broad genre of popular music. They variously refer to the popular (nontraditional) music played in the dance halls as "modern," "jazz," or "country and western," though all descriptions apply to the same style. Traditional music they refer to either as traditional or céilí music. Noncommercial venues also existed, such as Catholic parish halls.

11. Lynch interview.

12. Irish traditional musicians in this period were predominantly male. Therefore, my quoting more men than women is not an intentional bias, but one that reflects the subject matter.

13. Larry Reynolds, interview with the author, October 29, 2009, Boston.

14. Lynch interview.

15. Jimmy Ó Ceannabháin, interview with the author, January 8, 2011, Spiddal, Co. Galway.

16. Packie Browne, interview with the author, November 6, 2010, Ballyduff, Co. Kerry.

17. The sign is visible in a photograph by Paddy Fahey used in the documentary *Damhsa an Deoraí* [*The Immigrant Dance*], directed by Bob Quinn (2002). The original is in the Paddy Fahey Collection, Brent Museum and Archives, U.K.

18. Reg Hall, interview with the author, July 3, 2012, Croydon, London.

19. Mike Rafferty, interview with Jo Reed, 2010, National Endowment for the Arts. http://www.arts.gov/av/avCMS/Rafferty-stream.html. Accessed June 2016.

20. Jack Coen, interview with Mick Moloney, February 28, 1976, Mick Moloney Irish-American Music and Popular Culture Collection, Part II: Field Recordings, Archives of Irish America, New York University. Both Mike Rafferty and Jack Coen expressed and reinforced these same views in separate interviews with Tim Collins (2010, 498).

21. Sliabh Luachra (translation: rushy mountain) is a region on the Cork/Kerry border known for its distinctive musical style. Jimmy O'Brien, interview with the author, April 11, 2012, Killarney, Co. Kerry.

22. Mattie Connolly, interview with Mick Moloney, n.d., Mick Moloney Irish-American Music and Popular Culture Collection, Part II: Field Recordings, Archives of Irish America, New York University.

23. Joe Madden, interview with Mick Moloney, August 13, 1985, Mick Moloney Irish-American Music and Popular Culture Collection, Part II: Field Recordings, Archives of Irish America, New York University.

24. Louis Quinn, interview with Mick Moloney, May 17, 1977, Mick Moloney Irish-American Music and Popular Culture Collection, Part II: Field Recordings, Archives of Irish America, New York University.

25. This compares to 4 percent in the five counties that make up New York City and 3.6 percent in the Greater London area.

26. Larry Reynolds, interview with Scott Alarik, November 19, 2009, New England Folk Music Archive.

27. Jack Conroy, interview with the author, December 8, 2009, Boston.

28. Joe Derrane, interview with Brian Lawler, April 25, 2002, Irish Music Center, John J. Burns Library, Boston College.

29. Lynch interview.

30. Martin Mulhaire, interview with Mick Moloney, December 5, 1981; Dorothy Hayden Cudahy and John Cudahy, interview with Mick Moloney, December 31, 1982; Mattie Connolly, interview with Mick Moloney, n.d., Mick Moloney Irish-American Music and Popular Culture Collection, Part II: Field Recordings, Archives of Irish America, New York University.

31. Larry Reynolds, interview with the author, October 29, 2009, Boston.

32. Clancy interview.

33. Teresa McMahon, in Martin and Teresa McMahon, interview with the author, December 6, 2010, Shannon, Co. Clare.

2

CUMBIAS Y REBAJADAS

Aurality, Race, and Class in Monterrey's *Colombia* Culture

JUAN DAVID RUBIO RESTREPO

Cumbia, a music that emanated from the Colombian Atlantic-Caribbean to the rest of Latin America, has made its indelible mark in Monterrey, Mexico. Monterrey's chapter in the book of cumbia is certainly similar to others in the region. In studies by Pablo Vila et al. (2011) in Argentina, Raúl Romero (2007) in Perú, and Ketty Wong (2012) in Ecuador, to mention a few, we see a consistent dynamic: rural populations that migrate to big urban centers and find cumbia embrace it and make it a central part of their identity and their status in the metropole. Transnationally, cumbia is a music with a shared genealogy and whose aurality tends to index marginality across countries. While cumbia has developed into countless regional styles—from *chicha* to *tecnocumbia*, from *villera* to *amazónica*, and many more—Monterrey stands out as a city where cumbia's relevance is directly related to its Colombian origin. Residents of Monterrey not only acknowledge this, but the Colombian style they came to know is *their* style. In other words, cumbia in Monterrey *is* Colombian and it is performed and thought of as such. This is a non-diasporic process of musical transculturation that wasn't advanced by commercial or governmental interests.

In this chapter, I trace the evolution of cumbia in Monterrey and investigate the complex relation cumbia has had with issues of race and class. Using a decolonial approach, I argue that the sociopolitical dynamics this music practice articulates both testify to and resist long-lasting cycles of racialization, difference construction, and normalization of inequality. In other words, it constitutes both narrative and counternarrative. Cumbia in Monterrey has been studied in detail by Darío Blanco Arboleda (2014) and José Juan Olvera Gudiño (2005). Their studies, as well as my own fieldwork conducted over the summer of 2015, constitute the primary sources for my investigation. Here I also focus on a practice contained within the larger Monterrey cumbia phenomenon: *cumbia rebajada*. *Rebajadas*[1] are slowed-down cumbias made by lowering the revolutions per minute (RPM) of LPs; this produces a lower-pitched version of the original and constitutes a sub-practice that originated in Monterrey and that has been around for over thirty years. Little attention has been paid to rebajadas. Moving constantly between rebajadas and the overall Monterrey cumbia culture, I argue that while cumbia has made its way into the public sphere and has become popular among a broader audience, rebajadas have kept their marginal status and race/class connotation. At the same time, I argue that these musics constitute a rupture within the city's normativity and thus signal a decolonial ethos. This is a phenomenon in which the aural, the aesthetic, and the racial overlap and coconstitute each other.

A MAN, A TURNTABLE, A SONIDERO, AND A HISTORY OF THE MANY

On my very first day in Monterrey, José Juan Olvera Gudiño, a colleague, my local contact, and an expert on musics in the Mexican northeast (including *la colombia*), took me to the home of local *sonidero* Gabriel Dueñez. We went unannounced and my expectations were low. It was the middle of a weekday and we drove up La Independencia neighborhood blasting the AC, trying to counter the suffocating summer heat. The change of scene from downtown Monterrey to the Loma Larga hill (where "La Indepe" and other *popular*[2] neighborhoods are located) was quite striking. The Santa Catarina River (which is usually more of a canal) clearly divides the city. Up north is Monterrey's downtown with its tall buildings, fancy hotels, historical landmarks, and the colonial *barrio antiguo*, all of them catering to tourists and local consumers. Down south, a few hundred meters away and on the other side of the Puente del Papa bridge, are Loma Larga and La Indepe, its steep hills covered by countless houses going almost as high as the hill does.

From the north side of the bridge it seems that the houses landed on the hill. Its steepness and the precariousness of its access roads—which degrade and eventually become nonexistent as the hill rises—make me think of the quixotic endeavor building a house here must be. The overall aspect of Loma Larga resembles many other Latin American landscapes and histories in which the marginalized are concentrated on the mountains surrounding the city. On the other side of Loma Larga is the exclusive San Pedro Garza García zone. The borders enclosing La Indepe and other *popular* neighborhoods on the hill are not only socioeconomically but also geographically explicit. The Santa Catarina River and the peak of the hill act as a symbolic and physical

El Puente del Papa pictured from the north side, Loma Larga in the background. Photograph by the author.

signifier of a marginalized population. Loma Larga is the place where "*la colombia* de Monterrey"[3] was born.

Finally we found the Dueñez residency. My colleague greeted Don Gabriel and his wife Juanita and introduced me as yet another Colombian who wants to talk to him. Indeed, I was not the first one. Dueñez is an important figure in Monterrey *colombia* culture; visits by scholars, musicians, and enthusiasts—often from Colombia—are not rare for him. His house has one floor. In the first room, the one adjacent to the street, Juanita has a small store where she sells wrapping paper, sweets, gifts for special occasions, and the like. Next to some of the urns is Don Gabriel's current sound system. A turntable, a preamplifier, a small audio mixer, and a speaker form his "*sonido*," his (working) instrument. He told me he brings all of these to the *tocadas* (gigs). In the next room there is the kitchen and a small round dining table. The one next to it houses Dueñez's discotheque: hundreds and hundreds of LPs, mostly of Colombian cumbia[4] (and vallenato) performed by Colombian and Mexican artists dating back to the seventies and even sixties. One of Dueñez's daughters and some of his grandchildren were in the back room, where the master bedroom is. We sat down at the table and started chatting. Sonido Dueñez Hermanos is a staple in Monterrey, one of the most longstanding sonidos (sound systems) in the city. While sonideros are common throughout Mexico, some of the *regiomontanos* (from Monterrey) are peculiar in that they specialize in Colombian cumbia.[5]

Like many of the inhabitants of Loma Larga, Don Gabriel came from Zacatecas, a state that borders Nuevo León, the state in which Monterrey is located. Since the 1950s a crisis in the smallholding economy has triggered massive migrations from the neighboring states of Zacatecas, Coahuila, San Luis Potosí, and Tamaulipas into Monterrey.[6] Most of these immigrants settled in Loma Larga as squatters.

Sonideros have been around for a while. Don Gabriel remembers listening to the parties they hosted when he was a young man, as well as his determination to one day own a sonido. The main difference between those sonideros and Don Gabriel's generation is that the former played a wider variety of music, including all sorts of *música tropical*, different types of Mexican popular hits, and even "Anglo-influenced" music. By the 1970s Dueñez and other sonideros started specializing in Colombian cumbia.

Records were the umbilical cord that connected the emerging regiomontano *colombia* culture with its putative newfound home where cumbia was *adopted*—a word I choose carefully in order to underscore the sociocultural and politicoeconomic dynamics I find particular in this case. More specifically, I seek to distance myself from tropes that have dominated music scholarship dealing with transnational flows of music—namely, from concepts such as cultural appropriation and hybridity, often used to analyze the world music industry paradigm. In this type of vocabulary, I find an implicit power dynamic (center–periphery, first world consumers–third world creators, etc.) that implies a "North–South" dialogue. These notions can't account for "South–South" dialogues. In other words, a North–South dialogue, which encompasses issues of appropriation, hybridity, etc., carries within it specific epistemic, cultural, bio/geopolitical, and socioeconomical issues. Instead, I use *adopt*—from the Latin *ad* (to) and *optare* (choose)—to propose an alternative power relation that bypasses the economic and epistemological North, particularly its mainstream media industry machinery, through the creation of "piracy" networks. As I show, cumbia rebajada not only constitutes a transnational dialogue between people (Colombian and Mexican) with a similar colonial and racial past, but also affords the construction of alternative identities and political economies among marginalized populations.

In Monterrey, this process of adoption was advanced primarily through recordings. The Colombian artists whom regiomontanos had known for years primarily through LPs started coming more and more often to Monterrey, realizing that a lost piece of the Colombian Atlantic coast had surfaced in Loma Larga. Colombian LPs were scarce and rare. Though several recording labels in Colombia, particularly in Medellín, produced this type of music,

Gabriel Dueñez holding a photo picturing a group of local sonideros taken ca. 1970; part of his record collection is in the background. Photograph by the author.

they were not massively distributed in Monterrey (a topic I deal with below). As they built their collections, sonideros such as Don Gabriel would get their LPs from places like Houston (where his brother lives) and Dallas, cities with large communities of Latin American immigrants and that facilitated a more fluid trading circuit. Buying one of these rarities was (and still is) a luxury for people such as Don Gabriel. Only sonideros and a handful of enthusiasts were willing to spend what for them is an important part of their income on records. From the United States, Mexico City, or even Colombia, by mail or human carrier, the records would meet their inextricable destiny in Monterrey.

The role of sonideros is definitive. They are archivists, creators of taste, and active agents in the emergence of *la colombia*. Colombian music was established in Monterrey *through* them. Their LPs and sound systems (the duet that constitutes a sonido) were for years the only way regiomontanos could listen to cumbia. Sitting at his table, I could perceive the pride Dueñez has in his record collection and his accomplishments as a sonidero. He still lives in the same place he grew up in, upgrading the house little by little. His wife Juanita pulled out two running fans and pointed them toward us; the heat was almost unbearable. Right after introducing me, my colleague told Don Gabriel that I was interested in rebajadas. Immediately he reacted, exclaiming how beautiful and underrated the rebajadas are, then he added: "*nostros fuimos los que las sacamos*" [we (Sonido Dueñez Hermanos) came up with them].

SPREADING LA COLOMBIA, PIRACY, AND RESISTANCE: THE POLITICAL ECONOMY OF CUMBIA

Originally, sonideros were hired to play at *bailes* (dances) and miscellaneous celebrations. Hiring a live band or buying a sound system was expensive; sonidos were the most affordable option. This made sonideros a staple in *popular* neighborhoods. Though their speakers and turntables were crucial for the job, it was the LP collections the customers were after. Each sonidero built his collection carefully, trying to bring the most popular and exclusive items; sometimes they would even tear the labels from the LPs to keep the competition in the dark (a common practice in sound-system cultures). Sonideros are predominantly male. Nevertheless, as I discuss below, Dueñez's wife Juanita complicates a patriarchal account of the job. She has been a key figure in establishing Sonido Dueñez Hermanos and, consequently, in the emergence of *colombia* culture and rebajadas. Don Gabriel displays his first sonido proudly in his house: an old, quite heavy, and colorfully ornamented monophonic turntable and a *bosina*, a megaphone-shaped big and heavy speaker. He and a much-needed helper, he told me, used to carry the sonido and a selection of his records throughout Loma Larga to his gigs. Transporting the heavy instrument wasn't easy, especially on a hill so steep. Dueñez refers to some sectors of Loma Larga as *veredas*, implying these were not thought of as neighboring areas back then, but distant zones, hard to access. The higher you go, the harder it gets. Some sectors—usually the higher ones—were accessible only by foot or donkey (which is still the case in a few places).

Once he made it to the gig, Don Gabriel hung his speaker from the roof of the house or on a nearby tree, making the sound of the accordion, *guacharaca* (scraper), and *caja* (hand drum) move through the hill. In *popular* Latin American neighborhoods, particularly when the temperature is high, the divide between the public and private sphere is quite permeable. People often pull out some chairs in front of their houses and hang out, trying to catch a breeze and fight the heat. Similarly, in Loma Larga house parties are not necessarily a private matter. Part of a sonidero's gig is in fact to convoke the gathering. Through his hung speaker Don Gabriel would call *la raza*[7] to the celebration. Besides playing music, MCing is also an important part of the gig, calling out to people, sending salutations and shout-outs, inviting them to hit the dance floor, congratulating the ones being fêted, etc.

The parties would go for hours, Don Gabriel told me. In one of the gigs—probably during the early eighties, though he does not provide a specific date—he worked his now-retired turntable so hard that some of the metal pieces that move the platter wore off, and as a result the record started rotating slower and sounding, in his own words, "*aguado*" (literally, watered). The people liked it so much that back home he tried to emulate the malfunction with no success. He eventually settled on manipulating the slider that controls the turntable speed. Dueñez's story is no news to me. I encountered it in my preliminary research and it is one of the main reasons I came to see him first. In Monterrey, people who like Colombian music are aware of the existence of rebajadas, though few know how they came to be. Some don't think about it; others have heard stories, like about how the batteries of a stereo wore down; fewer have heard Don Gabriel's version. The fact is that Dueñez is recognized in Monterrey as the sonidero behind cumbia rebajada.

Sound technology became more affordable in the early eighties. This diminished considerably the work of sonideros. Still, they possessed something more precious than their sound systems. The LPs they had collected for years became their primary symbolic and financial capital. Selling the vinyl wasn't an option; Don Gabriel and every other sonidero hold an affective relationship with them. Instead, they started rerecording LPs onto cassette tapes. More affordable stereos meant sonideros weren't needed as much for parties, but also that there was a cassette player in every other house. Since the music that people of *la colombia* came to love was still unavailable, sonideros retained their position as the keepers of cumbia. Don Gabriel claims his wife Juanita was the first one selling tapes in the mideighties when she set up a stall on the Puente del Papa, the bridge connecting Loma Larga with Monterrey's downtown. This is a strategic point. The bridge is the main route connecting La Independencia with downtown and the rest of the city. Pedestrians—particularly those living in the hills—cross the bridge daily.

Juanita's initiative was crucial. She was a pioneer in switching the sonidero business from gigs to selling rerecorded music. This effectively opened a new circuit of music exchange and an alternative political economy through which the already engrained Colombian sound reached an even wider audience, further establishing the music's status in the city. More importantly, it was through this form of circulation that rebajadas became an established

Gabriel and Juanita Dueñez at their stall at the local pulga. Photograph by the author.

phenomenon. Over the years, Juanita and Don Gabriel have sustained their business, moving it through different flea markets (*pulgas*) and selling other merchandise such as shirts, USB flash drives, and pants, items of which Juanita is in charge. Don Gabriel's music continues to be the featured item and the main reason locals look for their stall. Hence, while Dueñez is certainly the visible head of Sonido Dueñez Hermanos, Juanita has been fundamental for the business, and thus, for the *colombia* culture in Monterrey. Soon enough, other sonideros followed her lead. The sound they spread for years through Loma Larga was reified in cassette tapes.

Keeping up with the digital revolution, Dueñez has started selling MP3s, CDs, and USB flash drives containing hundreds of tracks. This is a practice frowned upon by some of the few sonideros who remain in business. Like his attitude toward rebajadas, Don Gabriel's relationship with digital audio is closely in tune with his customers' preferences and the challenges brought by ever-changing sound technologies. This developed into a network of shared agencies in which technology, consumers, and producers create a unique, idiosyncratic and site-specific aesthetic practice shaped by the demands of the market, the affordances of sound technology, and the sonidero's expertise. The way in which this political economy unfolded, the feedback relation all the parts have, and the way this has impacted *la colombia*'s aurality certainly complicates simplistic and essentialized accounts of the "culture industry" and "music as commodity." In this case, we see how all these agents—producers, consumers, technology—and the exchanges of money and commodities taking place among them have developed not just into a para-economy that greatly benefits marginalized communities on many levels (financially, culturally, politically, etc.) but also into a robust music practice and culture.

Cassette tape was the vehicle through which rebajadas were established as a long-lasting phenomenon within *la colombia*. Don Gabriel told me that "*la raza las pedía*" [it was "the people" who kept asking for them], that he wasn't really trying to push the rebajadas. In his house, Dueñez would plug his turntable into a cassette recorder, push record and *rebajaba* the song "live." Imagining the craft inherent to such performance is fascinating: landing the needle on the exact place and pushing the record button; most importantly, deciding how much to *rebajar* each track. There is a particular audile technique involved and a degree of dexterity—after all, the sonido is the sonidero's instrument. How much can a track take? Where's the limit? There's a fine line before the song gets completely lost. The object being created and the performance taking place are in a sort of aesthetic limbo. What is being inscribed on the tape is not completely new, nor is it a copy of its original. On the side of Dueñez's performance, besides rebajadas, he also curated the songs that would go on the tape. As opposed to his "straight" repertoire, mostly constituted by rerecordings of entire LPs, rebajada tapes are compilations. While he curates most of them, there are some "custom" jobs as well. If a client brings a setlist and is willing to pay three to four times the amount of a regular copy, Don Gabriel goes through his collection and fulfills the request. Each of these compilations constitutes a "volume." Don Gabriel keeps stock of some of them in his stall. By now, counting Dueñez's compilations, the custom jobs, and editions dedicated to specific artists, he has close to 150 rebajada volumes, each of them carefully documented by Juanita in her own handwriting in a notebook that must be around thirty years old.

The monetary networks generated around *la colombia* are not just an economic phenomenon. In this case "piracy," I argue, has to do not only with issues of accessibility and affordability. Rather, piracy—together with sonidero parties—constitutes one of the most fluid networks through which *la colombia* has spread. On the side of the performers whose music is being traded, sonideros like Don Gabriel are greatly appreciated by Colombian and local cumbia performers. Iconic Colombian artists like Alfredo Gutiérrez recognize the key role sonideros have played in the arrival and establishment of their music in Mexico. Gutiérrez composed and performed the song "El sonidero" as an homage to them. Similarly, since the economy of local cumbia artists is based primarily on live performance, when local groups put out recordings (often made during concerts) it is not unusual for them to pass a copy to local sonideros hoping to make it into the sonideros' collections, and, by extension, their clients'.

This symbiotic relationship among pirate distributors, artists, and marginalized consumers is not unique. Similar dynamics have been found throughout Latin America. For example, in her study of popular music in Ecuador, Ketty Wong (2012) argues that local tecnocumbia artists hold a symbiotic relationship with pirate networks, as the latter function as a free distributor of sorts, aiding the artists in the process of getting fans and gigs, their main source of income (183). Wong's argument echoes Kathryn Mertz's (2013) study of tecnocumbia circuits in the Peruvian Amazon. Both these cases follow a similar pattern: not only are the performers uninterested in distributing their music, finding the process cumbersome and ultimately economically futile, but the networks created by these third parties effectively fill a circulation void. This is a void that is unlikely to be filled by the "mainstream" media machinery, as these musics are racialized and indexed to working-class populations.

What I find particular to Monterrey is: (1) while in Peru and Ecuador the emergence of "pirate" networks was directly related to the "digital revolution" and the flows of capital, equipment, and technology brought by neoliberalism,[8] Monterrey sonideros predate this, as they began selling analogue rerecorded music (LP to cassette) in the early to mideighties; and (2) as I have shown, sonideros are not mere music dealers. Their record collections are a source of cultural and financial capital that seems to have survived the arrival of the Internet. Their discotheques house an important part of *la colombia*'s history. Sonideros who remain active, like Don Gabriel, and even descendants of sonideros from the seventies and eighties, are respected figures among the *colombia* community.

Piracy in Monterrey may be illegal (though not a primary concern for local authorities), but it is also a locus of resistance where alternative economies and identities emerge. Piracy provides self-employment and income for members of a marginal population that has historically survived in the informal economy sector (Olvera Gudiño 2005). Furthermore, sonideros make cumbia accessible to their communities. This is true even now, as access to the Internet is not widespread among these populations. Most importantly, this para-economy and these alternative distribution networks afford close interaction between sonidero and listener. Their shared love for the music, the feedback loop between them, and the subsequent sense of shared identity created by cumbia, are the pillars on which *la colombia* was built. There is a direct connection between race, class, and capital. As I show below, it was the socioeconomic and racial status of the Monterrey cumbia consumer that triggered the emergence of pirate distribution.

While Colombian music was established in Monterrey in the early 1970s, it was mostly ignored by the local state and media. *La colombia* was born, established, and grew mostly alongside regiomontano "mainstream" culture. Radio shows programming this music did not emerge until the nineties. Nowadays, cumbia is becoming part of the city's musical catalogue. Walking through downtown Monterrey, where music is used to attract customers into stores, one hears every other type of Mexican popular music and, occasionally, as part of the cacophony, cumbia. Nevertheless, while a larger local audience is starting to consume cumbia, *rebajadas* have retained their marginal status, and their aurality continues to be highly classed and, hence, racialized.

RACE/CLASS, COLONIALITY, AND THE AURAL

In order to better understand the racial and sociopolitical dynamics cumbia rebajada articulates,[9] we ought to consider this music practice and *la colombia* vis-à-vis Monterrey's history and the broader narrative of difference construction in Latin America. It is important to understand marginalization and racialization as part of a historical continuum. Theorizing these larger narratives of classification of human life has been at the core of decolonial theory, particularly through the concept of *coloniality of power*, coined and developed by Peruvian sociologist Aníbal Quijano and further advanced by Latin American and Caribbean thinkers.[10] As Nelson Maldonado-Torres (2007) explains, "Coloniality is different from colonialism": while the latter "denotes a political and economic relation in which the sovereignty of nation or people rests on the power of another nation," the former "denotes long-standing patterns of power that emerged as a result of colonialism, but that define culture, labor, intersubjective relations, and knowledge production well beyond the strict limits of colonial administrations" (243).

Rather than following a linear theorization of human and state sovereignty (i.e., colonial to postcolonial and republican), coloniality conceptualizes the American colonial enterprise—being the first large-scale one of its kind— as a paradigmatic moment in history where the very basis of theories of the human, the less-than-human, and the subhuman were triggered by the encounter of the white European with his racialized Others.[11] Coloniality theorizes colonialism as a complex articulation of power that lingers. In the case of Monterrey, I conceptualize cumbia rebajada not simply as a phenomenon that emerged during the second half of the twentieth century but as part and agent of Monterrey's larger sociocultural landscape and its political economies. The aural opens the door of a silenced past and voices the marginalized—those whom Walter Mignolo (2011) would place on the "darker side of modernity."

Founded by conquistador Diego de Montemayor, Monterrey was part of a territory granted by the Spanish crown to Luis de Carvajal, a Portuguese businessman and slave trader. Carvajal colonized the territory known as the Nuevo Reino de León (a colonial territorial entity that encompassed most of the current state of Nuevo León, of which Monterrey is the capital) through a capitulation treaty that allowed him to occupy and exploit the land in exchange for paying tribute to the crown and establishing its power and faith (Cavazos Garza and Ceballos Ramírez 1998, 15). Carvajal was later arrested on suspicion of Judaism and judged by the Inquisition; he died in prison in 1591 (Backal 2011, 97). Montemayor, a member of Carvajal's expedition, founded the city in 1596. While colonization in Latin America was generally advanced by unmarried European white men, Monterrey's original population was comprised of European-born families that Montemayor brought from the nearby town of Saltillo, now the capital of the state of Coahuila. The nomadic indigenous populations of the area either were enslaved under the *encomienda* system (Flores Torres 2009, 44), forced to work in the mines with African slaves, or escaped from the invaders.

The economy of Monterrey and its peripheral areas relied primarily on silver mining, an activity that from the sixteenth to the eighteenth centuries responded to the crown's insatiable need for coin. Either in the mines or in the foundries, cheap—ideally free—labor was continuously in demand. After the encomienda system was abolished, with the imposition of wage-labor capitalist systems, the indigenous workforce kept feeding the mining industry. Also, Amerindians captured in wars (often orchestrated for that purpose) were forced to work as part of their sentence. Amerindians rebelled continuously against colonial power, attacking the city as well as nearby towns and ranches repeatedly during its early years. Indeed, even into the nineteenth century José María Pará, twice state governor (in 1825 and 1848), viewed these populations as a "plague" (Flores Torres 2009, 126).

After the US invasion of Mexico of 1846–48, Monterrey achieved a new level of importance. Although the city itself was invaded for almost the entire length of the conflict, Monterrey was the largest northern city of the newly delimited Mexican nation, which lost more than half of its territory to the United States in the Treaty of Guadalupe Hidalgo. Monterrey became a strategic point in Mexico's geopolitics. Its borderland status made Monterrey a financial and industrial hub that supported trade with the United States through trade corridors that remain active to this day. Amerindians kept resisting, caught up in a conflict of crowns, republics, and nations. Flores Torres notes: "The *indigenous devastations*, suffered since the conquest years, were *controlled* through an extensive military campaign in the decades of 1850 to 1880" (142, my emphasis). Aside from the author's interesting choice of words, we see how late into the nineteenth century the remaining and greatly diminished indigenous communities resisted and how their "devastations" were repelled by the city. Into the twentieth century, the racialized populations living in Monterrey and its peripheries were either a minority group with a servile past—most importantly, thought of as such by *criollo* urbanites—or a peripheral population, repelled and persecuted for over three centuries.

Hence, we can see how, as Blanco Arboleda (2014) argues, Monterrey is "a city that in its hegemonic worldview *thinks of itself* as being white-criolla" (40, my emphasis). This is the mentality with which the city entered its industrialization phase in the late nineteenth century. Monterrey's proximity to Texas made it an integral part of the trading route between Mexico and the United States (Cavazos Garza and Ceballos Ramírez 1998, 168). Its semi-arid climate made it unfavorable for agriculture, but its strategic location was ideal for the emerging industrial economy. By the beginning of the twentieth century, a major brewery and several concrete and metallurgic companies had settled in the city, following incentives offered by the local government (170–71). Monterrey would eventually become the second most important economy of the country and among the most productive cities of Latin America (Blanco Arboleda 2014, 44), a title it continues to hold.

Furthermore, the accelerated pace with which Latin American nations industrialized in the early to mid-twentieth century had a deep impact on both urban centers and their peripheries. Developing cities like Monterrey became the destination of massive waves of internal rural migrants seeking better prospects and escaping a pauperized agrarian economy neglected by the state. Within these peripheral migrant populations—and their loaded, racialized past—were people like Gabriel Dueñez and the bulk of the *colombia* from Monterrey.

Don Gabriel's story helps illuminate this history. He migrated from Estancia de Ánimas, a small town in Zacatecas. After he lost his father at a young age, his mother took him and most of her seven other children to

Monterrey after selling most of their farm, which was unproductive due to lack of infrastructure (Olvera Gudiño 2010). Entering Monterrey's mining industry (the same one built on the forced labor of indigenous populations not long before), Dueñez started working at a foundry at age twelve. This was a low-paid, burdensome job, which he complemented with his work as a sonidero for many years. It is through these loaded micro-histories that we can grasp the real significance cumbia has for people like Don Gabriel and how it came to be a fundamental part of his identity. The performers on the records, thousands of kilometers southeast in the Colombian Caribbean, told the marginalized rural immigrant about the beach they didn't have, about love stories in pastoral landscapes unthinkable when surrounded by urban concrete, and of mythical characters traversing a tropical savannah.

The conjunction of Monterrey's colonial-racial past and its industrial-capitalist present makes it the prototypical Latin American modern city: wealthy yet unequal, industrialized yet underdeveloped, multiracial yet segregated. Monterrey's history, as decolonial thought argues, is consistent with the construction of difference, inequality, and marginalization found throughout the former colonies. Race is definitive for class construction—or, in the words of Stuart Hall, "Race is thus, also, the modality in which class is 'lived,' the medium through which class relations are experienced, the form in which it is appropriated and 'fought through'" (Unesco 1980, 341). However, one of the most important interventions decolonial thought has performed on Marxian and post-Marxian accounts of class is precisely conceptualizing race not just as the "modality in which in which class is 'lived,'" but as its very foundation. Quijano (2007) observes:

> only processes of subjectivation, whose purpose is *the conflict around exploitation/domination*, are constitutive of processes of social classification. In world capitalism, the issues of labor, race and gender, are the three central instances around which these conflictive exploitation/domination relations are organized. (117)

Difference construction—race in this case—has been and continues to be key to Monterrey's history, and it is through these long-lasting legacies of violence that we can understand the role music plays in this larger scheme, and the potential it has as an agent of identity formation, denunciation, and resistance.

CUMBIA AND CUMBIA REBAJADA: CLASSED AURALITIES

In the introduction to their edited volume *Cumbia! Scenes of a Migrant Latin American Music Genre* (2013), Héctor Fernandez L'Hoeste and Pablo Vila propose the verb *to articulate* to express the capacity certain musics have to both "construct" and "reflect" processes of identity formation:

> We believe that, quite often, a particular musical practice helps to articulate ... particular imaginary, narrative identifications when performers or listeners of this very music feel that it (complexly) resonates with (obviously following a complex process of negotiation between musical interpellation and argumentative storyline) the narrative plots that organize their variegated narrative identities. (15)

In other words, music practices and every activity they afford—what Christopher Small (1998) calls *musicking*—are complex performances with many elements (playing, listening, dancing, selling/buying, etc.) that are not limited by a single "object" or "event" (concert, recording, etc.). Rather, musicking is both agent and testament of the complex aesthetic, socioeconomic, and political processes behind the production/consumption of music.

One of the most salient characteristics of cumbia and cumbia rebajada is their "class indexicality." By this, I mean the process through which certain practices of music and sound come to be perceived as related to, or identified with, certain socioeconomic groups. This is by no means a prescriptive concept; on the contrary, it is a constructed notion. As I have shown, in the case of Monterrey this has been concomitant with long-standing processes of racialization. In the local context, these genres were not just fundamental to processes of identity formation for the marginalized groups I discuss above, but their consumption was simultaneously linked to these groups by the middle and upper classes. Thus, cumbia in Monterrey—particularly in its early decades—was a marker of socioeconomic status. To reiterate, race and class coconstruct each other in Latin America; therefore, a music that articulates class also indexes racial dynamics. In this section, I trace such "articulation," arguing that, although cumbia in Monterrey emerged among the *popular* classes and was thought of as particular to their identity, this has slowly changed after this music began to be featured in mass media and consumed by other socioeconomic groups. Nevertheless, rebajadas have kept their marginal status and class indexicality, coming to be disparaged even within the *colombia* population.

Both Olvera Gudiño (2005) and the testimonies of sonideros I collected indicate that Colombian cumbia arrived to Monterrey in the late 1960s as part of the larger música tropical phenomenon. This category, coined primarily by media industries throughout Latin America for marketing purposes, is loosely used to refer to different types of musics with an Afro-Latin/Colombian/Antillean origin. These musics are closely associated with social dancing. Roughly from the middle of the twentieth century to the present, música tropical has included styles like the danzón, mambo, cha cha chá, and other Afro-Cuban rhythms; the Dominican merengue; Venezuelan band music, like that of Billo's Caracas Boys and Los Melódicos; and, of course, Colombian cumbia in all its variations.[12] Though these musics emanated from different countries, the role Mexico played was fundamental. Being the most important and powerful media industry of the region throughout the twentieth century, most cultural products that were consumed transnationally were either produced in Mexico (recorded and often performed by local musicians) or had to pass through this country before an artist could be validated as truly transnational. On top of that, the biggest stars in the Mexican recording industry were often also active in the Mexican film and later television industries.

In Monterrey during the late 1960s, besides the aforementioned musics, a "mexicanized" type of cumbia originating in central Mexico and along the northeastern border was also included in the música tropical category: music by artists like Mike Laure y sus Cometas and Rigo Tovar y su Costa Azul. Colombian cumbia was just a minor player in this huge music selection and, importantly, it wasn't produced and backed by the powerful Mexican media industry. Most likely, cumbia produced in Colombia arrived at Monterrey via the limited number of recordings distributed by Mexican labels and through a few people who brought records directly from Colombia. It is remarkable, then, that the rural migrants who arrived in Monterrey in the fifties and sixties adopted this music, choosing it over a rather wide musical supply that included local genres like música norteña and other types of regional music from the northeastern Mexico–US border.[13] The cumbia distribution networks were so narrow and the demand for it so overwhelming that, as I discussed above, sonideros came up with alternative networks of supply and distribution.

According to Olvera Gudiño (2005), the first Colombian recordings that made it to Monterrey were by orchestras like those of Manuel Villanueva and Conjunto Típico Contreras. Soon enough "superband" Los Corraleros de Majagual would make it, too. Los Corraleros continue to be one of the most iconic cumbia bands, widely popular in Colombia and one of the musical pillars of *colombia* culture in Monterrey. From Los Corraleros, solo artists—all of them singers/accordionists/composers—like Alfredo Gutiérrez, Aniceto Molina, and Lisandro Meza emerged, becoming seminal figures of la *colombia* themselves. Andrés Landero, known as "the king of cumbia" and the father of accordion cumbia,[14] is arguably the other pillar of cumbia in Monterrey. All these performers come from the Colombian Caribbean coast, several of them from a rural background. For instance, Landero came from a peasant family and continued to work the land during his performing career. The population of this part of Colombia is predominantly of Afro-Indigenous decent, as are most cumbia performers.

The city of Cartagena de Indias, located on the Colombian Caribbean coast, was among the first ports colonized by the Spanish crown in the early sixteenth century. An important part of the trade of the southern territories, including African slaves, passed through this port. Furthermore, several indigenous groups inhabited this area before the colonial invasion. Since the early colony, this city and its surrounding areas have been multiracial and miscegenated. While the political, theological, and economic power of the crown was concentrated in the urban centers, many racialized peoples (*cimarrones* [maroons], rebellious indigenous groups) resisted in the peripheries, where their knowledge of the territory, as well as its vastness and insurmountability, protected them. It was among these peripheral, marginalized communities that cultural expressions like cumbia first emerged. Thus, in Colombia, cumbia was connected to racialized perceptions of sexuality, culture, and morality by the colonial (and then republican) white-mestizo elite. Before making it to the national sphere in the mid-twentieth century, cumbia went through a process of cultural "whitening" (Hernández Salgar 2007; Wade 2000). However, cumbia's "brownness" (or, better, its lack of whiteness) was never completely erased. This is something we can find not only in the music that made it to Monterrey but also in the art on the LP covers, where artists that fell outside the normative whiteness required by the recording industry were often portrayed in "rural" attire (shirt, pants, and indigenous sombrero) and "tropical" scenarios (palm trees, beaches, sand, etc.).

In contrast, the Mexican media industry held highly stylized production values. From the tangos of Libertad Lamarque, to the boleros of Los Panchos and Agustín Lara, to the corridos of Antonio Aguilar, to Dámazo Pérez Prado's mambos (to name a few), there is a consistency. Visually, fashionable suits, tuxedos, and dresses in line with the latest trends were used as well as fashionable hairstyles. Whether in a film or TV settings, mise en scène was carefully produced, stages were built, and the supporting band was uniformed. If a song was performed as part of a movie—as was often the case for artists like Lamarque and Aguilar—production values were in tune with Hollywood's "Golden Age." Francisco Crespo (2003) describes films produced during Mexico's "Golden Era of Cinema" as

> noirish melodramas mixed with extravagant musical productions. They featured lively dance numbers, in which traditional and then-fashionable Afro-Cuban music was used metaphorically to express modernity, decadence, and the effects of urbanization and "foreign elements" on Mexican society of the time. (227)

The Mexican entertainment industry was a key agent in setting the aesthetic standard for the rest of the region.

Mike Laure was among the first Mexican artists experimenting with cumbia. Starting in the early sixties, Laure became one of the pioneers of Mexican-made cumbia, an effort that was shortly followed by artists such as Rigo Tovar, who was particularly popular in the northeastern Mexico–US border region.[15] Musically, they rearranged cumbia and performed exclusively on western—and often electric—instruments. Their bands were essentially rock 'n' roll ensembles (electric bass, electric guitar, drum set, keyboards, sometimes saxophone) with Afro-Latin instruments added (congas, guiro, cowbell). Besides the timbral component, the cumbia pioneered by Laure and Tovar simplified its polyrhythmic structures and diluted its strong syncopated feel. Visually, both of them presented a "clean" look, wearing suits and fashionable hairstyles.

All in all, musics produced by the Mexican media industry went through a systematic process of whitening. In the Latin American musical context, this concept has been developed by race thinkers like Peter Wade (2000) and advanced by music scholars like Oscar Hernández Salgar (2007). Whitening is a complex idea; for my purposes, it suffices to define it as the processes through which non-European musics are altered to fit a racially "whiter" imaginary by incorporating elements derived from the European concert music canon. Instrumentation, forms, harmonic structures, (in film and television) mise en scène, and any of the elements that comprise musicking may take part in whitening processes. As the United States became a dominant economic and epistemic power throughout the twentieth century, its musics also entered such an imaginary.[16] Whitening processes certainly took place in the Colombian style that arrived in Monterrey (Wade 2000). This can be found in the incorporation of instruments, structures, and aesthetics from Western musics. Nonetheless, we see a less whitened aesthetic in the work of artists like Los Corraleros de Majagual and Andrés Landero vis-à-vis that of Mike Laure or Rigo Tovar.

In summary, in the late sixties and seventies when cumbia first arrived to Monterrey within the larger música tropical wave, it was adopted by the incoming migrants who identified with the music and the imaginaries it portrayed, while the middle and upper classes preferred the musics produced and whitened by the Mexican media industry.[17] The music produced by the mainstream media industry articulated their socioeconomic and political status in the city, as it portrayed an "aura" of ethnic, cultural, and racial whiteness. Thus, cumbia was simultaneously adopted by racialized and working-class immigrants and shunned by Monterrey's normative population.

SLOWING DOWN LA COLOMBIA: COLOMBIA YOUTHS AND CUMBIA REBAJADA

In the 1980s cumbia rebajada emerged in Monterrey simultaneously with the first local cumbia and vallenato artists, such as Celso Piña y su Ronda Bogotá,[18] La Tropa Colombiana, and Los Vallenatos de La Cumbia. A novel musical development after two decades of listening to Colombian cumbia, rebajadas marked a milestone in the assimilation process. Together with the early local bands, rebajadas constituted the first truly local type of cumbia emanating from *la colombia*. Reducing the speed of the LPs they had heard for decades and rerecording them onto cassette tape constituted a complex aesthetic practice, a technological process that advanced a long-standing culture into a sort of "local(ized) aurality," a music that stood somewhere between its Colombian performers and Monterrey's technological manipulation, and that was, finally, their own. Rebajadas were embraced by younger generations, the descendants of the rural immigrants. These generations found themselves in an equally bad or perhaps even more marginal situation. During the eighties and nineties, these youths reproduced, reinforced, and re-performed the culture they inherited.

Like their parents, once these youths finish high school—and often even before that—they find work in the informal sector or in low-paying posts in construction, cleaning services, factories, etc. The systematic process of pauperization these racialized/classed populations have endured is the very thing on which the city's development has relied for centuries. Furthermore, the ghettoization process they suffered via a series of state-sponsored housing projects starting in 1973—initially directed toward fighting squatting by internal migrants arriving to Loma Larga (Blanco Arboleda 2014, 158–61)—has developed into territorial disputes among youth groups. This hostile environment set the ideal conditions for the emergence of gangsterism. *Colombia* youths (*chavos colombia*) have been stigmatized within the city. This is the product of a successful campaign led by state and media, which renders them as criminal (170–200) and treats their constructed delinquency as the illness of the city, instead of as a symptom of systematic processes of racialization and classification of human life.

Colombia youths have appropriated their aural legacy and expanded it into a statement, not only asserting their long-standing marginalization but also denouncing it by making it visible. One of the most effective ways this has happened recently has been through the radical fashion trends that have emerged among *colombia* youths and that are documented at length by British photographer and fashion designer Amanda Watkins (2014) in the book *Cholombianos*, in which Leticia Saucedo, a local scholar and activist who has worked directly with these youths for several years in programs aimed at disarticulating gang violence and stigmatization, writes:

> Being "Colombia" is an identity taken up primarily by the youth of different working-class neighborhoods through the city. Its aesthetic continues to transform: from tight denim jeans, flannel shirts, Converse tennies [*sic*], and hairdos [a popular hairstyle in Mexico in the eighties and nineties "with bangs almost to the eyebrows, short on top, sometime with a small tail in the back, or with sideburns"], to the brightly colored Hawaiian shirts ..."Colombia" as a synonym for palm trees near the ocean, the image being a distant cry from a city encircled by a semi-dessertic [*sic*] zone, far away from the water and lush foliage of Central American climates.
>
> Being "Colombia" in this city of mirages carries with it the burden of being observed by others with a stigmatizing gaze. So there are those on one side who take pride in who they are, but also those who are almost bothered by this look and taste, by this youth culture's unhindered ostentatiousness, which first and foremost reveals a social class in which the fears, prejudices and frustrations of the middle and upper classes are placed. (33–34)

Saucedo's insightful account outlines the positionality of the *colombia* youth in the city and the disruptive quality of their very presence. More than a trend, identifying as *colombia* constitutes a statement and a transgressive manifestation of their subalternity.

Interloping in Monterrey's status quo comes at a price. Around 2010, a few years before Watkins published her book, the presence of the *colombia* youth was made more explicit by their gathering outside their peripheral neighborhoods and concentrating in Monterrey's downtown. Showcasing their marginality proved to be a highly disturbing performative statement of the city's normativity. When they gather outside "their territory"[19] in their extravagant outfits, these youths are constantly harassed by the local police via "random" frisks. For all practical purposes, this continuous, targeted police state resembles what Stuart Hall calls "policing the crisis."[20] This is accounted for in the fanzine *¡Qué pasó raza!* (What's Up, People!), edited by José Carlos Zarazúa and indexed in Watkins's book, which contains several testimonies by *colombia* youths.[21] In the texts, we find firsthand accounts of several of the issues I have discussed. Testimonies of police harassment and the stigmatization that comes with being *colombia* are found throughout, as well as accounts of the consumption of cheap drugs such as paint thinners (which seems to be fairly common), and pressure from family members and employers to look "normal." The repercussions for sticking to their identity range from simple nagging to being fired or even hit by the police. These are consequences that are harder to afford as they get older and acquire family responsibilities.

Talking to local musicians, cumbia enthusiasts, and even youths who do not identify themselves as *colombia*, it was striking to see how closely associated cumbia rebajada is with *colombia* youths. While visiting the local co-op Cruce de Caminos Ayaguara, Kooperativa Rayenari—an organization with a wide practice that includes cultural research, academic advising, project management, and teaching, located in Monterrey's old town—I met with a group of six youths (five males, one female), ranging in age from fifteen to the midtwenties, and Cristóbal López and Nydia Prieto, who run the organization, in what turned out to be an impromptu focus group. I was able to confirm how imbued cumbia is in the city and in their personal memories. These youths recalled with amazing detail the music's history back to the nineties and even the eighties, way before they were born. According to them, they have listened to cumbia and rebajadas since they can remember because "it's been around since we were born." Nevertheless, they associated rebajadas primarily with *colombia* youths, gangsterism, and drug consumption. Particularly interesting was the fact that one of the interviewees claimed that while he might know more about cumbia and vallenato than *colombia* youths, the difference between them lies in the fact that the latter make this music a fundamental part of their identity.

This differentiation is telling as it nuances the *colombia* phenomenon. The interviewee was not distinguishing himself from *colombia* youths so much in terms of race or class (he does not come from a privileged background), but in terms of musical taste and identity. Though all the people in the focus group admitted they listened to cumbia and rebajadas, they were clear in stating that it is just one of the many musics they consume. They claimed *colombia* youths not only have a very particular style of dancing cumbia,[22] but also that some of their moves mimic the act of getting high on paint thinners, pretending to have a plastic bag in one hand and breathing in and out of it.

The aural space *colombia* youths create through cumbias and rebajadas also constitutes a public statement. These musics are often consumed in public spaces like concerts, sonidero parties, *tardeadas* (parties for underage kids that usually take place in public open spaces in the afternoon), or simply on the street with some beers (also referred to as *caguamear*[23] by the locals). Cumbia fills these spaces. Through its aurality, a way of being in the city has been built. When the aural meets the imaginary, the utopian emerges. An idealized Colombian Caribbean runs throughout these youths' identity. Their colorful looks (often containing the yellow, blue, and red of the Colombian flag) and the tropical shirts "being a distant cry . . . from the water and lush foliage of Central American climates" gives us a glimpse of the utopian place they have constructed.

Roshanak Kheshti (2015) argues that sound has the capacity to "materially structure social relations, formations and actors" (12–13). Over the years, *la colombia* has transformed from a predominantly aural and cultural space to a microcosm that often manifests itself in quite material forms. Such is the case of Mario Duarte's store, "Artesanías Colombia," a little shop located near downtown Monterrey and close to one of the city's busiest zones (the intersection of Cuauhtémoc Street and Francisco Madero Avenue). Duarte—who started selling Colombian music on tape and travels yearly to Colombia to bring back merchandise—sells apparel, souvenirs, posters, music, paintings, miscellaneous items, and even musical instruments, all of them an homage to Colombia and its most popular vallenato and cumbia artists. Duarte's is a place where musicians, connoisseurs, *colombias*, slackers, and everyone who enjoys Colombian music and culture meet. The yellow, blue, and red of the Colombian flag cover every corner of the locale, illustrating the utopian Colombian Caribbean some regiomontanos envision through the music.

Artesanias Colombia and business owner Mario Duarte. Photograph by the author.

This utopian imaginary was a notion I found constantly during my fieldwork. A sort of longing for returning to a place most of them have not been to runs through *la colombia*. Perhaps even more telling was the fact that I received special treatment due to my nationality, something unheard of for someone carrying a Colombian passport. During my visit, people were keen to talk to me and respond to my questions, but also inquiring about Colombia, its music, and how well-known *la colombia* of Monterrey is over there, perhaps sending a symbolic shout-out. Musicians were also eager to play for me and even jam. That was the case with a local accordionist and *cajero* (the person who plays the caja vallenata) who happened to drop by Mario Duarte's store while I was there. After talking, they played one of my favorite vallenato songs upon my request: Adolfo Pacheco's "El mochuelo," featuring shop owner Duarte on the guacharaca. While we were talking, another two random men in their late thirties/early forties came in, bringing sodas and food. When the music began they started dancing. In only an instant, *la colombia* unveiled itself before me.

A FLOATING BOAT: "LA PIRAGUA"[24]

On the first volume of rebajadas, edited by Don Gabriel in the mideighties, the very first track is a rebajada rendition of "La piragua." This song is an unofficial anthem in Colombia and its composer José Barros is an iconic composer in the country. On the track, the first thing we hear is the aural double trace left by the white sound of the rolling tape overlaid by the needle. Dueñez skillfully lands the needle a few seconds before the song starts. Contained in these few seconds, prior to the actual song, is a palimpsestic inscription carrying part of the rebajada's history. A friction between the original version and its re-performed doppelgänger emerges from the very beginning. We hear a music that emanated thousands of miles away being re-performed and indexed to its putative home via a simple but fundamental technological operation. Technology made its indelible aural mark in rebajadas: a glitch that developed into a music practice; a practice that became a way of being. Technology's agency is heard in the hissing, the distorted pitches, the guttural voices, and a sense of time that seems to stretch back and forth. Instead of trying to mask the glitch, it is front and center. It is the very essence upon which this culture is made. The aesthetics of failure are turned into skill; malfunction becomes taste. A metaphor builds itself.

Then comes the guitar, moving from its lower to middle register. However, in its rebajada iteration, these visual metaphors seem to fold. Rebajadas put in evidence the arbitrariness of the spatial abstractions we use to describe sounds. In this case, the change of register seems more like a change of timbre, as if a different instrument engages in a duet with its other self. After a short introductory phrase, the guacharaca and bass guitar follow. The former provides the quintessential cumbia groove, three sixteenth notes phrasing toward the downbeats—the never-ending loop that spread throughout an entire continent. This and the bass guitar's two eighth notes, also landing on the downbeat, are among the only identifiable musical features found in most of cumbia's countless incarnations. It is indeed interesting that the two traits that endured in many of the musics that are known as cumbia throughout Latin America, the few things that seem to bind this convoluted genealogy, are the rhythmic augmentations and diminutions of the same groove. Put together, the bass guitar and guacharaca create a simple yet overwhelming polyrhythmic structure that constitutes cumbia's engine. In its rebajada self, this loop even feels endless, heavy and hypnotic, almost transcendental and ritual.

Over the groove, the guitar plays its melodic line; a series of three notes originally intended to mimic a sustained sound. The song's doppelgänger reveals all the creases. Each of the plucks unfolds and becomes perceptible, thus revealing the performer's technique. This is one of the things Don Gabriel says he likes about rebajadas. He claims the tracks he re-performs put in evidence the performers' quality and separates the exceptional from the good and the bad. I concur with him. It was through rebajadas that I was able to fully experience the masterfulness of Alfredo Gutiérrez's accordion. His rhythmic precision, the many and subtle ornaments and passing notes he uses so often to beautifully anticipate a good destination, but that in its rebajada guise seem to last for ages, creating a shocking and beautiful dissonance unheard of in this music: every little detail—timbral, rhythmic—emerges. An augmented aurality. The hypersensitive ear grasps every single sound and allows full engaging.

Rebajadas become more explicit through the voice. The rest of the instruments change, certainly, but the human voice mutates into something else. It sounds more like a terrible, deep scream. It is terrible in its darkness: a sort of angst or urgency emanates from it. The once "tropical" song is now filled with the guttural voicings of a mechanized voice telling us about "la piragua"; a pirogue that sailed long ago and far away, but that is almost palpable for the regiomontano listener. To rebajar a sung track is to cross a boundary. This becomes evident by analyzing Dueñez's catalogue. His earlier compilations are made up mostly of instrumental cumbias. As his practice, repertoire, and technique evolved, he began including fewer instrumental and more sung numbers. Eventually, full volumes dedicated to specific singers came out. As Juanita's meticulously kept archive tells us, after more than a hundred albums of mixed compilations, Don Gabriel started making volumes entirely dedicated to key cumbia performers like Andrés Landero (whose minor accordion cumbias reach a new level of heaviness after they pass through Dueñez's needle), Los Corraleros del Majagual and its offspring (Alfredo Gutiérrez, Lisandro Meza), the Binomio de Oro de América, Diomedez Díaz, local artists like Celso Piña and Super Grupo Colombia, and other rarities found in his collection, such as cumbias performed by mariachi bands.

The canoe in the song seems to freeze in time and elevate itself from the water. Sailing turns into floating, and in its journey the boat passes through several places of the Colombian Caribbean. As mythical as these may sound, the port of El Banco mythicized in the song by Barros is the very stage on which he was born, the same place from which in 1919—a few years after his birth—a wooden boat, property of a local merchant, sailed for the first time to the nearby town of Chimichagua transporting goods. These places, a few hundred miles away from the tropical beaches regiomontanos yearn for, are also lands of water. It is the place where the Magadalena River, Colombia's most important fluvial route, flirts with countless *ciénagas* and tributaries; places where racialized populations resisted the Spanish yoke and settled free towns of *cimarrones* and bellicose Amerindians whose many encounters are told by the miscegenated expression that is cumbia.

The rebajada iteration of "La piragua" has an effect both narcotic and perturbing. The relationship many people in Monterrey draw between listening to rebajadas and the consumption of cheap drugs like marijuana and paint thinners by *colombia* youths is a racialized stereotype but also a utopian aural practice. In the city, many argue, rebajadas replicate the psychotropic state induced by these drugs.[25] The convergence of the aural, the psychotropic, and the imaginary develops into a complex multisensory experience, communal and ritual, that provides *colombia* youths with a space in the city and a longing for a fantastic place on the Colombian Caribbean coast that they have never been to, but that they have built on aurality. In any case, while rebajadas are in fact consumed by these youths, they are also listened to by a wide variety of regiomontanos, in the same way cumbia is not a music exclusive to Loma Larga and its diaspora.

In this track states, ports and cities, waters and ancestors are mentioned in this quasi-mythical story that serves as the basis for an equally quasi-mythical imaginary: a piece of Colombia that surfaced in Monterrey. After the somber voice finishes telling us about the feats of the little wooden boat, challenging rough waters and storms, the beat accelerates little by little, in this case not through a technological maneuver but by the performers, as if the song wanted to return from its drowsy self. At the end it is not enough. "La piragua" suddenly stops, leaving just resonances and its technological trace—the needle over the tape. The aural, the oral, and the technological merge into a single object that leads the way into an entire microcosm that breaks through the hardships of an unequal modern metropole.

CONCLUSION

Since the 1990s, cumbia has established itself in Monterrey's public sphere via the entertainment industry—primarily radio and, to a lesser degree, television. Its race/class connotation has been gradually changing, as it has become one of many musics consumed by the general population. Furthermore, the popularity of the genre has brought a professionalization of the local cumbia scene. Many regiomontano performers play either Colombian or original tunes (always maintaining the Colombian aesthetic) regularly in local clubs that, though not the "hippest" or most exclusive in town, cater to a clientele much wider than the *colombia* population. A few music academies teaching Colombian music have emerged, as have local festivals devoted to it. Overall, cumbia seems to be making a transition from *popular* to "folk" music, from marginal cultural expression to music "tradition."

These changes are in line with more recent developments in cumbia in other Latin American countries. Many of the cumbias that have emerged in places like Peru, Argentina, Colombia, and Mexico, which initially carried a race/class association not much different from the one I have discussed, have been "reclaimed" by more diverse populations. This does not imply cumbia is making a "comeback." It has always been around. Rather, the fact that cumbia has been reappropriated (or, better, re-*adopted*) has exposed it to wider audiences. The people making and listening to these musics nowadays are not the same as thirty, twenty, or even ten years ago. This complicates its racialized connotation and, by extension, recent scholarship on the topic.

A new generation of musicians has turned to cumbia. These artists, often urban, middle-class, and even academically trained, have taken its aurality and reworked it through the techniques the globalized world has to offer. Sounds and aesthetics originating in the global north have been merging with local cumbia practices. DJing, jam bands, distorted instruments, pop aesthetics, experimentalism and much more are now part of the practice. Not only is the music's aurality in constant motion but its sociocultural context also is mutating and diversifying. Moving between its racialized past, projects of construction of national (and even regional) identity, the (dis)encounters of the neoliberal world, and the tensions between the local and global, now, more than ever, cumbia is exponentially expanding its already convoluted genealogy. This is a phenomenon that is beyond the purview of this chapter and that I explore further in other work.[26]

In the case of Monterrey, Colombian cumbia arrived via alternative circulation circuits and became a fundamental part of a generation of rural immigrants turned marginalized urbanites and their descendants. Sound systems, vinyl, cassette tapes, USB flash drives, and the sonideros behind them have been key agents in the process of establishing these musics in the city. Independent networks and piracy are the very basis of *la colombia*. This non-diasporic community has built its identity on the music circulated through these circuits; the cumbia that sounded in the fringes of the city eventually blended with it. While a knowledgeable group of local musicians, connoisseurs, and enthusiasts has emerged over the last few decades—perhaps destigmatizing this music and making it less of an interloper—rebajadas have seemed to retain their marginal status. Many of these connoisseurs step away from rebajadas and its racialized/classed connotation, render it as a "lesser" practice, a corruption of the original that contravenes the artist's intentions. In my conversations with local cumbia musicians and enthusiasts, the vast majority claim they dislike rebajadas, often arguing issues of fidelity and purity of practice that resemble the Eurocentric conception of "work." This is indeed a problematic claim. By the time regiomontanos adopted cumbia, this music had already gone through many transformations directly related to issues of politics, race, commercialism, and class in Colombia (Wade 2000).

For chavos *colombia*, cumbia and cumbia rebajada are not just taste, but a way of being, of existing in the city. While many people listen to rebajadas, this music continues to be closely associated with these youths. But, why are rebajadas and the *colombias* they are associated with the target of so much animosity in Monterrey? Why do rebajada's bizarre sonority and the extravagant fashion that goes with it generate so much anxiety? I suggest that rebajada's aurality and the culture built around it constitute a decolonial performative practice, what Mignolo (2009) calls "body politics." These are performatives that uncover, denounce, and resist the systematic marginalization these youths and their families have endured for generations. Unveiling modernity's dark side comes at a cost. In this case, going against the grain of the city's normativities makes this music and its consumers a target for further repression. Be that as it may, in Monterrey cumbias and rebajadas are not just markers of subalternity but also agents of disturbance that articulate resistance, and even a sense of futurity and utopia.

ACKNOWLEDGMENTS

I thank Gabriel and Juanita Dueñez, José Juan Olvera Gudiño, and to all the people I interacted with in Monterrey for their generosity and warmth. I am also grateful to the coeditors Martha Chew Sánchez and David Henderson, and to the peer reviewers for their invaluable comments. I dedicate this chapter specially to the memory of Celso Piña, "El Rebelde del Acordeón" (1953–2019), who passed during the final stages of producing this piece. Unless otherwise noted, all translations are my own.

BIBLIOGRAPHY

Backal, Alicia G. de. 2011. *La memoria archivada: los judíos en la configuración del México plural*. México: Universidad Nacional Autónoma de México: Facultad de Estudios Superiores Acatlán-UNAM: Comunidad Ashkenazí de México: Centro de Documentación e Investigación de la Comunidad Ashkenazí de México.

Baker, Geoffrey. 2015. "Digital Indigestion: Cumbia, Class and a Post-Digital Ethos in Buenos Aires." *Popular Music* 34 (2): 175–96.

Blanco Arboleda, Darío. 2005. "La música de la costa atlántica colombiana transculturalidad e identidades en México y Latinoamérica." *Revista Colombiana De Antropología* 41: 171–203.

Blanco Arboleda, Darío. 2007. "Mundos de frontera: colombianos en la línea noreste de México y Estados Unidos." *Trayectorias: Revista De Ciencias Sociales De La Universidad Autónoma De Nuevo León (México)* 09 (25).

Blanco Arboleda, Darío. 2014. *Los colombias y la cumbia en Monterrey: identidad, subalternidad y mundos de vida entre inmigrantes urbanos populares*. San Nicolás de los Garza, N.L., México: Facultad de Filosofía y Letras, Universidad Autónoma de Nuevo León.

Cavazos Garza, Israel, and Manuel Ceballos Ramírez. 1998. *Monterrey 400: estudios históricos y sociales*. Monterrey, México: Universidad Autónoma de Nuevo León.

Crespo, Francisco J. 2003. "The Globalization of Cuban Music through Mexican Film." In *Musical Cultures of Latin America: Global Effects, Past and Present*, edited by Steven Loza, 225–31. Los Angeles: UCLA Ethnomusicology Publications.

Delgado, Mariana, and Marco Ramírez Cornejo. 2012. *Sonideros en las aceras, véngase la gozadera*. Creative Commons Attribution-NonCommercial-ShareAlike 4.0 International License.

Fernández L'Hoeste, Héctor D., and Pablo Vila. 2013. *Cumbia! Scenes of a Migrant Latin American Music Genre*. Durham, NC, and London: Duke University Press.

Flores Torres, Oscar. 2009. *Monterrey histórico*. San Pedro Garza García, N.L., México: Centro de Estudios Historicos UDEM.

García Usta, Jorge, and Alberto Salcedo Ramos. 1994. *Diez juglares en su patio*. Santafé de Bogotá, D.C.: Ecoe Ed.

González Castillo, Eduardo. 2015. *Juventud, espacio urbano e industria cultural: un estudio del medio sonidero*. New York: Peter Lang.

Grosfoguel, Ramón, and Santiago Castro-Gómez. 2007. *El giro decolonial: reflexiones para una diversidad epistémica más allá del capitalismo global*. Bogotá: Siglo del Hombre.

Hall, Stuart. 2013. *Policing the Crisis: Mugging, the State and Law and Order*. London and Basingstoke, UK: Macmillan.

Hernández Salgar, Oscar. 2007. "Colonialidad y postcolonialidad musical en Colombia." *Latin American Music Review* 28 (2): 242–70.

Kheshti, Roshanak. 2015. *Modernity's Ear: Listening to Race and Gender in World Music*. New York: New York University Press.

Madrid, Alejandro L. 2008. *Nor-tec Rifa!: Electronic Dance Music from Tijuana to the World*. New York: Oxford University Press.

Maldonado-Torres, Nelson. 2007. "On the Coloniality of Being." *Cultural Studies* 21 (2–3): 240–70.

Metz, Kathryn. 2013. "*Pandillar* in the Jungle: Regionalism and *Tecno-cumbia* in Amazonian Peru." In *Cumbia! Scenes of a Migrant Latin American Music Genre*, edited by Héctor D. Fernández L'Hoeste and Pablo Vila, 168–87. Durham, NC, and London: Duke University Press.

Mignolo, Walter. 2009. "Epistemic Disobedience, Independent Thought and Decolonial Freedom." *Theory, Culture and Society* 26 (7–8): 7–8.

Mignolo, Walter. 2011. *The Darker Side of Western Modernity: Global Futures, Decolonial Options*. Durham, NC: Duke University Press.

Ochoa Gautier, Ana María. 2014. *Aurality: Listening and Knowledge in Nineteenth-Century Colombia*. Durham, NC: Duke University Press.

Olvera Gudiño, José Juan. 2005. *Colombianos en Monterrey: origen de un gusto musical y su papel en la construcción de una identidad social*. México: Consejo para la Cultura y las Artes de Nuevo León.

Olvera Gudiño, José Juan. 2010. "Los caminos de la vida son de migración y diversidad . . . además de la 'colombia.'" In *Colores y ecos de la colonia independencia*, 135–50. México: Municipio de Monterrey.

Pagden, Anthony. 1982. *The Fall of Natural Man: The American Indian and the Origins of Comparative Ethnology*. Cambridge: Cambridge University Press.

Quijano, Anibal, and Michael Ennis. 2000. "Coloniality of Power, Eurocentrism, and Latin America." *Nepantla: Views from South* 1 (3): 533–80.

Quijano, Anibal, and Michael Ennis. 2007. "Colonialidad del poder y clasificación social." In *El giro decolonial: reflexiones para una diversidad epistémica más allá del capitalismo global*, edited by Ramón Grosfoguel and Santiago Castro-Gómez, 93–126. Bogotá: Siglo del Hombre.

Radano, Ronald Michael, and Tejumola Olaniyan. 2016. *Audible Empire: Music, Global Politics, Critique*. Durham, NC: Duke University Press.

Romero, Raúl R. 2007. *Andinos y tropicales: La cumbia peruana en la ciudad global*. Lima: Pontificia Universidad Católica del Perú, Instituto de Etnomusicología.

Rubio Restrepo, Juan David. 2020. "'Una cosa es el indio y otra cosa es la antropología': Racial and Aural (Dis)Encounters in Cumbia's Current Circulation." *Twentieth-Century Music* 17 (1).

Santamaría Delgado, Carolina. 2014. *Vitrolas, rocolas y radioteatros: hábitos de escucha de la música popular en Medellín, 1930–1950*. Bogotá, D.C.: Editorial Pontificia Universidad Javeriana.

Small, Christopher. 1998. *Musicking: The Meanings of Performing and Listening*. Middletown, CT: Wesleyan University Press.

Tucker, Joshua. 2013. "From *The World of the Poor* to the Beaches of Eisha: Chicha, Cumbia, and the Search for a Popular Subject in Peru." In *Cumbia! Scenes of a Migrant Latin American Music Genre*, edited by Héctor D. Fernández L'Hoeste and Pablo Vila, 138–67. Durham, NC, and London: Duke University Press.

Unesco. 1980. *Sociological Theories: Race and Colonialism*. Paris: Unesco.

Vila, Pablo, Pablo Semán, Eloísa Martín, and María Julia Carozzi. 2011. *Troubling Gender: Youth and Cumbia in Argentina's Music Scene*. Philadelphia: Temple University Press.

Wade, Peter. 2000. *Music, Race, and Nation: Música Tropical in Colombia*. Chicago: University of Chicago Press.

Watkins, Amanda. 2014. *Cholombianos*. México, D.F.: Trilce Ediciones.

Wong, Ketty. 2012. *Whose National Music? Identity, "Mestizaje," and Migration in Ecuador*. Philadelphia: Temple University Press.

Wynter, Sylvia. 2004. "Unsettling the Coloniality of Being/Power/Truth/Freedom: Towards the Human, After Man, its Overrepresentation—an Argument." *CR: New Centennial Review* 3 (3): 257–337.

NOTES

1. *Rebajar* is partially translatable to "bringing down" or "cutting down."

2. I use *popular* (italicized) in its Latin American connotation where, broadly speaking, it is used to signify something characteristic of the working classes. This is directly related to the complex *música popular* (popular music) category in Latin America, a topic I don't deal with in this essay. For ethnomusicological studies relating race, class, and the *música popular* category, see Carolina Santamaría Delgado's chapter on *El giro decolonial* in Grosfoguel and Castro-Gómez (2007) and chapter 2 of Ana María Ochoa Gautier's *Aurality* (2014).

3. I will continue to use the term *la colombia* (italicized and lowercased) to refer to the *colombia* from Monterrey culture I analyze below.

4. I use *cumbia* (not to be confused with *cumbia rebajada*) as a broader signifier that includes Colombian cumbia, vallenato, and porro (another rhythm from the Colombian Caribbean coast) as well as mixtures of some or all of them performed by both Colombian and Mexican artists. Cumbia has a similar connotation in Monterrey. Though many locals are aware of the difference between these rhythms (and some of them even identify the subgenres of vallenato), *cumbia* often works as an umbrella term used to refer to the entire musical practice of *la colombia*. In this paper I occasionally use "Colombian music" interchangeably with cumbia as I have described it above.

5. For extended discussions of the sonidero culture in Mexico, see Delgado and Ramírez Cornejo (2012); González Castillo (2015); Cathy Ragland's chapter in Fernández L'Hoeste and Vila (2013); and Josh Kun's chapter in Radano and Olaniyan (2016).

6. Olvera Gudiño (2005) tracks the migration and establishment of the *colombia* culture. He argues that most of the immigrants that arrived to Monterrey from these states—which had rural-based economies—were part of an unskilled/uneducated workforce that found work mainly in the informal economy sector: construction, domestic work, and the like. Dueñez himself started working at age twelve at a foundry.

7. *La raza* (the race) is a concept ingrained throughout Mexico. It is particularly used among working-class populations to talk about what they conceive as "their" people. The underlying racial component of this expression has to do with a shared acknowledgment of their shared mestizo (European-Indigenous) ancestry. *La raza* is a complex, loaded, and problematic race/class signifier I don't deal with in this essay.

8. While the neoliberal economic turn is usually thought of as taking place throughout the 1980s—especially during the Reagan and Thatcher administrations—this economic model wasn't fully established in Latin American countries until the 1990s. Several governments implemented neoliberal reforms in the eighties and even the late seventies, but it wasn't until the nineties, with the implementation of NAFTA in Mexico and the economic reforms of presidents like Cesar Gaviria in Colombia and Carlos Menem in Argentina, that the neoliberal agenda was in full throttle in the region.

9. *To articulate* is a concept I develop in the next section based on Fernández L'Hoeste and Vila's (2013) formulation in their introduction to their edited volume. Broadly speaking, it is the capacity music—as cultural practice—has to both "construct" and "enact" processes of identity formation. As I use it in this essay, *to articulate* is not related to Stuart Hall's idea of articulation.

10. Elaborating on the work of Quijano as well as Enrique Dussel, thinkers like Walter Mignolo, Santiago Castro-Gómez, Nelson Maldonado-Torres, Silvia Wynter, and Arturo Escobar have contributed to what some have called "the decolonial turn." An introduction to Latin American decolonial thought can be found in Grosfoguel and Castro-Gómez (2007).

11. For extended discussions on the matter, see Wynter (2004); Padgen (1982); and Quijano and Ennis (2000).

12. For a substantial study of the intricate development of cumbia and *música tropical* in Colombia, see Wade (2000).

13. Blanco Arboleda (2014) and Olvera Gudiño (2007) propose different explanations for the locals' proclivity to listen to Colombian music over regional musics. While this is beyond the purview of this essay, these theories revolve around issues of self-identification (i.e., cumbia often portrays rural topics/imaginaries that may have connected with the immigrants' rural origin) and the prominence of the accordion, the primal instrument of many regional musics in the area.

14. Accordion cumbia is a subgenre of cumbia whose development is credited to Landero. By adapting the melodies traditionally performed by the indigenous *gaita* (a flute-like instrument autochthonous to the Colombian Caribbean), Landero's extrapolation brought the Afro-Indigenous roots of cumbia to the accordion. While there is a wide array of musics performed with accordion in this region, Landero's style—and the style of his pupils—is recognized as a discrete category.

15. For an extended discussion of Laure and Tovar see the chapter by Olvera Gudiño and Madrid in Fernández L'Hoeste and Vila (2013)

16. I'm aware that many (if not all) the musics that emanated from the United States to Latin America throughout the twentieth century are Afro-American in essence (jazz, rock, hip hop) and that this may contradict the whitening dynamics I am proposing. While this may sound counterintuitive, it is important to note that most US musics that made it to Latin America via the media industry from the fifties to the seventies were performed mostly by white musicians (Bill Haley & His Comets, Elvis Presley, the Beatles, the Rolling Stones, etc.). On top of that, musics coming from the United States and England (countries perceived as "developed," "civilized," and economically advanced) are—under coloniality's standards—often more desirable than those from Latin American countries (perceived as "backward," "underdeveloped," and poor), particularly among the middle and elite classes.

17. During my fieldwork, I attended a dance hosted in an open square of the Palacio Municipal (the city's government headquarters) free of charge with a full orchestra mostly playing the aforementioned Afro-Cuban rhythms and attended primarily by senior and elderly couples. Although it was a free event, open to the public, it was interesting that most of the attendants wore elegant-casual clothes and were lighter-skinned, indicating they were not necessarily wealthy, but arguably from well-off backgrounds. The few darker-skinned couples (some of them families with children) mostly sat around watching the people dance. To my knowledge, this dance takes place every Sunday afternoon.

18. Piña was *the* pioneer of regiomontano Colombian cumbia, among the first to pick up an accordion and learn Colombian tunes by ear.

19. Especially in early 2010s, chavos *colombia* started congregating in downtown Monterrey. A wave of violence (mostly associated with drug cartels) interrupted this phenomenon. *Colombia* youth culture is highly dynamic and volatile. The trends and cultural movements documented by Watkins (2014) are constantly changing and reinventing themselves.

20. I am drawing a parallel with Hall's study *The Politics of "Mugging"* (2013). Focusing on the period 1972–73, Hall argues, "The on-going [sic] problem of policing the blacks [youths] had become, for all practical purpose, synonymous with the wider problem of policing the [economic] crisis" (332). Though this is a different context, I read similar dynamics in my study. Policing *colombia* youths (and here I want to highlight a race/class relation very similar to the one Hall studies) became not only a form of policing the crisis, but of reinforcing and safeguarding Monterrey's normativities and the inequality on which these are built.

21. The exact origin of the fanzine—whether it was produced for the book or a reissue of an existing publication—is not clarified in the book.

22. Contrary to the more traditional couple dance style used for most "tropical" music by the older *colombia* generations, *colombia* youths are known for dancing communally to cumbias and vallenatos. They dance in circles that can reach the hundreds. In them, each person dances alone following the circular motion of the group and the beat of the song in what can better be described as a "cumbia swarm."

23. In Mexico 32 oz./940 ml beer bottles are called *caguamas*. Due to their size, drinking *caguamas* is often thought of as a social experience. *Cagueamear* refers to the act of hanging out (often in the street) around *caguamas*.

24. This section is partially based on Alberto Salcedo Ramos's piece on José Barros, collected in García Usta and Salcedo Ramos (1994), and "La historia de 'La piragua' y su compositor Andariego," kienyke.com, last modified March 12, 2017, available at https://www.kienyke.com/historias/jose-barros-y-la-piragua.

25. This is something not unheard of. It closely resembles the chop and screw movement that emerged a few years later and hundreds of miles up north in Houston where, in the early 1990s, instead of cumbia they had hip hop, and instead of paint thinners they had codeine. I have not found evidence connecting the rebajada movement in Monterrey to Houston's chop and screw.

26. See Rubio Restrepo (2020). For other studies on the diversification of cumbia at the turn of the millennium, see Madrid (2008); Tucker (2013); and Baker (2015).

3

CUBATÓN'S TRANSNATIONAL CREOLIZATIONS

WILLIAM GARCÍA-MEDINA

The 2014 musical hit "Bailando," performed by the Afro-Cuban duo Gente de Zona and the Spanish singer Enrique Iglesias, took the Latin music industry by surprise with the song's timba-reggaetón fusion. When reggaetón music was beginning to rise on the *Billboard* charts during the early 2000s, several artists in Latin American countries began searching for success by creating innovative songs capable of reaching a mainstream audience. Despite reggaetón's notoriety—with dances replicating sexual intercourse and lyrics about material capitalism—"Bailando," by contrast, elicited emotions of love, friendship, and passion, ushering in new possibilities for marketing Cuban music.

This new sound that infuses melodic Cuban timba with reggaetón beats—cubatón—now overshadows the famed Cuban hip hop genre that was once a near-obsession for many US scholars, journalists and documentarians. As Sujatha Fernandes (2006) describes, Cuban hip hop is necessarily political and entails rejection of any form of capitalism. Cubatón has become a highly aesthetic alternative that fuses various Caribbean musical styles, including dembow, merengue, bachata, and timba. However, unlike Puerto Rican artists who oscillate freely between reggaetón and hip hop, cubatón artists are restricted to either hip hop or reggaetón, mainly because of the harsh criticism cubatón music has received from many hip hop artists, who claim cubatón's explicit sexual lyrics glorify wealth and violence. The Cuban government has also previously regulated cubatón precisely because of its stark contrast to what they considered authentically Cuban music (Rueda 2012). Cubatón is particularly appealing to young crowds because, unlike Cuban hip hop, it is ideally suited for crowds wishing to escape, at least temporarily, from the constraints and hardships of Cuba's communist party rule.

The explosion of cubatón came late in the Special Period, a euphemism for an extended period of time of economic dissolution caused by the fall of the Soviet Union in 1991 and, by extension, the COMECON (Council for Mutual

Economic Assistance). As a result, the country lost approximately 80 percent of its imports—especially affecting agriculture, healthcare, and the industrial sector—and experienced severe food shortages. The rupture between Cuba and the Soviet Union resulted in the Cuban government opening its doors to mass tourism in order to bring income to the country. Eventually, many Cuban hip hop artists, disenchanted by their lack of success amidst the crisis, crossed over to cubatón music in search of financial success and greater artistic freedom to produce different styles of music. Since 2002, with little official support or airtime on state-controlled radio, many cubatón artists have recorded in makeshift studios lined with egg cartons for sound isolation and equipped with laptops, circulating their music in the streets through homemade CDs and flash drives. Cubatón has both captivated the youth and enraged a cultural establishment with its vulgar lyrics and transcaribbean sounds of reggaetón, hip hop, and other musical styles.

Well-known Cuban hip hop artists like Aldo from Los Aldeanos, in songs like "Lo que te mereces," have indirectly criticized cubatón, claiming it is an "unconscious" and "corrosive" genre of music that encourages Cuban society to embrace the ailments of capitalism. Artists such as Aldo are paradoxically fascinating. On one hand, they advocate for more individual freedom, the eradication of racism, the elimination of government social control, and the creation of Cuban prosperity overall. On the other, they align themselves with conservative Cuban values, such as self-control, anti-capitalism, and Cuban nationalism, values that have been imposed by the island's government.

Although a host of scholars have underscored Cuban hip hop's revolutionary anti-capitalist discourse, few have written both at length and critically on the indirect cultural politics of cubatón. Cuban hip hop scholars such as Sujatha Fernandes (2006), Nora Gámez Torres (2013), and Marc Perry (2015), among others, have minimally written about cubatón precisely as its popularity has emerged. After receiving support from the Cuban government, hip hop in Cuba, with its anti-American and anti-capitalist appeal, was understood as a transmission and reproduction of a Cuban discourse of *revolución* that created a collective identity even if it opposed state institutions. British musicologist Geoffrey Baker was one of the first scholars to provide a more in-depth analysis of Cuban revolutionary hip hop (hip hop *revoluciónario*) in dialogue with the new musical genre that was superseding it. In *Buena Vista in the Club: Rap, Reggaetón and Revolution in Havana*, Baker argues:

> The degree of interest in the subject [of hip hop] by foreign writers and filmmakers is out of all proportion to its role in the Cuban cultural scene:

in terms of audiences and media space, rap has been utterly overshadowed first by timba (Cuban salsa) and then by reggaetón, yet these forms of commercial popular music, the most eagerly consumed by young Cubans, have received considerably less attention from overseas.... The enthusiasm for rap and lack of curiosity about reggaetón are revealing of the scholarly agendas that dominate the academic study of popular music, which tend to give greater priority to logocentric, supposedly resistant, niche musical forms than to more widely consumed commercial dance genres. (2011, 19–20)

Baker elaborates on the cultural politics and history of hip hop in Cuba and its contentious relationship to reggaetón's insurgent populism. In highlighting the importance of cubatón, Baker observes two recurring ideas expressed in critical response to it:

[The first, that] reggaetón is an authentic Caribbean musical genre that has been corrupted by the hyper-commercialism of the global music industry and by a lack of discernment on the part of the Cuban media, rather than being an inherently problematic cultural form. The second, that the threat of commercialized, globalized reggaetón could be readily reduced by a great effort toward local adaptation (glocalization), and that such Cubanization would be the result of natural evolution. (157)

Just as reggaetón had to modify its lyrics in order to attract cross-generational support, cubatón is a fusion of local music. The interplay of nationalizing hip hop and explicit politics was suddenly riding two overlapping waves in the late 1990s: the Black August–inspired hip hop revolution and the music-inspired tourist boom. As Baker notes, many of Los Aldeanos' songs, such as "Aldito el guzanito," depict Havana as an urban space full of heartless people, while other songs, such as "La niña robot," "Crisis de fe," "El joven fantasma," and "Vampiros," criticize Cuban society. Cuban rappers criticize the pretensions of urban dwellers and claim that they are responsible for the problems in Cuba. They criticize Habaneros for flaunting their wealth and living a cosmopolitan lifestyle in a country in need of change, meanwhile stressing humility and a disdain for capitalism.

Nora Gámez Torres, in "Rap Is War: Los Aldeanos and the Politics of Music Subversion in Contemporary Cuba" (2013), emphasizes her disagreement with Geoffrey Baker, who suggests that the Cuban Revolution and hip hop are "two branches of the same tree." Gámez Torres argues that Cuban hip hop is subversive, considering Los Aldeanos as an example of radical opposition to the socialist state in the cultural public sphere (4). She argues that Los Aldeanos employ effective strategies through their music: the public legitimation of their voice as representatives of the people; the construction of social antagonism via the deconstruction of state ideology and the presentation of historical leadership as illegitimate; and the reappropriation of revolutionary ideology to promote action through confrontation (6). In addition, they deny receiving any money from foreign agents or from the opposition based in Miami (which is perceived as anti-national and opportunistic).

Marc Perry dedicates a few paragraphs to cubatón, concluding that the genre will eventually end up reproducing rather than undermining dominant representations and hierarchies of gendered difference (2015, 208). Although Perry's prediction on the global marketing of cubatón is in accordance with the genre's present situation, he also overlooks the multiple layers of cubatón at the local and underground level. However, I do not wish to depart from or make light of Perry's formulation of cubatón's corporate cooptation, as it is a present reality difficult to ignore and one that requires consideration. Clearly, Perry mentions cubatón as a response to Baker's critique of US scholars framing Cuba as an anti-capitalist nation and as a center of Black radical consciousness. Perry's argument fails to explore different ways of understanding Caribbean creolizations through informal politics of subversiveness. By the same token, Baker fails to understand that Cubanness is also inextricably connected to the African diaspora, and does in fact have a shared history with Black Americans, so that Cubanness effectively transcends the confines of nationhood from a transnational lens. In this chapter, I suggest that we look at the contending forces of homogeneity and differentiation as a Caribbean manifestation of more universal trends—from racial inequality to musical innovation to economic uncertainty. I argue that cubatón, as a musical genre and creolized cultural production, challenges dominant narratives of nationalism, race, and gender, as seen through the work of cubatón artists Osmani García, Alkana, and El Micha. I highlight two things: (1) the creolization that is cubatón when we approach it from a transnational and transcaribbean lens; and (2) the fact that, although as a popular music genre it is now a globalized one, cubatón is still a music of escape and nostalgia but in a transnational, globalized, pan-Latin framework. Because of this, it functions both subversively and in tandem with a corporate transnationalism of cubanidad/latinidad.

CUBATÓN CREOLIZATIONS

The term *creolization* has been defined in various ways over the past decades, in part because the term "creole" has varied considerably over time and space. Edouard Glissant has maintained that creole cultures emerged in the Caribbean as a result of colonization and the mixing of indigenous, African, and European peoples, who created new identities (2010, 90). In Manthia Diawara's documentary *Edouard Glissant: One World in Relation* (2010), Glissant discusses creolization as being about unity and multiplicity as well as the constant changes that rearrange those multiplicities. Furthermore, he describes identity formation by centering on the rhizomatic: identities are formed in relation to the Other but also in contrast with the Other. Glissant would argue that the idea of contrast is a type of relation, formed to create an ambivalence and avoid any kind of negation. Yet, we understand that these negations, contrasts, differences exist in epistemologically violent environments. Does Glissant overlook the human condition when he theorizes creolization and the rhizomatic? Humanity is not built for what Glissant was proposing—it is utopian in the same way that pan-Latinidad is also a utopian identity and notion. The Spanish Caribbean question that is posed when people deny their Blackness—"Y tu abuela 'onde está?" ("And your grandma, where she at?")—is your rhizomatic approach to Blackness in a pan-Latino context. It is our Spanish Caribbean transnational world in relation. Geoffrey Baker is on to something in his research around Cuban hip hop and reggaetón, but his lack of acknowledging this very complexity of the Caribbean makes his analysis limited. This is the Caribbean human condition.

I agree with Glissant in the way that I see cubatón as having unfixed conclusions and that it is constantly changing. The attempt to decide where cubatón starts and ends is in tension with creolization. In a transnational context, one can argue that pan-Latinidad, as a political rationality, discursively encompasses certain elements of multiplicities that have value in unity. This phenomenon of the unidentifiable and the multiple has been used as a marketing and political strategy that overlooks current and continuous local racial hierarchies and geographies, as discussed by scholars such as Arlene Dávila, Raquel Rivera, and Petra Rivera-Rideau. Glissant is well-intentioned but at the same time overlooks the neoliberal power of political interests, appropriation, consumption, and commodification. Pan-Latino unity as a dichotomous manifestation against the background of racial formations in the United States is what sells. It becomes rhizomatic for the wrong reasons. Corporations are good at making Cuban music, like cubatón, tenable for a transnational Latino audience by making connections with the local characteristics of the genre but then extracting them from their sociopolitical context.

In *Globalisation and the Post-Creole Imagination: Notes on Fleeing the Plantation* (2009), Michaeline Crichlow offers a continuation of creolization that takes into account its multidimensional aspects, including politics and imperialism, in ways that look beyond the theories of peasant creolizations, plantation-based economies, and Glissant's romanticized understanding of Caribbean "points of entanglements"—his idea of a *tout monde* (all-encompassing world). Crichlow's main argument invites us to move creolization debates beyond the plantation and the ideological constructions of Caribbean homogeneity. Her positionality situates the local within the global in relation to the remaking of geographical boundaries through a dystopian lens:

> While creolization has been popularized in relation to Caribbean forms originating with plantation and slavery generally, giving rise to cultural forms in worlds made anew in the Americas, it seemed to me that one could justifiably argue that creolization was a process that transcended an emphasis on its originary places, populations and spaces. (xiii)

Crichlow also posits:

> Analyzing the creolization process beyond any plantation, and historicizing it, results in a *dynamized* creolization, that helps supersede the romanticization of peoples and politics, especially those considered "peasant folk" who often become the central figures of the production of "Caribbean culture." Historians in this sense must rework around literary, artistic, sociological, historical, hermeneutic, political, economic, ethnographic, and philosophical insights of Caribbeans and other citizens of the present space of the global world. (xiii)

On the whole, how concretely do Caribbean creolizations, as a process of selective creation and cultural struggle, find expression in this postcolonial, neoliberal economic era? In this sense, creolization cannot be simply read through conflictual, economistic, binaristic, or deterministic scripts but rather through exercises of a cultural politics expressed in the conducts of modern governmentality. Crichlow attributes the essentialisms of creolization to state/elite-mobilized notions of culture, misrecognizing or simply ignoring differences and contestation over the meaning of creole citizenship. Crichlow also reveals the hegemonic restructuring of popular notions of uniqueness, spooled around ideas about the national, the community, and self-development, threaded in a particular optic that becomes "common sense" for most Caribbeans in much the same way the ideology of racial democracy works for Brazilians (8).

By the end of the twentieth century it was clear that people in highly technological societies preferred to maximize differentiation. Racial, regional, and ethnic communities resisted benign imperialism and developed separate identities by reconfiguring and disseminating new traditions through the use of off-the-shelf technologies. Glissant's scholarship regarding globalization in the Caribbean region showed how these global transformations gave rise to new cultural contact zones, expanding the processes of creolization.

In this way, Juan Flores's framework, in his article "Creolite in the Hood: Diaspora as Source and Challenge," becomes a mainstay for future research encompassing migration, return migration, and globalization beyond the traditional realms of economic remittances and traditional Caribbean frameworks. Furthermore, Flores puts forward two related arguments about contemporary Caribbean culture identified within the cauldron of globalization. The first asserts that the most active site for contemporary Caribbean creolization and intercultural entanglements can be found not so much within the region but rather among the large transnational diasporic communities dwelling in the large global cities abroad. The second argument is that many of the creolized cultural forms and values adopted through social interactions in the diaspora travel back to the home territories through return migration or the media. Issues of race, gender, and class relations, in particular, resurface in new ways within the local national population as a "cultural remittance," with profound effect on the conceptualization as well as commodification of national cultures and traditions (2005, 17).

Antonio Benitez-Rojo adds:

> For me, creolization is a term with which we attempt to explain the unstable states that Caribbean artifacts, continuously transformed by a series of performers, present over time; for me this is not a process—a word that implies forward movement—but a broken series of recurrences, of happenings, whose only law is change.... I think that in the coming together and pulling apart of the innumerable fragments that circulate through the Caribbean sociocultural space many kinds of forces are at work. To begin with, there is an assortment of competing desires; not simple desires but complex ones which we can relate to anthropological terms like retention, resistance, assimilation, acculturation, enculturation and so forth. (2003, 19)

It is through these multiple Caribbean thinkers and scholars of the Caribbean that I want us to think of cubatón's creolization: as a process, but also as an ongoing pull and tug that centers how globalization, neoliberalism, and colonialism are constantly shaping transnational identities. Cubatón's creolization grapples with the traction of race, gender, and citizenship—the good, the bad, and the ugly—as both subversive and complicit. Furthermore, I want to push us to think in the ways that, for these thinkers I have discussed, creolization is not placed at the crossroads of the political as well as the neoliberal and globalized commodification that is cubatón, or in this sense, cubanidad. For example, here I am referring to the global success of Gente de Zona and the proliferation of cubatón within the Zumba fitness music repertoire. I want us to think of creolization not only as that which is unattainable and impossible to put in a box, but also in the way that this same unidentifiability has been commodified for global pan-Latino consumption. It is the moment of sitting in the car with my Dominican immigrant mother-in-law and her Afro-Ecuadorian partner as they sing along and rejoice in Gente de Zona's "La gozadera" when I realize the way non-Cuban immigrants in the United States are also living through their own sense of nostalgia and escape from everyday working-class life. Cubatón's creolization globalized is evidence of what Juan Piñón argues in his essay "Corporate Transnationalism: The U.S. Hispanic and Latin American Television Industries." He writes, "I argue that the line between the national and the foreign in U.S. Hispanic and Latin American television has become blurry because of the increasing presence of transnational capital, productions, and formats" (2014, 23). He traces corporate transnationalism in US/Latin American media companies, including Sony. Meanwhile, Cuban hip hop artists and scholars have criticized cubatón as foreign or vulgar; it is some of these same tropes that make it subversive in acknowledging people's subjectivity, agency, and transnational identities. It is also complicit with this neoliberal era we live in, where it is appropriated and commodified for everyone's consumption.

RECONSIDERING CUBATÓN'S CREOLIZATION AND THE CORPORATE TRANSNATIONALISM OF CUBANIDAD

Cuban hip hop artists criticize the commodification of hip hop fashion, which, since its inception, always had a "well-dressed swag" mentality; at the same time, they themselves followed the same fashion trends. Even though Los Aldeanos have been critical of the Cuban government and their anti-industrial developmental imperative, they fail to acknowledge the historical connections of capitalism and creolization. We can ask, how has the relationship between profit and creolized cultures been in tension? Capitalism and creolization have a history together—it is the Caribbean. The same cubanidad that Aldo refers to is also the same cubanidad that is tied to capitalism and creolization. In "Creolization in Havana: The Oldest Form of Globalization," Benitez-Rojo argues that Cuban tourism has always been an important force for converting Havana into a cosmopolitan city (2005, 79). He states that by the eighteenth century,

> Above and beyond gambling and other vices, music and dance were the principal entertainments that Havana offered the traveler. In 1798, the chronicler Buenaventura Ferrer estimated that the city had some fifty balls per day. At the same time, in the *cabildos* blacks danced and sang, to the rhythm of drumbeats, the *piqui piquimbin* or *Engo teraneme* or *Cangala lagonto*, and in the brothels they danced the *chuchumbe*, a creolized dance that can be taken as an antecedent of the *rumba*. (85)

This lively scene influenced many visitors and writers, such as Alejo Carpentier, James Baldwin, and Nicolás Guillén. Benítez-Rojo disagrees with many Cuban scholars (and rappers such as Aldo) who refuse to expand and reconfigure contemporary Cuban identity, transnational music histories and their place in the Caribbean. He writes:

> Thanks to commercial contacts and economic dependence on the United States, Afro-Cubanism was transmitted in the 1920s to the island's entire population via the first radios, victrolas, and disc recordings; later vehicles would be the movies and television. Meanwhile the proximity to the United Sates contributed (through tourism, the recording industry, and the interchange of music and performers) to the development of both local creolization and its influence abroad. At present, thanks to the post-Soviet crisis, Havana has started to resemble what it was: a cosmopolitan port city with a complex, creolized culture whose population looks towards the sea with hope. (95)

In other words, to think of cubanidad as insular would be a mistake. Instead, we should think of cultural productions such as cubatón from a transcaribbean and transnational perspective of creolization. Benítez-Rojo does not wholly criticize tourism as a negative aspect of Cuban history and does not advocate complete disengagement from capitalist economic circuits. During the first thirty years of Castro's government, he notes, the island lost almost all touristic value. In this light, raperos' prioritization of individual market pursuits stands in juxtaposition to more collaborative modes of political cohesion and solidarity, precisely a kind of nostalgic loss with the rise of Cuban reggaetón. Perry quotes DJ Alexis D'Boys, saying that "many raperos are now doing reggaetón because of the Cuban Rap Agency, so they're destroying the culture of hip hop by commercializing it" (2015, 211). While he mentions reggaetón in Cuba, he does not acknowledge the multidimensional aspects of cubatón. In contrast, Baker places Afro-diasporicity in his work, perhaps unintentionally, by placing cubatón as contradictory to the national imaginary due to its syncretic musicalizations and neoliberal involvement. Perry in particular seems to avoid the "having fun" aspect of enjoying good music, marked by communal sharing, dancing, singing, toasting, and boasting. The idea to consider, then, is: are acts of protest limited to picketing and openly standing against social injustices? In his essay "Looking for the Real Nigga: Social Scientists Construct the Ghetto," historian Robin D. G. Kelley suggests that there are informal and formal forms of politics and refers to them, respectively, as "infrapolitics" and "organized resistance" (2004). But, importantly, these are two sides of the same coin.

Ignoring the Cuban diaspora in the United States is a necessary ingredient for claiming Cuba as a country without external influences, whether from the perspective of Cuba or its exile community. Unlike Cuban hip hop artists who refuse to mention the Cuban diaspora (mainly in Miami) in their songs in order to avoid their historical connections to the United States (despite accepting Cuban exile remittances), cubatón artists' collaborations in the United States, mainly in Miami, highlight a new era of Cuban–Puerto Rican–Dominican relations that is becoming prominent in Latin America and in US Latino communities.

A very good example of a cubatón artist striving to use infrapolitics is Osmani "La Voz" García, whose notorious song "Chupi chupi" was denounced in November 2011 by Cuban Minister of Culture Abel Prieto and the president of the Cuban Institute of Music, Orlando Vistelas, as "degenerate" for its sexual overtones. García has nonetheless made connections with many reggaetón artists in Puerto Rico and the United States. García's goal in his music is to entertain and give his audience and fans a chance to experience life through dance, laughter, and a connection to the sexual self. In other words, cubatón allows Cubans an expressive space that is ambivalently supported by corporate transnationalism. Some would say that this is not radical, but neither is state surveillance. Cubatón's performance is liberating for Cubans in that they can attend to their own humanity and sense of self, and connect to others across Caribbean diasporas even while being pan-latinized. Moreover, Osmani García also emphasizes his collaborations with Puerto Rican artists Farruko and J Alvarez, among other artists on the island, with songs like "Chupi chupi," "La puteri," "Estoy pa' Dartela," and "Emperifollarse." García is now based in Miami and is signed with Legacy Recordings, a division of Sony Music; many of his songs are also distributed through the Zumba fitness program's music and choreography. In this sense, García's creolized music, which was once a glocalized phenomenon, is now a globalized one through corporate transnationalism.

As previously noted, many cubatón artists were hip hop artists who wanted to make a living from their talent or wanted to fuse their music with different Caribbean rhythms. Havana Cultura, a cultural showcase initiated by Havana Club (the rum company) for diffusing Cuban music and art to the world, began to interview many of these artists or groups on their distinctive approaches to producing cubatón music. It has published detailed interviews with cubatón groups Gente de Zona, Candyman, Los Cuatro, Insurrecto, Baby Lores, Los Confidenciales, Kola Loka, Micha, Alkana, and El Chacal, among others.

From Santiago de Cuba, Afro-Cuban Alkana (Mileidys Gonzales) identifies as a reggaetónera, rapper, and feminist MC who advocates for a women's music label. A former member of the hip hop group Alto Voltaje, she grew up with folkloric dance, music, and theatrical performances, and these inspired her to become a musician. She believes that regardless of musical style, what matters is that the message entails reflection and positive thinking. Her preference is for reggaetón and hip hop rhythms, where she finds "a true freedom of speech" that "gives you the freedom to say what you want, how you want and when you want." Alkana's intricate and versatile approach to music in Cuba is problematic to many Cuban hip hop purists, not only because of the constant stigma against reggaetón but also because reggaetón represents Cuba as a twenty-first-century Caribbean country undergoing change ("Alkana [Havana Cultura]" 2011).

Where does Alkana fit between Aldo's cubanidad/Cuban cultural argument and the corporate transnationalism of cubatón? Alkana is a Black Cuban woman artist that many still do not know about. She is a local artist who creates a creolized cultural production that is rendered unextractable by Aldo's sense of cubanidad and corporate transnationalism. Also, where is the engagement of Cuban hip hop scholars with Alkana's work?

Meanwhile, other reggaetón artists openly state that they are not interested in political affairs and are mainly concerned with making people dance. Born in Havana, Afro-Cuban reggaetón artist El Micha (Michael Sierra Miranda), in a video made by Havana Cultura, states that his aspiration is "to try that in every house, in every car, in every place, people hear my raspy voice telling people the truth, telling them to dance and telling them to forget about everything else, and that quality is quality" ("El Micha [Havana Cultura]" 2011). Interviewed in a poor neighborhood, underneath a mural of Fidel Castro wielding a machete, he adds:

> Yo no sé la música que yo hago. Yo trato de fusionar los ritmos bien tradicionales Cubanos, con el ritmo de ahora de reggaetón. Le pongo el ritmo, le pongo la voz mía, empastan bien y el ritmo es eso. Y el ritmo mío es eso, un sazón ahí que es lo que hecho yo. Verdaderamente no se ni que ritmo es. ("El Micha [Havana Cultura]" 2011)

> [I don't know the music that I make. I try to create a fusion between traditional Cuban rhythms and the rhythms of today of reggaetón. I put together the rhythm, my voice, they mesh well and that is the rhythm. And the rhythm is that: a seasoning there is what I've made. Truthfully, I don't even know what rhythm it is.] (my translation)

His style of reggaetón, which he seems reluctant to categorize, offers a new way to represent poor neighborhoods in Cuba. Moreover, it hits home with Glissant's idea of opacity—the idea of knowing and not knowing in a way that does not adhere itself to a particular essence—and that these multiplicities comes from unknown places. For El Micha, there is no fixed conclusion for the music he creates. He reconstructs and remixes from what is available to him. During an interview, he walks around his neighborhood while rapping freestyle a cappella, with a competitive street overtone very similar to hip hop freestyles in Puerto Rico. Micha's comment on "not knowing what kind of music he plays" accentuates the social systems, interactions, and intricacies of the circum-Caribbean (Roach 1996).

The transnational diffusion of reggaetón to Cuba resembles the diffusion of other Caribbean music, such as merengue, dancehall, reggae, and bachata, to Cuba; these are what Flores calls "cultural remittances" that continue to thrive in Cuba (2009, 4). One of the most successful reggaetón groups in Cuba, Gente de Zona, was formed in 2005 by Alexander Delgado, Yeiko, Dando Pro, and Jacob Forever. Gente de Zona aimed to revolutionize and fuse music in Cuba, such as combining chachacha, mambo, and son with other musical genres such as bachata, reggaetón, and rock. They have recorded with heavyweight artists such as Orishas, Vacaciones, and Pitbull, and also recorded the merengue hit "Con la ropa puesta" with Dominican rapper-producer El Cata. They have released three studio albums: *Lo mejor que suena ahora* (2008), *A full* (2010), and *Visualízate* (2016). In an interview with Havana Cultura, Alexander complains that music in Cuba is too often viewed through a traditional lens, and points out, "The music has revolutions. We are the new generations of musicians" ("Gente de Zona [Havana Cultura]" 2013).

Gente de Zona's music, although currently one of the most globalized cubatón groups, is also creolization. Although he doesn't comment on the debate about reggaetón's polemical arrival in Cuba, Alexander states: "I've always tried to tell the truth, to narrate what's happening around me without breaking into obscenity or resulting into vulgarity. Besides I use a lot of double entendres. Innuendo is a Cuban specialty" ("Gente de Zona [Havana Cultura]" 2013).

Hip hop artists have lost a lot of their fan base in the twenty-first century because their fans desire instead material ostentation. While technology and change are deemed problematic for Cuban nationals and Cuban rappers, technology is a valued index of change for others. For Baker, "the cellphone is a symbol of recent changes in political, social, economic and musical fields: permitted at last by the government, embraced by reggaetóneros and scorned by rappers precisely because it embodies consumerism and inequality" (2013, 139). Furthermore, while reggaetón was first viewed as the expression of marginalized communities, it later found support among higher classes: "When Gente de Zona plays at the Salon Rojo of the Hotel Capri, the venue is filled to the rafters with Havana's dressed up, money-eyed crowd, ready to pay 35 CUC (Cuban convertible pesos) for an evening of music" (140). Parallel to Cuba's musical golden age during the early twentieth century, reggaetón is attracting the *farandula*—the young, fashionable, upwardly mobile, predominantly female crowd. Now people are going to reggaetón concerts in posh venues, wearing designer clothes and laden with jewelry, and both marginal and dominant class support for reggaetón has branded La Havana as a site of aspiration for poor urban youth. All of these are ingredients for the corporate transnationalism of Gente de Zona's global creolization.

New access to technologies continues to change local forms of music. In Santiago, old-school dancehall, raga, and Panamanian reggae have been a big influence in the birth of reggaetón. Trespeso's Silega y Joe, an all-reggaetón-and-perreo group from Santiago, make use of Santiago Afro-Cuban styles that people in Havana thought were from Puerto Rico but are in fact Cuban rhythms. Puerto Rican reggaetón and North American hip hop influence the music in Santiago, allowing it to explore its long entanglement with other parts of the Caribbean. In the twenty-first century, reggaetón and Cuban hip hop depend on technology: songs and videos are uploaded to YouTube to make them available to audiences worldwide. The reggaetón generation in Cuba, especially in La Havana, has positioned itself against the state and intellectuals, forging a new place and a new sense of agency. The rise of cubatón reminds us of what Benítez-Rojo has written about post-Soviet Havana: "a cosmopolitan city re-emerging with a complex, creolized culture whose population looks toward the future with hope" (2005, 95). Reggaetón in Havana can be understood as music of pleasure and as an escape, a temporary freedom from hardships with transnational consequences.

The importance of both hip hop and reggaetón not solely as political commentary but also as artistic genres that bring people pleasure should be emphasized, as both hip hop and reggaetón have thrived through global economic systems, expanded telecommunications networks, and the interplay between corporations and subjugated peoples. In addition, Roberto Zurbano's work suggests a need for further research on various kinds of glocalized Cuban music, such as that of X-Alfonso, Kelvis Ochoa, and Goza Pepillo, the sounds of the maraca, jazz innovations in rumba, and Cuban rock music. These creolized forms of Cuban music suggests that cubatón is just part of a wider matrix of invention and tradition in Cuban music. What needs further exploration are the process, production, and limitations of glocalization, and how the process is inflected by race, gender, sexuality, and social class. Regardless of the ongoing debate around reggaetón and hip hop and their commercialized or noncommercialized diffusion, it is the Caribbeanization of the Hispanic Caribbean that deserves more attention, and the study of this process should not favor a pan-Latin or national discourse at the expense of excluding the Caribbean and the United States. As many Caribbean peoples are increasingly dispersed across the United States, circulatory musical remittances are only accelerating. In the case of the Caribbean, it is important to continue the exploration of inter-Caribbean linkages and not to rely solely on Afrocentric approaches. It is important for Cuban identities to be contextualized in transatlantic slavery and its continued effect on ongoing reconfigurations of Caribbean music and culture, especially in light of colonial and neocolonial legacies and realities. It is time we look toward our neighboring countries and the centrifugal migrations that have connected us and will continue to influence our way of life.

It is in the precarious origins of cubatón and hip hop that there exists a common ground. In Cuba and the United States, racial discourses are rooted in the contestation over space and the marginalization of populations that occurred hand in hand with urbanization. Hip hop and reggaetón both enact urban practices and urban knowledge as a means of claiming and representing the environment in which youth live. The Caribbean version of this was precipitated by many Cuban rappers' denial to fuse hip hop with other Cuban musical genres (such as salsa, merengue, rumba, or son). Corporate transnationalism's stronghold on creolized Caribbean music, such as cubatón, is a glimpse of a historical trend that needs to be contested. However, the way to contest this is by making sure we don't start essentializing what we believe creolization to be. One way that Cuban music scholars should look at corporate transnationalism is by critiquing the "free" market and being cognizant of the relationship between the undefinable or that which lacks definition and the collective unconsciousness of what people think it is. Otherwise, when we start essentializing, creolization becomes an obscurity. Creolization in literature, music and cultures cannot be understood in essentialist terms. In dialogue with Glissant, I ask: how can we be one world in relation when we are in constant change? El Micha and Alkana as Black Cuban artists should not be ignored. We must come to understand the complexity of creolization by centering the voices of artists and how they understand what they are doing, since they are the ones tracing and reconstructing Caribbean legacies of distraught memories.

BIBLIOGRAPHY

Baker, Geoffrey. 2011. *Buena Vista in the Club: Rap, Reggaetón, and Revolution in Havana*. Durham, NC, and London: Duke University Press.

Benitez-Rojo, Antonio. 2003. "Creolization and Nation-Building in the Hispanic Caribbean." *Matatu* 27: 17–28, 539–40.

Benitez-Rojo, Antonio. 2005. "Creolization in Havana: The Oldest Form of Globalization." In *Contemporary Caribbean Cultures and Societies in a Global Context*, edited by Franklin W. Knight and Teresita Martínez-Vergne, 75–96. Chapel Hill: University of North Carolina Press.

"Castro Government Bans Reggaetón on the Radio and TV." 2012. Fox News, December 4. https://www.foxnews.com/world/castro-government-bans-reggaeton-on-radio-and-tv.

Crichlow, Michaeline A. 2009. *Globalization and the Post-Creole Imagination: Notes on Fleeing the Plantation*. Durham, NC, and London: Duke University Press.

Diawara, Manthia. 2010. *Edouard Glissant: One World in Relation*. Video. New York: Third World Newsreel.

Dyson, Michael Eric. 2007. *Know What I Mean? Reflections on Hip-Hop*. New York: Basic Civitas Books.

Fernandes, Sujatha. 2006. *Cuba Represent! Cuban Arts, State Power, and the Making of New Revolutionary Cultures*. Durham, NC, and London: Duke University Press.

Flores, Juan. 2004. "Creolité in the Hood: Diaspora as Source and Challenge." *Centro Journal* 16 (2): 282–93.

Flores, Juan. 2009. *The Diaspora Strikes Back: Caribeño Learning and Turning*. New York: Taylor & Francis.

Gámez Torres, Nora. 2013. "Rap Is War: Los Aldeanos and the Politics of Music Subversion in Contemporary Cuba." *Trans: Revista Transcultural de Musical* 17. http://www.sibetrans.com/trans/public/docs/trans-17-11.pdf/.

Glissant, Edouard. 2010. *L'imaginaires des langues: Entretiens avec Lise Gauvin (1991–2009)*. Paris: Gallimard.

Guridy, Frank Andre. 2010. *Forging Diaspora: Afro-Cubans and African Americans in a World of Empire and Jim Crow*. Chapel Hill: University of North Carolina Press.

Israel, Esteban. 2009. "Reggaetón Fever Shakes Up Cuba's Culture." *Reuters*, June 29. http://www.reuters.com/article/2009/06/29/us-cuba-reggaetón-idUSTRE55S6EK20090629.

Kelley, Robin D. G. 2004. "Lookin' for the 'Real' Nigga: Social Scientists Construct the Ghetto." In *That's the Joint: The Hip-Hop Studies Reader*, edited by Murray Foreman and Marc Anthony Neil, 134–52. New York and London: Routledge.

López, Antonio. 2012. *Unbecoming Blackness: The Diaspora Cultures of Afro-Cuban America*. New York: New York University Press.

Perry, Marc. 2015. *Negro Soy Yo: Hip-Hop and Raced Citizenship in Neo-Liberal Cuba*. Durham, NC, and London: Duke University Press.

Roach, Joseph. 1996. *Cities of the Dead: Circum-Atlantic Performance*. New York: Columbia University Press.

Rueda, Manuel. 2012. "Cuban Government Censors Reggaeton and 'Sexually Explicit' Songs." *ABC News*, December 6. https://abcnews.go.com/ABC_Univision/News/cuba-censors-reggaeton-sexually-explicit-songs/story?id=17888666&page=2.

VIDEOGRAPHY

"Alkana [Havana Cultura]." 2011. Havana Cultura, November 3. YouTube. https://youtu.be/YEhKPaxpDME.

"El Micha [Havana Cultura]." 2011. Havana Cultura, November 10. YouTube. https://youtu.be/LPA_TnTTGvg.

"Gente de Zona [Havana Cultura]." 2013. Havana Cultura, April 18. YouTube. https://youtu.be/8k3YMYaP32U.

4

LETTER TO GAUTAM GUPTA

EYVIND KANG

Dear Gautam,

"There is no need to dance, there is no need to sing, there is no need to make music anymore!" What prompted that memorable outburst of yours, which still makes me laugh after twenty years? For several months a group of us had been gathering daily at the artist Ashish Swami's apartment in Mumbai. The gathering was a coincidence, a result of what you might call the *karma* of Swami and myself to have become next-door neighbors. I was a student of music, studying the *gayaki ang* at that time with the great master Dr. N. Rajam. As I recall, you were working as a set designer, Avinash as an actor, Mr. Rajan was a retired professor and active photographer; along with several others we formed a study group in a style of artistic research that might have been called transmodern—as well as a kind of support system for the partially and completely unemployed.

Almost all of us were recent graduates or dropouts of art schools. Each of us lived in a zone between art, research, and the world; each of us were members of that ever-expanding class of freelance artists and temporary workers, individuals obliged to skirt from gig to gig, project to project. Despite our many differences, this common condition, along with the desire to learn, brought us together. There was much to discuss in terms of comparative situations on the ground in the so-called West and Global South. Poverty, partition, and war were constant themes of Swami's painting, collage, video. The year was 1998 and anti-globalization was a constant theme in our conversations, which tended to accumulate energy over spans of many hours, and often found its conclusion in one of your great, pithy exclamations—followed by much laughter all around.

It is touching to recall the way we used to cook every evening, gathered together around a Coleman stove. To defray the cost of food, cigarettes, and other expenses, you, Avinash, and Swami would take your paintings downtown and sell them on the street across from the National Gallery. One night upon return you told an interesting story: apparently an American musician by the name of Ornette Coleman had been walking past and your watercolors had caught his eye. After purchasing a few of your paintings he had invited you up to his hotel room where he entertained by playing the saxophone. It was, you had said, "the best jazz music we have ever heard." Of course, you had wanted to know more about this man. One of the many questions you posed to me was: "What is the position of Sri Ornette in America?"

At the time I might have said something like "Sri Ornette is a *pandit* or an *ustad*, whose position in jazz is similar to that of Kumar Ghandarva in North Indian classical music in terms of the high estimation in which his art is held, as well as the controversy that surrounds the question of his mastery over traditional forms. His performance style—as you were able to hear for yourselves—may be compared to Pannalal Ghosh in its tactility, urgency, originality. His great achievement in musicology—the origination and practice of a new and very strange theory called Harmolodics, which reconceptualizes elements of harmony, melody, and form liberated from governance by notions of progression and resolution—might be compared to those of Pandit Omkarnath Thakur, whose reclassification of the ragas *contra* Bhatkhande liberates raga from the overarching categories of *that*."

The Harmolodics theory was of special interest to you, and its imperative to "remove the caste system from sound," per the statement spelled out in the promotional materials for *Tone Dialing* (Harmolodic, 1998)—one of the few CDs I happened to have with me in India—found a particular resonance within our conversations. Titles such as "Ustad," "Pandit," "Sri," and so forth carry with them an elitism according to which other musicians, those of other cultures or races, and especially those who practice the so-called popular or folk genres, would be considered inferior, if not actively despised. But if we retained the honorific "Sri" in the case of Ornette, we must have recognized that the Harmolodic imperative goes beyond calling for removal of the caste system among musicians: he calls for removing the caste system from sound itself. In this respect the theory seems to be oriented at the outset toward a more general form of itself, one which extends beyond any particular musical practice. Sri Ornette himself states: "to remove the caste system from all information . . . I have been practicing that in sound as well as in humanism."[1]

The Harmolodic imperative speaks of "caste" rather than "race" or "class" precisely for the transitive scope of the term—caste can apply equally to sound or to the nonhuman. The Sanskrit word translated as caste is *jaat* or *jaati*, which can also refer to a type of musical mode or scale, or even the generic relation of ascending and descending quantities within the mode.

By way of the pun of caste and sound, one can begin to distinguish music, in the first place, from humanist sound practices, placing music on the side of the nonhuman, a move which follows from the traditional division of sound (Skt. *nada*) into *ahata* and *anahata nada*, or struck and unstruck sound. Nonhuman sound practices could mean many things: those of nature, of gods, of demons, of persons not considered human, of animals, of objects, and so forth. To extend the term as far as *anahata nada*, in effect completely transposing the cultural to the natural, would entail the existence of a sound completely absent of human intention. Thus we affirmed in our own terms the validity of an antique principle of Indian classical music—that the degree of musicality of a sound hangs on the balance of the relation of intentionality to nonintentionality, of the struck to the unstruck, of action to nonaction, of culture to nature, of human to nonhuman.

Within the term "human sound practices," I include all that you meant to quit when you said—to much laughter—"there is no need to dance, there is no need to sing, there is no need to play music anymore." If what Rosa Maria Rodriguez Magda calls the "transmodern totality" of globalization does not point toward an end of history per se, at least it may lead to the end of art history.[2] A comedic effect arises from the combination of this statement of the obvious—that there should be no need for frivolity in a dangerous political and environmental global situation—with the absurd, as though dancing, singing, music were ever strictly necessary, and as though we could voluntarily and immediately discontinue doing them.

After twenty years, I have thought of a rejoinder: I suggest that rather than humans giving up sound practices, sound itself should give up the human. What would this mean for music and musicians? A massive shift in perspective will be required; I claim that a general theory of Harmolodics provides the tools. In brief, by using the Harmolodic techniques of *transposition*, on the level of nature, and of *translation*, on the level of culture, musical thought could be navigated such that music is defined not as the sum of its sonic elements ("organized sound" per Varèse's banal definition), but the inverse: sound as a totality of musics. Music is not made by sound, sound is made out of music. We can see that in the word Harmolodics there is a concatenation of the words *harmony* and *melody* around the central yet occulted term *movement*—represented only by the transposition of E to O at the center of the word—which seems to propose a wager on the mutually embedded nature of timescales of harmony and melody. Its general form would be constituted by an expansion of the cultural terms "harmony" and "melody" to natural terms—let's call them the "simultaneous" and the "sequential"—where translation indexes movement along the cultural domain, and transposition along the natural domain.

Moving from Sri Ornette's Harmolodics to General Harmolodics, one sees recursive formations along both cultural and natural axes: the expansion of the register of music-historiographical time—the time of stories about music—annexes musicology (comparative, ethnological, critical, etc.), allowing for a harmolodic redefinition of the sciences of musical objects, repertoire, traditions, and so forth, as simple elements of music, and in turn of sound itself. Conversely, the expansion of naturalized conceptions of temporality, from the microcosmic envelopes within the simultaneous, to the long arc of what we are obliged to call the age of the universe on the macrocosmic-sequential scale, reduces the dynamics of *ahata/anahata* to dynamics within the scientific image of the Big Bang at one end, and the cosmic heat-death on the other. I use the terms culture and nature provisionally, to simply point out that if a General Harmolodics *qua* translation rests upon a unified field of music and musicology, *qua* transposition it rests upon a unified field of nature and culture.

As an example take this letter itself. Among the factors that prompted me to write it: at the time we parted ways none of us, save Swami, had a phone number, nor a physical address, even email. Now there is internet, the world is much smaller, but there are just far too many people with your same name to find you on Facebook or elsewhere. Like a phone number, the proper name is a code which is dialed to refer to the person. However, if there are more people than there are names for them, with each new generation, the difference in quantity is raised by another order of magnitude. *Gautam Gupta*: how many have shared names with you since the time of the Lord Buddha? *Swami* too more often denotes a religious leader rather than being used as a proper name. As for my own name, I can't be sure that you ever knew it since all of you used to call me (again it is amusing to recall) *A Wind*.

I remember how sometimes Swami used to criticize: "A Wind, the more you learn Indian classical music, the more you lose your originality." I had a retort ready at the time, but I also agreed with him to some extent. What constitutes an "original" music, and how could you learn it? An ideal education in music would be commensurate with the personality of the musician taken as a whole: with their family, ancestry, teachers, lineage, *guru-shishya selseleh*—in short, with their culture. Still—to paraphrase the author Jyoti Prakash Dutta, whose beautiful short stories I was reading at the time—"what happens in most cases also happens here." In most cases, and in my own case too, the personality of the musician is fragmented by the world, its histories, its capacities for injustice, oppression, and so on.

Sri Ornette, in a remarkable conversation with Jacques Derrida documented in 1997, puts it like this: "being black and the descendent of slaves, I have no idea what my language of origin was."[3] Derrida empathizes, "I (too) have no contact of any sort with (the) language of my supposed ancestors." Sri Ornette then formulates two questions: "Do you ever ask yourself if the language that you speak now interferes with your actual thoughts? Can a language of origin influence your thoughts?" Harmolodics entails the transposition of these questions—actually the same question asked from two perspectives—from the linguistic to the musical register. In the same conversation Sri Ornette says, "I'm trying express a concept according to which you can translate one thing into another." Within a few short exchanges he sketches an idea of recursive translatability from thoughts to words along vectors of interference and influence.

These considerations place the Harmolodic within a broad philosophical tradition, the possibility of a general or universal language. This tendency is normally associated with the name Leibniz, whose Characteristic was intended to operate as an alphabet of human thoughts. *Of Universal Synthesis and Analysis* describes such an alphabet in terms of a "*summa genera . . . such as A, B, C, D, E, F out of whose combination inferior concepts would be formed.*" Inferiority here indicates the gradated particularities formed by expanding combinations of the genera—let's call them dyads, triads, etc. A map of combinations whose routes from generality to particularity is then enhanced with respellings and letter substitutions to allow for simulations of thought-movements from the genera to what he calls *concepts* and *predicates*. Leibniz illustrates the process with the following example: "suppose that there is a species Y, whose concept is ABCD, and suppose for AB there is substituted L; for AC, M, for AD, N; for BC, P; for BD, Q; and for CD, R, all of which are groups of two; and suppose that for ABC there is substituted S; for ABD, V; for ACD, W; and for BCD, X, which are groups of three. All of these will be predicates of Y, but the convertible predicates of Y will be the following only: AX, BW, CV, DS, LR, MQ, NP."[4]

Leibniz's Characteristic employs combinatorial methods toward the goal of universal intelligibility; Sri Ornette's Harmolodics describes a combinatorial process that is oriented toward the emancipation of predicates. Where the Characteristic designates a universal alphabet to represent concepts, the Harmolodic expands the dimensions and possibilities of reading. Sri

Ornette: "I think that sound has a much more democratic relationship to information, because you don't need an alphabet to understand music."[5] Rather than adding another layer of theory to music or sound, Harmolodics initially takes the form of a method for undoing the structures of various theories by means of a fourfold expansion, which Sri Ornette describes as "a base of expanding the melody, the harmonic structure, the rhythm, and above all the free improvised structure of a composition."[6] In Sri Ornette's discourse on transposition, this process of expansion begins at the level of letter substitutions in the reading of the names of pitched sound according to conventions of music notation.

> When you play the piano you're playing in the G clef, that's the treble clef, but the soprano, alto, tenor, and the bass clefs are independent of the treble clef. If you take the soprano C, which is on the E line, you take the bass C, which is on the second space, the alto C, which is on the third line, and the tenor C which is on the fourth line, you'll have A, B, D, and E. Now, the B natural that's on the treble clef is totally independent from these four notes, therefore most people transposing those voices to the treble clef are not transposing the natural notes of the unison. That's why you have harmony, changes, and improvising, because the treble clef doesn't transpose, it's only for range. If you have A, B, D, and E in the bass clef, you would be reading C, D, F, and G. In the treble clef, when you play A, B, D, and E, that A is C [for bass], the B is a C for alto, the [D] a C for the tenor, and the E is the C for the soprano. So, it's not really four different notes, it's the same four notes.... If I asked you to play the soprano G natural on the piano, that's C natural for the treble clef. C natural for the soprano would be E. You can't hear those as voices, you have to call them chords and keys. In harmolodics those four voices are transposed into one voice. For instance, the A, B, D, and E would be a B, C, E, and F on the alto clef, and G, A, C, and D on the tenor clef. The same notes. So, you have a different unison for the same notes.[7]

For Sri Ornette, clef is the indicator of pitch and letter substitutions, giving combinatorial particulars in the place of semantic unisons and arriving at what Leibniz calls "convertible predicates" by way of the transposition of "the same notes" into "different unisons." Again, the Harmolodic differs in orientation from the Characteristic by affirming the process of transposition—the move from the general to the particular—as the guarantor of "harmony, chords and changes," rather than the other way around. For Leibniz, harmony is established by what he describes as a "Divine anticipatory artifice," exemplified in the image of two clocks ticking in perfect unison, and guaranteed by the fact that all substances are "representations of one and the same universe."[8] Yet it is the notion of the oneness and sameness of the universe as the basis of this pre-established harmony which is itself in question in Sri Ornette's discourse on transposition. By affirming a "different unison for the same notes," Sri Ornette counters the Leibnizian image of two clocks with that of one clock which tells multiple times at the same moment.

When the Harmolodic triple expansion exceeds thresholds between and beyond the harmonic, melodic, and formal domains (the latter of which I take to be equivalent to "free improvised structures"), the process of transposition might be better understood in terms of *transduction*. If *trans* means across, over, beyond, and *ducere* means to lead, transduction is the crossing of the threshold. A closely related definition, "to convert variations in (a medium) into corresponding variations in another medium," supplements the conception.[9] Taken together in approaching the Harmolodics, these senses of transduction describe a capacity to non-destructively remove hierarchical structures from a medium while corresponding to different, or new, information across levels of mediation. On its most general level, writes Sri Ornette, "Harmolodic is a noun that can be applied for the use of participating in any form of information equally without erasing or altering the information."[10]

"Harmolodics can be used in almost any kind of expression. You can think harmolodically. You can write fiction and poetry in Harmolodic."[11] Rather than being a philosophy in itself, Harmolodics might be understood as a system for generating transductions between philosophies. Furthermore, Harmolodics provides a platform for transductions between philosophy and domains of thought outside of philosophy, those domains which are again appropriated by philosophy and designated non-philosophical by thinkers such as Francois Laruelle. In non-philosophy we may find another approach to what Sri Ornette calls the free improvised structure, a structure which sustains multiple methods of simultaneous construction without recourse to that posture which Laruelle calls the "Decision in Advance." Thus the expansion of these methods on the bases of General Harmolodics would lead not only to a method of music making that takes place *In All Languages*, per Sri Ornette's album of the same name, and which applies to those Sri Ornette will refer to as *People Existing in All Colors Eternally*, but equally to a *non-music* that withdraws from all musical systems in the manner that non-philosophy withdraws from all systems of thought.

At some point it had occurred to me that, while you had heard him play in person on that fateful day, neither you, Swami, nor Avinash had heard any of Sri Ornette's albums. By way of a parting gift, I gave Swami the CD *Tone Dialing*. That recording, which was the most recent of Sri Ornette's albums at the time, and which remains one of my personal favorites, features an interesting cover image that provides an illuminating illustration of the Harmolodic: a white touch-tone telephone on whose buttons, which would normally bear numerals, are written the following words: Hearing (1), Quality (2), Smell (3), Taste (4), Present (5), Sight (6), Action (7), Receiving (8), Touch (9), Territories (0). A key to the diagram is provided inside, which reduces these categories from ten to five, pairing terms as follows: Smell=Present, Taste=Qualities, Hearing=Receiving, Touch=Action, Sight=Territories.

Obviously the diagram with its array of perceptual names reminded us of the classical *Samkhya*, with its descriptions of five subtle elements (Skt. *tanmatras*)—sound (*shabda*), touch (*sparsha*), form (*rupa*), taste (*rasa*), and smell (*ghanda*)—each of which are integrated in turn with what the Sages called "external instruments," the five sensory organs that facilitate perception. The Samkhya system posits a system of evolution where Touch evolves from Hearing, Vision from Touch, Taste from Vision, and Smell from Taste; these physiological evolutes and their elemental correspondents are positioned alongside psychological and metaphysical nodes in a diagrammatical formation that suggests the possibility of navigation along transcendental lines.

Diagrams like this, which abound in so-called magical thinking, and which posit that a change in one realm can be operated to effect a change in a corresponding realm, were our daily bread and butter. I still have one here that I copied down from Swami's notebook. Names of animals, colors, pitched sounds, times of day, days of week, seasons, moods, or emotions are enumerated and made to correspond with one another in an expansive regime of relations. In a sense, any transcendental system is a magical system that traces the networks of correspondence to the most general, or Godlike, level. Samkhya, too, can be characterized by a great enthusiasm for lists of elements organized into more or less consistent groups, which are made to correspond to one another across metaphysical lines and which tend toward the production of diagrams, figures, or mandalas. Deleuze and Guattari define the mandala as "a projection on a surface that establishes correspondence between divine, cosmic, political, architectural, and organic levels as so many values of one and the same transcendence."[12] The force of Samkhya is to describe the projection of *Purusa*, the transcendental principle of consciousness, into the material principle, *Prakriti*, equivalent to what Deleuze and Guattari, following Spinoza, call the plane of Immanence. "The transcendence that is projected onto the plane of Immanence paves it or populates it with Figures . . . it is (only) from this point of view that Chinese hexagrams, Hindu mandalas, Jewish Sephiroth, Islamic 'Imaginals,' and Christian Icons can be considered together."[13]

However, the *Tone Dialing* diagram is not a projection of the transcendental. Rather, it describes a world in which the names of each external instrument (sense perception) and subtle element can be freely dialed or recombined or networked with every other element, just like the icons on the face of a telephone. The implication is that sequences formed by the combinations of names of perceptions and material/temporal elements converge in a code that "dials" a specific address or agent. There is no indication of a singular transcendent address, whether cause or objective, in this plane of immanence. There are as many addresses as there are codes dialed. Thus Purusa is multiplied to the infinite, but not in a fashion that emanates toward a greater or lesser level of infinity in relation to Prakriti. By endowing Purusa with an infinite amount of addresses rather than one general address, Purusa is located at the level of Prakriti, the transcendental at the level of the immanent. The musical implications are too numerous to mention; for now, it will suffice to note a univocal circuit between sound and musician, the first step toward a generalized form of Harmolodics. In the words of Sri Ornette, "When you play a sound and you hear yourself playing, that's you. That's Tone Dialing."[14]

Operations described by the *Tone Dialing* diagram might unfold as follows: a set of subtle elements (Present/Quality/Receiving/Action/Territories) are paired with the external instruments and arrayed in dyads along a spectrum from the harmonic "present" to the melodic "territories" such that Smell=Present names the state of simultaneity, harmony, verticality; on the other side of the spectrum, Sight=Territories names sequentiality, melody, horizontality. The middle term of Harmolodics, Movement, corresponds to the dyad Hearing=Receiving. On this reading, Movement denotes the agency of the hearer/receiver to determine the received harmonicity or melodicity of a particular duration. Again, Hearing=Receiving is synonymous with the gesture of the E to the O in the spelling of "Harmolodic," indicating the shift from structure to function of sound.

The movement of perspectives of sense perception on the real can be illustrated with examples that compare human perspectives with those of animality. The French composer Gerard Grisey explains this shift by reference to the relativity of what he calls the time constants among radically different kinds of hearer-receivers:

> Think of whales, humans and birds. When you hear the songs of the whales, they are so spaced out that what sounds like a gigantic, drawn-out and endless moan is perhaps only one consonant to them. This means that it is impossible to perceive their speech with our constant of time. Similarly, when we hear a bird sing, our impression is that it sounds very high pitched and agitated, for its constant of time is much shorter than ours. It is difficult for us to perceive its subtle variations of timbre, while it may perceive us, perhaps, as we perceive the whales.[15]

Those familiar with classical Skepticism will recognize this argument as a mode of suspension of judgment. Sextus Empiricus, in his masterpiece *Outlines of Pyrrhonism*, compares the conflicts of appearances from the perspectives of animals such as mosquitos, gnats, frogs, maggots, dung beetles, bees, wasps, humans, birds, bears, etc., to the pitch ranges of musical instruments in a manner curiously similar to Sri Ornette's discourse on transposition:

> just as one and the same breath blown by a musician into a flute becomes in one place a high note and in another a low note, and the same pressure of the hand on a lyre produces in one place a low sound and in another a high one: in the same way it is reasonable that external existing objects should be observed as different depending on the different constitutions of the animals that receive the appearance.[16]

The distinction in kind rather than in degree between humans and animals constitutes an essential element of modern thought, principally associated with the name Descartes. Premodern conceptions of the relation between humans and animals, which form such an integral part of the Skeptical challenge to philosophy, are rehabilitated to some extent in Deleuze and Guattari's notion of "becoming-animal," which includes "becoming-music" wherein "music takes as its content a becoming-animal."[17] The materiality of the musical instrument provides a good example of this. In a violin, catgut strings and horsehair bow produce sound by their perpendicular interaction. But if the the agency of transposition is attributed by Sextus to "the different constitutions of the animals that receive the appearance," the dynamics between becoming-animal and becoming-music become more complex than Deleuze and Guattari seem to have imagined. The hearer-receiver, or *sruti*, in the middle term of the *Tone Dialing* schematic, is the one who receives becoming, since "becoming" itself is a musical function. Therefore "becoming-music" is a recursive structure, one which continually generates novel emergences of animal and music.

This sense of the Harmolodic coincides with those sciences of human-animal transduction that anthropology has conflated under the Ural-Altaic term shamanism. Though the word has been much criticized for its overcoding of diverse Indigenous practices, scholars seem to find the term indispensable in its distinction between various medical and magical practices and a specific science that annexes the time of myth or of the long-ago, the time before humans and animals were different, to the now. "Shamanism is a mode of action entailing a mode of knowledge," writes Eduardo Viveiros de Castro, where "to know is to personify, to take the point of view of what should be known, or rather, the one who should be known."[18] A universe constructed out of these points of view would correspond to what de Castro calls a *multinatural* universe, in opposition to a multicultural one.

The *Tone Dialing* Present—that singularity which forms the center of multiple time constants during which the future and the past converge in a network of harmonic lattices approaching the infinitesimal, and during which multinatural universes become knowable to each other—is paired here with Smell, the olfactory as the limit of unicity. On the spectrum of animal-human perceptivity, scent can be said to lie on the side of the animal; for many species, an acute and refined sense of smell forms the basis of orientation, navigation, and communication in the world, where for most humans it remains the least objectifiable, the least measurable, describable, communicable, and therefore the least knowable, on a scientific level, of sense perceptions.

On a phenomenological level, however, scent has been considered one of the most evocative of sense perceptions, one whose affect ranges from the abject to the sublime. A beautiful essay, "A Note on Sanskrit Ghanda" by the great philologist Minoru Hara, compiles scriptural and poetic uses of the Sanskrit term *Ghanda*; we learn that among the sense perceptions and corresponding subtle elements or *tanmatras* of the Samkhya schema, Gandha is particularly abundant in associations: as an attribute, *guna*, of the Earth, *bhumi*, diverse in sources such as flowers, trees, incense, and so forth, "born by herbs and waters" in the Atharva-veda, and rich in character, as in the scent of the face of the beloved Rama lamented by King Dasartha in the Valmiki Ramayana.[19] Varieties of gandha such as "root-scent, heartwood scent and flower scent" are explored in Pali Buddhist texts; from the Gita we get the composite term *vaha-gandha*, denoting the wind as a diffuser of scent. If the colloquial meaning in Hindi denotes a mundane sense of filth, if not an abject state, neither is the sublime far away. A pertinent example lies in the name of the celestial musicians. The Ghandarvas are extensively described in Hindu, Buddhist, and Jain texts as messengers who transduce music between heaven and earth, and who take the form of hybrid between animal (specifically birds or horses) and human.

For Sri Ornette, Smell=Present is an indicator of the harmonic structure of gandha, with an earthly, physical, immanent, and even abject (stinky/funky) fundament yielding overtones that ascend through increasingly finer grades of interval, approaching ever-subtler realms, including those of the Ghandarvas themselves. It is a gathering of the abject and sublime in an apparent simultaneity that is not so much a *moment* as it is a *state* of becoming-music, within which the hearer-receiver is endowed with the agency to transpose, to transduct, and to trace multiplicities. These multiples correspond in turn to what Grisey, with the Spectral composers, is obliged to refer to as *envelopes*, partial domains, each with their own proper dynamic against the whole. Yet within each state of apparent simultaneity the one dynamically and combinatorially relates to its predecessors and successors, forming an apparent continuity in combination with the faculties of memory and imagination within the hearer-receiver. In this way, the relation of the one and the many yields two: the many *within* the one, and the many *without* the one, corresponding to the concepts of harmony and melody respectively. Harmolodic thought emphasizes the phenomenon that each of these in combination with the other yields one again, making the process regenerative and reflexive while corresponding to that occulted middle term which Sri Ornette calls "movement."

To be clear, the hearer-receiver at the center of the *Tone Dialing* spectrum is the one endowed with the agency to name—that is, to transpose, translate, and transduct—information. That is why the term *sruti* has a double meaning, referring both to hearing, the concept, and to microtonality, the object. On this point, from the perspective of Harmolodics, the name of the sruti matters little since its data is always provisional and susceptible to renaming; every letter can be transposed, every word can be translated, every phrase can be transduced. Rather, it is the fact that there is a name at all, whether it is of a sight, a territory, a smell, or a moment, which provides metadata, marking the fact that something is heard and named, which is the constitutive act of the *sruti*. By way of this general Harmolodic metavocabulary, both senses of the sruti converge on the hearer-receiver, privileging neither (what amounts to) the cognitive bias of apparent simultaneity nor that of apparent continuity, and yet provisionally naming the act of naming "one."

Thus if the dyad Smell=Present corresponds to the harmonic individuation, or the one-within-the-many-within-the-one, the melodic individuation will correspond to the dyad Sight=Territories, or the one-without-the-many-without-the-one. Edmund Husserl, in *The Phenomenology of Internal Time Consciousness*, provides the following account of the relations of apparent simultaneity (Smell=Present) and continuity (Sight=Territories) hanging on the example of melody:

> The matter seems very simple at first; we hear a melody, i.e. we perceive it, for hearing is indeed perception. While the first tone is sounding, the second comes, then the third and so on. Must we not say that when the second tone sounds I hear *it*, but I no longer hear the first and so on? Therefore, I hear at any instant only the actual phase of the tone, and the Objectivity of the whole enduring tone is constituted in an act-continuum which in part is memory, in the smallest part is perception, and in a more extensive part expectation.[20]

Anticipating the objection that "although A itself is past, a new content A with the character 'past' may be in consciousness by virtue of the primordial association," Husserl proposes:

> the actual [*leibhafte*] tonal now is constantly changed into something that has been; constantly an ever fresh tonal now, which passes over into modification, is peeled off. However, when the tonal now, the primal impression, passes over into retention, this retention is itself again a now, an actual existent. While it in itself is actual (but not an actual sound), it is the retention of a sound that has been. A *ray of meaning* [*Strahl der Meinung*] can be directed towards the now, towards the retention, but it can also be directed towards that of which we are conscious in retention, the past sound.[21]

By this account, tones are temporal objects retained and protended by the hearer-receiver and oriented by "rays of meaning" that penetrate the movement of the before to the after, resulting in a binding together of the tonal objects in apparent melodic continuities. The binding agent, variously referred to as *primordial association* or *primary retention*, is supplemented by the memory of the melody itself, referred to as *secondary retention*. On the Harmolodic account, by contrast, melodic tones are not to be construed as temporal objects within a given time flow; rather, each tone constructs its own time scale, its own orientation within that time scale, and its own set of harmonic and melodic envelopes, while simultaneously becoming a witness to itself and to the other member tones. For example, if the equivalence of formal structures on different time scales (harmonic, melodic, and free improvised structures) entails that the primary retention take the form of a refrain embedded within another refrain, it is the microphysical frequency of the first refrain, or the tone itself, that would recapitulate the primary retention of the first refrain on a psychological level, and simultaneously transduce it to a phenomenological register. The secondary retention—the memory of the melody—can then be described as not only a refrain within a refrain within a refrain, but as *all* of the combinations and permutations of *all* the refrains within each tone in the primary retention. To the extent that one can speak of meaning as illumination, rather than a ray that emerges from the side of the hearer-receiver, it will take the form of an effulgence that emerges from within each tone and can be directed to every other tone as well as to the hearer-receiver; this is why the name of "tone" in Sanskrit is *svara*, or self-emergence. From the dynamics of these self-emergent time scales arise those confluences of melodies named *Raga*. Raga, which has been variously translated as *that which pleases*, as *body*, or as *desire*, is not to be conflated with any vitalist construct, but rather as the emergence of a Real comprised of multinatural temporalities in continuous modes of individuation.

Gautam, in this letter I have tried to weave together stands of speculation from more or less distantly related discourses that hinge on the terms *Nada, Sruti, Svara, Raga*. Since it may not be possible to gather these threads and fragments into a conclusion, I will leave off with a small story.

I had initially refused to be the bearer of Swami's letter to Sri Ornette, telling him that the post office would be more reliable, and trying other ways to beg off the errand. Nevertheless, Swami prevailed. Although it had seemed unlikely to me that I would ever meet Sri Ornette in person, within a few months I received an invitation to a party at his loft in the Garment District of New York City. The elevator opened straight into the vast loft, and the master graciously greeted me and several other guests who arrived at the same time, taking our coats and draping them over the bed. I promptly delivered the letter, which I hadn't taken out of the breast pocket of my jacket since returning from India.

"This is a letter from Swami."

"Which Swami?"

"Ashish Swami..."

He vaguely appeared to recognize the name. "That man wrote something beautiful about art...."

Sri Ornette then opened the envelope and unfolded the letter. I recognized the handwriting. The page began: "Dear Sri Ornette, *a wind* came to India and gave us your music...."

Even as the master praised the letter, I was disturbed that that my own name, misspelled, mispronounced, and misconstrued, was mentioned in the opening sentence. This gave rise to the doubt that since the proper name Swami is easily mistaken for a religious position; even if the question, "Which Swami?" was an appropriate one, I couldn't be sure if I had answered it correctly.

In an effort to put my mind at rest, I called Swami the next day—in fact, this was the last time I spoke with him. I reported that I had delivered the letter, described the encounter, and I asked him if he had ever "written something beautiful about art." He denied it.

In retrospect, I can't be sure that Sri Ornette knew Ashish Swami, nor can I be sure that Swami, you, and Avinash ever actually met Sri Ornette. Perhaps you were mistaken, or perhaps you met somebody else who identified himself as Sri Ornette. Or perhaps you simply made up the story in the first place.

I'm sure you have heard by now: Sri Ornette has been gone from this Earth for some years. But even in his absence—especially in his absence, and for all the reasons I have described—the Harmolodics theory must exist, and in speaking of a "general" Harmolodics, I'm thinking of a Harmolodics that will live on. In fact, because of its great generality, it could outlive every other music theory.

But, now that I have written you this letter, I myself am going to renounce this language; I only wanted to reclaim a portion of the Harmolodic from the many imbeciles who have never understood it, but who insist on speaking of it now that the master is gone. Additionally, to paraphrase the great poet Hafez, "henceforth I will renounce of renouncing." I have to admit that it is unlikely you will ever read this. Although this letter is actually meant to be a piece of writing which shifts registers in the manner of the Harmolodic, as I write it I notice that it doesn't shift at all, since it keeps coming back to the same point.

In any case, wherever you are, I just want you to know that I'm still thinking of you, Swami, Avinash, and the whole crew fondly. Thank you for the many great conversations, which I remember in detail to this day.

Your friend,

Eyvind

BIBLIOGRAPHY

Coleman, Ornette. 1996. "Tone Dialing." *Bomb* 56. https://bombmagazine.org/articles/tone-dialing/.
Deleuze, Gilles, and Félix Guattari. 1994. *What Is Philosophy?* Translated by Hugh Tomlinson and Graham Burchell. New York: Columbia University Press.
Deleuze, Gilles, and Félix Guattari. 2004. *A Thousand Plateaus: Capitalism and Schizophrenia.* Translated by Brian Massumi. London: Continuum.
Derrida, Jacques, and Ornette Coleman. 2004 [1997]. "The Other's Language: Jacques Derrida Interviews Ornette Coleman, 23 June 1997." Translated by Timothy S. Murphy. In "Blue Notes: Towards a New Jazz Discourse," part 1, edited by Mark Osteen, special issue of *Genre: Forms of Discourse and Culture* 37 (2): 319–29. Originally published in *Les Inrockuptibles* #115 (August 20–September 2).
Hara, Minoru. 2010. "A Note on Sanskrit Ghanda." *Studia Orientalis* 108: 65–86.
Husserl, Edmund. 1971. *The Phenomenology of Internal Time Consciousness.* Translated by James Churchill. Bloomington: Indiana University Press.
Leibniz, Gottfried Wilhelm. 1995a. "Monadology." In *Philosophical Writings.* Translated by Mary Morris and G. H. R. Parkinson, 179–94. London: Orion.
Leibniz, Gottfried Wilhelm. 1995b. "Of Universal Synthesis and Analysis; *or,* Of the Art of Discovery and of Judgement." In *Philosophical Writings.* Translated by Mary Morris and G. H. R. Parkinson, 10–18. London: Orion.
Mandel, Howard. 2008. *Miles, Ornette, Cecil: Jazz beyond Jazz.* New York: Routledge.
Rodríguez Magda, Rosa María. 2004. "Globalization as Transmodern Totality." In *Transmodernidad,* by Rosa María Rodríguez Magda, 22–46. Barcelona: Anthropos. Posted, in English translation, on December 27, 2008, at http://transmodern-theory.blogspot.com/2008/12/globalization-as-transmodern-totality.html.
Sextus Empiricus. 1985. *Outlines of Pyrrhonism,* line 54. Quoted in *The Modes of Scepticism,* by Julia Annas and Jonathan Barnes, 33. Cambridge: Cambridge University Press.
Shoemaker, Bill. 1995. "Dialing Up Ornette." *Jazz Times* 25 (10): 42–44.
Viveiros de Castro, Eduardo. 2014. *Cannibal Metaphysics.* Translated by Peter Skafish. Minneapolis: Univocal.

DISCOGRAPHY

Coleman, Ornette. 1987. *In All Languages.* Fort Worth: Caravan of Dreams.
Coleman, Ornette. 1995. "Search for Life." From *Tone Dialing.* New York: Harmolodic.
Grisey, Gerard. 2005. "Conjectures and Ideas in Two Paragraphs." From *Solo Pour Deux.* Vienna: Kairos.

NOTES

1. Mandel 2008, 189.
2. Magda 2008.
3. Derrida and Coleman 1997.
4. Leibniz 1995b, 11.
5. Derrida and Coleman 1997.
6. Shoemaker 1995, 56.
7. Shoemaker 1995, 56.
8. Leibniz 1995a, 192.
9. From *Oxford English Dictionary*.
10. Coleman, quoted in Shoemaker 1995.
11. Coleman, quoted in Shoemaker 1995.
12. Deleuze and Guattari 1994, 89.
13. Deleuze and Guattari 1994, 89.
14. Coleman, quoted in Shoemaker 1995.
15. Grisey 2005.
16. Sextus Empiricus 1985, 33.
17. Deleuze and Guattari 2004, 335.
18. Viveiros de Castro 2014, 60.
19. Hara 2010, 65.
20. Husserl 1971, 43.
21. Husserl 1971, 50.

5

CONNECTING IDENTITY

The Rasta Reggae Diaspora in Columbus, Ohio

IVY CHEVERS

ROOTS, ROCK, REGGAE

George Easton, a professor at Oberlin College in Ohio, conducted the first study of Rastafarian culture in Kingston, Jamaica. In his *Personal Reflections of Rastafari in West Kingston in the Early 1950s*, he wrote:

> I could not have imagined in 1953 that the Rastafari movement would give birth to reggae, embraced by people throughout the world, and would develop a culture that would spread to North America, Europe, and even Africa; nor could I have envisioned that Rastas would travel abroad to represent their culture at places such as the Smithsonian Institution, Howard University, Johns Hopkins University, York University in Toronto, as well as in South Africa and other international conferences of social scientists and other scholars. (1998, 226)

Reggae musicians from England, Jamaica, and South Africa have performed in Ohio from the 1970s to the present; and certainly Columbus, Ohio, like other cities across North America, has its own reggae musicians. Sound systems and reggae music are Jamaican cultural codes that have been thoroughly assimilated into the contemporary Ohio landscape. This chapter includes twelve narratives collected between 2006 and 2016 from musicians, promoters, and fans of reggae in Ohio, as well as experts in the fields of Rastafarian culture and reggae from Jamaica and California. The narratives give insight into some of the ways in which reggae transcends differences and creates solidarities within various communities. This chapter contextualizes how the aesthetic codes and values associated with indigenous Jamaican reggae rhythms and Rastafarian culture are performed in Ohio. The chapter also examines the historical events and people that bridge the African diaspora in Ohio, Jamaica, and Ethiopia.

RASTA AND REGGAE BEGINNINGS

I credit my father, Elmer Johnson, for my Afrocentric worldview. His library of Afrocentric books filled my teenage years in Dayton, Ohio. As an undergraduate at the University of Cincinnati, I grew my first dreadlocks and began purchasing reggae albums at a used record shop in Cincinnati. Following my graduation in 1980, I traveled to Kingston, Jamaica, as a Peace Corps volunteer and was drawn to Rastafarian culture.

Witnessing firsthand the performance and production of reggae music in the early 1980s in Kingston, Jamaica, was a reggae lover's dream come true. Zinc Fence, Third World's studio on Dumfries Road in New Kingston, sponsored steady doses of live reggae and dub poetry performances. I saw, among others, Half Pint and Black Uhuru (with Junior Reid and the late Puma Jones) perform at Zinc Fence. Watching Jean Breeze, Linton Kwesi Johnson, and Mutaburuka on stage there as well, I became an admirer of their dub poetry style. Witnessing the early beginnings of some of reggae's best musicians, I felt as if I was a part of something special. The red, gold, and green colors of flying Rastafarian flags, the smell of street vendors' ital food, and the pounding heartbeats of reggae made these performances at Zinc Fence some of my most memorable experiences.

After five years of Peace Corps volunteer service, I returned to Ohio. Three years later, I returned to Jamaica, where I spent the next thirteen years teaching art and crafts at a high school in rural St. Ann. I became immersed in a Jamaican and RastafarI lifestyle. In 2001 I returned to Ohio, and began graduate studies at the Ohio State University a year later. As a graduate student, I traveled abroad to Ghana and Brazil, where I observed Rastafarian culture and reggae music spaces. In Goiânia, Brazil, I met professor Alex Ratts, a scholar of reggae, who took me to a reggae dancehall session. The DJ, in rapid Portuguese, "talked over" dubbed versions of dozens of familiar Jamaican reggae tunes. The dance floor remained full until early morning. Reggae spaces, Alex told me, were the only spaces in Brazil where dark- and light-skinned Brazilians, mostly young, come together to socialize and dance. In Ghana, I met Rasta men who spoke highly of Haile Selassie and offered me herb to smoke. My experiences of reggae spaces reflect both William Spencer's description of reggae as a vehicle of social change that "can transcend cultures and work powerfully to alter attitudes toward injustice and prejudice" (1998, 280) and Verona Reckford's view that "not all reggae fans accept the Rastafarian philosophy and doctrine, but many had identified with Rasta's symbolic beating down of Babylon with militant chants and Nyabinghi dancing and drumming, which are at once both entertaining and assuring" (1998, 249). This chapter focuses on my experiences of reggae and Rasta spaces primarily in and around Columbus, Ohio; my experiences are consistent with both Spencer's and Reckford's observations.

RASTAFARIAN CULTURE

The Rastafarian movement in Jamaica has been documented in Rex Nettleford's *Identity, Race and Protest in Jamaica* (1970), Leonard Barrett's *The Rastafarians: Sounds of Cultural Dissonance* (1998), and Joseph Owens's *The Rastafarians of Jamaica* (1976). Out of the Rastafarian movement emerged a language that combines Jamaican dialect with the movement's philosophical symbolism. Scholars of Rastafarian literature vary in their use of spellings and terms related to RastafarI. The words "you" and "me" are rarely used in Rastafarian speech. Instead, the term "I and I" is used to signify a singular reference to the self or a plural reference to the self and others. The term "Rastafarianism" is generally avoided in favor of "Rastafarian," "Rastafari" or "RastafarI." For purposes of this chapter, I use RastafarI and Rastafarian interchangeably to denote both plural and singular references.

REGGAE MUSIC

Reggae is one of the primary bearers of Rastafarian culture. Many reggae musicians are Rastafarians and the lyrics of some reggae music reflect Rastafarian ideology. Nyabinghi drumming is a traditional style of Rastafarian music that is characterized in reggae rhythms. Nyabinghi drumming emerged with the growth of RastafarI during the 1930s in Kingston, Jamaica, and is derived from African Burru and Kumina influences (Edmonds 2003; White 1998; Salewicz and Boot 2001). Burru drumming was made popular in Jamaica by master drummer Oswald Count Ossie Williams, a Rastafarian musician who founded Mystic Revelation of RastafarI and trained and mentored many aspiring Rasta musicians (Reckford 1998). By the early 1970s the proliferation of RastafarI singers and instrumentalists had become dominant influences in communicating the philosophical ideology of RastafarI through reggae. Reggae was made popular internationally by the group Bob Marley and the Wailers, which originally included members Peter Tosh and Bunny Livingston Wailer. Marley performed in Columbus, Ohio, on May 24, 1978, at Memorial Hall as part of the Kaya Tour. Bob Marley died in 1981; in 1994 he was inducted into the Rock and Roll Hall of Fame in Cleveland, Ohio.

The Ark Band, All Star Jammerz, and the Flex Crew in Columbus; SeefarI in Wilberforce; and Carlos Jones and the Plus Band from Cleveland are well-established reggae bands in Ohio. Roots Records in Columbus and Enlightenment Promotions in Cincinnati provide these cities and surrounding towns with reggae music events and promotions, such as Bob Marley Day celebrations, the celebration of Haile Selassie's coronation on November 2, and the celebration of Selassie's birthday on July 23.

THE AFRICAN DIASPORA IN OHIO

Reggae music promoter Carl Newman in Columbus has estimated that 60 percent of reggae supporters in Columbus were continental Africans (personal communication, 2007). As Mary Mederios Kent (2007) has found, between 2008 and 2012 Columbus was one of the fifteen metropolitan areas in the United States with the largest foreign-born populations from Africa, the greatest numbers from Somali and Ghanaian parentage: "in 2005, more than one million U.S.-born Black children were immigrants or had at least one foreign-born parent" and "about two-fifths of these were from African families and three-fifths from Caribbean families" (12). Kent puts Columbus at fifteenth on the list of top United States metropolitan areas for foreign-born Blacks in the United States, with Jamaica first among Caribbean countries that send Black immigrants to the United States (4). She notes that "the growing number and size of Black immigrant communities, with their distinct dress, language, music, and food, are raising their visibility" and "bring a diversity of skills and experiences, along with rich cultures and traditions" (3). At most of the reggae venues and Rastafarian events I attended in and around Columbus, the majority of patrons were continental Africans, people of Caribbean heritage, and African Americans.

ETHIOPIANISM, RASTAFARI, AND THE AFRICAN DIASPORA IN OHIO

The 1896 battle of Adwa was a unifying event that stirred the hearts and minds of Africans in the diaspora. That year Italy sent an army of more than fourteen thousand men to Adwa, Ethiopia, in an attempt at colonialization. Ethiopian emperor Menilek II's army defeated Italy in what became an historic battle. Ethiopia's victory united and strengthened relations between Jamaicans, Ethiopians, and African Americans. Fikru Negash Gebrekidan states, "Adwan mythology rendered East Africa an important place in modern Black thought, and Ethiopianism consequently became the direct harbinger of twentieth-century nationalist expressions, among them Garveyism, pan-Africanism, and Rastafarianism" (2005, 39). As a result of the battle of Adwa, African Americans in Columbus, as elsewhere in the United States, attached sentiment to Ethiopianism. The *Ohio State Monitor*, a leading Black Baptist newspaper in Columbus, included the poem "The Ethiopian" by Mrs. J. E. White in a 1919 issue. The poem emphasized the conditions of diasporic Africans in America: "the wise and the noble, bound under the iron chain, we are fighting for our freedom, and little by little we gain."[1]

Marcus Garvey, a Jamaican descendent of maroons, was an early prophet of the Rastafarian movement (White 1998). During the early 1900s, Garvey founded the Universal Negro Improvement Association (UNIA), a reform association dedicated to educational and racial uplift for Blacks. In 1920 the *Ohio State Monitor* published an article describing the activities of Garvey supporters in Columbus. An April 10 headline read, "Colored People of Columbus, O., to Organize Branch of the U.N.I.A and A.C.L.," publicizing a meeting held on April 12 at the A.M.E. Zion Church at 485 East Long Street.[2] A September 25 headline of the *Cleveland Advocate* read, "Garvey's Men Invade Ohio's Capital."[3]

On September 25, 1923, Marcus Garvey spoke to a large crowd of supporters in Columbus at what is referred to by Mark Christian as the "lost parade" (2004). A crowd of over 2,300 people gathered at Memorial Hall to hear Garvey speak. Each of the major cities in Ohio—Cincinnati, Cleveland, and Columbus—had a strong UNIA presence. Smaller towns in Ohio—especially Hamilton, Middletown, Youngstown, and Dayton—could also claim strong support of Garveyites. Christian documents that the area most populated by African Americans in Columbus in 1923 was the East Long Street and Champion Avenue district located on the near east side of Columbus and the Mount Vernon Avenue area near Champion Avenue. East Long Street was almost totally comprised of African Americans and other African-descended groups, such as the migrant Jamaicans (Christian 2004). This area of Columbus remains a hub of Caribbean activity, and is home to Miss Ena's Caribbean Kitchen, a staple on Cleveland Avenue for over thirty years.

Garvey prophesized that Black people should look to Africa, where a Black king would be crowned. This king, Garvey prophesized, would be the redeemer. In 1930 Tafari Mokonnen, Ras Tafari, prince regent of Ethiopia, was crowned emperor of Ethiopia, Haile Selassie I, King of Kings, Lord of Lords, Conquering Lion of the Tribe of Judah. This event was well publicized in Jamaica and abroad and the followers of Garvey cited Biblical references to support their belief that Haile Selassie was God. Those Biblical references include Revelations 19:16, which states, "And he hath on his vesture and his thigh a name written, King of Kings, and Lord of Lords," and Psalms 68:31, which reads, "Princes shall come out of Egypt; Ethiopia shall soon stretch out her hands unto God." The most fundamental belief of RastafarI is that Haile Selassie is the one and only true living God.

During the reign of Emperor Haile Selassie, international ties between the United States and Ethiopia strengthened. Haile Selassie sent young Ethiopian scholars to the United States to study, among them Maleku Bayen, who received a bachelor's degree in chemistry from Muskingum College in Ohio in 1928. He spent a year at the Ohio State University in Columbus as a graduate student and later transferred to Howard University as a medical student in Washington, DC. In 1935, Italy invaded Ethiopia again in another attempt to colonize the country. This "sparked a number of protests, demonstrations, physical clashes, boycotts, fund-raising activities, and recruitment and volunteer efforts in the African diaspora" and "created an emotional reaction that strengthened the bonds of pan-Africanism among descendants of Africans around the world" (Harris 1994, 24, 35). African Americans participated in the Ethiopian cause during the war. Colonel John Robinson, an African American pilot, led Ethiopian air forces against the Italians and trained pilots in Ethiopia. Bayen became an advocate of the pan-African cause, and in 1936, during the height of the Italian invasion of Ethiopia, he founded the Ethiopian World Federation (EWF). "The EWF held as its objective the unity of all blacks and black organizations under the Ethiopian banner" (Gebrekidan 2005, 104). A branch of the EWF remains active in Columbus.

Hattie Koffie, from Harlem, was part of a congregation of African Americans who migrated to Ethiopia in 1930. Koffie, a jazz pianist, lived in Addis Ababa, where she became a well-known musician. Koffie repatriated from Ethiopia in September 1934, when Italy's invasion of Ethiopia appeared imminent. She settled for a time in Columbus, Ohio, and continued to envision a flourishing community of African Americans in Ethiopia. While in Columbus Koffie advocated for the Ethiopian cause and wrote letters to President Roosevelt regarding the Italian invasion of Ethiopia (Harris 1994, 17). Her story is one of the many I found that linked Ethiopianism in the African diaspora. Like the narratives in the following section of this chapter, her experiences gives insight on how solidarity is created within various communities in the African diaspora.

PARTICIPANT NARRATIVES

Hatch and Wisniewski (1995) maintain that personal narratives connect the lives and stories of individuals to the understanding of larger social phenomena. These narratives "help establish collective memories and imagined communities; they tell of the concerns of their time and place and bridge cultural history with personal biography" (Plummer 2001, 289). Between 2006 and 2016 I conducted twelve interviews with musicians, promoters, and fans of reggae in Ohio, as well as experts in the fields of Rastafarian culture and reggae from Jamaica and California. Their narratives were transcribed from face-to-face interviews, recorded phone calls, and emails. They illustrate how reggae and Rastafarian philosophy are performed, practiced, understood, and communicated in personal, local, and global contexts.

Cedric "Im" Brooks

Cedric Brooks, now deceased, was a well-known elder Jamaican RastafarI man, accomplished saxophone player, and founding member of the Light of Saba band and later member of the Skatalites. I met Cedric in Jamaica in 1982. He was godfather and mentor to my ex-husband, Akete. When Akete and I married, Light of Saba played at our reception at a private home in Stony Hill, Jamaica. I kept up with Cedric over the years and on the evening of September 5, 2007, I spoke with him on a recorded phone call.

I asked Cedric if he believes that reggae has the power for social transformation and change. "Yes," he replied, "it is a part of the legacy of all music." He recalls that in Jamaica music was banned by the colonial powers because of the recognition of the communicative spirit and intensity of the music. Cedric pointed out that two of Jamaica's national heroes, Sam Sharpe and Nanny, used the music as part of their organizing force to help raise the spirit of Black people to resist slavery.

Cedric maintained that, during the time of Bob Marley, the music made a significant turn in its message. Marley became an icon to many people. People seemed to idolize him more than His Imperial Majesty Haile Selassie, Cedric said, and that is something that is a little bit troubling to him sometimes. He said that he "needs to see a return to the real traditional drumming chanting of the RastafarI movement." Although reggae seems static in some Western countries and transformed by the power structures that oppress people of color from an active, revolutionary form to a passive, enjoyment type of fare, Cedric claimed that there are still some African countries and Black communities that are taking on reggae as their voice in the revolution. "Reggae music is still very potent in a lot of the depressed Black communities," he said.

Basil Walters

Basil Walters, a Jamaican journalist and Rasta man, has written extensively about reggae and pan-African affairs for the *Jamaica Observer* and as a freelance journalist. His reflections on Rasta and reggae echo some of Cedric Brooks's sentiments. When I returned to Jamaica the second time in 1988, I met Basil through a friend and former Peace Corps volunteer. Through a series of emails and phone calls in 2007, Basil and I discussed authenticity, globalization, and the Rastafarian experience in and outside of Jamaica. Basil wrote:

> If I Overstand it correctly, you are asking in essence, if the culture/philosophy of RastafarI can be practiced in places like Columbus, Ohio without it losing its authenticity. If that's the question then the answer is yes, a RESOUNDING YES. The culture/philosophy of Rastafari is a UNIVERSAL AFROCENTRIC PERSPECTIVE. It is because of its universitality why it has crossed borders, continental borders, and today a Rastafarian can be found in the most remote part of the world. Rastafari is EVERYWHERE. Of course, thanks to the international impact and power of Reggae Music this has become a voice, a vehicle and an avenue of expression for Rastalogy.

Cedric and Basil have lived authentic Jamaican experiences. They both agreed that reggae gives voice and expression to RastafarI in and outside of Jamaica.

Roots Records

My first visit to Roots Records on High Street in Columbus was in 2006, on a rainy Thursday afternoon in October. The shop sells a large collection of reggae records and CDs as well as incense, reggae magazines, and T-shirts. The owner of the shop, Carl Newman, was not there at the time. I visited the shop again on a Tuesday afternoon the following month with the intention of speaking with Newman, and also to buy two tickets to the upcoming Sizzla reggae show. I spoke to a Black dreadlocked Jamaican named Cush for about ten minutes. He was from the parish of St. Ann, Jamaica, where I lived for thirteen years. Though we had never met, we seemed to have known some of the same people in Jamaica. Cush went upstairs to the office to tell the owner I was there. I was invited up to meet Carl, a middle-aged, slightly balding white man. We talked informally for about forty minutes about my research and his work as a promoter of reggae. He agreed that I could interview him and do observations in the shop. I did not officially interview Carl until a year later, on a Tuesday afternoon in October. I was impressed by his knowledge of reggae and his role as a promoter in bringing some of Jamaica's finest reggae acts to Columbus. Carl bought Roots Records from his friend and mentor, Hugo Cabrera, in 1998. Carl shared a wealth of archives with me, including newspaper articles and posters documenting Cabrera's works as a reggae promoter. One of his employees, Modou Bah, a young African dreadlocked brother from the Gambia, joined the interview. He said that he has been listening to reggae since he was a child in the Gambia. Modou Bah grew up in a Muslim country and professes Islam; he does not consider himself a Rasta though he relates to the importance the movement gives to African unity, history, and pride.

Carl has been into reggae since the beginning of its movement in the United States in the mid-1970s. He was moved by the positive, uplifting lyrics of the music, its drum and bass rhythms, and syncopation. He travels to Jamaica often to conduct business. Carl feels that reggae provides a space for relaxation, dancing, and forgetting about worries, quoting Bob Marley's lyrics, "forget your worries and dance." He stated, "I think most of the lyrics come straight from the good book like Proverbs. The music brings it to a level where everybody realizes and understands it and gets into a harmonious relationship with themselves." Carl says he has read Marcus Garvey and can understand his teachings. He has not read too much about Haile Selassie, but says, "that is very strong stuff, it's all good and needs to be understood." Carl says he doesn't know if he is Rasta; to him Rasta means a pure and clean way of thinking.

He considers himself just a "messenger" or "mailman" carrying the torch that was passed to him by Hugo Cabrera. He says he feels blessed to be a part of it.

I asked Carl about the evolution of reggae. He says that reggae remains a countercultural, alternative, underground music that neither African Americans or white Americans have fully embraced. "Reggae artists need to get back to more Rasta stuff and get into kids' minds," he added. He asserts that continental Africans are the biggest supporters of reggae in Columbus, estimating that 60 percent Africans, 20 percent African Americans and West Indians, and 20 percent whites make up the customers at his shop. Carl was instrumental in arranging interviews for me with Hugo's daughter, Jennifer Cabrera, and reggae historian Roger Steffens.

Jennifer Cabrera

Jennifer is the daughter of Hugo and Donna Cabrera, the former owners of Skankland and Negril and Jamaica Records in Columbus, Ohio. She, like Carl, is white. I accompanied Carl to Jennifer's home in Bexley, Ohio, in the fall of 2008, where I conducted a two-hour interview. Jennifer's father, Hugo, visited Jamaica over forty times in his life. He opened a booking agency in 1981 that brought Jamaican acts to local clubs in Columbus. In 1987 he founded Skankland, one of Columbus's first reggae clubs, and brought international reggae acts to the city. Jennifer was seventeen then. She remembers that Skankland drew a crowd of college professors, Ohio State University students, graduate teaching associates, people from Cincinnati, and a large continental African following. Her parents did not profess to be Rastas, but her father had dreadlocks and both mother and father were "hippies big-time, open-minded people who loved everything and everybody, especially reggae music." Jennifer does not subscribe to any particular religion nor participate in any RastafarI activities. She says if you're a good person, you live well, do good to other people, and do right by yourself.

Jennifer traveled extensively to Jamaica as a young child and as an adult. She is a hardcore reggae and dancehall fan and is married to a member (and manager) of the All Star Jammerz, a reggae, soca, calypso, and dancehall band. Jennifer feels that because people in American do not understand the lyrics of reggae, it makes it difficult for the music to become mainstream. She loves the energy of the music and describes her experiences at Jamaica's reggae events as fabulous: "there is nothing like being in an open-air outdoor venue under the beautiful stars with thirty to fifty thousand people waving their arms—nothing like that—a very interesting experience, lots of energy there."

Roger Steffens

Roger Steffens is cofounder of the *Beat Magazine* and editor of its annual Bob Marley Collectors' Edition; he has been chairman of the reggae Grammy committee. Stevens started listening to reggae in 1973; he has a collection of reggae paraphernalia that fills six rooms of his home in Los Angeles. Through emails between late 2007 and early 2008, Roger and I discussed cultural appropriation and reggae. In response to my questions, he wrote:

> Your questions cut to the quick about the consequences of cultural appropriation, but those borders have been evanescent for centuries already. Like it or not, the lion escaped the leash when Bob, especially, became the international face of the philosophy of Rastafari. Reggae is the soundtrack or the Movement of Jah. What is appropriation, and what is inspiration? And how can you own something as ephemeral as a sound? One of the biggest toasters on the international reggae scene in recent years is a German named Gentleman, who stirs it up in Western Kingston as easily as he does for tens of thousands of rapt skankers at European festivals. It is the wonderous message of Rasta-inspired reggae ("King's Music") that is the lynchpin of its success throughout the globe. Roots-conscious DJs with yarmulkes crowning their dreadlocks play the latest 7-inches from Yard in a Rasta kibbutz in the middle of the Negev Desert; physically mountainous Samoans, Tongans and Hawaiians play together in Honolulu in a reggae band called Ookla-the-Moc, adding the holy rhythm to songs of local protest and native land rights, just as do their Maori cousins in New Zealand.

Steffen's statements, like those of Cedric Brooks and Basil Walters, affirm the expansive influence of reggae and Rastafarian culture internationally.

The Ark Band

The Ark Band is a local Columbus reggae group. Two of its founding members are from the island of St. Lucia; I interviewed one of them, Terry Bobb. I called Terry to discuss my research and make arrangements for an interview. His response to my call was kind, and before our interview I visited the Scarlet and Grey Café, near the Ohio State University, twice to hear the band play their regular Thursday night gig. This is where I interviewed Terry on Thursday, August 30, 2007.

Terry Bobb is a dreadlocked, middle-aged man from St. Lucia. His father and grandfather were musicians. He has traveled to Jamaica, where he has learned a lot about reggae. He describes himself as a Biblical Christian. Terry does not profess RastafarI, though at the age of nineteen in St. Lucia he was thrown into jail for growing his dreadlocks and associating with Rastafarian elders. He feels that people grow dreadlocks because in their heart they decide it is a peaceful thing to do. Like many other youth who grew their dreadlocks in the early 1970s, Terry's mom was greatly concerned about her son's future and insisted that he be sent to America. Instead Terry chose to go to the hills of St. Lucia and gain knowledge of RastafarI from Rasta men who lived there. I asked Terry how he came to know RastafarI in St. Lucia. He said, "It is through Bob Marley we come to know Rasta in St. Lucia. The whole world comes to know Rasta through Bob Marley."

In 1976 Terry moved to Brooklyn, New York. He saw Bob Marley twice at the Apollo. He says "people just worshipped Bob Marley" and noted that "Marley is the biggest inspiration in my life." In 1986 Terry and his brother Eustace moved to Columbus, where they have resided ever since. He says that people called both Eustace and him "Bob Marley" and that Columbus was like a "breath of fresh air." In 1987 Terry and Eustace founded the Ark Band, which is now one of the longest-existing reggae bands in the city. The band plays originals and cover versions of calypso, reggae, and soca music. The band has traveled throughout the United States, Canada, and Jamaica. The Ark Band's website states that their music is "designed to entertain, educate and enlighten all types of people. THE ARK BAND continues to be a dynamic force on the American scene after two decades, their songs expressing the love, peace, togetherness and spirituality needed in our world today!" I asked Terry if he thinks reggae is transformative. He replied, "Reggae is a powerful peaceful music and the cry of the people."

Haile Israel

Haile Israel, a vocalist and guitarist, has performed with the reggae group Ras Michael & the Sons of Negus. Haile has also acted as a personal priest to Ras Michael. I met Haile in 1985 in Ohio through one of my older sisters. Years later they were married, but after almost twenty years together, they were divorced. I interviewed Haile on Sunday, July 14, 2008. Haile, a Rasta man of African American/Caribbean descent, describes himself as chief minister and "I Priest" of the Order. Haile has been involved in the RastafarI movement for over thirty years. He has traveled extensively throughout the

United States, the Caribbean, Hawai'i, and Africa, playing reggae and spreading the word of RastafarI. In Hawai'i he founded a Reggae Church. Of the Reggae Church Haile states, "The mission of the Reggae Church is to both entertain and inform listeners of the message in the music—'Jah Music' as we referred to it in the seventies." Haile described RastafarI as an indigenous, esoteric Jamaican cultural and oral tradition that cannot be explained in Western terms. He reasons that climate and geographical location affect how people practice a Rasta lifestyle. On the future of RastafarI and reggae, Haile commented that the future of RastafarI is to get out of Babylon. He added that one of the major pillars of RastafarI is repatriation, and that we need to fulfill prophesy by leaving Babylon and returning to Africa.

SeefarI

Tom Carroll (SeefarI) is the founder of SeefarI, a reggae band located in Wilberforce, Ohio. SeefarI is a white Rasta man with dreadlocks. He has been a musician since he was a teenager. I met SeefarI in 1985. At that time, he and Haile often shared the same reggae stages together. In the early 1980s SeefarI began listening to Bob Marley's music, and as a result he began to profess RastafarI. SeefarI sees Haile Selassie as an avatar of Christ, a Christ messiah personality. The first time he recalls seeing Haile Selassie was on television at the funeral of John F. Kennedy. He says the "fact that he came back as an African king is really important because his presence helped to restore balance in the world regarding the impression of Africa," adding that "it's a real important symbol to the world that we have an African Christ figure."

SeefarI adheres to a strict vegetarian diet and like many RastafarI, he adheres to the Nazarite vow. The Nazarite law was one of the legislations of Sinai that required one who was devoted to God to keep himself ceremonially clean and devoted to God by not cutting his hair or drinking wine or strong drink. Of Bob Marley SeefarI states, "Bob has a universal appeal that seems to go beyond any kind of racial, religious or societal barriers, rich, poor, black, white from all different countries. They all love Bob." SeefarI believes that Bob Marley is the reincarnation of Yared, an Ethiopian songwriter. Like Terry Bobb of the Ark Band, SeefarI also credits Bob Marley and reggae as major influences on his life and music.

Matt Stinson

Matt, an African American male with dreadlocks, was born and raised in Columbus. I was introduced to Matt by a fellow graduate student at OSU. I met and interviewed Matt on October 25, 2007, at the coffee shop of Barnes & Noble near the OSU campus. Matt started listening to reggae in the late 1980s. His curiosity about the message in the music led him to research RastafarI on his own and talk to other Rastafarians in Columbus. "I was attracted to what I heard" in the music, he said. "It was something that I was never told before in school or in my own household." Through RastafarI he learned about the teachings of Marcus Garvey and Haile Selassie. He says that through Rasta he learned about a more positive image of Africa.

Matt says Rasta keeps him grounded, focused, humble, and on the right path to be successful in life. He has traveled to Jamaica on numerous occasions. Like SeefarI and Terry Bobb, Matt's journey to RastafarI began with the lyrics of reggae.

Andrew Buck

The first time I encountered Andrew was at a high school in Hilliard, Ohio, in November 2007. He was a guest speaker at an Invisible Children presentation. On stage, he wore all white with African drums as props. His white, male perspectives on Uganda and the Peace Corps held my interest. In January 2008 I saw Andrew again at OSU in a course in which we were both enrolled, on experimental writing in qualitative research. I recognized him from the Invisible Children presentation, introduced myself, and spoke about my research on RastafarI and reggae. Andrew shared with me his story about a "mystical" encounter with a RastafarI man he met in Uganda. Later in the semester I interviewed him. About RastafarI and reggae, he stated:

> I consider myself Rasta, because it is undeniable in my heart. I consider myself one with God and all of Creation. The prophets of this movement have had great influence in my awareness of "who I am" and "where I belong." Also, Nesta Robert Marley, his life and mission, the message he spread through his music has led me to know him as a true prophet. His message is Gnostic, and Christian, but is overwhelmingly about LOVE, Respect, Oneness, the battle against the evil forces of the devil's philosophy, and he knows that "righteousness shall cover the earth like water cover the sea" well. It is all summed up in one word for me: Oneness. This is Rasta

to me, and why I attempt to follow the tenets and philosophies provided by political and social leaders like Marcus Garvey (acceptance of our true nature, the appreciation of the mother land), Haile Selassie, Nesta Bob Marley . . . plus, reggae music is the life blood of this socially conscious philosophy. I love it. It moves me. I am a spiritual dancer.

Andrew's experience echoes those of most of the interviewees—that reggae is a driving force to Rastafarian philosophy.

Sister Queen

I met Queen in Columbus at a 2007 coronation celebration for His Imperial Majesty Haile Selassie. Queen is an African American artist, seamstress, and vendor of Afrocentric and Rastafarian accessories, clothes, and educational items. She grew up in Cleveland, Ohio, in a Muslim community before professing RastafarI. She says that everything she has done in her life is directed toward the struggle for freedom from oppression. Queen often vends at reggae shows and is instrumental in organizing and participating in Rastafari holy day events in Ohio.

Queen came to RastafarI through reggae. She attended a reggae concert in Cincinnati in 1980 where Ras Michael & the Sons of Negus were performing. "It was like you was in church, such a spiritual thing." Queen states that ever since that day Rasta has been in her heart. But it was not until after she fulfilled a commitment she made to Allah to raise her children in the Muslim faith that she began to fully participate in a RastafarI way of life.

Queen feels that reggae is nothing like it used to be but her commitment to RastafarI is strong. She says that if people would just listen to His Imperial Majesty's Emperor Haile Selassie's words they would understand that we are peaceful people and all we want to do is just live in peace.

Leah Saho

Leah, an African American woman living in Cincinnati, Ohio, performs and promotes reggae and RastafarI cultural events through her business, Enlightenment Promotions. I met Leah in Columbus, while I was a consultant at the King Arts Complex in 2008. At that time I helped curate the exhibits "Columbus Rastafari" and "The Men, the Message, the Music, and the Movement: Martin, Malcolm, and Marley." In February 2009 the King Arts Complex opened the exhibits and, in conjunction with a screening of *Africa Unite*

(2007), a tribute to and documentary film about Bob Marley, I conducted a forum and Q&A with members of the Rastafarian and reggae community in Ohio and James Henke, author of *Marley Legend: An Illustrated Life of Bob Marley*. Leah brought a group from Cincinnati, which provided drumming and entertainment for the evening.

I interviewed Leah in May 2016. She shared with me her involvement in the RastafarI community, which began in the 1980s when Enlightenment first began promoting and supporting educational opportunities for Black, Afrocentric, and RastafarI communities in Cincinnati. In 1981 Leah helped found the All Seasons Reggae group and sang lead and background vocals. She partnered with other female reggae performers and created Enlightenment in an effort to form alliances with Afrocentric women. An initial promoter of the Empress Menen Educational Center[4] and Ethiopian African Orthodox RastafarI Church in Cincinnati, Enlightenment continues to contribute to the reggae and RastafarI cultural landscape in and around Cincinnati.

DAYTON REGGAE FESTIVAL

During my eighteen-year residence in Jamaica, I attended countless reggae concerts. In Ohio I have also enjoyed seeing some of the finest reggae acts perform, including Sizzla, Barrington Levi, Half Pint, Tony Rebel, Capleton, Luciano, Buju Banton, Ziggy Marley, Jimmy Cliff, Beres Hammond, the Wailers, the Meditations, Morgan Heritage, Third World, and Pato Banton and the Now Generation Band. My experiences at those shows always left me feeling uplifted and hopeful. I attended my first Dayton Reggae Festival in September 2007. The festival was celebrating its twentieth year. I arrived at the festival to see the Ark Band perform. The crowd was diverse: old and young, black and white. Vendors sold Rasta-inspired arts and crafts including skullcaps, red, gold, and green scarves, and T-shirts with images of Bob Marley, Marcus Garvey, and Haile Selassie.

The following day the article, "Reggae Festival Rocks Downtown," by Ben Southerly, headlined the local section in the *Dayton Daily News*. Southerly, as well as people he interviewed for the article, had high praises for the festival. One attendee said of the festival, "it's real multicultural, multigenerational. It's not one specific crowd. The music is real kid-friendly and has a lot of positive messages." Another attendee said she "enjoyed the festival because the Rastafarian scene emphasizes peace, freedom and love, we're all one in the big scheme of things, and at events such as the Reggae Festival, we learn to understand each other's culture, each other's beliefs."[5] I myself left the festival, sponsored in part by Michelob, feeling conflicted: happy to see friends and listen to reggae, but lukewarm and overwhelmed by the apparent overindulgence of beer by some of the patrons. Based on Old Testament teachings, RastafarI considers the body a temple. Many Rastafarians follow a strict vegetarian diet and do not drink alcohol. While not all reggae fans are Rastafarians, many are. In traditional RastafarI settings alcohol and cigarette smoking are discouraged in favor of healthy natural alternatives and foods.

CONCLUSION: SOCIAL MOVEMENTS AND COLLECTIVE IDENTITY

In *Music and Social Movements: Mobilizing Traditions in the Twentieth Century,* Eyerman and Jamison (1998) claim that the cultural effects of social movements live on through songs, art, and literature in the absence of the particular political platforms and struggles that brought them into being. They contend that social movements are key agents of cultural transformation and see music and art as carriers of the truth-bearing, knowledge-producing forces inherent to social movements (163). Individuals and groups who play reggae are inclined to produce truth-bearing knowledge based on the music's interconnectedness with its Rastafarian philosophy and Jamaican roots. For some, the rhythms and the pulse of the drums are an appealing sound, while others are more closely drawn to a Rastafarian philosophy. Borrowing from Eyerman and Jamison, I observed that reggae and RastafarI in Ohio create a "context in which the traditions carried through art become actualized, reinvented, and revitalized" (46) and recognize the fine line that distinguishes art from ideology. While some reggae listeners may not fully understand the ideological influences of the music, there are others who do. And while pleasure is part of listening to reggae, its lyrics in many cases still reflect the cries of Rastafarian musicians and fans who continue to "chant down Babylon" with music. For the most part I have observed that reggae reinforces bonds in the African diaspora, bridging cultures and histories by connecting the lives and stories of individuals to collective identities.

Kebede, Shriver, and Knottnerus argue that "since the movement's inception the Rastafarian collective identity has revolved around a number of core themes associated with language, music, rituals, and appearance" (2000, 315). Eight out of the twelve people I interviewed in this chapter identify with RastafarI culture. All twelve are inspired and uplifted by reggae. In Cleveland, Columbus, and Cincinnati, RastafarI aesthetics, codes, and values are scattered where reggae is performed. Black, red, green, and gold flags and accessories; portraits of Haile Selassie, Empress Menen, Bob Marley, and Marcus Garvey; and African-centered history books are bartered, traded, and sold. With the music's rhythms and lyrical chants pulsating, continental Africans, African Americans, West Indians, white Americans, and others come together to dance, socialize, have a good time, gain knowledge, share with one another, and network together.

The practice and consumption of RastafarI culture outside of Jamaica and the interactions between agency and play are complex issues. This chapter provides my personal reflections and experiences with reggae and Rastafarian culture, connecting the histories of African Americans in Columbus, Ohio, to those of the Jamaican and Ethiopian diaspora. The narratives woven with my lived experiences speak to the ways in which Rastafarian culture and reggae music is maintained, contextualized, and transformed in the African diaspora.

BIBLIOGRAPHY

"The African American Experience." 1920. *Ohio State Monitor*. Volume 2, number 43. http://www.ohiomemory.org/cdm/ref/collection/p16007coll28/id/593. Accessed February 2007.

Barrett, Leonard. 1998. *The Rastafarians: Sounds of Cultural Dissonance*. Boston: Beacon.

Brodber, Erna, and John Edward Green. 1998. *Reggae and Cultural Identity in Jamaica*. Kingston: University of the West Indies Institute of Social and Economic Research.

Christian, Mark. 2004. "Marcus Garvey and the Universal Negro Improvement Association (UNIA): With Special Reference to the 'Lost' Parade in Columbus, Ohio, September 25, 1923." *Western Journal of Black Studies* 28 (3): 424–34.

Easton, George. 1998. "Personal Reflections of Rastafari in West Kingston in the Early 1950s." In *Chanting Down Babylon: The Rastafari Reader*, edited by Samuel Murrell, William D. Spencer, and Adrian Anthony McFarlane, 217–28. Philadelphia: Temple University Press.

Edmonds, Ennis. 1998. "Dread 'I' In-a-Babylon: Ideological Resistance and Cultural Revitalization." In *Chanting Down Babylon: The Rastafari Reader*, edited by Samuel Murrell, William Spencer, and Adrian McFarlane, 199–216. Philadelphia: Temple University Press.

Edmonds, Ennis. 2003. *Rastafari: From Outcasts to Culture Bearers*. Oxford: Oxford University Press.

Eyerman, Ron, and Jamison, Andrew. 1998. *Music and Social Movements: Mobilizing Traditions in the Twentieth Century*. Cambridge and New York: Cambridge University Press.

Gambino, Christine P., Edward N. Trevely, and John Thomas Fitzwater. 2014. "The Foreign-Born Population from Africa: 2008–2012." U.S. Census Bureau. https://www.census.gov/content/dam/Census/library/publications/2014/acs/acsbr12-16.pdf.

"Garvey's Men Invade Ohio's Capital City." 1920. *Cleveland Advocate*. Volume 7, issue 20, 1. http://dbs.ohiohistory.org/africanam/html/page4a36.html?ID=9800. Accessed March 2007.

Gebrekidan, Fikru Negash. 2005. *Bond without Blood: A History of Ethiopian and Caribbean Relations, 1896–1991*. Trenton, NJ: Africa World Press.

Gilroy, Paul. 1997. "Diaspora and the Detours of Identity." In *Identity and Difference*, edited by Kathryn Woodward, 301–42. London: Sage.

Harris, Joseph. 1994. *African-American Reactions to War in Ethiopia 1936–1941*. Baton Rouge and London: Louisiana State University Press.

Hatch, Amos, and Richard Wisniewski, eds. 1995. *Life History and Narrative*. London: Falmer Press, 1995.

Kebede, Alem, Thomas Shriver, and David Knottnerus. 2000. "Social Movement Endurance: Collective Identity and the Rastafari." *Sociological Inquiry* 70 (3): 313–37.

Kent, Mary Mederios. 2007. "Immigration and America's Black Population." *Population Bulletin* 62 (4): 3–16.

Nettleford, Rex. 1970. *Identity, Race and Protest in Jamaica*. Kingston: Collins and Sangster.

Owens, Joseph. 1976. *Dread: The Rastafarians of Jamaica*. London: Heinemann.

Plummer, Ken. 2001. "The Call of Life Stories in Ethnographic Research." In *Handbook of Ethnography*, by Paul Atkinson, 395–406. London: Sage.

Reckford, Verona. 1998. "From Burru Drums to Reggae Riddims: The Evolution of Rasta Music." In *Chanting Down Babylon: The Rastafari Reader*, edited by Samuel Murrell, William Spencer, and Adrian McFarlane, 231–52. Philadelphia: Temple University Press.

Salewicz, Chris and Adrian Boot. 2001. *Reggae Explosion: The Story of Jamaican Music*. New York: Harry Abrams.

Southerly, Ben. 2007. "Reggae Festival Rocks Downtown." *Dayton Daily News*, September 3, 2007, 4.

Spencer, William. 1998. "Chanting Change around the World through Rasta Ridim and Art." In *Chanting Down Babylon: The Rastafari Reader*, edited by Samuel Murrell, William Spencer, and Adrian McFarlane, 266–82. Philadelphia: Temple University Press.

White, J. E. 1919. "The Ethiopian." *Ohio State Monitor*, volume 1, number 45 (April 19), 1. http://dbs.ohiohistory.org/africanam/html/pagece57.html?ID=2759. Accessed March 2007.

White, Timothy. 1998. *Catch a Fire: The Life of Bob Marley*. New York: Henry Holt.

NOTES

1. White 1919.
2. "The African American Experience."
3. "Garvey's Men Invade Ohio's Capital City."
4. Born April 3, 1891, Empress Menen Asfaw, the wife of Emperor Haile Selassie, is also a RastafarI cultural icon.
5. Southerly 2007.

6

MICHIE MEE

Rap Music, Cultural Representations, Identity, and the Caribbean Diaspora in Toronto

ATHENA ELAFROS

The Caribbean diaspora in Toronto has played a germinal role in the creation, formation, and dissemination of rap music and hip hop culture in Canada. This chapter aims to outline the importance of the Caribbean diaspora in the formation of rap in Toronto, Ontario, by situating rap within the larger field of popular music production in Canada, and in doing so, illustrating the importance of a diasporic understanding of cultural fields. Drawing upon Pierre Bourdieu, Rinaldo Walcott, and Stuart Hall, this chapter uses Michie Mee, Canada's "first lady of Toronto hip hop," as a case study of diasporic cultural identity, diasporic cultural production, and diasporic "Black cultural capital" (Carter 2003; Wallace 2016). I will first outline the historical, social, and economic conditions of Caribbean migration in Toronto. Second, I will discuss the marginalization of rap music and people of color within the music industry in Toronto. Finally, I will provide an analysis of interviews and a selection of the musical works of Michie Mee to answer the following questions: (1) How does she use rap to showcase her diasporic roots/routes? (2) How does she help redefine Canadian identity in ways that emphasize the importance of diasporic identities? (3) How does she use rap to challenge racist and racialized conceptions of Canadian identity (e.g., as predominantly European)? The goal of this chapter is to show how diasporic cultural identity and diasporic cultural production can productively inform Bourdieusian analyses of culture.

CULTURAL PRODUCTION, CULTURAL IDENTITY, AND DIASPORAS

Bourdieu discusses how various types of capital—economic, social, cultural, and symbolic—are resources that are struggled over within all cultural fields

(1991, 1993, 1996). This chapter posits that, similar to economic, social, cultural, and symbolic capital, cultural identity is also a resource that is struggled over within cultural fields. Historically, identity is a hard-to-define concept and is used in a variety of different ways within sociology (Bottero 2010, 3). As I have noted in previous work, identity can be defined in personal, collective, and cultural terms. Personal theories of identity focus on identity as a stable entity, or essence. Identity within this framework reflects the self, which is seen as a stable structure. These views of identity draw upon symbolic interactionist perspectives and the works of George Herbert Mead and Herbert Blumer. Collective theories of identity focus on how identities can be mobilized in terms of collective action with others. Cultural theories of identity focus on the situational, social-structural, and cultural elements of identity that are located outside of the individual. These definitions of identity focus on similarities, differences, and solidarities with others. The work of Stuart Hall is important in this regard. He provides two definitions of cultural identity that are most relevant to the current discussion: cultural identity as product, and cultural identity as solidarity. Cultural identity as product focuses on how identity is simultaneously socially constructed yet also determined and constrained by social differences such as race, class, gender, sexuality, and ability, among others. Cultural identity as solidarity focuses on the ways in which identity is used by people to promote social change and justice.

For Bourdieu, identity emerges from the interrelations between habitus and field. The habitus is a collection of dispositions that shape how actors operate within the field. The field is "a structured space of positions in which the positions and their interrelations are determined by the distribution of different kinds of resources or 'capital'" (Thompson 1991, 14). Bourdieu envisions the field as a network of objective relations between positions (1996, 231) that is structured by the distribution of available positions and by the objective characteristics of agents occupying those positions (Johnson 1991, 16). Positions in the field may be occupied by different social entities, such as organizations, groups, or individuals (Regev 1994, 86). Broadly speaking, there are three types of positions within the field: *dominant positions*, those who possess various forms of capital and recognition within the field, such as well-known artists; *newcomers*, those who are new to the field; and *dominated positions*, those who have been in the field for some time but lack capital and recognition, such as striving artists (Bourdieu 1993, 83). Each of these types of positions within the field is defined by its objective relationship to other positions (Bourdieu 1996, 231).

Within this framework, Bourdieu's work emphasizes the dispositional nature of subjectivity (Bottero 2010, 10), with cultural identities reflecting the dispositions of social actors within the field. Cultural identity is a product of the field. However, Bourdieu's understanding of cultural identity does not adequately address how identity emerges from the intersubjective relationships between people in the field (5). How and why do dispositional identities (which are entrenched and involuntary "products" of fields) transform into reflexive identities (which involve conscious calculation, struggle, and solidarity) (8)? The solution to this problem, as posed by Bottero, is that reflexivity needs to be reframed in intersubjective terms. Reflexive identifications are a reflection *on*, not *of*, dispositional practice (19). Cultural identity, within this revised framework, is objectively structured and subjectively experienced, as well as dispositional and reflexive. This chapter uses an intersubjective understanding of cultural identity, which sees cultural practice as the negotiated outcome of intersubjective coordination (20). This reframing of Bourdieusian cultural identity allows us to focus on how cultural identities are strategically employed and represented within cultural fields. This chapter examines cultural identity as dispositional *and* reflexive and applies this understanding of cultural identity to an analysis of cultural fields.

Of particular interest here is how cultural identity (with an emphasis on solidarity) and diasporic belonging[1] contribute to an improved understanding of fields of cultural production. Drawing upon the works of Rinaldo Walcott and his analyses of Caribbean/Black popular culture in Canada (1997; 2000; 2001), I explore how diasporas and transnational contexts are crucial components of most (if not all) cultural fields. For example, Walcott argues that Caribbean popular culture (for example, rap, calypso, reggae, and dancehall) in Canada is always constructed in ways that fit "local concerns and contexts, but still always [lead] somewhere else" (2001, 126). These forms of diasporic cultural production are always created with both local concerns and contexts, but also concerns with "elsewhere" (Walcott 2011). Fields of cultural production need to be reconceptualized in ways that include theorizations of "elsewhere," ones that move beyond traditional analyses rooted in the nation-state.

Previous Bourdieusian analyses of popular music (Lopes 2000; Moore 2007; Prior 2008; Regev 1994; Thornton 1996) have tended to focus on fields at the local and/or national level of analysis and do not focus on the diasporic and/or transnational character of these same fields. However, there is a growing literature on transnational or global fields. Examples include the works of Buchholz (2016) on theorizing global fields; Go (2008) on global fields;

Kuipers (2011) on the role of cultural intermediaries in the globalization of television as a transnational cultural field; Fligstein and McAdam (2012) on strategic action fields; Meuleman and Savage (2013) on transnationality and highbrow consumption in the Netherlands; Savage and Silva (2013) on field analysis in cultural sociology; Verboord, Kuipers, and Janssen (2015) on institutional recognition in the transnational literary field; and Elafros (2013a) on the distinctions between local and translocal authenticity among the cultural producers of hip hop culture in Athens, Greece. However, greater emphasis needs to be placed on the diasporic character of national and/or local fields. Whereas much of this previous research focuses on how global fields are distinct from national fields, this work aims to illustrate the ways in which global, transnational, and/or diasporic concerns permeate all fields of cultural production. By focusing on a single artist, Michie Mee, this chapter aims to illustrate how a diasporic analysis is of benefit to all cultural fields.

A BRIEF HISTORY OF THE CARIBBEAN DIASPORA IN TORONTO

Toronto, Ontario, a city with a total of 2.6 million residents, boasts one of "the most cosmopolitan urban populations in the world" (Burman 2001) and is often seen as a "diasporic city" (Burman 2010). The province of Ontario accounts for 53.3 percent of Canada's foreign-born population, and 70.3 percent of Ontario's immigrant population lives in Toronto, with just under half (46 percent) of Toronto's total population being foreign-born (Ontario Ministry of Finance 2011). This makes Toronto one of the most diverse and cosmopolitan cities in the world. There are many thriving diasporic communities within Toronto, one of which is the Caribbean diaspora.

The people in the Caribbean diaspora in Toronto are a diverse group, consisting of individuals with African, Indian, Asian, white, and West Indian ethnic and cultural backgrounds. As Karen Flynn notes, "Caribbean people are not only diverse as a result of their colonial heritage; the communities in Canada are demarcated by race, color, gender, ethnicity, and sexual orientation" (Flynn 2013). Within Canada, most members of the Caribbean diaspora have settled in Toronto and Montreal, Quebec. In the 2006 census, 578,695 Canadians reported that they originated from the Caribbean, and the overwhelming majority of these people have immigrated to Canada since the 1970s for economic reasons (Labelle, Larose, and Piché 2015). Prior to the 1960s there was very little immigration from the Caribbean to Canada. This is because, prior to the 1960s, the field of immigration in Canada was shaped by the government in ways aimed to maintain a "white" society by providing preferential treatment to white immigrants from Europe, the United States, and certain Commonwealth countries (Hiebert 1994, 255). In the 1960s the distinction between "preferred" and "non-preferred" countries was replaced with a points system. Instead of providing preferential treatment based on country of origin, the points system allotted each applicant points based on predetermined selection criteria (there are currently six used in the federal government skilled workers program: language skills, education, work experience, age, arranged employment in Canada, and adaptability). The higher the points allotted, the greater the likelihood of being allowed to immigrate to Canada. The outcome of this change was significant. The vast majority of immigrants prior to 1967 were of European background, while immigration since that time has been much more international in character (255). The contours of the field of immigration greatly shifted as a result of legislative changes and the establishment of the points system. Larger-scale migration from the Caribbean began after the introduction of the points system in 1967, and by 1973 Caribbean immigration accounted for 13 percent of all immigration to Canada, though after 1974 and until the 1990s it declined. Since the 1990s the population of Canadians of Caribbean origin has grown more quickly than the Canadian population as a whole, with the majority (90 percent) of Caribbean Canadians living in Ontario and Quebec (Labelle, Larose, and Piché 2015).

The field of immigration in Canada is hierarchically organized. Focusing on the history of the movement of Caribbean peoples into Canada highlights how that hierarchy reflects systemic racism. Historically, there have been several periods of Caribbean forced slavery and migration to Canada (Labelle, Larose, and Piché 2015). The first people from the Caribbean in Canada were enslaved men and women brought to Halifax, Nova Scotia, in 1688 (Flynn 2013). A much larger group brought to Canada in 1796 against their will were the Maroons, a group of Jamaicans who resisted British colonial rule and were transported to Halifax (Flynn 2013). Between the years 1900 and 1960, very few immigrants were allowed to migrate to Canada from the Caribbean due to the "preferred" country of origin legislation. The exception during this time was the West Indian Domestic Scheme (1955–60), wherein women from Jamaica and Barbados immigrated to Canada to work as domestic workers. Under this scheme, single women between the ages of eighteen and forty with no dependents and at least an eighth-grade education could move to Canada as landed immigrants on the condition that they remain in live-in domestic service for at least one year (Foner 2008, 10). From 1960 to 1971 there was a growth in Caribbean migration due to the "liberalization" of the Canadian Immigration Act. This period marked a growth in immigration from the Caribbean due to the eventual adoption of the points system. Most of the Caribbean immigrants during this time were technical and professional workers, such as teachers and nurses (Flynn 2013). From the 1970s until roughly 1996, immigration from the Caribbean declined. However, between 1996 and 2001, the Canadian population grew by 4 percent, while the Caribbean Canadian population grew by 11 percent (Labelle, Larose, and Piché 2015). Michie Mee (Michelle McCullock) was born in 1970 and immigrated in her youth to Canada from St. Andrew, Kingston, Jamaica, with her family.

In addition to the long-standing history of racism against Caribbean migrants noted above, there is also a history of racism against Caribbean immigrants within Canada. The current contours of the immigration field reflect deep-seated systemic racism and inequality. This racism has been well-documented by Frances Henry's groundbreaking study (1994) on the Caribbean diaspora in Toronto. In this study, Henry outlines how the Caribbean community faces racism within a variety of social institutions, such as the immigration system, the job market, the search for housing, the education system, and in their relations with police and the criminal justice system. This is particularly pronounced within the job market. For example, although Caribbean immigrants often possess the required qualifications for jobs, racist hiring practices have historically forced Caribbean migrants to accept jobs that were not commensurate with their qualifications, which has resulted in many Caribbean immigrants being overrepresented in service and manual sectors in the Canadian economy (Flynn 2013). As Warner illustrates in his study (2006) of Afro-Trini immigrants in the Greater Toronto Area (GTA), members of the Caribbean diaspora experience everyday racism, cultural racism, individual racism, and institutional racism within the larger Canadian society and job market. These sentiments are mirrored in the 2003 Ethnic Diversity Survey published by Statistics Canada that found nonwhites were more likely than others to say that they felt uncomfortable or out of place in Canada at least some of the time because of their ethnicity, culture, race, skin color, language, accent, or religion. Furthermore, in "The Black Experience Project [BEP] in the GTA" (James 2017), the majority of respondents (individuals sixteen years old and older living in the Greater Toronto Area who self-identify as either Black or of African heritage) identified shared experiences of Black identity in spite of diversity. BEP participants almost unanimously agreed that being Black is important to their identity and their social relationships, and shared the conviction that Black people in the GTA are treated unfairly because of their race (James 2017). Given these long-standing social and historical conditions within the immigration field in Canada, it is important to note that the Afro-Caribbean community in Toronto possesses a shared sense of solidarity and shared cultural identity based on shared experiences. This shared sense of cultural identity is reflected in the work of Michie Mee, and these are the historical and social conditions of the Afro-Caribbean community in Canada within which her work needs to be situated.

THE POPULAR MUSIC FIELD IN TORONTO AND THE HISTORICAL MARGINALIZATION OF RAP MUSIC

> Once the non-existent infrastructure catches up to the current quality of the music, the artists should be good. I mean we all know that a large percentage of young people love hip hop music and culture. But Canadian radio does not even remotely reflect the demand for the music and touring companies do not support Canadian hip hop artists for whatever odd reasons. I believe there is a large amount of racism and "not wanting to lose our spots/jobs in the industry" attitudes going on, or maybe even some unwarranted fear of the music. ("Gee Wunder Interview" 2008)

In the above quote, Gee Wunder clearly outlines two of the most important struggles that are ongoing in Toronto hip hop (despite the successes of artists such as Drake and The Weeknd): struggles over material resources and struggles against marginalization. The economic conditions within which rap artists make music are marked by increased struggles over material resources at the national, provincial, and city levels. At the national level, Canada is the world's sixth largest music market (Spendlove 2004). In 2007 Canadian artists accounted for 18 percent of all album sales in Canada, and the majority of the top ten Canadian artists were rock and pop musicians (Nielsen SoundScan 2008). In terms of sales by genre:

> according to the International Federation of the Phonographic Industry and the Canadian Recording Industry Association (CRIA), rock and pop recordings accounted for 51 percent of total sales, followed by country (6 percent), hip hop (6 percent), world music (5 percent), classical (4 percent), jazz (3 percent), R&B (3 percent), and soundtrack (2 percent). Other genres combined for a 30 percent share. (Spendlove 2004, 15)

Of the new releases, the number of annual new recordings by Canadian artists increased 63.3 percent, from 1,261 in 1999 to 2,059 in 2003 (Spendlove 2004). However, though the number of recordings annually has increased, the percentages of recordings released have remained the same, with rock/pop receiving the largest number of new releases. In 2003 rock/pop accounted for 54.9 percent of new albums released by Canadian artists, with urban and dance accounting for only 9.8 percent (Spendlove 2004).

At the provincial level, according to data collected by Statistics Canada, from 1998 to 2003 the sound recording industry in Ontario also became increasingly competitive. During this time period, the number of new releases, sales, and profits as a percentage of total revenues for Canadian musicians fell and the sale of recordings by Canadian artists decreased by 35.6 percent, compared with a 22.7 percent decline in sales of foreign artists. These declines in sales are significant since in 2003, Ontario accounted for 82.1 percent of sound recording industry revenue in Canada, with most of that revenue in the year 2000 coming from operations within the Toronto Census Metropolitan Area (Coish 2006).

At the city level, popular music makers in Toronto argue that the disparities in terms of new releases and sales of "urban" music are the result of a lack of material resources for Black popular music makers and the marginalization of these musical forms. According to Will Strickland, the former president of the Urban Music Association of Canada, and Solitair, a well-known producer, artist, and songwriter in Toronto, there is the widely held belief among popular music makers that Canada is a "rock country." By saying this, Strickland and Solitair are arguing that there are biases toward Black popular music in the Canadian music industry that have resulted in urban music being undersupported.[2]

At the city level, within Toronto, there are also important social conditions within which Black popular music making needs to be situated. Ron Nelson, a well-known and well-respected radio DJ in Toronto, recalls that in the mid-1980s the major Canadian record labels showed no interest in Black music: "What is keeping rap from taking off is a general misunderstanding and rejection of this type of music and its audience, not to mention media and public prejudice against the power of Black urban music" (quoted in Chamberland 2001, 309). This is the time period within which Michie Mee was first emerging on the scene. Roger Chamberland argues that within Canada "the production, distribution, and broadcasting of rap remains confined to the margins" (311–12). For Strickland, Solitair, and many others, this marginalization of Black popular music making in Toronto has resulted in a lack of infrastructure, opportunity, and support for Black popular music makers (Elafros 2013b, 465). First, in terms of a lack of infrastructure, DJ Grouch, a turntablist, radio DJ, and DJ instructor, argues that, at the local level, "money is not being put into the development of urban artists the way that it is being put into indie music, or rock music, which are well-oiled machines in terms of infrastructure. The bottom line is that urban artists are not getting the support that they need."[3] Because of this lack of infrastructure, L'Oqenz, a DJ, producer, and manager, notes that "you basically hit a glass wall if you are on an urban tip. It is different if you are in rock and roll. If you are a rock band, you have a good chance. If you are an urban artist, it is much harder. It is an uphill battle because labels are not interested."[4] This lack of infrastructure manifests itself in many ways, such as having fewer managers willing to work with you and less major-label investment. Second, there is a lack of opportunities to showcase musical talent in live venues within Toronto and across the country. Addi "Mindbender" Stewart, a rap artist, journalist, and actor, believes that:

> On the rock side, there is the traditional infrastructure which has been set up for touring and getting other forms of support. This is because rock and roll is well established in Canada. Hip hop culture on the other hand is much newer to Canada. It is also really difficult to go to rock people with hip hop music. They sometimes don't understand the music and because of that they are less likely to invest.[5]

Third, there is a lack of radio support. At the time of data collection, FLOW 93.5 was an R&B and hip hop radio station located in Toronto that was expected to service the whole country and also reach an international audience. Since that time, FLOW 93.5 has changed formats several times and has since become a rhythmic adult contemporary radio station. This has resulted in fewer radio venues for Toronto-based rap music. The frustrations regarding a lack of radio support were felt by many artists during the first ever "It Starts with the DJ" conference (at the Toyota Yaris 2008 Stylus DJ Awards). During a panel titled "Bridging the Gap," a hip hop artist from Toronto in the audience outlined the lack of radio support for Black popular music in Canada. He said: "Yo, I got an album out right now, know what I'm sayin'. I shoulda got service right across Canada. They [commercial radio] told me the single was 'too urban,' 'too hip hop,' they don't wanna play it.... Outside of Toronto, they're not playing hip hop" ("Bridging the Gap" 2008). This artist's comments clearly illustrate how some forms of Black popular music making are marginalized by commercial radio in Canada, which is geared toward "non-urban" forms of musical expression of the predominantly rock/pop variety. These are the economic and social conditions that support Solitair's claim that rock music is at the "top of the mainstream food chain" in terms of radio play, video play, corporate sponsorship, and A&R representation at major labels.[6]

The support for rock/pop music in Canada often reflects the interests of an older generation that is still in control of the major record labels and media outlets. According to Craig "Big C" Mannix, EMI consultant and one of Canada's first Black music executives, the Canadian hip hop scene "has never been properly nurtured. It never developed like the indie rock or the country scene. It's like 'Okay, here's our Black artist. This is the one we're going to let through, the one we're going to have succeed,' yet there can be 100 indie rock bands that get written about" (quoted in Stewart 2008). Solitair believes that the reason for this disproportionate support for indie rock is that there are not many people in positions of power who understand Black popular music. For Solitair, "there has never been a changing of the guard in terms of having people who grew up with and understand the culture, where hip hop music came from, and urban music came from, what it is, [in order] to be able to market it on a mass scale."[7] More or Les, a rap artist and DJ, agrees: "there are a group of people who are in charge of the outlets who do not reflect the interests of the audience. The people who run organizations have spent a lot of time in folk, or pop music or dance music. The people who run the organizations do not have a background in urban music."[8] This is not to say that infrastructure resources for musicians do not exist in Canada, but that these resources are tailored toward rock artists. As Mel Boogie, radio and club DJ, notes, "the main thing to remember is that the stuff that works for a rock artist doesn't translate for a hip hop artist. What works for one genre won't work for another. There is no cookie cutter way to do things."[9]

The lack of infrastructure and material resources and a lack of control of the means of production and distribution has contributed to the construction and maintenance of a popular music hierarchy in Toronto where Black popular music is marginalized in comparison to rock/pop music genres. At the national level, the popular music field is marked by the economic dominance of Canadian rock and pop recordings. At the provincial level, the popular music field is marked by increased competition for limited resources. At the city level, the popular music field is marked by racism and bias toward Black popular music broadly, and rap in particular. Within this context, rap historically has occupied a newcomer and dominated position within the field of popular music in relation to rock and pop. It is within this doubled historical context of marginalization, both in terms of immigration and assimilation and in terms of popular music, that Michie Mee's work will be situated.

THE CARIBBEAN DIASPORA, RAP IN TORONTO, AND MICHIE MEE, "THE FIRST LADY OF TORONTO HIP HOP"

The Caribbean diaspora has played an incredibly influential role in the formative years of rap music in Canada and in Toronto in particular. Mark V. Campbell (2014), Remi Warner (2006), Roger Chamberland (2001), and Rinaldo Walcott (1997; 2000; 2001) have provided excellent analyses of the important role that the Black Canadian diaspora has played within the Toronto hip hop community. Campbell examines hip hop in Toronto from 1986 to 2000 and illustrates how rap artists from the Afro-Caribbean diaspora used hip hop music to forge complex definitions of "home." Warner examines, through interviews with K-os, Sol Guy, DJ Power, and Emcee Motion, how rap and hip hop culture were influenced by what Paul Gilroy has dubbed the "Black Atlantic." Chamberland outlines the immigrant roots of rap music in Toronto and the rest of Canada. And in his numerous works, Rinaldo Walcott examines the complex interconnections between Black popular culture, racism, rap, the Caribbean diaspora, and the sense of belonging to the Canadian nation-state.

The influence of the Caribbean diaspora on rap in Toronto has been particularly pronounced. According to Campbell, there are two periods in the formative years of rap and hip hop culture in Toronto: 1986–93 and 1993–2000. Both were deeply influenced by Caribbean cultures in the city. Campbell argues that in the first period, "Toronto-based hip hop artists were engaged in creolizing their locales, importing and prominently presenting their Caribbean diasporic roots," while during the second period "articulations of home and belonging in the music became more localized and less abstractly sketched as directly linked through the Caribbean" (2014, 273–74).

One of the most important voices of the Caribbean diaspora in the Toronto hip hop scene is Michie Mee. Born in St. Andrew, Kingston, Jamaica, and having moved to Toronto at a young age, Michie Mee was the first Canadian MC to sign a record deal with First Priority/Atlantic Records in the United States in 1988. She is one of the founding figures of Canadian hip hop, one of the first artists to combine rap music with dancehall and reggae, and one of the first artists to use Jamaican patois in her rap music. In addition to being a successful MC, she is also an actor and radio host. She is considered by many to be a Canadian hip hop icon, a germinal figure in the Toronto hip hop scene, and "the first lady of Toronto hip hop" (Cowie 2015).

Michie Mee gained international fame after her performance at a concert in Toronto in 1985. She was introduced to the audience by Scott La Rock and KRS-One (of Boogie Down Productions), both of whom she had met while visiting her aunt in the Bronx. Michie Mee shortly thereafter teamed up with DJ L.A. Luv and Beat Factory (a now-defunct Toronto-based production company and independent label founded by Ivan Berry and Rupert Gayle), and in 1988 they released the duo's first single, "Elements of Style." This single earned Michie Mee her first record deal with a major American label and started her international rap career. In 1991 Michie Mee and L.A. Luv released their debut album *Jamaican Funk—Canadian Style*, which showcased Michie Mee's unique style of blending rap and reggae with Jamaican-infused patois.

Drawing on Rinaldo Walcott's work on Caribbean Black popular culture, we can say her work is simultaneously "local and nationally local" (2001, 126). To fully understand her impact and importance, we need to situate her within what Larissa Buchholz has dubbed "vertically nested" fields (2016). In this instance, the vertically nested fields of importance include: the diasporic field of Black and Caribbean popular music production (within which global rap music is situated), the popular music field in Canada, and the local rap field in Toronto. Michie Mee's diasporic "roots" and "routes" illustrate the important role of identity, capital, and cultural production in each field. In an interview with Del Cowie for *Vice* magazine in 2015, Michie Mee discusses the concrete transnational connections between Toronto, the Bronx, and Kingston, Jamaica, in the formative years of hip hop. Even in those formative years, the field of cultural production for rap within Toronto was already diasporic in nature and transnational in character. As Walcott notes, "Caribbean popular culture in Canada is lodged between the continuing relations of Canadian proximity to the United States and, simultaneously, an imagined and real relation to the . . . Caribbean . . ." (2001, 125). The overlapping of the transnational, national, and local is clearly illustrated in the case of Michie Mee. In Toronto, Michie Mee was deeply influenced by Jamaican poet Lillian Allen, whom she saw perform at her school. She was influenced by Allen's speaking, her singing, and her poetry, and that made her want to become a cultural producer and "write in the accent" (Cowie 2015). Another important mentor in Toronto was Itah Sadu, a community worker, author, and current owner of A Different Booklist bookstore in Toronto, who taught classes in Toronto's

Flemingdon Park neighborhood that Michie Mee attended (Cowie 2015). She also followed the Sunshine Sound Crew, a crew from Kingston, Jamaica, that started playing in Toronto in the 1970s and exposed Toronto audiences to rap through "blockos" or block parties (Warner 2006, 52). Another mentor was Ivan Berry, a native of St. Kitts, entrepreneur, artist manager, record label owner, talent development executive, and music publisher, who told her to use her Jamaican accent and "rap how [she] talk[s]" (Cowie 2015). Lillian Allen, Itah Sadu, and Ivan Berry, members of the Black diaspora in Canada, each helped shape Michie Mee into the artist she would become. In the Bronx, Michie Mee spent a great deal of time at her aunt's house, where she had direct mentorship in West Indian and hip hop culture through her interactions with legendary artists MC Lyte, Scott La Rock, and KRS-One. She rapped for them outside of a Manhattan hip hop venue and eventually recorded with the duo who would later become known as Boogie Down Productions (BDP). Finally, in Kingston, Jamaica, her father had worked in the entertainment industry and there she met one of the country's most famous performers, Louise Bennett (aka Miss Lou), who moved to Toronto in 1987. Miss Lou brought Jamaican folklore, Jamaican patois, and cultural oral traditions to the forefront and gained a great deal of international acclaim in her lifetime. While still in Jamaica, Michie Mee was one of the children feature on Miss Lou's children's show *Ring Ding*. Her father was one of the producers and promoters of the show, so Michie Mee "was an original *Ring Ding* girl" (Cowie 2015).

Michie Mee drew upon these diverse transnational and diasporic cultural resources in Toronto, New York, and Kingston in order to better position herself within the popular music field in Canada. This was accomplished through her cultural production style and her cultural representations within the field of popular music. Through her song lyrics, style of dress, language, self-presentation, music videos, and interviews, Michie Mee became an integral figure of diasporic cultural production within the field of popular music. Central to her cultural production was her diasporic cultural identity. As Mark V. Campbell notes, many children of the Caribbean diaspora in Toronto have used hip hop as "the vehicle for exploring the fluid and hybrid identities of being both Canadian and 'Other'" (2014, 274). Michie Mee's music clearly illustrates Campbell's argument. For instance, in her interview with Del Cowie, she states: "I knew that I was rapping, I knew that I was dressed like dancehall, and I knew that I wanted to say 'I'm Jamaican.' But I didn't know if I wanted to do it and meanwhile everyone was cursing me out. So, in the face of that, all I could do was become Michie Mee" (Cowie 2015).

Here she notes the initial tensions she had about blending rap and reggae, and how she overcame them to create her signature sound and image and "become Michie Mee." The importance of Jamaican culture within her works is clearly outlined by Scobie, who notes:

> In her performance practice, Michie Mee articulates Jamaican culture through linguistic, sartorial, and sonic signifiers of dancehall reggae. These signifiers are juxtaposed with markers of Canadian and North American musical and cultural identities; for example, she often switches between rapping with and without a Jamaican accent and mentions both Jamaican and Toronto locales in her lyrics, articulating a distinct hybrid identity in her music. (Scobie 2015, 19)

This distinct hybrid and diasporic cultural identity is evident in songs such as "Run for Cover" (1987), "Victory Is Calling" (1988a), "On this Mic" (1988b), and in particular on the album *Jamaican Funk—Canadian Style* (1991) (Scobie 2015). These songs are representative of a Caribbean/Black popular culture that fits the "local and nationally local" (Walcott 2001, 126) context of her cultural production. These "local and nationally local" influences are represented in her lyrics, style of dress, and music videos. These cultural representations are a central element of her diasporic cultural production within the field. For example, "Run for Cover" was her first song to feature patois. "Victory Is Calling" features "patois banter" in the intro and outro (Scobie 2015, 68) while also making clear references to her hometown of Toronto in the lyrics: "In a world of style, this one stands alone, Michie Mee is from Toronto, no American clone." As Scobie notes, on this track, Michie Mee clearly expresses her allegiances to "her hometown, her production team (Beat Factory), and her record label (First Priority). In doing so, she affirms her Canadian identity, but also a specific allegiance to Toronto" (70). However, it was not until the release of "On This Mic" that Michie Mee signified her Jamaican identity and indicated her local (Toronto) and national (Canada) allegiances by using patois in the actual song verses and by specifically using a dancehall rhythm (73). She also once again makes specific references to her regional Canadian identity in the lyrics: "I live in Canada, my area's good to go, don't you know good things grow in Ontario." (This lyric is a direct reference to a famous ad campaign by Foodland Ontario, the musical jingle for which was "good things grow in Ontario.")

These diasporic sensibilities reach their full maturation on *Jamaican Funk—Canadian Style* (1991), an album that she conceptualized as being half rap and half reggae. As Scobie notes, the "album's title track and other examples, continues her presentation of dual cultural sensibilities, but increases the Jamaican content by way of strong reggae influences. The video for 'Jamaican Funk—Canadian Style' provides rich examples of Jamaican cultural signifiers" (22). These cultural signifiers include the use of patois and the adoption of dancehall rhythms, hairstyles, clothing, jewelry, and attitude that signify her Jamaican roots and her Jamaican Canadian identity. In the video Michie Mee and L.A. Luv are in front of an indoor audience. The Jamaican flag is prominently on display, and there is graffiti in the background in the colors of red, green, black, and gold. For the majority of the video, Michie Mee wears dancehall clothing styles: jean jacket, short shorts, red frilled sleeves, and red leather boots. Her jewelry is big, chunky, and gold, as was common in the late 1980s and early 1990s. Dancehall culture similarly inspires her hairstyle, with large curls and a big blond streak. However, in other parts of the video she also wears a red dress, a white and pink track suit, and a jean jacket with silver trim. As Scobie observes, "in combination, these sartorial elements constitute a prime example of the video's articulation of Michie Mee's hybridized identity that is equal parts Jamaican, Canadian, and hip hop" (90).

The song entitled "Canada Large" from the same album is an ode to Canada (and specifically, Greater Toronto) in which she aims to "big up Canada." In the track she claims her Canadian identity, makes links to members of the Black diaspora in Canada, and also distinguishes herself from Americans. The track starts by asking the question, "Step up you wanna know where I come from?" and her response is "Canada is where I conceived the vibe for this album." In the track, she specifically emphasizes the importance of Canada as a source of rap music and how the Canadian rap scene is ready to become "large." The track references many greater Toronto area communities, such as Mississauga, Thornhill, Brampton, Markham, and Scarborough, while also specifically mentioning many Toronto neighborhoods, such as Regent Park, Jane and Finch, and "Jungle" (Lawrence Heights). These communities and neighborhoods are areas that traditionally have been associated with the Black diaspora in Canada. On "Canada Large" Michie Mee also distances herself from the United States: "Some claim we try to imitate many Americans, but like a true Canadian, I know I can, I know I can, I know I can." The track is mostly rapped in Canadian English, but dispersed throughout there are words and phrases that draw upon Jamaican patois.

These examples from her musical career illustrate how her "speech codes, dress styles, musical preferences, and other attributes" can be seen as non-dominant forms of cultural capital or resources that lower-status groups convert into capital for status purposes (Carter 2003, 139). These are cultural representations that aim to celebrate Blackness and diasporic forms of belonging. These forms of diasporic "Black cultural capital" (Carter 2003; Wallace 2016) are of central importance to the performative strategies Michie Mee uses to express "a dual Canadian/Jamaican identity that reflected her experience as a Jamaican immigrant in a diasporic city" (Scobie 2015, 73). These forms of diasporic "Black cultural capital" are cultural signifiers of the Afro-Caribbean community in Toronto that aim to create a shared sense of solidarity and shared cultural identity.

Finally, this emphasis on the diasporic and transnational within Michie Mee's music is important because it showcases how she uses rap to challenge racist and racialized conceptions of Canadian identity and racism within the music industry more broadly. As Walcott reminds us, Black popular culture in Canada articulates a "dual citizenship" that forces the "recognition of a different kind of Canadianness" (2001, 139)—in this instance a "Canadianness" that is diasporic, transnational, and hybrid in nature. It is marked by multiple local contexts within a field of popular music that is transnational in character, and these local contexts are linked through the concrete connections between members of the Caribbean diaspora. The recognition of a "different kind of Canadianness" is important given the historical marginalization of Caribbean immigrants in Canada, and of rap within the Canadian music industry. For nonwhite artists, this marginalization has often translated into racism and discrimination. In January 2016 *Now* magazine released a special issue on racism within the Toronto music scene, and one of the people interviewed was Michie Mee. For Michie Mee, the most obvious way she has experienced inequities in the music industry in Toronto has been economic:

> The most obvious way [I've experienced racism in the music scene], and one that trickles down in every aspect, whether it's being female, being a Jamaican woman of African descent and all that good stuff, has been financial: not getting paid, not getting opportunities. (Michie Mee 2016)

The intersections of race, nationality, and gender are perfectly illustrated in Michie Mee's discussion of how racism has limited both her economic capital and social capital opportunities within Toronto. These intersectional connections are further solidified later in the interview when she notes: "no one wants to hear what this rapper girl has to say. They want to know, 'Okay, who is the Black guy in charge of her and then who is the white guy in charge of him?' Even though I am the one creating things." Although Michie Mee is the "first lady of Toronto hip hop," she has nonetheless experienced a great deal of discrimination in the industry.

CONCLUSION: THE CARIBBEAN DIASPORA AND CULTURAL PRODUCTION

This chapter draws on Bourdieu (1991; 1993; 1996), Walcott (1997; 2000; 2001), and Hall (2003) to illustrate both the importance of diasporic communities within fields of cultural production and how cultural fields need to be reconceptualized within a diasporic framework. Drawing on Bourdieu, this chapter offered a qualitative case study of Michie Mee's collective identity work within the larger field of Caribbean/Black diasporic cultural production, the field of popular music in Canada, and the field of rap music in Toronto. Based on this analysis, this chapter makes the following contributions to Bourdieusian understandings of cultural production.

First, cultural identity as a resource, similar to other forms of capital, is struggled over within *all* cultural fields. Cultural identity is "a 'production' which is never complete, always in process, and always constituted within, not outside, representation" (Hall 2003, 234). By framing cultural identity as a resource that is struggled over within cultural fields, I illustrate how cultural identity may be reflexively and strategically used as a form of collective action (Bernstein 1997, 537). In this instance, Michie Mee's identity work challenges understandings of Canadian identity that treat nonwhites as Other within the Canadian nation-state. Like Choclair, Kardinal Offishall, and other artists, Michie Mee refuses "a particularly marginalizing narrative of Blackness as unCanadian" by redrawing definitions of Canadian identity and placing herself "firmly within the nation" (Campbell 2014, 274).

Second, crucial to the formation and contestation of cultural identities are various practices of representation. In this instance, song lyrics, interviews, and music videos are the representational mechanisms use to perform a collective identity for members of the Caribbean diaspora within a Canadian context. Michie Mee uses Jamaican patois, reggae rhythms, and reggae clothing styles and jewelry, coupled with rap music and hip hop sensibilities, to represent a vision of Canadian identity that is hybrid and diasporic in nature. However, she always reminds the listener of her "Canadianness" as well by referencing Canada, Ontario, Toronto, and specific neighborhoods in Toronto. Field theory in this instance illustrates how music is used as an objectified representation (similar to flags, emblems, badges, etc.) of ethnic identity (Bourdieu 1991, 220) in the cultural struggle for recognition. In other words, cultural fields not only produce practices, or ways of acting, but also representations, or ways of seeing, which are used in struggles over both identity and the mechanisms of identification. Therefore, all cultural fields are also fields of representation, and all cultural fields involve the struggle over representations and cultural identities (221). Of central importance to these struggles over cultural identity and representation are various forms of capital. In this instance, Michie Mee draws upon localized and diasporic forms of "Black cultural capital" (Carter 2003; Wallace 2016), such as patois, clothing, hairstyles, and jewelry, in her representational practices within the field of popular music in Toronto. Thus, cultural identity and cultural representations are crucial elements of diasporic "Black cultural capital" within the cultural field.

Finally, this chapter illustrates the importance of reconceptualizing fields of cultural production with "elsewhereness" (Walcott 2001) in mind. It is not possible to understand rap music in Toronto, or rap in Canada, without paying attention to the ways in which "vertically nested" fields (Buchholz 2016) overlap with one another. In this instance, the focus on a singular artist illustrates the interconnections between the diasporic field of Black and Caribbean popular music production (within which global rap is situated), the popular music field in Canada, and the local rap music field in Toronto.

In closing, this chapter has illustrated how a transnational approach to Bourdieusian field theory illuminates the important contributions of diasporic communities to the formation, dissemination, and maintenance of hip hop culture. Future research can draw upon this study in building a transnational approach to Bourdieusian studies of cultural production and consumption. By moving beyond the confines of the nation-state and insisting on transnational and diasporic understandings of cultural production and consumption, this chapter has aimed to deepen our knowledge of how cultural fields operate.

BIBLIOGRAPHY

Bernstein, Mary. 1997. "Celebration and Suppression: The Strategic Uses of Identity by the Lesbian and Gay Movement." *American Journal of Sociology* 103: 537.

Bottero, Wendy. 2010. "Intersubjectivity and Bourdieusian Approaches to 'Identity.'" *Cultural Sociology* 4 (1): 3–22.

Bourdieu, Pierre. 1991. *Language and Symbolic Power*, edited by J. B. Thompson, translated by G. Raymond and M. Adamson. Cambridge: Harvard University Press.

Bourdieu, Pierre. 1993. *The Field of Cultural Production*. New York: Columbia University Press.

Bourdieu, Pierre. 1996. *The Rules of Art: Genesis and Structure of the Literary Field*. Stanford, CA: Stanford University Press.

Braziel, Jana Evans, and Anita Mannur. 2003. "Nation, Migration, Globalization: Points of Contention in Diaspora Studies." In *Theorizing Diaspora*, edited by Jana Evans Braziel and Anita Mannur, 1–22. Malden, MA: Blackwell Publishing.

"Bridging the Gap." 2008. Panel. Stylus Spinfest/Stylus DJ Awards at It Starts with the DJ Conference. May 31. Robert Gill Theatre, Toronto, Canada.

Buchholz, Larissa. 2016. "What Is a Global Field? Theorizing Fields beyond the Nation-State." *Sociological Review Monographs* 64 (2): 31–60.

Burman, Jenny. 2001. "At the Scene of the Crossroads 'Somewhere in This Silvered City': Diasporic Public Spheres in Toronto." *Public* 22/23: 195–202.

Burman, Jenny. 2010. *Transnational Yearnings: Tourism, Migration, and the Diasporic City*. Vancouver: University of British Columbia Press.

Campbell, Mark V. 2014. "The Politics of Making Home: Opening Up the Work of Richard Iton in Canadian Hip Hop Context." *Souls: A Critical Journal of Black Politics, Culture, and Society* 16 (3–4): 269–82.

Carter, Prudence L. 2003. "'Black' Cultural Capital, Status Positioning, and Schooling Conflicts for Low-Income African American Youth." *Social Problems* 50 (1): 136–55.

Chamberland, Roger. 2001. "Rap in Canada: Bilingual and Multicultural." In *Global Noise: Rap and Hip-Hop outside the USA*, edited by Tony Mitchell, 306–25. Middletown, CT: Wesleyan University Press.

Coish, David. 2006. "Profile of Selected Culture Industries in Ontario." In *Culture, Tourism and the Centre for Education Statistics*, 1–106. Ottawa: Statistics Canada.

Cowie, Del. 2015. "Michie Mee Is the First Lady of Toronto Hip Hop." *Vice*. https://noisey.vice.com/en_ca/article/6vgdj3/michie-mee-dancehall-rap-toronto-interview-2015. Accessed July 30, 2016.

Elafros, Athena. 2013a. "Greek Hip Hop: Local and Translocal Authentication in the Restricted Field of Production." *Poetics: Journal of Empirical Research on Culture, the Media and the Arts* 41 (1): 75–95.

Elafros, Athena. 2013b. "Locating the DJ: Black Popular Music, Location and Fields of Cultural Production." *Cultural Sociology* 7 (4): 463–78.

Elafros, Athena. 2014. "Cultural Identity." In *Music in the Social and Behavioral Sciences—An Encyclopedia*, edited by William Forde Thompson, 299–302. California: Sage Publications.

Fligstein, Neil, and Doug McAdam. 2012. *A Theory of Fields*. Oxford: Oxford University Press.

Flynn, Karen. 2013. "Caribbean Migration to Canada." In *The Encyclopedia of Global Human Migration*, edited by Immanuel Ness. February 4, 2013. https://onlinelibrary.wiley.com/doi/abs/10.1002/9781444351071.wbeghm093. Hoboken, NJ: Blackwell Publishing.

Foner, Nancy. 2008. "Gender and Migration: West Indians in Comparative Perspective." *International Migration* 47 (1): 3–29.

"Gee Wunder Interview." 2008. MegaCityHipHop. http://www.megacityhiphop.com/interviews/geewunder_feb2008.html. Accessed July 29, 2016.

Go, Julian. 2008. "Global Fields and Imperial Forms: Field Theory and the British and American Empires." *Sociological Theory* 26 (3): 201–29.

Hall, Stuart. 2003. "Cultural Identity and Diaspora." In *Theorizing Diaspora*, edited by Jana Evans Braziel and Anita Mannur, 233–46. Malden, MA: Blackwell Publishing.

Henry, Frances. 1994. *The Caribbean Diaspora in Toronto: Learning to Live with Racism*. Toronto: University of Toronto Press.

Hiebert, Daniel. 1994. "Focus: Immigration to Canada." *Canadian Geographer* 38 (3): 254–70.

Carl E. James. 2017. "The Black Experience Project in the GTA." https://www.theblackexperienceproject.ca/wp-content/uploads/2017/07/Black-Experience-Project-GTA-OVERVIEW-REPORT-4.pdf. Accessed August 21, 2017.

Johnson, Randal. 1993. "Editor's Introduction: Pierre Bourdieu on Art, Literature and Culture." In *The Field of Cultural Production*, by Pierre Bourdieu, 1–25. New York: Columbia University Press.

Kuipers, Giselinde. 2011. "Cultural Globalization as the Emergence of a Transnational Cultural Field: Transnational Television and National Media Landscapes in Four European Countries." *American Behavioral Scientist* 55 (5): 541–57.

Labelle, M., Serge Larose, and V. Piché. 2015. "Caribbean People." In *The Canadian Encyclopedia*. http://www.thecanadianencyclopedia.ca/en/article/caribbean-people/. Accessed July 29, 2016.

Levitt, Peggy, and Nina Glick Schiller. 2004. "Conceptualizing Simultaneity: A Transnational Social Field Perspective on Society." *International Migration Review* 38 (3): 1002–39.

Lopes, Paul. 2000. "Pierre Bourdieu's Fields of Cultural Production: A Case Study of Modern Jazz." In *Pierre Bourdieu: Fieldwork in Culture*, edited by Nicholas Brown and Imre Szeman, 165–85. New York: Rowman & Littlefield.

Meuleman, Roza, and Mike Savage. 2013. "A Field Analysis of Cosmopolitan Taste: Lessons from the Netherlands." *Cultural Sociology* 7 (2): 230–56.

Michie Mee. 2016. "Michie Mee: Rapper, Songwriter, Actor." *Now*. https://nowtoronto.com/music/racism-in-music/michie-mee/. Accessed July 30, 2016.

Moore, Ryan. 2007. "Friends Don't Let Friends Listen to Corporate Rock: Punk as a Field of Cultural Production." *Journal of Contemporary Ethnography* 36 (4): 438–74.

Nielsen SoundScan. 2008. "The State of the Canadian Music Industry." *Canadian Music Week*. Toronto, Ontario, Canada.

Ontario Ministry of Finance. 2011. "2011 National Household Survey Highlights: Factsheet 1." http://www.fin.gov.on.ca/en/economy/demographics/census/nhshi11-1.html.

Prior, Nick. 2008. "Putting a Glitch in the Field: Bourdieu, Actor Network Theory and Contemporary Music." *Cultural Sociology* 2 (3): 301–19.

Regev, Motti. 1994. "Producing Artistic Value: The Case of Rock Music." *Sociological Quarterly* 35 (1): 85–102.

Savage, Mike, and Elizabeth B. Silva. 2013. "Field Analysis in Cultural Sociology." *Cultural Sociology* 7 (2): 111–26.

Scobie, Niel. 2015. "'Jamaican Funk—Canadian Style': Diasporic Dialogue and Hybridized Identity in the Music of Michie Mee." Master's thesis, Carleton University.

Spendlove, Paul. 2004. "The Canadian Music Industry 2004 Economic Profile." Minister of Public Works and Government Services Canada. http://publications.gc.ca/collections/Collection/CH41-11-2004E.pdf. Accessed July 29, 2016.

Statistics Canada. 2003. *Ethnic Diversity Survey: Portrait of a Multicultural Society*. Ottawa: Catalogue no. 89-593-XIE. http://publications.gc.ca/Collection/Statcan/89-593-X/89-593-XIE2003001.pdf. Accessed July 29, 2016.

Stewart, Addi "Mindbender." 2008. "Toronto Hip Hop's Bad Rap." *Now*, March 2008. https://nowtoronto.com/music/toronto-hip-hops-bad-rap/. Accessed July 29, 2016.

Thompson, John. 1991. "Editor's Introduction." In *Language and Symbolic Power*, by Pierre Bourdieu, 1–31. Cambridge: Harvard University Press.

Thornton, Sarah. 1996. *Club Cultures: Music, Media and Subcultural Capital*. Hanover and London: Wesleyan University Press.

Verboord, Marc, Giselinde Kuipers, and Susan Janssen. 2015. "Institutional Recognition in the Transnational Literary Field, 1955–2005." *Cultural Sociology* 9 (3): 447–65.

Walcott, Rinaldo. 1997. *Black Like Who? Writing Black Canada*. London, Ontario: Insomniac Press.

Walcott, Rinaldo. 2000. *Rude: Contemporary Black Canadian Cultural Criticism*. London, Ontario: Insomniac Press.

Walcott, Rinaldo. 2001. "Caribbean Pop Culture in Canada; or, the Impossibility of Belonging to the Nation." *Small Axe: A Caribbean Journal of Criticism* 5 (1): 123–39.

Wallace, Derron O. 2016. "Re-Interpreting Bourdieu, Belonging and Black Identities: Exploring 'Black' Cultural Capital Among Black Caribbean Youth in London." In *Bourdieu: The Next Generation*, edited by Jenny Thatcher, Nicola Ingram, Ciaran Burke, and Jessie Abrahams, 37–54. London and New York: Routledge.

Warner, Oswald S. 2006. "Encountering Canadian Racism: Afro-Trini Immigrants in the Greater Toronto Area, Canada." *Wadabagei* 9 (1): 4–37.

Warner, Remi. 2006. "Hiphop with a Northern Touch!? Diasporic Wanderings/Wonderings on Canadian Blackness." *Topia: Canadian Journal of Cultural Studies* 15: 45–68.

DISCOGRAPHY

Michie Mee. 1987. "Run for Cover." Justice.
Michie Mee. 1988a. "Victory Is Calling." First Priority Music.
Michie Mee. 1988b. "On This Mic." First Priority Music.
Michie Mee. 1991. *Jamaican Funk—Canadian Style*. First Priority Music/Atlantic Records.

NOTES

1. There are multiple meanings associated with the term *diaspora*, which can often refer to "communities of people dislocated from their native homelands through migration, immigra-

tion, or exile as a consequence of colonial expansion, but etymologically suggests the (more positive) fertility of dispersion, dissemination and the scattering of seeds" (Braziel and Mannur 2003, 3). However, the term is increasingly used by many scholars to "describe the mass migrations and displacements of the second half of the twentieth century, particularly in reference to independence movements in formerly colonized areas, waves of refugees fleeing war-torn states, and fluxes of economic migration in the post–World War II era" (4). The Caribbean diaspora can be situated within the influx of post–World War II economic migration to Canada. The term "diasporic belonging" refers to the experience of plural identifications (for example, Jamaican Canadian) that are constitutive of diasporic forms of identity.

2. Will Strickland (president of the Urban Music Association of Canada) in discussion with the author, 2008; Solitair (producer) in discussion with the author, 2008.

3. DJ Grouch (turntablist, radio DJ, and DJ instructor) in discussion with the author, 2008.

4. L'Oqenz (DJ, producer, and manager) in discussion with the author, 2008.

5. Addi "Mindbender" Stewart (artist, writer, actor) in discussion with the author, 2009.

6. Solitair in discussion with the author, 2008.

7. Solitair in discussion with the author, 2008.

8. More or Les (artist and DJ) in discussion with the author, 2008.

9. DJ Mel Boogie (radio and club DJ) in discussion with the author, 2008.

7

JOURNEY TO JAH

The Discourse of Internationalization in German Reggae and Dancehall Media

BENJAMIN BURKHART

In 2002, the German reggae singer Gentleman released his second studio album *Journey to Jah*. By this time, a vibrant reggae and dancehall scene had already emerged in Germany. Twelve years later, Gentleman and Alborosie, a reggae musician from Italy, were portrayed in a movie with the same title. This movie tells the story of two musicians from Western European countries who tried to create their own version of reggae. But, as the title implies, the journey has not ended yet. Certain aspects of Jamaican reggae and dancehall are yet to be appropriated by European musicians. The case of Gentleman and Alborosie exemplifies the transcultural flows, the processes of recontextualization and reinterpretation that are essential for the globalization of popular music.

Jamaican popular music has become a global phenomenon over the past few decades. Since the advent of roots reggae in the early 1970s, Jamaican musical styles and cultural codes have been globally appropriated and local scenes are forming all over the world. Ever since then, the ongoing internationalization of reggae and dancehall music has also become the subject of academic conferences and research (see Cooper 2012b; Hope 2013, 2015) and has been investigated, with a focus on local reception, in Japan (Sterling 2010), Finland (Järvenpää 2015), Oceania (Clough 2012), and Brazil (Godi 2001), to name just a few examples. Authors of early publications on Jamaican popular music were already aware of reggae's global dimension, even while paying attention to the development of the British scene (Clarke 1980; Davis and Simon 1982; Hebdige 1979). Ever since immigrants from the Caribbean settled in great numbers in the U.K. during the 1950s and 1960s, their music has been widely heard, played, and composed, even by British-born musicians (Hall 2003). Furthermore, the British music industry played an important role for the globalization of Jamaican popular music, since producer Chris Blackwell successfully promoted Millie Small and Bob Marley as international pop stars during the 1960s and 1970s (Stratton 2014). The internationalization of Jamaican popular music is frequently discussed in academia and it is widely known that the influences of Caribbean cultures are especially notable in the societies of former European colonial powers such as Great Britain, France, and the Netherlands (Trakulhun 2007, 75–77).

In Germany, the situation is different. Since the late 1990s there has been a growing German scene with commercially and internationally successful artists and several festivals and magazines, even though there have never been large numbers of immigrants from the West Indies. So in an article on the history of reggae in Germany, the editors of the German reggae and dancehall magazine *Riddim*, Ellen Köhlings and Pete Lilly, pose the entirely legitimate question: "How did it come about that youths from European countries without significant Caribbean communities are able and motivated to recreate something that is genuinely Jamaican in origin but can, to a certain extent, even compete with what is happening in Jamaica today?" (2012, 72). In the following, I will keep this question in mind in order to describe the discourse of internationalization in German reggae and dancehall media. The following additional questions form the basis of my chapter: Is the global dimension of reggae and dancehall music important for the members of the German scene? How do Germans evaluate Jamaican artists (the "originals")? How can artists from Germany even be authentic reggae or dancehall musicians? What role does the music's Caribbean roots play in Germany?

In recent years, only a few scholars from German-speaking countries have published writings on aspects of Jamaican popular music in general (e.g., Helber 2015; Pfleiderer 2001; Wynands 1995; Zips 2014) and on its cultural appropriation in Germany in particular (e.g., Karnik 2006; Karnik and Philipps 2007; Köhlings and Lilly 2012, 2013; Pfleiderer 2011). Furthermore, little attention has been paid to the evaluation of Jamaican artists in the German scene. But this should be a central issue if one wishes to understand how Jamaican popular music is negotiated in Germany, since reggae and dancehall artists often address subjects that are unconventional for many European listeners—e.g., Black empowerment, Rastafarianism, or homophobia.

The article is divided into three sections. First, the concept of "transculturality" ("Transkulturalität") as proposed by the philosopher Wolfgang Welsch will be outlined as a methodological framework (Welsch 1999, 2010). Welsch argues that modern societies cannot be rigidly regarded as homogeneous or monolithic entities. Second, I shall present results of a discourse analysis that I undertook for another research project.[1] Using qualitative empirical methods, I analyzed several hundred articles, interviews, and reviews published in the German reggae and dancehall magazine *Riddim*. The internationalization of the scene was identified as an essential part of the discourse. Third, a discussion of the movie *Journey to Jah* (2014) will show how the global popularity of reggae and dancehall music is negotiated in other contemporary German media. At the core of the movie, which portrays the European artists Gentleman and Alborosie, lies the phenomenon of cultural appropriation. The movie can tell us about the ongoing processes of reinterpretation and adaptation of Jamaican popular music in Europe.

TRANSCULTURALITY AND THE STUDY OF POPULAR MUSIC

In the 1990s, Wolfgang Welsch introduced the concept of "transculturality." His aim was to show that the study of contemporary cultures should not, for the main part, refer to normative and separatist ideas formulated by eighteenth- and nineteenth-century scholars. Johann Gottfried Herder, in particular, devised a concept of culture that can be described as holistic (Trakulhun 2007, 81): he propounded a model of clearly separated cultures when speaking of "social homogenization, ethnic consolidation and intercultural delimitation" (Welsch 1999, 204). Welsch, in contrast, argues that modern cultures should be conceived of as deeply interwoven, as a result of complex processes of assimilation and amalgamation. While describing this general hybridization as the macro-level of a society, he further proposes another level, the micro-level of the individual—that is to say, each single member of a society can be influenced by diverse cultural patterns. When adapting Welsch's concept for further research, it is important to keep in mind that his aim was not to investigate the contact between two homogenous cultures and, as a result, to identify the formation of a new culture. But his theory also does not deny the existence of different cultural spheres, which is decisive for the study of cultural exchange. It is essential to be aware of the constant pluralization of cultures and of the complex processes of exchange between societies (macro-level) and individuals (micro-level) (see also Helff 2012, 198; Trakulhun 2007, 76). For this reason, Welsch defines transculturality as being different from concepts such as "interculturality" or "multiculturality." Since these are focused on the exchange between separate cultures (intercultural) or on the struggles of different cultures existing within a single society (multicultural), he describes such ideas as inappropriate and as outmoded as the traditional holistic model propounded in the writings of Herder (Welsch

1999, 196). That is to say, modern societies should be understood as being intrinsically transcultural. The question should not be *whether* cultural transfers are constitutive for modern societies, but *how* they can be systematically described and understood (Trakulhun 2007, 84). To sum up, the concept of transculturality sketches a picture of cultural exchange that is characterized by "entanglement, intermixing and commonness. It promotes not separation, but exchange and interaction" (Welsch 1999, 205).

As (popular) music has always been global (White 2012, 2), it seems appropriate to keep ideas of transculturality in mind when studying the interdependencies of music making and globalization. According to Isabelle Marc, "Popular music is one of the main cultural fields in which the flows of global culture are particularly noticeable" (2015, 4). She further notes that "contemporary popular music is especially prone to movement as transcultural flows are reinforced by the global economy, by ubiquitous access to technologies of music distribution, and by increasingly complex and intensifying migratory movements, as well as by cosmopolitan cultural practices" (Marc 2015, 4). It seems obvious that today's music markets are not restricted by national boundaries. That is, styles of popular music all over the world are characterized by transnational flows that prompt the transformation and renegotiation of musical meaning. To quote Marc again: "travelling styles are not globally uniform but are modified by the different contexts in which they are produced and received" (2015, 5). Accordingly, popular music travels between different cultural spheres and is transferred into new contexts where the recipients—for example, members of subcultures such as the German reggae and dancehall scene—can transform the musical material, as well as its meaning, according to their culturally and socially determined preferences. A transcultural society can therefore feature several subcultures with influences from various cultural spheres which can interact with each other: as modern societies are intrinsically transcultural, so are popular music scenes.

Due to these complex entanglements of modern societies in general and popular music scenes in particular, these cultures must be studied from a non-normative perspective. As stated above, music's meaning is not inherent in musical sounds but is instead negotiated by listeners and producers according to their cultural and personal backgrounds. It is therefore essential for the study of popular music scenes to investigate the specific values and meanings that are relevant for the members of certain subcultures (Mendívil 2013, 47). In order to understand the production and negotiation of the meaning potentials[2] of musical sounds and cultural patterns, one can concentrate on the discourses of the musical subcultures in question. Stuart Hall elaborates the term "discourse" as follows:

> The very term "discourse" refers to a group of statements in any domain which provides a language for talking about a topic and a way of producing a particular kind of knowledge about that topic. The term refers both to the production of knowledge through language and representation and the way that knowledge is institutionalized, shaping social practices and setting new practices into play. (1997, 222)

According to Hall, discursive practice not only creates and communicates meaning in cultural domains, but also produces knowledge. So to understand the results of transcultural flows in musical subcultures one can attempt to explore the aesthetic discourses that are important for meaning-making. That is, an understanding of the values of popular music from a transcultural perspective requires an investigation of the rules of meaning-making: we must find out how music signifies within certain cultural and societal contexts for certain social groups.

RIDDIM MAGAZINE: NEGOTIATING JAMAICAN POPULAR MUSIC IN GERMANY

Discourses on popular music communicate specific values: for example, what is understood as beautiful music, how artists ought to promote themselves, or how music should be produced. Before undertaking a discourse analysis, it is necessary to consider which sources would appear to be appropriate and most likely to contain relevant information. Applying methods of cultural sociology, previous studies have shown that printed music magazines with a focus on single genres of popular music are highly suited for this kind of research (Diaz-Bone 2002; Pfleiderer and Zaddach 2014). In these magazines, professional critics as well as musicians, and to some extent even fans, discuss musical styles and the cultural values linked to the music, and they negotiate what can be understood as bad or good music. Diana Crane describes magazines as being part of what she calls the "peripheral domain." While conceptualizing culture in terms of three cultural domains, she separates media such as books and magazines from television, film, or major newspapers ("core domain") and from the domain of concerts and performances ("urban domain") (1992, 5–6). According to her, magazines are typically distributed nationwide, but are dedicated to "distinct subgroups usually based on age and life style" (Crane 1992, 5). In brief, music magazines contain highly specialized discourses on popular music, and an understanding of the social and musical values inherent in these discourses can be analyzed with the use of qualitative empirical methods.

In Germany, there is one magazine that can be analyzed constructively in terms of discourses of reggae and dancehall music, as well as of transcultural flows: *Riddim*. The magazine was founded in 2001, has a current circulation of 45,000 (six issues per year),³ and reports mainly on Jamaican and German artists but also on musicians from other countries. It also refers in part to musical styles such as ska, dub, or electronic dance music. Furthermore, *Riddim* tries to mediate Jamaican culture as well as foster an awareness of the historical roots of reggae and dancehall among its readers (Köhlings and Lilly 2012, 90). Besides artist features, artist interviews, and reviews, *Riddim* also contains articles about Jamaican society, often with a focus on poverty and violence, and interviews with Caribbean politicians or scholars. Focusing on styles of popular music that are Jamaican in origin but have by now been widely appropriated in Germany, the magazine not only reflects discourses on reggae and dancehall but is also a result of transcultural adaptation. With regard to the ideas of transculturality mentioned above, magazines like *Riddim* can communicate and create meaning both in subcultural communities and for individuals (Renger 2002, 486)—or, in other words, "media cultures are a kind of thickening of translocal articulation of meaning" (Hepp 2009, 4).

For another research project on reggae and dancehall aesthetics in Germany, I used *Riddim* as a source for a discourse analysis.⁴ I analyzed all texts contained in the 2014 volume (six issues, around 700 articles) using qualitative empirical research methods and the software MAXQDA. First of all, I read all the texts and tried to systematize all the topics and criteria for evaluation I could find in the articles. Upon completion of this first step, I controlled my findings by reading all passages grouped together by topic. Then I took a break for several weeks and read all the articles again, in order to improve the quality of my data. In a final step, I controlled every coded passage a second time and marked the most convincing utterances that appeared helpful for reconstructing the essential parts of the discourse. In doing so, I tried to optimize my findings and make them intersubjectively intelligible.

After completing this discourse analysis, I identified the internationalization of reggae and dancehall music as one of the key topics in *Riddim*. This seems remarkable because, as stated above, the magazine is itself a result of transcultural appropriation and mediates Jamaican popular music in

Germany. It can be assumed that members of the German scene are themselves aware of this cultural hybridism.

Many authors in *Riddim* write about the internationalization of reggae and dancehall in general, and they are aware that this music has been a global phenomenon for some years now. But many of them are apparently still surprised at the fact that original Jamaican music is still played and produced on a professional level by musicians in, for example, New Zealand (Münch 2014, 85) or the Canary Islands (Kramer 2014, 23). Nevertheless, some journalists remind their readers that certain elements of the Jamaican culture cannot be easily understood by European listeners. According to some of them, fans should keep in mind that reggae music in the early days was—and often still is—an expression of Black empowerment, and the artists sing about subjects such as slavery and colonial history (Anonymous 2014, 3). But in general, artistic open-mindedness seems to be essential. Accordingly, singer Maxi Priest told journalist John Masouri that great reggae musicians such as Bob Marley, Dennis Brown, or Jimmy Cliff had always made music for the whole world, and that it was therefore his aim to cross musical borders (Masouri 2014, 32). Sam Gilly, drummer of the Austrian band House of Riddim, claims that it should be all about the music, and that it is in his opinion of no interest whether reggae or dancehall is made in Austria, Germany, Jamaica, or Uzbekistan (Hautmann 2014, 21). The internationalization of reggae and dancehall is therefore an important issue for the musicians and the listeners, one that is also seen critically. *Riddim*'s writers attempt to communicate that the music originated in another cultural sphere and that the readers should appropriate the codes of reggae and dancehall carefully. Still, the global dimension of the music under discussion is generally appreciated.

Furthermore, there is an occasional emphasis on the idea that successful artists do not necessarily have to be Jamaicans and that good reggae and dancehall can be produced all over the globe. In a review of an album by the French band Dub Inc, Helmut Philipps states that for some time now, the big stars of the genre are no longer from Jamaica. In his opinion, Jamaican artists such as Busy Signal or Damian Marley play a major role internationally, but average musicians cannot compete with the new generation of artists from Italy, Germany, the United States, or the Ivory Coast (Philipps 2014, 77–79). The British producer Kris Kemist mentions that, for a long time, "real" reggae had to be produced in Jamaica, but that artists from Great Britain were currently more successful, since Jamaicans were no longer creating "authentic" music, but rather "island pop" (Lindorfer 2014, 23). In general, some authors argue that contemporary Jamaican productions are focused on "shock value" rather than on musical quality, whereas European productions made references to the old reggae and dancehall "originals." The assumption that the production of "good" reggae and dancehall music is not restricted by national boundaries anymore would therefore appear to be common sense. Nevertheless, there are also artists who view Jamaica as a major point of reference and try to reproduce certain elements of the "original" sound as well as possible in order to be accepted by Jamaican audiences. For example, singer Jah Sun from California admits that, at the start of his career, he tried to imitate the Jamaican patois and wanted to sound like his Caribbean role models (Zill 2014b, 25), and Pressure Busspipe from the Virgin Islands explains how he closely studied Jamaican culture before making his music public (Taylor 2014, 44). Jamaica would therefore still seem to be highly important for many artists, even though individual authors currently view some international artists as the new stars of the genre.

The special role played by Jamaica in global reggae and dancehall becomes obvious when artists talk about their travels to the Caribbean island: the fact that international artists travel to Jamaica in order to get in touch with the culture and to produce authentic-sounding music is frequently mentioned. German singer Sebastian Sturm reports experiencing a special atmosphere when recording in Jamaica that could not be reproduced in Europe (Zill 2014a, 53), as do the Italian band Mellow Mood (Landolt 2014, 9), Dutch singer Ziggi Recado (Zill 2014c, 27), and Elijah from Switzerland (Bücheler 2014, 25). They all describe Jamaica as an inspiring place to play, produce, and record music. To sum up: in discussions of authentic sound, it still seems important for many artists to be inspired by Jamaican musicians or by the island itself. When trying to play reggae or dancehall, getting in touch with Jamaican culture is generally viewed as a reasonable strategy. The collaborations of Jamaican and European musicians when recording and producing music especially confirms the impression that reggae and dancehall are already highly transcultural.

Music magazines usually contribute to the definition of the most important artists in a certain genre of popular music. Not every musician will be featured in magazines, and with defining lists such as *Rolling Stone*'s "Greatest Albums of All Time" the media can help their readers decide which artists appear to be important (as well as, by extension, which artists appear to be unimportant). *Riddim*'s writers make it relatively clear which artists they believe are the most significant for reggae and dancehall. First of all, there are the artists who played a highly important role in the origins of reggae: the famous singers of the roots reggae era, such as the "king of reggae" Bob

Marley, the "crown prince" Dennis Brown, and Peter Tosh, as well as bands such as Black Uhuru or producers such as Lee "Scratch" Perry. Secondly, singers of 1990s dancehall and neo-roots such as Buju Banton, Sizzla, Shabba Ranks, and Bounty Killer are seen as pioneering artists. Singers of the so-called "reggae revival"—for example, Chronixx, Jah9, and Kabaka Pyramid—are considered important for the future development of Jamaican popular music, as are dancehall artists such as Vybz Kartel, Alkaline, and Popcaan. It is conspicuous that for the most part only Jamaican artists are mentioned in this context—only Gentleman from Germany plays a similar role in the articles published in *Riddim*. What does this tell us about the discourse of internationalization? It makes clear that Jamaica still functions as a major and highly important point of reference for the German scene, even though the global dimension of reggae and dancehall is frequently discussed in the analyzed articles by journalists, musicians, and fans. Still, the impact of German artists has remained relatively small.

One article by editor-in-chief Pete Lilly is striking with regard to these findings (2014, 45). Lilly admits that, for a long time, journalists writing for *Riddim* avoided speaking of "German reggae" when reporting on artists from Germany. According to him, the reggae and dancehall music produced in Germany over the last years could not be conceived of as an independent musical style, since both musicians and listeners were highly influenced by and focused on Jamaican artists. But while summarizing some current developments, he also claims that the time has come to think about naming reggae and dancehall made in Germany. One has to keep in mind that the German scene did not begin to grow noticeably until the early 2000s, when artists like Gentleman and Seeed became popular stars signed to major record labels, and German labels such as Rootdown Records or Germaican Records were founded.

> While in the 1990s, dancehall was restricted to a certain set of well-informed insiders within Germany, the new millennium not only ushered in an era of much easier access to information about the culture, but also generated a measurable, more lasting success for reggae in the German mainstream. (Köhlings and Lilly 2012, 89)

At this time, Jan Delay and Seeed had released commercially successful records with German lyrics and Gentleman and Patrice became well-known artists, while making clear references to the Jamaican roots reggae originals. Over the last years, there have been several artists presenting reggae and dancehall with German lyrics, some of them even in regional dialects, but English is still the widely preferred language.

The current situation of reggae and dancehall in Germany could therefore be interpreted as an ongoing process of transcultural flows. There are many artists who developed musical and lyrical styles that can be considered a German version of Jamaican popular music; there is a professionalized infrastructure as well, but the focus on Jamaica is still apparent. A vital subculture originated in Germany where the constant appropriation of musical styles and cultural codes led to something new, which can by now—according to Lilly—be referred to as German. Still, Jamaicans are seen as the big stars, and Jamaica remains an important influence.

In order to understand the discourse on reggae and dancehall in Germany, it is furthermore necessary to concentrate on matters that are *not* a subject of the discussion in the articles published in *Riddim*. It is widely known that many Jamaican artists often promote homophobia and violence in their lyrics as well as on stage, and that many song lyrics deal with sexually explicit content, which is also presented visually in their music videos.[5] Wider German audiences are often put off by these topics, and gay rights activists have even tried to prevent concerts by artists such as Sizzla or Beenie Man. In fact, Jamaicans sometimes have to sign contracts and confirm that they will not sing homophobic lyrics on stage when performing in Germany. These aspects of the original culture are not readily accepted in Western European societies, which is why they do not play an important role in songs composed by German artists (Pfleiderer 2011). The results of my discourse analysis show that homophobic or violent lyrics in songs by Jamaican artists are not a major topic in the articles either—if they are, the authors generally distance themselves from these or view them neutrally. The discussion of Rastafarianism can be interpreted in a similar fashion. When writing about or interviewing Jamaican artists, Rastafarian faith is frequently discussed, but in the everyday lives of most German musicians it does not seem to be of importance. Jamaican artists even define Rastafarianism as a central aspect of their identity, and they especially highlight the negotiation of African heritage through this religion (Köhlings 2014, 42). European musicians, such as the Austrian Danny Ranks, rather characterize respect or discipline as relevant for their understanding of a spirituality inspired by Rastafari (Lukas 2014, 12). Since Rastafarianism is deeply linked to African heritage and colonial oppression, it is obvious that white people who grew up in a wealthy industrial nation find it inappropriate to adopt essential aspects of this religion easily. This is therefore also a crucial part of transcultural flows: elements of the Jamaican original that cannot simply be "translated into a 'white' lifestyle" (Köhlings and Lilly 2012, 78) are of no significant importance for the German discourse, since most of the German musicians and audiences are of European descent. The following section will show that similar issues are also at the core of the movie *Journey to Jah*.

JOURNEY TO JAH—GLOBALIZED MUSIC AND FOREIGN SPIRITUALITY

Journey to Jah, a project by the German producers Moritz Springer and Noël Dernesch, was shown for the first time in 2014. The idea dates back to 2000, when Springer got in touch with Rastafarianism while traveling in Ethiopia and decided to make a film about people in search of spirituality in foreign cultural spheres. The producers chose to focus on the German reggae singer Gentleman, who is also well-known in Jamaica, and Alborosie, a reggae artist from Italy who has been living on the island for many years. Other people featured in the film include artists Damian Marley, Richie Stephens, Bounty Killer, and Terry Lynn, academic Carolyn Cooper, and cab driver Devon Gayle. Because the film focuses on people in foreign cultural contexts, and the most prominent reggae artist from Germany is one of the main characters, *Journey to Jah* can tell us a lot about the discourse of internationalization.

At the very beginning of the movie, we hear Gentleman ask: "This isn't really my own culture, am I actually allowed to do this? And German is really my mother tongue. Doesn't that come across as totally ridiculous?" Then Alborosie states: "I came to Jamaica to find myself, to start a new life." Obviously, both artists are aware of cultural differences and both have tried to incorporate certain aspects of Jamaican culture. The aforementioned tendency of many European artists to imitate Jamaican artists as closely as possible also plays an important role in the careers of Gentleman and Alborosie. Richie Stephens, who helped Gentleman become an accepted artist in Jamaica, describes his first encounter with the German singer:

> What I was impressed by is the ability that Tillmann[6] has to speak the Jamaican patois. . . . I said to him, "Excuse me, you live here in Jamaica?" And he said, "No!" I said, "Wow, amazing! How did you learn to talk like that, to speak Jamaican language like that, in such a clear way?" And he said, "Well, I just love the culture and the music and everything, so I just learned it."

Stephens adds that it was hard for Jamaicans to believe that a white singer from Germany could sound that authentic when singing reggae songs. The ability to sound like a Jamaican can therefore be considered an essential aspect of Gentleman's international success. Alborosie's wife similarly describes his adoption of Jamaican culture and language: "Alberto speaks Italian like he's talking Jamaican. . . . He is not an Italian anymore—he is a Jamaican now. . . . He has that Jamaican vibe." Both musicians are described as foreign artists who were able to represent parts of the Jamaican culture in such an authentic manner that they are now treated as Jamaicans. Gentleman and Alborosie are not well-known for their ability to create a distinct kind of European-sounding reggae—instead, their music is viewed as largely Jamaican. This finding conveys the impression that Europeans still have to imitate the original sounds, to a certain extent, to achieve international success. Nevertheless, both musicians ask themselves if they are at all allowed to live Jamaican culture as intensively as this.

As the title *Journey to Jah* implies, spirituality is one key topic of the movie. Carolyn Cooper, professor of literature and cultural studies at the University of the West Indies, speaks on Jamaican culture and religion. She explains Rastafari as "mental emancipation from the slavery of colonialism,"[7] so it initially seems paradoxical for white Europeans to profess their faith in Rastafari. But neither of the two protagonists characterize their spirituality as dogmatic nor do they promote a thoughtless understanding of Rastafarianism. They instead emphasize the spiritual dimensions of music, explaining that they do not need a church to experience spirituality. So spirituality, as linked to Jamaican popular music, can be important for some European musicians, but Gentleman and Alborosie do not simply take over elements of a religion that is deeply linked to Black empowerment. Even though they are considered authentic reggae musicians and are both accepted by Jamaican artists and audiences, there are still elements of a foreign cultural sphere that they find unsuitable for adoption.

Interestingly, both artists talk about the cultural differences between Europe and Jamaica that are apparent in everyday life. They actually emphasize the differences between the mentalities of affluent Europeans and lower-class Jamaicans from the garrisons of Kingston, and Gentleman even speaks of a "culture shock" when recounting his first stays in Jamaica. Just as many articles in *Riddim* address themes such as poverty and violence in Jamaica, the main figures in *Journey to Jah* try to draw a realistic picture of current Jamaican society as well. For those who have deep insights into both cultural spheres, it seems to be important to make people aware of the various differences between life in Europe and in Jamaica. But as the careers of Gentleman and Alborosie show, a holistic model of culture would be unable to explain these complex processes of transfer and interaction.

Another important aspect of the movie is its title song, "Journey to Jah." We can see the artists recording the song in the studio, and later on performing it together on stage at the Summerjam festival in Cologne, Germany. *Journey to Jah* is also the title of Gentleman's second studio album, released in 2002 on Four Music. For a movie that portrays musicians in search of foreign spirituality, the title seems to fit as well: at one point, when the musicians are shown in the studio together, Gentleman says, "The 'Journey to Jah' song, that's our story."

The song is a typical neo-roots reggae composition, recorded with drums, bass, guitar, piano, keyboard, saxophone section, backing vocals, and the two lead singers. With the use of digital sound effects and various overdubs, and a slightly higher tempo, this modern kind of roots reggae differs from the original analog roots recordings of the 1970s. The first verse describes traveling through a valley as well as the need to break out of the daily grind: "Hundred percent devotion and you never give no less / And everyday you're surrounded by stress." In the chorus, the artists sing about their journey to Jah in order to cross borders and find spirituality: "Crossing border, divine is the order / Now I'm on my journey, on my journey to Jah Jah / And now is the time and I don't wait no more / Divine is the order, we liberate the border / Now I'm on my journey, on my journey to Jah Jah." In the second verse, Gentleman describes his search for spirituality abroad, since he was no longer able to find meaning in "the words that the preachers preach." In the third verse, he claims that everyone should find their own spirituality, without being restricted by cultural borders: "Modern wisdom, ancient philosophies / It's your decision and you choose who you want to be." These lines are similar to a statement he made in an interview with the German authors Olaf Karnik and Helmut Philipps, in which he said that as the son of a protestant priest he would rather find truth in Jamaican music than in the ideologies of Christianity (Karnik and Philipps 2007, 127). At the end of the movie, we see Gentleman and Alborosie performing the song at Summerjam, the biggest reggae festival in Germany—so the journey ends where it has begun, with an expanded transcultural sensibility.

CONCLUSION

So what is the discourse of internationalization in the German reggae and dancehall scene really about? Generally, it is crucial for processes of musical transfer that the "original" is appropriated, reinterpreted, and renegotiated in such a way that distinctively new musical styles and new meaning potentials arise. I mainly agree with Köhlings and Lilly, who take the view that German reggae and dancehall enthusiasts "began by first copying the Jamaican blueprint before turning initial misunderstanding into something productive, something that is Jamaican in form, but European in content" (2012, 92). We can see the results of these renegotiations when looking at artists such as Seeed and Jan Delay, who have produced German-language reggae and dancehall in recent years. But when we look carefully at the manner in which journalists and musicians discuss the internationalization of the scene, we have to admit that Jamaica still plays a highly important role. Many musicians travel to the Caribbean island in order to create an authentic sound. While some try to sound like Jamaican artists, very few musicians outside of Jamaica are valued as being great stars of the genre. Nonetheless, it can be very helpful for Germans (or Europeans in general) to imitate Jamaican sounds and language as accurately as possible if they want to be (inter-)nationally successful; Gentleman and Alborosie are prominent examples. But there are also aspects of the Jamaican reggae and dancehall culture that the German scene has not appropriated extensively up until now—for example, lyrics infused with homophobia or valorizing gun violence. And Rastafari does not play a key role for German artists, even though Gentleman's statements show that certain elements of Jamaican spirituality might attract Europeans—such as the spiritual dimension of music-making, the decisive role of Jah in daily life and conversations, and a non-dogmatic understanding of spirituality.

There is a vital reggae and dancehall scene in Germany, but even so, to date it has been difficult to speak of "German reggae" (Lilly 2014, 45). The decisive role that Jamaica still plays for German musicians and listeners seems remarkable in comparison with other musical scenes in Germany that originated under the influence of foreign musical styles and codes. Pfleiderer and Zaddach have shown that, for German jazz musicians, jazz from the United States is nowadays only one important point of reference among many others (2014, 84)—but it should also be noted that jazz has been played in Germany since the early twentieth century. In the case of rap music, which was first heard and played in Germany in the 1980s, there has been less time for intensive processes of assimilation. Nevertheless, there is an established and commercially successful German scene and the musical style is even called "Deutschrap." One important reason for the success of rap music in Germany may be the fact that American rap was presented as the music of Black ghetto youths, that many young immigrants in 1980s Germany were able to identify with these role models, and brought the music to public attention (Elflein 1998). Furthermore, the past decades have featured internationally famous musical styles that were labeled as German, such as "Krautrock" and "NDW" ("Neue Deutsche Welle"), while a similar term such as "German reggae" has not yet been established. Since reggae and dancehall music are both undoubtedly linked to the Afro-Caribbean diaspora, the cultural codes might be hard to understand for the majority of Western European listeners. Nevertheless, German reggae and dancehall artists strongly articulate their affinity with their Jamaican role models and even try to "sound Jamaican." An autonomous German adaption of Jamaican popular music may need more time to fully develop.

Obviously, the reception of reggae and dancehall cannot be understood properly when conceptualizing culture in a traditional holistic manner. It can, though, be comprehended in terms of transcultural flows in a globalized, media-saturated society (macro-level) within which human groups and individuals (micro-level) interact and are organized into subcultural spheres in order to create new models of musical style and meaning potentials over time. In this article, I have tried to show that the idea of transculturality can be suitably applied to the study of popular music in a global context. As popular music scenes are intrinsically transcultural, it could be argued that musical styles generally exist both in their "original" cultural spheres and in various diasporas. Musicians and listeners are probably aware of these cultural borders, even though they are constantly crossed. It is therefore essential to concentrate not only on the locations where the music is received, but also on the role the originals play for musicians and listeners when they come into contact with foreign musical styles. In the case of reggae and dancehall outside of Jamaica, it is necessary to describe the "local context of production, performance and reception, and not the fact that Jamaican music has become global" (Rommen 2006, 257).

BIBLIOGRAPHY

Anonymous. 2014. "Editorial." *Riddim* 14 (1): 3.
Bücheler, Daniel. 2014. "Elijah. Reifes Früchtchen." *Riddim* 14 (3): 24–25.

Clarke, Sebastian. 1980. *Jah Music: The Evolution of the Popular Jamaican Song*. London: Heinemann.
Clough, Brent. 2012. "Oceanic Reggae." In *Global Reggae*, edited by Carolyn Cooper, 265–83. Kingston: Canoe.
Cooper, Carolyn. 1993. *Noises in the Blood: Orality, Gender and the "Vulgar" Body of Jamaican Popular Culture*. New York: Palgrave Macmillan.
Cooper, Carolyn. 2004. *Sound Clash: Jamaican Dancehall Culture at Large*. New York: Palgrave Macmillan.
Cooper, Carolyn. 2012a. "Reggae Studies at the University of the West Indies." In *Global Reggae*, edited by Carolyn Cooper, 301–25. Kingston: Canoe.
Cooper, Carolyn, ed. 2012b. *Global Reggae*. Kingston: Canoe.
Crane, Diana. 1992. *The Production of Culture: Media and the Urban Arts*. London: Sage.
Davis, Stephen, and Peter Simon, eds. 1982. *Reggae International*. London: Rogner and Bernhard.
Diaz-Bone, Rainer. 2002. "Diskursanalyse und Populärkultur." In *Populäre Kultur als repräsentative Kultur. Die Herausforderung der Cultural Studies*, edited by Clemens Albrecht, Winfried Gebhardt, and Udo Göttlich, 125–50. Cologne: Halem.
Elflein, Dietmar. 1998. "From Krauts with Attitudes to Turks with Attitudes: Some Aspects of Hip-Hop History in Germany." *Popular Music* 17 (3): 255–65.
Godi, Antonio J. V. dos Santos. 2001. "Reggae and 'Samba-Reggae' in Bahia: A Case of Long-Distance Belonging." In *Brazilian Popular Music and Globalization*, edited by Christopher Dunn and Charles A. Perrone, 207–19. Gainesville: University Press of Florida.
Hall, Stuart. 1997. "The Centrality of Culture: Notes on the Cultural Revolutions of Our Time." In *Media and Cultural Regulation*, edited by Kenneth Thompson, 207–38. London: Sage.
Hall, Stuart. 2003. "Calypso Kings." In *The Auditory Culture Reader*, edited by Les Back and Michael Bull, 419–25. Oxford and New York: Berg.
Hautmann, Markus. 2014. "House of Riddim. Der Rest ist Geschichte." *Riddim* 14 (2): 21.
Hebdige, Dick. 1979. *Subculture: The Meaning of Style*. New York: Routledge.
Helber, Patrick. 2015. *Dancehall und Homophobie. Postkoloniale Perspektiven auf die Geschichte und Kultur Jamaikas*. Bielefeld: transcript.
Helff, Sissy. 2012. "The Missing Link: Transculturation, Hybridity and/or Transculturality?" In *Literature for Our Times*, edited by Bill Ashcroft, Julie McGonegal, Ranjini Mendis, and Arun Mukherjee, 187–202. Amsterdam: Rodopi.
Hepp, Andreas. 2009. "Transculturality as a Perspective: Researching Media Cultures Comparatively." *Forum: Qualitative Social Research* 10 (1). http://www.qualitative-research.net/index.php/fqs/article/view/1221/2657. Accessed April 26, 2016.
Hope, Donna P. 2010. *Man Vibes: Masculinities in the Jamaican Dancehall*. Kingston: Ian Randle.
Hope, Donna P., ed. 2013. *International Reggae: Current and Future Trends in Jamaican Popular Music*. Kingston: Pelican.
Hope, Donna P., ed. 2015. *Reggae from Yaad: Traditional and Emerging Themes in Jamaican Popular Music*. Kingston: Ian Randle.
Järvenpää, Tuomas. 2014. "Listening to Intergalactic Sounds—Articulation of Rastafarian Livity in Finnish Roots Reggae Sound System Performances." *Temenos* 50 (2): 273–97.
Karnik, Olaf. 2006. "Reggae." In *Contemporary Youth Culture: An International Encyclopedia*, vol. 1, edited by Priya Parmar, Birgit Richard, and Shirley Steinberg, 329–37. London: Greenwood.

Karnik, Olaf, and Helmut Philipps. 2007. *Reggae in Deutschland*. Cologne: Kiepenheuer & Witsch.
Köhlings, Ellen. 2014. "Reggae Revival. Mehr als nur zwei Worte." *Riddim* 14 (1): 42.
Köhlings, Ellen, and Pete Lilly. 2012. "The Evolution of Reggae in Europe with a Focus on Germany." In *Global Reggae*, edited by Carolyn Cooper, 69–93. Kingston: Canoe.
Köhlings, Ellen, and Pete Lilly. 2013. "From One Love to One Hate? Europe's Perception of Jamaican Homophobia Expressed in Song Lyrics." In *International Reggae: Current and Future Trends in Jamaican Popular Music*, edited by Donna P. Hope, 2–29. Kingston: Pelican.
Kramer, Simon. 2014. "Dactah Chando. Wellenreiter." *Riddim* 14 (1): 22–23.
Kress, Gunther, and Theo van Leeuwen. 1996. *Reading Images: The Grammar of Visual Design*. New York: Routledge.
Landolt, Michael. 2014. "Mellow Mood. Eineiig." *Riddim* 14 (5): 9.
Lilly, Pete. 2014. "Reggae aus Deutschland. Nenn' es beim Namen!" *Riddim* 14 (1): 45.
Lindorfer, Peter. 2014. "Kris Kemist (Reality Shock Records). Gute Nachbarschaft." *Riddim* 14 (3): 23.
Lukas, Adam. 2014. "Danny Ranks. Social Rasta." *Riddim* 14 (4): 12.
Marc, Isabelle. 2015. "Travelling Songs: On Popular Music Transfer and Translation." *iaspm@journal* 5 (2): 3–21. http://www.iaspmjournal.net/index.php/IASPM_Journal/article/view/738. Accessed April 26, 2016.
Mendívil, Julio. 2013. "Transkulturalität revisited: Kritische Überlegungen zu einem neuen Begriff der Kulturforschung." In *Transkulturalität und Musikvermittlung. Möglichkeiten und Herausforderungen in Forschung, Kulturpolitik und musikpädagogischer Praxis*, edited by Susanne Binas-Preisendörfer and Melanie Unseld, 43–61. Frankfurt am Main: Peter Lang.
Masouri, John. 2014. "Maxi Priest. Gentleman Rasta." *Riddim* 14 (5): 32–33.
Münch, Ursula. 2014. "Dancehall Riddims." *Riddim* 14 (2): 85–86.
Pfleiderer, Martin. 2001. "Riddim & Sound. Dub Reggae und Entwicklungen der neueren Popularmusik." In *Populäre Musik im kulturwissenschaftlichen Diskurs II*, edited by Thomas Phleps, 99–114. Karben: CODA.
Pfleiderer, Martin. 2011. "'Come inna mi ramping shop.' Slackness und Schwulenhass in der jamaikanischen und deutschen Dancehall." In *Thema Nr. 1. Sex und populäre Musik*, edited by Dietrich Helms and Thomas Phleps, 165–87. Bielefeld: transcript.
Pfleiderer, Martin, and Wolf-Georg Zaddach. 2014. "Der gegenwärtige Jazzdiskurs in Deutschland. Versuch einer empirischen Rekonstruktion anhand von Jazzzeitschriften." In *Jazz Debates/Jazzdebatten*, edited by Wolfram Knauer, 61–89. Hofheim: Wolke.
Philipps, Helmut. 2014. "Dub Inc. Paradise." *Riddim* 14 (1): 77–79.
Renger, Rudi. 2002. "Populäre Printprodukte transkulturell." In *Grundlagentexte zur transkulturellen Kommunikation*, edited by Andreas Hepp and Martin Löffelholz, 474–99. Konstanz: UVK.
Rommen, Timothy. 2006. "Protestant Vibrations? Reggae, Rastafari, and Conscious Evangelicals." *Popular Music* 25 (2): 235–63.
Sterling, Marvin D. 2010. *Babylon East: Performing Dancehall, Roots Reggae, and Rastafari in Japan*. Durham, NC: Duke University Press.
Stratton, Jon. 2014. "Melting Pot: The Making of Black British Music in the 1950s and 1960s." In *Black Popular Music in Britain Since 1945*, edited by Jon Stratton and Nabeel Zuberi, 27–45. Farnham, UK: Ashgate.

Taylor, Angus. 2014. "Pressure Busspipe. Grassroots Chanter." *Riddim* 14 (2): 42–45.
Trakulhun, Sven. 2007. "Bewegliche Güter. Theorie und Praxis der Kulturtransferforschung." In *Musik-Sammlungen—Speicher interkultureller Prozesse*, vol. A, edited by Erika Fischer, 72–94. Stuttgart: Steiner.
van Leeuwen, Theo. 2005. *Introducing Social Semiotics*. New York: Routledge.
Welsch, Wolfgang. 1999. "Transculturality: The Puzzling Form of Cultures Today." In *Spaces of Culture: City, Nation, World*, edited by Mike Featherstone and Scott Lash, 194–213. London: Sage.
Welsch, Wolfgang. 2010. "Was ist eigentlich Transkulturalität?" In *Hochschule als transkultureller Raum? Kultur, Bildung und Differenz in der Universität*, edited by Lucyna Darowska, Thomas Lüttenberg, and Claudia Machold, 39–66. Bielefeld: transcript.
White, Bob W. 2012. "Introduction: Rethinking Globalization through Music." In *Music and Globalization: Critical Encounters*, edited by Bob W. White, 1–14. Bloomington: Indiana University Press.
Wynands, René. 1995. *"Do the Reggay!" Reggae von Pocomania bis Raggamuffin und der Mythos Bob Marley*. Munich: Piper.
Zill, Valentin. 2014a. "Sebastian Sturm & Exile Airline. Überflieger." *Riddim* 14 (1): 52–53.
Zill, Valentin. 2014b. "Jah Sun. Paradigmenwechsel." *Riddim* 14 (5): 25.
Zill, Valentin. 2014c. "Ziggi Recado. Selbsttherapie." *Riddim* 14 (5): 26–27.
Zips, Werner. 2014. "'The Good, the Bad, and the Ugly.' Habitus, Feld, Kapital im (Feld des) jamaikanischen Reggae." In *Ethnohistorie. Rekonstruktion, Kulturkritik und Repräsentation. Eine Einführung*, edited by Karl R. Wernhart and Werner Zips, 221–38. Vienna: Promedia.

NOTES

1. This discourse analysis is part of my doctoral research. I would like to thank the Ernst-Abbe-Stiftung (Ernst Abbe Foundation) for the financial support that made the work on this article possible.

2. Following social semiotics, I use the term "meaning potential" because it is sensitive to the changing of meaning in different cultural and societal contexts. Additionally, it does not promote the existence of a naturally fixed meaning (see Kress and van Leeuwen 1996; van Leeuwen 2005).

3. In 2001 it was four issues per year, and that has been true since 2016 as well.

4. Discourse analysis is one fundamental part of the study. The results were also systematically used to describe visual and sounding characteristics in order to reconstruct the aesthetics of reggae and dancehall as negotiated in Germany.

5. A discussion of these complex phenomena is beyond the scope of this article. For details see Cooper 1993, 2004; Helber 2015; and Hope 2010.

6. Gentleman's real name is Tillmann Otto; Alborosie's birth name is Alberto d'Ascola.

7. She refers to a quote of pan-Africanist Marcus Garvey that became world famous when Bob Marley paraphrased it in "Redemption Song" in 1980: "We are going to emancipate from mental slavery because whilst others might free the body, none but ourselves can free the mind" (Cooper 2012a, 301).

8

"WE'RE CALLED NECK, AND WE PLAY PSYCHO-CEILÍDH—IT GOES SOMETHING LIKE THIS . . ."

GARETH DYLAN SMITH

INTRODUCTION

This chapter provides perspectives on aspects of the Irish diaspora through a personal account of working with the London Irish punk "psycho-ceilidh" band Neck, from 2002 to 2016. I played drums with Neck in festivals, clubs, and pubs around the UK, Europe, and the United States. The band has long had a "revolving door" membership, with "permanent" members fluctuating, and many (including this author) returning to play with the band when required and as available; I know more than twenty musicians who have performed as part of Neck, which goes out as a five- or six-piece band. I have played at least 115 shows with the band in five countries.[1] This chapter draws on autoethnographic data from participant observations and field notes, and from an audio-recorded interview and informal conversations conducted with the band's leader, singer, songwriter, banjo player, and main guitarist Leeson O'Keeffe; all direct quotes from O'Keeffe in this chapter are taken from the interview, conducted in June 2012, unless otherwise indicated. Further rich data constructing and construing diasporic experiences are included in the form of the band's lyrics, all penned by O'Keeffe.[2]

Neck plays "psycho-ceilidh" music—a term adopted by O'Keeffe from its inventor and his former bandleader (and employer) Shane MacGowan, to describe the band's particular brand of Irish music, which is intrinsically connected to O'Keeffe's upbringing in Britain and identity as Irish. O'Keeffe usually opens a Neck performance with the words "We're called Neck, and we play psycho-ceilídh—it goes something like this," followed immediately by shouting "a haon, do, trí, ceathair!" to count the band into the first song of the set.

The sound of the band is intoxicating; that is why I played with them for so many years, and for so little material gain (certainly, in fact, a net loss). The music is raucous, fast, loud, chaotic, and unrefined. It is also incredibly tight, punchy, and focused, belting along with the pace and exuberance of a powerboat catapulting at full throttle. There is a danceable lilt to the breakneck reels and jigs, and a singalong predictability to the headlong, double-time pogo-punk-rock anthems. (I auditioned for the band because their music reminded me of the Celtic folk and English folk-rock music my parents used to listen to at home when I was growing up.) Neck has a sweaty, dive-bar, old-school rock aesthetic—I would often play shirtless, for instance, and Leeson, given the chance, would run and slide across a big-enough stage on his knees mid-guitar solo. These traits are mixed with a carefully rehearsed set and song structures, showcasing note-perfect, lightning virtuosity from the violin, banjo, uilleann pipes, and tin whistle. The experience of drumming in Neck is exhilarating. As I have noted elsewhere, "I am only ever really satisfied if I come off stage or out of a rehearsal sweaty as hell, having worked out hard and long and known the power of a huge flowing groove for the best part of an hour or more" (Smith 2017). Neck is the perfect environment for achieving these ends. Férdia Stone-Davis suggests that "the physical character of musical experience discloses a first-order mode of being, one that involves a suspension of the distinction between subject and object (promoting instead their mutuality)" (2011, 158–59). This was absolutely my experience of drumming in Neck. I wanted to know only the now, to experience it to its—and my—fullest.

Sean Campbell notes the "enduring" and "diverse" contribution of "musicians of Irish descent in the history of British pop," observing that, despite the considerable attention paid to many of these musicians, "there has been relatively little address . . . to their Irish context." This oversight "has obscured the role of Irish ethnicity in the musicians' lives and work" (Campbell 2011, 1). In this short case study of Neck, I aim to provide insight, albeit limited, into "second-generation Irish music-making as a complex cultural process that exceeds both Irish ethnicity and English assimilation" (Campbell 2011, 2). Neck and O'Keeffe—the only constant member of the band since it was first formed in 1994—serve as singular examples of the tremendously diverse musicking undertaken by members of the Irish diasporic community in England. Their case is not typical, and should not be taken as a point from which to generalize with regard to music or musicians of the Irish diaspora; it is, however, uniquely and intrinsically fascinating. I hope the account and discussion that follow in this chapter will prompt at least as many questions as they may answer, serving as one step along the road to a deeper, more nuanced understanding of the roles that diasporic experiences play in music making.

EXPRESSING IRISHNESS

Harris and Rampton (2003) provide two helpful, overlapping definitions of "ethnicity" that help to frame the Irishness expressed and embodied by Neck. They explain:

> (1) It is assumed that individuals possess (or belong to) cultures that are relatively discrete, homogenous and static, and that . . . ethnicity provides us with tacit, but ingrained dispositions.
> (2) Ethnicity is regarded as something that people can emphasize strategically, in a range of different ways according to their needs and purposes in particular situations. . . . [E]thnicity is viewed more as a relatively flexible resource. (5)

Throughout this chapter, these passive and active realizations[3] of ethnic identity (Smith 2013) are evidenced through the discussion of Neck and the band's lyrics. When discussing the idea of "otherness" and its manifestations, music education scholar Deborah Bradley explains:

> By employing the social construct of race, humans designate Otherness through labels they attach. The concept of race may categorize people according to physical characteristics (including skin color), by ethnic heritage, by shared language, by religion, by geographic location—it is a long and fluid list of factors determining who currently makes up society's others. (Bradley 2015, 191)

This notion of otherness, and the experience of othering, are central to the experience and identity of O'Keeffe, who struggles with and thrives on the fact that he does not feel completely at home either in England or Ireland. His life and his musical work are, to a large extent, about managing, reinforcing, and navigating what it means to be at home in neither and both places. As Malone and Dooley note, people identifying as "('London') Irish have a particular and distinct sense of their own respective 'insider'/'outsider' status" (2006, 12). O'Keeffe also loves to visit the US cities of Boston and

New York, feeling empathy with Irish diaspora community members there who are *from* Ireland but not *of* Ireland. Neck has played more times in New York City than anywhere else outside the band's hometown of London, and O'Keeffe, who at one time had an Irish American girlfriend, even considered relocating to New York.

The band's name, Neck, allies it to the Irish music community. It is an overt reference to an Irish saying about being tough, thick-skinned, or resilient: "to have a neck like a jockey's bollocks," O'Keeffe often says from the stage, adding that the band has this name "because we're cheeky fuckers." He jokingly admits that the name may be "too Irish," acknowledging it is deliberately somewhat obscure because "if you're not Irish you don't get it," and that is precisely the point. The band had previously gone under the name of the Craic Dealers, which, while appropriately referring to its aspiration of purveying the experience of a good time ("craic" in Gaelic) to audiences, this allegedly caused no end of trouble when trying to secure bookings by telephone.

O'Keeffe discovered at the age of twenty-one the centrality of Irishness and Ireland to his life and to his sense of self when his mother took him and his brother home to Dublin for the first time to visit their "cousins with funny names." Born to an immigrant Irish mother, and living with extended family in the English town of Hemel Hempstead for most of his life to that point, he had always sensed that "something was missing" while growing up, but had no idea that this something would turn out to be Ireland and a deeper connection to his Irishness. Upon arriving in Dublin on the ferry with the sunrise, he describes the experience as "like being hit by a thunderbolt; I was going home. It was so profound, so overwhelming, that my mam and me just cried on the bus all the way into Dublin from Dun Laoghaire." In our interview O'Keeffe wept at the memory, struggling briefly to talk, acknowledging, "that was what was missing," and "that's why" he does Neck: "because it's [Ireland is] home." On trips to Ireland with Neck, I have seen the same thing happen to Leeson. He will insist on taking over driving duties of the van upon arrival in Ireland, and drive, weeping, into the green hills of the Irish countryside. This feeling is captured in the last verse and chorus of his song, "Diaspora" (O'Keeffe 2003b):

> It's all about who I am & where I come from,
> it's all about my identity,
> & without doubt it's a well I draw deep from,
> it's my salvation, my sanctuary:

> Diaspora!—the spawn of immigration,
> Diaspora!—flung wide upon the seas,
> Diaspora!—the haemorrhage of a Nation,
> Diaspora!—& there's millions there like me.

It was a period of employment in Shane MacGowan's post-Pogues band, the Popes, eleven years later in 1993, that provided the further epiphany that set O'Keeffe's life on a new course, with Neck coalescing in 1994 because "I wanted to portray my Irish roots as well as the punk thing, and playing 'psycho-ceilídh' in the Popes was really inspiring—I was fired up by it, and I knew I could take it further." Six months in the Popes and "going to Ireland with Shane was cathartic, it was life-changing." The transformative experience in Ireland centered on rehearsing for and performing at a festival in Tramore, County Waterford—the hometown of well-known Irish impresario Vince Power. The trip began with a drunken ferry crossing from Swansea, Wales, to Cork, and a drive to MacGowan's family cottage in Tipperary. Upon arrival in the vicinity of the dwelling, the torrential rain that had followed them from the ferry cleared. The sheer joy of the literal and figurative parting of the clouds is captured in the song, "Blue Skies Over Nenagh" (O'Keeffe 1995a), of which the first verse, bridge, and chorus are:

> Oh we left our homes in London Town
> In the last few days of May,
> Over the sea, Tipperary-bound,
> In ould Ireland for to play . . .
>
> Oh, the clouds have gone, the future's bright,
> Though the pressure's on, we'll be alright,
> Through storms & doubt, we'll boldly face it out,
>
> For we've found blue skies over Nenagh,
> For we've found blue skies over Nenagh.

O'Keeffe recalls that on that trip, "the first day I started writing Irish music." From Tipperary the band travelled to Dublin, to continue rehearsals for the forthcoming festival show. During this time in Dublin, O'Keeffe was able to cement relationships with local family members, and penned a clutch of songs, including what would become a frequent set-opener, "Loud and Proud and Bold" (O'Keeffe 1995b), which portrays some of the romance and revelry that the city holds for O'Keeffe:

> The swirling Liffey waters rush,
> Down between The Quays,
> The clouds scud along north-westerly,
> While the moons' silver light smiles down on me,
>
> The wind may blow and the rain may spray,
> And the night air may be cold,
> But I love to be in Dublin's fair city,
> Bein' loud 'n' proud 'n' bold!

According to the lyrics of "Blue Skies Over Nenagh," following rehearsals in Dublin the band "kicked arse at Tramore" (O'Keeffe 1995b). O'Keeffe's friends, cousins, brother, and girlfriend were in the audience for this performance, and in front of him on stage he had a picture of his mother. He says that this gig "was like playing for Ireland," and he recalls playing through tears of pride, because "being second-generation Irish, playing in Shane's band, it validated what I was." O'Keeffe, his songs, and their vehicle in Neck exemplify "the dilemma faced by second-generation Irish people, many of whom locate themselves as 'half-and-half' and 'very much both' or 'caught right down the middle.' The musicians thus adopt a range of hyphenated positions (such as London-Irish . . .), and inflect their affinities uniquely" (Campbell 2011, 2, quoting Hyder 2005, 166), according to the city or region in which they live (Malone and Dooley 2006). As O'Keeffe put it, there is a common perception that "you're not English, you're not Irish, what the fuck are you?!" His distinct identity is portrayed and performed in his songs (West 2016, 148).

Central to O'Keeffe's sense of self is that "I've got my grandfather's voice." His aunt told him she could hear her father's singing voice in O'Keeffe's when he sings:

> Fittingly, my aunt said this while she was listening to an early demo of a song I wrote about my grandfather, and which would become the title song of Neck's first album, *Here's Mud in Yer Eye!* (taken from what he used to say prior to taking a drink). She was dying of cancer, so the sound and the lyrics brought her great comfort. Another touching thing was that my then-eighteen-year-old cousin was present, and, due to my aunt having married into an originally Northern Irish Protestant family, who were quite

derogatory towards her because she was an Irish Catholic, my cousins weren't allowed to know much about their Irish background, so my cousin found out more about her grandfather in the five minutes of that song than she had done in the previous sixteen years she'd been alive! So it's amazing that the gift I inherited from him was informing his family about him.... you can see how it's all linked and why it's so important to me.

O'Keeffe takes tremendous pride in his inherited vocal qualities, which he says contain the distinctive Irish "nyaa" that is common to singers of Irish heritage, including John Lennon, Paul McCartney, and George Harrison of the Beatles, Liam and Noel Gallagher of Oasis, and John "Johnny Rotten" Lydon of the Sex Pistols. According to O'Flynn (2009, 155, citing Barthes 1977, 179–89), the "nyaa" "tends to be regarded as a particular and unique kind of (Irish) 'vocal grain'" and can refer to the slightly nasal timbre that characterizes O'Keeffe's voice. Through this connection to his grandfather, O'Keeffe also feels a direct familial connection to politics and patriotism in Ireland, since his grandfather had fought in both the Anglo-Irish war and the Irish Civil War, later becoming a member of the Garda Síochána, the Irish police. Through Neck, O'Keeffe is "doing my bit for my country, my culture, for my family," although, he concedes, "I'm not completely altruistic, obviously."

The notion of there being something distinctly Irish about O'Keeffe's voice and Neck's music is acknowledged by O'Flynn (2009, 21) as the attribution of an "Irish sound" to "accents . . . and other paramusical aspects of the music." This sound is related to the "essential Irishness" of Irish music (21), wherein Irish traditional music is equated with "Irish music." The inclusion of traditional Irish instruments is indeed critical to the sound of Neck. O'Keeffe acknowledges the trail blazed for the second-generation Irish community by the London-Irish band, the Pogues, fronted by Shane MacGowan, saying that, from the birth of Neck, "the idea was to take things further than the Pogues . . . be quite aggressive about it in terms of the sound . . . but obviously to write Irish music." Neck has become quite well known in London, the UK, Europe, and the United States, and many people recognize the band as part of a lineage that, as O'Keeffe notes, "comes from the Clancy's via the Dubliners, to Finbar and Eddie Furey, via the Chieftains to Planxty, Horslips, Thin Lizzy and Moving Hearts, to the Pogues; and then from them come Dropkick Murphys and Flogging Molly. It's all Irish music." O'Keeffe notes that Neck has "always been the envy of [Dropkick Murphys and Flogging Molly], even though they're bigger than us, because our trad players are proper, authentic trad Irish players—they've told me as much." Indeed, one of the distinguishing features of Neck's sound—and one of the exhilarating things for me about first learning the music of Neck and then playing with them—is that the level of musicianship of the musicians playing traditional Irish folk instruments (fiddle, tin whistle, uilleann pipes, banjo, and occasionally accordion) is frequently truly outstanding.

IDENTITY STRUGGLES

Being in Neck serves as a vehicle for O'Keeffe (along with some band and audience members) to express the unique identity and shared experiences of the fact that "over there you're English, over here you're a Paddy." Neck performs a song called "Plastic and Proud" (O'Keeffe 2012), repurposing the derogatory term, "Plastic Paddy," which describes those who are "not English . . . not Irish—what the fuck are you?!" The band has appropriated the phrase and "turned it on its head like Black people say 'n***a' to each other [because] if you own it, you're turning [the term] on its head." O'Keeffe says, "I might be a Plastic Paddy, but I'm still a Paddy," framing what to some may appear a paradox, wherein "while I'm proud to say, 'I'm an Irish musician,' I would not change where I grew up. . . . I'd rather be a Plastic Paddy than be no Paddy at all." Ireland and England are both central to his identity as a musician; as he notes, "I don't just play Irish music—I've got a punk background" and "I'm fortunate to have grown up in the UK [where] the music scene here, I think, is second to none." This complexity speaks to the experience of second-generation diasporic community members who understand that "you're a hybrid, you're a freak," an experience captured in the caption on the band's best-selling Plastic 'n' Proud T-shirt, the back of which reads, "it's a second-generation Irish identity crisis thing—you wouldn't understand." Aptly, Gilroy, when describing diaspora, notes that the term places "emphasis on contingency, indeterminacy and conflict" (1997, 334).

In the original lineup of Neck, three of the six musicians were from Ireland or were Irish-born, and the others were second-generation Irish living in London. I have no Irish blood. While I have always felt welcome in the band, and thrilled to be playing in Neck, I have struggled with my identity in a band about whom O'Keeffe says "we're writing from an Irish perspective, because that's what we are." It is not what I am; I am just a drummer, playing great music with a fantastic band and for a man whom I respect and admire. However, my affiliation with Neck played an important role in my personal life. When my now-wife moved to London from New York, she came to multiple Neck gigs with friends, ostensibly to see me play, although I wonder if she also sought some affirmation of her identification with Irishness—both her parents are Irish Americans, so she could be Irish in the United States and the UK. Most of the other musicians I know who have played with Neck have had an Irish family connection, with the exception of a long-standing fiddle player, who is Scottish.

The line between who Neck is and who I am was never more clearly drawn than when I played with Neck at a regular stop on the band's gigging calendar at the Ardoyne Fleadh. This community music festival takes place on the grounds of the Holy Cross Boys' Catholic Primary School, in the predominantly Irish, Catholic, working-class Ardoyne area of north Belfast. Being an Irish Catholic enclave surrounded by the sectarian majority of British Protestant communities, the area and the Holy Cross school have seen violent sectarian protests, including a bombing of the entrance to the school. I have never felt as uncomfortable being British as I did walking through the audience ahead of our set, seeing children as young as ten wearing t-shirts that declared, "Thatcher wanted for state terrorism," and posters for sale featuring fighter jets in Irish tricolour livery dropping bombs over an outline of England. I hurried backstage, afraid to open my mouth and reveal my starkly English accent; O'Keeffe has an Irish accent that he deploys with great effect, while I had just my plummy English tones, inherited from my father's grammar school days in the 1950s. It was exhilarating later that evening to play music to a large audience who were captivated by the music and dancing to the groove we created. I experienced one of the most moving moments of my drumming career when we played David Bowie's song "Heroes"—about divided, Cold War Berlin—to the crowd at the Ardoyne Fleadh, who O'Keeffe described from the stage as "heroes," living in a city divided by invisible lines and eight-foot-high brick "peace walls" (which began to be taken down by authorities in 2016). We topped off that trip to Belfast by smuggling an American guitarist back to London with us. He had apparently booked flights *to* Belfast and home *from* London, so we had him lie down between us on the floor of the band van and covered him with coats and instrument cases. Fortunately for us, immigration officials were none the wiser; they also conveniently overlooked our cargo of illicit poitín ("potcheen," a distilled traditional Irish beverage typically with high alcohol content) hiding in plain sight on one of the front seats in a three-quarters-full bottle bearing a Smirnoff vodka label.

EXPRESSING IRISHNESS IN PERFORMANCE

An aspect of Irishness that is stereotyped, celebrated, and assumed the world over is a culture of heavy alcohol consumption (Mullen, Williams, and Hunt 1996). Neck has always been home to hard-drinking musicians. I never play drums when I have been drinking, and often find that the band's rider of beer will be gone by the time I get around to helping myself to a bottle after performing and taking my drums off the stage. I recall a St. Patrick's Day gig with the band, where the venue we were playing was offering a Guinness-branded top hat for every four pints of Guinness purchased; by the close of Neck's first set, the six of us had collectively accrued six hats, and I had not touched a drop. The Irish drinking culture, particularly the hard-drinking night of St. Patrick's Day, is celebrated in the Neck song "Every Day's St Patrick's Day" (O'Keeffe 2003c). O'Keeffe introduces this staple of the Neck set with the words, "People all over the world know the 17th of March, St. Patrick's Day, as a day to get drunk and celebrate being Irish. Wrong. Where we come from in north London, every shaggin' day's St. Patrick's Day!" The last verse and chorus of the song explain the revelry:

> In London every weekend, see the feckers dance and sing,
> From The Archway, Swan & Fiddler, to The Lark and Claddagh Ring,
> And [from] New York to California, Prague to Amsterdam's the same:
> The hooley's the intention, the diaspora the name!
>
> Well, every day's St. Patrick's Day! There's no needin' an excuse,
> Every night works out this way, it's too easy cuttin' loose!
> Every day's St. Patrick's Day! If you know what I mean,
> There's no need to wear a shamrock, or paint your mickey green!

Neck's music is accessible in different ways or on several levels: to those who feel kinship with Ireland or Irishness, to punks, to rockers, to traditional Irish musicians, and to anyone wanting to party the night away. Their live shows—the band's bread-and-butter for a quarter-century—touch and move audiences, inviting and drawing them in, and rewarding them amply for their engagement. O'Keeffe is the consummate frontman, captivating the crowd (of any size—I have played to ten and to 10,000 with the band) with lighthearted banter, serious political commentary, and utter devotion to performing the songs with total conviction. He sings his heart out, plays every show like it's the last one he'll do, and the band rises to the occasion. Magic is made at Neck shows, which enacts and enables a sort of expanded diaspora or diasporic moment, through a shared musical-diasporic experience.

Kevin Kenny advises that "diaspora" can be understood as an idea that helps us understand the world created by human migration (2013, 1), and that it serves especially well to explain "particular forms of coerced migration, involving slavery, genocide, famine, and political oppression." Garratt and Piper (2008) explain how "particular people, groups and ethnicities become knowable as a category and are seen as a fixed commodity.... [T]herefore, identities continue to be produced and reproduced in systems of power" (80). There is evidence of this in the Neck song "Ourselves Alone" (O'Keeffe 1987), which calls for a united Ireland, free from British foreign rule, as highlighted in the bridge, pre-chorus, and chorus:

> England spawned a monster, and tried to wash their hands,
> If things can change in South Africa, then why not the same in Ireland?
>
> No we do not need them to occupy our minds,
> This ascendancy precedes them from another time,
> We are prisoners of our history—a grip that won't let go,
> If there's justice then our destiny is by . . .
>
> Ourselves alone, Ourselves alone, Ourselves alone, Ourselves alone,
> Ourselves alone, Ourselves alone, Ourselves alone, Ourselves alone.

The "monster" to which the song refers here is the centuries-old history of war, imperialism, and oppression that has existed between Britain and Ireland, culminating most recently in the Troubles from 1968 to 1998 and beyond. "Ourselves Alone" or "We Ourselves" is the English translation of the Irish words "Sinn Fein," the Irish Republican political party dedicated to the unification of Ireland and the end of British rule in Northern Ireland (Sinn Fein 2017); links between Sinn Fein and the Provisional IRA have been alleged by governments in the UK and the United States.

In my youth, the specter of the Provisional IRA loomed large. I grew up close to Brighton on England's south coast, and was seven years old in 1984 when the IRA bombed the Grand Hotel in the city with the aim of killing Prime Minister Margaret Thatcher. The attempt on her life failed because she had been at breakfast while the bomb went off in her bathroom. The blast caused massive damage to the property, and even now when I drive past I still think of the hotel as newly refurbished, remembering the grim day. I recall, too, the mortar attack on the prime minister's residence in 1991, and the Paddington and Victoria train station bombs later that year; my father was a frequent London commuter, and I feared for his life every day he traveled. When I moved to London in 2001, my friends and I found cheaper-than-usual rent in the Ealing area, due to the local shopping center having been devastated by an IRA bomb three weeks prior.

O'Keeffe sings candidly and emotively about the Troubles in the powerful Neck song "Blood on the Streets" (O'Keeffe 2003a), which recalls several violent incidents from the period. These are the sectarian deaths of Robert Hamill in 1993 and Rosemary Nelson (the human rights lawyer hired by Hamill's family to investigate his death) in 1999, the murder by British police in London of IRA volunteer Diarmuid O'Neill in 1996, and the racially motivated murder of Black teenager Stephen Lawrence in London in 1997. The reference to Lawrence's case serves to contextualize the Troubles, and the London-Irish experience, within broader British establishment racism; Lawrence's murder was poorly handled by London's Metropolitan Police, leading to long-running investigations into institutional racism on the force. Lawrence is also featured—his name shouted out—in Neck's anti-racism song and single release, "Everybody's Welcome to the Hooley" (O'Keeffe, 2006).

As Kenny notes, Irish diasporic communities have tended to blame Britain entirely for the potato famine of the 1840s, viewing it as an act of deliberate negligence bordering on genocide, a view "that became foundational in Irish American ethnic identity: that emigration was a matter of British-imposed exile rather than voluntary choice" (2013, 31). This is a perspective that holds up to an extent, although the reality is arguably more nuanced. As a British national with no special connection to Ireland outside of playing drums with Neck, I have considered the complexity and anguish that must reside in a perceived need to leave Ireland and, for some, to leave to live and work in the land of the oppressor. The enmity between the countries is deep-seated, evident in Britain through centuries of racism and stereotyping (Parekh 2000; Szwed 2005). As a child at school, I recall the Irish were always the butt of jokes; I repeated these into my adulthood, unthinkingly perpetuating the racism and division of my country's imperial culture, much as I unquestioningly repeated the words of the British national anthem about willing God to bring victory and glory to "our" queen. In my late twenties, I discovered that what was absent from my schooling was the history of why, for instance, the IRA might feel they had just cause to bomb my country, or why the Irish spoke to one another mainly in, of all things, English.

The theme of the coerced migration of the Irish at the hands of the British is also expressed in the song "The Fields of Athenry" (St. John 1979). This song tells the story of an Irish couple who are forced into crime by the Irish potato famine of the mid-nineteenth century; the man is sent to the British prison colony of Australia as punishment, separated from his wife and child. This song is also the anthem for fans of the Irish football team, and is inseparable for me from my experience of the day in June 2004 when Ireland played Spain in the quarterfinal of the World Cup, and Neck was hired to play at one of our regular venues on the London Irish bar circuit, O'Donoghue's Pub in Shepherd's Bush. (This was the same venue where we set up to play one night later that year, only to be told that there would be no punters arriving, since the police had closed off all surrounding roads due to fights and a riot breaking out between Queen Park Rangers and Cardiff football team fans. It was also the venue that refused ever to work with us again after we cancelled on them with less than twenty-four hours' notice in order to play a headline slot at a festival in Graz, Austria; that was a hit worth taking.)

We must have played "The Fields of Athenry" two dozen times in the course of the afternoon. We played it loud and hard, with conviction every time, and we played more than an hour longer than we were booked for. The pub was packed to more than double the legal capacity, with hundreds of people singing and shouting along to the music, with a level of collective enjoyment and *joie de vivre* that I have not experienced anywhere since. On this occasion, as usual, the landlord had the band plug the power for our gear into a power supply in the pub's kitchen, which was on a different circuit from the room in which we played. This was so that we could play as loudly as we wanted, watching the decibel meter register permanently in the red with no regard at all.

The other song we played upward of a dozen times that afternoon was the song O'Keeffe (2002) wrote specially for the Irish World Cup team, "May the Road Rise with You / Go N-éiri an bóthair leat," based on a well-known Irish blessing. This song epitomizes the "Irish" predilection both for refusing to admit defeat, even in the face of it, and for having a good time regardless of the outcome of a game; it reflects what Yeats (2003, 301) refers to as "Indomitable Irishry." The song's chorus captures a sense of devotion to Ireland through using words from the blessing, and, in the last line, emphasizing the spirit of collective participation:

> May the road rise with you,
> Go N-éiri an bóthair leat [phonetically, "go nie-ree an bowher lat"]

> May you succeed in everything you do,
> And if we win or lose,
> We'll sing a song for Ireland,
> 'Cos if we're still singin' then we're still kinda winnin' too!

This song epitomizes also one of the key functions of the use of the term "diaspora." Kevin Kenny explains:

> "diaspora" flattens out social and temporal distinctions, lumping all members of a given migrant group into a single undifferentiated category, based on their place of origin . . . refer[ring] to all people who happened to migrate from [e.g.] Ireland or Italy, along with their descendants, regardless of the circumstances of their migration or the nature of their history abroad. (2013, 16)

This construal of diaspora recalls what John O'Flynn (2009) refers to as the evocation of a "mythical Irishness" in Irish music, one that "engender[s] feelings of nostalgia for an idealized and undifferentiated Irish society of the not-so-distant past" (23). This view of the Irish diaspora is exemplified in the first verse of "May the Road Rise with You" (O'Keeffe 2002):

> We are a tribe that has wandered the world,
> Whether through choice or not at all,
> But there's one cause that bids us gather in one place,
> That's to answer Ireland's call.

This reference to both the figurative, emotional call of Ireland, and "Ireland's Call"—the Irish rugby team's "alternative national anthem" (written due to the team being drawn from both the Republic of Ireland and the six counties of the British Statelet of Northern Ireland, so representing the island of Ireland as a whole, such that an appropriate, less sectarian anthem was required)—highlights both diversity and similarity, further emphasized through the song's second and third verses:

> From the banks of the places that we've made home,
> The Thames, the Hudson, the Charles, Clyde and Mersey,
> We flow out across the wild raging foam,
> From the Shannon, the Liffey and the Lee.

Galway, Limerick, Cork, Waterford,
Dublin, Belfast, Derry, Glasgow,
Liverpool, Manchester, Birmingham, London,
Boston, Chicago, New York—the whole wide world!

In order to appeal to a crowd, perform to a packed room, and sell albums, one has to generalize.

CONCLUSION

I hope this short case study of Neck might go a small way toward developing an understanding of the multivariate, idiosyncratic, and complex phenomenon of Irish musicians in Britain as "insider-outsiders" (Parekh 2000, 21), shedding light on a small area of the "complex and diverse contours that constitute Britain's multi-ethnic margins" (Campbell 2011, 156). Neck is an incredible live band, and no amount of writing can approximate or do justice to the fantastic, energetic, visceral experience of seeing, hearing, and feeling them perform (notwithstanding my attempts herein to do so). Most of my experience of Neck has been in performance, and in traveling to and from gigs in the UK, Europe, and the United States. I have seen them perform once; otherwise, I know them from the stage, the road, and the occasional rehearsal. A gig with Neck is always emotional. It is very much about the music, but the music is about so much more. As noted by Anthias (1998), a characteristic of diaspora is that "a new identity becomes constructed on a world scale which crosses national borders and boundaries" (560). O'Keeffe says that, while most rock is about narcissism, "with Irish music, you're part of something bigger than yourself.... [I]t should be about doing the best you can for the music, and spreading it out to the world, which is what we do."

BIBLIOGRAPHY

Anthias, Floya. 1998. "Evaluating 'Diaspora': Beyond Ethnicity?" *Sociology* 32 (3): 557–80.
Barthes, Roland. 1977. *Image–Music–Text*, translated by Stephen Heath. London: Fontana.
Bradley, Deborah. 2015. "Hidden in Plain Sight: Race and Racism in Music Education." In *The Oxford Handbook of Social Justice in Music Education*, edited by Cathy Benedict, Patrick Schmidt, Gary Spruce, and Paul Woodford, 190–203. New York: Oxford University Press.
Campbell, Sean. 2011. *Irish Blood, English Heart: Second Generation Irish Musicians in England*. Cork: Cork University Press.

Garratt, Dean, and Heather Piper. 2008. *Citizenship Education, Identity and Nationhood: Contradictions in Practice?* London: Continuum.

Gilroy, Paul. 1997. "Diaspora and the Detours of Identity." In *Identity and Difference*, edited by Kathryn Woodward, 299–343. London: Sage.

Harris, Roxy, and Ben Rampton. 2003. "Introduction." In *The Language, Ethnicity and Race Reader*, edited by Roxy Harris and Ben Rampton, 1–14. London: Routledge.

Hyder, Rehan. 2006. *Brimful of Asia: Negotiating Ethnicity on the UK Music Scene*. Aldershot, UK: Ashgate.

Kenny, Kevin. 2013. *Diaspora: A Very Short Introduction*. Oxford: Oxford University Press.

Malone, Mary E., and John P. Dooley. 2006. "'Dwelling in Displacement': Meanings of 'Community' and Sense of Community for Two Generations of Irish People Living in North-West London." *Community, Work and Family* 9 (1): 11–28.

Mullen, Kenneth, Rory Williams, and Kate Hunt. 1996. "Irish Descent, Religion, and Alcohol and Tobacco." *Addiction* 91 (2): 243–54.

O'Flynn, John. 2009. *The Irishness of Irish Music*. Farnham, UK: Ashgate.

O'Keeffe, Leeson. 1987. "Ourselves Alone."

O'Keeffe, Leeson. 1995a. "Blue Skies Over Nenagh."

O'Keeffe, Leeson. 1995b. "Loud and Proud and Bold."

O'Keeffe, Leeson. 2002. "May the Road Rise with You / Go N-éiri an bóthair leat."

O'Keeffe, Leeson. 2003a. "Blood on the Streets."

O'Keeffe, Leeson. 2003b. "Diaspora."

O'Keeffe, Leeson. 2003c. "Every Day's St. Patrick's Day."

O'Keeffe, Leeson. 2006. "Everybody's Welcome to the Hooley."

O'Keeffe, Leeson. 2012. "Plastic and Proud."

Parekh, Bhikhu. 2000. *The Future of Multi-Ethnic Britain: The Parekh Report*. London: Commission on the Future of Multi-Ethnic Britain.

Sinn Fein. 2017. Homepage. http://sinnfein.ie.

Smith, Gareth Dylan. 2013. *I Drum, Therefore I Am: Being and Becoming a Drummer*. Farnham, UK: Ashgate.

Smith, Gareth Dylan. 2017. "Embodied Experience of Rock Drumming." *Music & Practice* 3. Available at: http://www.musicandpractice.org/volume-3/embodied-experience-rock-drumming/.

St. John, Pete, performed by Neck. 2005. "The Fields of Athenry." From *Here's Mud in Yer Eye*. Recorded March 2002. Hibernian CD.

Stone-Davis, Férdia. 2011. *Musical Beauty: Negotiating the Boundary between Subject and Object*. Eugene, OR: Cascade Books.

Szwed, John. 2005. "Race and the Embodiment of Culture." In *Crossovers: Essays on Race, Music, and American Culture*, edited by John Szwed, 79–90. Philadelphia: University of Pennsylvania Press.

West, Andrew. 2016. *The Art of Songwriting*. London: Bloomsbury.

Yeats, William Butler. 2003. "Under Ben Bulben." *The Collected Poems of W. B. Yeats*. Ware, UK: Wordsworth Editions.

NOTES

1. I looked back through my old paper diaries and smartphone calendars. The figure is approximate, as it does not include ad hoc acoustic sessions after regular shows, and in some instances it is unclear as to exactly with whom I was playing on a given date.

2. All song lyrics included in this publication are reproduced with permission of Leeson O'Keeffe, using his original punctuation.

3. Passive identity realization refers to understanding aspects of oneself and one's self. Active identity realization denotes living out and performing identities.

9

REWORKING THE *BRASILIDADE* NARRATIVE

Dekassegui, Música Sertaneja, and the Performance of Identity in the Japanese Brazilian Expatriate Community

JUNKO OBA

Joe Akio Hirata is a *Nikkey* Brazilian (Brazilian of Japanese descent)[1] *música sertaneja* (Brazilian country music) singer. To be more precise, that appeared to be the persona he was trying to enact in his performance when I first met him during his tour in Japan in 2005. Wearing his trademark cowboy hat, Hirata walked into the small lecture hall at Musashi University in Tokyo, where he was to give a special lecture performance that afternoon.[2] He had just embarked on a tour of Brazilian communities in Japan, performing for different community events and promoting his newly released mini-album CD, *Reencontro* (Reunion, Reconnection, or Rediscovery). Although I had no idea who he was, nor what música sertaneja was at that time, Hirata was already a celebrity in the Nikkey community. Some of us in the audience, including a reporter from *International Press*, a Portuguese-language newspaper in Japan, and myself, made a special trip to this lecture to listen to his "dream-come-true" story of going from being a migrant worker in Japan to being a professional singer.

Hirata was of medium build, probably in his midthirties at that time. He was dressed in an authentic música sertaneja outfit—a plain black shirt, blue jeans complete with a leather belt with a large metal cowboy buckle, and a stylish white cowboy hat. Although I was used to seeing people wearing cowboy hats in rural Tennessee, my home at that time, a cowboy in a Japanese college classroom was a curious sight. Hirata, however, looked very relaxed in this environment. Waiting for the sound check to be completed, he exchanged friendly greetings with the staff and a few people in the audience.

Standing beside Hirata was the sociology professor, Angelo Ishi, who coordinated this special visit from the star singer for his media studies class. Ishi himself is a third-generation Nikkey Brazilian. He has lived in Japan since

Joe Hirata in a música sertaneja outfit. Photograph courtesy of Joe Hirata.

1990 and has conducted extensive research about the Brazilian community in Japan. As a journalist and scholar, Ishi has also been involved in many efforts to empower Brazilian migrants in Japan and to raise public awareness of their predicament. Following Ishi's brief introduction, Hirata took the stage and began his story, taking the audience back to his childhood in Maringá, in the state of Paraná, Brazil. Like many stories recounted in typical música sertaneja songs (Dent 2009; Reily 2008), Hirata's life story revolves around themes of urban migration and the search for identity prompted by a sense of displacement, feelings of loss and fragmentation, and a nostalgic longing for home. As a native of Maringá, Hirata's experience and sentiment well resonate with thousands of other Brazilians who left their homes in the south-central interior during the country's rapid modernization and centralization in the past several decades. This is the population with which música sertaneja is typically associated. Hirata's story, however, is also deeply intertwined with the unique experiences of Nikkey Brazilians, and their recent *dekassegui* return migration to their ancestral home of Japan.

In this essay, I investigate música sertaneja in the Japanese Brazilian expatriate community, following its unique trajectory of transnational migration from Brazil to Japan, and, in some cases, back again to Brazil in the past few decades. Música sertaneja is a style of "country music" that originated in the Brazilian countryside and is currently the most popular musical style in Brazil. It evokes life in the countryside, landscapes of loss, and the distinctive Brazilian sentiment of *saudade*, or nostalgic longing. As Brazil underwent a process of rapid urban development and large-scale rural-to-urban migration starting in the mid-1940s, música sertaneja spoke and continues to speak for people's shared experiences and nostalgic longing for what they left behind, both in their real life and in their romantic imagining. In its earlier form, música sertaneja was performed by one or two male singers accompanying themselves on stringed instruments of colonial origin such as the *viola caipira* and *violaõ*. Over time, the musical style has changed, incorporating different regional styles, elements of other Latin American traditions, and, more recently, strong influences of US country music. While many música sertaneja performances nowadays include an electric guitar and a synthesizer in their standard instrumentation, the vocal harmony produced by the male vocal duo, called *dupla*, and the sounds of acoustic guitar and *sanfona* (accordion) still most unambiguously define música sertaneja. For many listeners of música sertaneja, these sounds, combined with the aforementioned nostalgic imagery of the bucolic countryside, conjures an image of *brasilidade* (Brazilianness) as their cultural roots. Historically, however, Japanese-Brazilian immigrants' similar life stories were banished (or ridiculed and dismissed as being misfit, as in Lourenço e Lourival's música sertaneja song, "Os Três Boiaderos Japoneses") from the narrative of this quintessentially Brazilian experience and deemed irrelevant to the music or the *brasilidade* that it inspires.

Despite the perceived disconnect, música sertaneja has become an important site of identity negotiation for Brazilians of Japanese descent in the past few decades, when the massive economic migration known as *dekassegui*, which literally means "go out and earn," propelled many middle-class Japanese Brazilians to "return migrate" to their ancestral home as unskilled laborers. Their experiences of geocultural and socioeconomic displacement and alienation in Japan forced them to reexamine their identity in relation to their new environment. I discuss how this recent dekassegui experience provoked Japanese Brazilian expatriates to reconfigure their identities, and how, in the process, they not only used música sertaneja to negotiate their space in the diaspora, but also reworked the traditional *brasilidade* narrative in their favor.

A PERSONAL STORY

Despite the fact that the industry greatly owes the current popularity of música sertaneja and its commercial success in urban cosmopolitan areas to the innovative mind of a Nikkey Brazilian producer, Ivan Miyazato (Becker 2010), música sertaneja has never been a genre of music that people typically associate with the Nikkey population. Currently only a handful of Nikkey Brazilian música sertaneja singers are active performers. Their performances mostly take place inside their local communities and/or Nikkey ethnic enclave, and are hardly known to people outside. Among these Nikkey música sertaneja singers, Hirata is the most celebrated figure in the community. Back home in Brazil now, Hirata's iconic presence is an indispensable element in all major Nikkey cultural festivals and community events. He also occasionally appears in events that Nikkey community members organize for charity and fundraising. In June 2016, Hirata's extensive contributions to the Nikkey community were recognized with a prestigious award in the *108 Anos da Imigração Japonesa no Brasil* (108 years of Japanese immigration to Brazil) celebration. His work as a música sertaneja singer is particularly remarkable, as it has questioned and complicated the images of Nikkey—both the socially constructed and self-imposed stereotypes, which tend to emphasize their Japaneseness and an ethnically and culturally defined otherness, and tend to neglect their Brazilianness.

Joe Hirata was born in Maringá, a son of Nikkey immigrants. The entire family was musically adept and supportive of Hirata's dream of becoming a singer. At his parents' encouragement, Hirata began singing in *nodojiman* and karaoke singing competitions in the Nikkey community at the age of eight and won many prizes and championship titles, including a national championship.

Nodojiman (のど自慢), which literally means "throat boast," is a form of public singing competition that was popularized by the radio program disseminated by NHK (Japan's semi-governmental radio and TV network) in post–World War II Japan. The show began in January 1946 to provide entertainment to a nation recovering from war. While the popularity of nodojiman was more recently replaced by karaoke, the show is still broadcast every Sunday afternoon on both TV and radio, and its grassroots appeal remains consistent. In the current format adopted in the early 1970s, the show tours different cities and towns all over Japan each week and holds open public auditions for local amateur singers. About twenty qualified singers chosen out of hundreds of contestants are given opportunities to sing in the competition that is broadcast nationwide. At the end of each year, the local champions chosen in these weekly competitions are invited to compete in the grand championship nodojiman held at the prestigious NHK Hall in Shibuya, Tokyo.[3] The progressive hierarchical structure of nodojiman, like many other audition or talent search programs, recognizes individual musical talents and promotes a sense of healthy competition. However, the real attraction of nodojiman for both audience and participants is the show's strong emphasis on regionalism, a sense of community, and personal stories.[4] The finalists, therefore, typically include contestants who are not necessarily the most musically talented, and the show highlights and "prizes" these ordinary people's lives and the songs that are an integral part of their personal life experiences.

When the program became available for overseas audiences, nodojiman provided not only a form of Japanese-language entertainment but also an important diasporic connection for many Japanese expatriates. In Brazil, in particular, nodojiman has occupied a special place in the life of Nikkey immigrants, as they also created a public competition circuit of their own in addition to simply enjoying the satellite broadcast of the Japanese show. "[O]perat[ing] within a highly structured hierarchical network, [nodojiman] linked Japanese-Brazilians together into a broadly based ethnic enclosure" and "[w]ithin the competition, the negotiation of 'Japanese-Brazilian-ness' took place" (Hosokawa 2000, 95). In 2009, when NHK Nagoya launched *Concurso Latino Nodojiman* (Latino Nodojiman Competition) for Nikkey Brazilians living in the Nagoya area, it attracted many contestants from Brazilian communities all over Japan.[5] The overwhelming response indicated how deeply nodojiman singing competitions were engrained in Nikkey Brazilian culture.

As noted, Joe Hirata began singing in local nodojiman and karaoke contests back home in Maringá at an early age. Another Nikkey música sertaneja singer, Marcia Kawashima, from Londrina, Paraná, had similar childhood experiences (Skype interview, 2011).[6] However, Hirata himself had never seriously pursued his dream of becoming a singer while he was in Brazil. Had he not left for Japan as a dekassegui migrant worker, Hirata's successful career as a professional singer would have never been conceivable (Ishi 2003, 215–16) since dekassegui provided him with both the framework and elements essential for his story.

Dekassegui is a Portuguese-language adaptation of the Japanese word *dekasegi* (出稼ぎ), a compound noun made up of two verbs *deru* (go out) and *kasegu* (earn). It means "working away from home for money" and refers to the temporary staffing arrangement that migrant workers, mostly manual laborers, seek. In the era of Japan's rapid economic growth in the 1960s and

1970s, the term commonly referred to the seasonal employment that many farmers took in the big cities to earn some extra income during agricultural off-seasons. The term *dekasegi*, as well as this type of seasonal migrant labor, seemed to become rather obsolete in the late 1980s. Interestingly, however, the term returned to common usage with a new, global meaning in the early 1990s when a large number of Nikkey Brazilians "return migrated" to Japan, their ancestral homeland, as dekassegui (デカセーギ) workers.

The massive influx of dekassegui migrants was incited by an immigration law amendment passed by the Japanese government. In June 1990, the government revised the Immigration Control and Refugee Recognition Act (出入国管理及び難民認定法), commonly referred to as the Immigration Law (入国管理法), for the first time in many years. Business leaders, concerned about domestic labor shortages and hoping for alternative resources from abroad, drove the push for the revision. Although the "new immigration law" maintained its overall restrictive principles concerning the entry of unskilled laborers from abroad, the amendment created space to selectively open the labor market to Japanese emigrants living overseas and their families and descendants. In the following fifteen years, the number of return migrants from South American countries, predominantly from Brazil, continued to rise. At the time of my initial research in 2005–2006, over 320,000 dekassegui workers and their families from Brazil had taken up residence in different parts of Japan, forming the third-largest ethnic minority after Koreans and Chinese. Although the number significantly decreased after the financial crisis in 2008, many who had been in the so-called "permanent sojourner" status in 2005–2006 more permanently settled in Japan.

Hirata came to Japan as a dekassegui worker in 1988 and engaged in various blue-collar jobs for six or seven years before his singing career unexpectedly took off in 1995. Leaving his pregnant wife in Brazil, Hirata had no intention to try his luck as a singer in a country ten thousand miles away from home. However, one of his coworkers, recognizing Hirata's musical talent in singing karaoke, secretly sent in an application for Hirata to compete in the NHK nodojiman. Hirata won the local competition and proceeded to the grand championship held in Tokyo in order to compete with all other local champions. Hirata recounted his excitement at being in the prestigious NHK Hall for the grand championship. "I was elated, as I was standing on the same stage that those famous singers sang on at the time of the *Kōhaku Utagassen*.[7] I saw them on TV!" (Hirata, lecture performance at Musashi University, 2005, translated from Japanese by the author). When he successfully won the grand championship in 1994, Hirata became the first "foreigner" to do so.

Winning the grand championship and standing in the spotlight was undoubtedly a life-changing experience for a nameless dekassegui worker and an important milestone in Hirata's success story. However, while Hirata's "dream-come-true" story celebrates his first major professional accomplishment, the narrative lacks a strong-willed protagonist who strives to realize his personal dream and would not mind sacrificing all else, which is often a critical element of a success story, as in many música sertaneja songs. Other episodes incorporated into Hirata's success story also essentially reject such heroic but "selfish" pursuits by emphasizing Hirata's initial disinterest in the opportunity (it was not Hirata but his coworker who sent an entry application) and depicting him as a responsible family man. The narrative also establishes the extremely personal nature of his singing. "I cried every time I remembered my wife and my son who was born after I left Brazil. I had seen him only in pictures ..." (Hirata, quoted in Ishi 2003, 215). When the distress of separation and alienation became unbearable, Hirata sought solace in singing to overcome his homesickness and to bemoan his loneliness; he sang nightly in his solitude, sometimes in his small apartment and other times out in the nearby rice field. After the grand championship nodojiman competition in 1994, Hirata eventually opted to return to Brazil to reunite with his wife and son, turning down a recording contract offered by a Japanese record company (Ishi 2003, 215). Notwithstanding the "stupid" decision to pass up the big chance, this episode only added another favorable characteristic to his reputation and his identity narrative as a responsible family man.

FROM PERSONAL STORY TO CORPORATE NARRATIVE

In the university lecture hall, Hirata's perfectly timed lecture continued flawlessly, using a video clip from the grand championship competition, his singing, and jokes as punctuation points.[8] In the video clip of the grand championship competition, Hirata did not wear a cowboy outfit but a nice white jacket with a black ribbon tie and a pair of black pants. In the background, an image of his baby was projected on a large screen as the MC of the grand championship competition introduced Hirata and his dekassegui story. After nervously answering the MC's questions, the young, shy Hirata started singing a J-pop song that would win him a grand champion title at the end of the day.

Hirata, who lived in Japan for a total of ten years, spoke to the audience in the lecture hall in fluent Japanese. Although Ishi jumped in here and there to

Joe Hirata telling his life story at Musashi University, Tokyo, July 2005. Photograph by the author.

help Hirata as an interpreter, the singer had a good command on stage and knew how to get the audience's attention. I was attracted to Hirata's polished presentation as much as its dramatic content. It was almost too well-crafted for a singer's stage talk, and the gap between the young, shy Hirata in the video clip and the confident demeanor of the singer in front of me was quite fascinating. I later found out that Hirata had delivered similar presentations hundreds of times and that this was a performance of his identity narrative that he had perfected when he worked for a São Paulo–based health insurance company, Nipomed Sistema de Saúde (Nipomed Health System). The company, whose primary business was health insurance, had recently launched a new business of selling a self-motivation program, "Basic Courses for Success," designed for aspiring dekassegui workers in Japan. Learning about Hirata's now widely disseminated story, thanks to the *Nodojiman* broadcast, Nipomed recruited Hirata as the company's "official artist," or image character, so to speak.

> The company claimed that Hirata's character matched Nipomed's spirit. He was chosen not because of his sweet voice, but because of his tough life history. Hirata began to entertain the guests at every Nipomed event. He

was not a mere singer; between songs, the organisers projected videotapes narrating Hirata's dramatic life history, to show how he suffered and how hard he worked until he obtained success—the experience of working in a factory, winning the TV contest, defeating Japanese rivals, and giving up a big music career in the name of the "family." (Ishi 2003, 215–16)

While it is of no doubt that the company deployed Hirata's personal story for its own benefit, Ishi analyzes Hirata's decision to become an image character for Nipomed's self-motivation program as a strategic choice—his response to the new possibilities available in the era of global marketing. During his time with Nipomed, Hirata took full advantage of the transnational company's marketing network while bringing them profit. "He did not need his own concerts, since the 'Basic Courses for Success' were his main 'stage.' His first CD sold around 30,000 copies, thanks to a 'direct mail' campaign within the 'Nipomed family'" (Ishi 2003, 216). When Hirata decided in 1999 to cut his ties with Nipomed and move his base to Brazil, instead of going back and forth between Nikkey communities in Brazil and Japan, he had already established a good reputation in both countries—a solid foundation for a successful career as an ethnic community singer (Ishi 2003, 216).

SONHO DE UM BRASILEIRO (DREAM OF A BRAZILIAN)

Dekassegui provided a narrative framework for experiences of separation, loss, fragmentation, and homesickness shared by many Nikkey immigrants. For Hirata, as noted above, these experiences and emotions were extremely private affairs. The personal story, however, became part of this collective identity narrative, as it found an audience and a market via Nipomed's image character campaign for "Basic Courses for Success." Hirata recorded his first CD, *Lembranças* (Memories),[9] during his Nipomed years. It consists of two popular J-pop songs: "Lembranças," a Portuguese cover of "Saigo no Iiwake" (The Last Excuse) by Tokunaga Hideaki, and Nakanishi Yasushi's[10] "Last Call," which Hirata sang in Japanese. Being a J-pop cover, and musically not in the música sertaneja style, "Lembranças" set the basic characters of the identity narrative that Hirata would continue to enact in his later música sertaneja songs. While both Hirata's Portuguese version and Tokunaga's original lyrics deal with separation, in Hirata's version the male protagonist reminisces about the love he left behind, whereas Tokunaga's male protagonist agonizes over the relationship that is about to end, feeling helpless as his lover had already made up her mind to leave him. In contrast to the sad, regretful tone of Tokunaga's story set in the sleepless night, Hirata sings about the love that still endures after many years of separation in a much more positive tone, remembering the good old days with dreams, sunshine, and the beautiful moon. Hirata's version contains all the formulaic expressions of música sertaneja; the lyrics alone would pass as a música sertaneja song.

Although Hirata continues to incorporate a wide variety of Japanese popular songs into his recording and concert repertoire for his Nikkey audience in Brazil, he began to rework his identity narrative more consciously and chose música sertaneja as a vehicle for performative expression after he returned to São Paulo in 1999. On the jacket of his second CD, *Sonho de um Brasileiro* (Dream of a Brazilian), released in June 1999, Hirata presented himself as a música sertaneja singer for the first time. Dressed in a gray plaid/striped shirt and a cowboy hat, Hirata poses as a young cowboy against the backdrop of a rural farm in this picture. As he stands behind the weathered farm fence, which serves as the lower border of the picture, the viewer encounters a young *brasileiro* looking straight into her/his eye from the other side of the boundary. The fourteen-track album includes covers of different Brazilian popular songs, the aforementioned "Lembranças," as well as a few original songs, all sung in Portuguese. The album's title song, "Sonho de um Brasileiro," is one of the original songs, and its lyrics are decidedly autobiographical. The story, which begins with a young man's departure for Japan from his native place of Maringá, Paraná, follows the trajectory of Hirata's personal journey. Although the lyrics do not use the word dekassegui, it makes many clear references to the life of dekkasegui migrant workers and their hardships integral to the story: for example, inclusion of the Japanese word *zangyo* (work overtime), which many dekassegui workers are quick to learn at work. However, Hirata's "success story" highlighted in the corporate narrative vanished from this new identity narrative; the central thread of the story is the young man's return to his home, where nothing has changed, and the reunion with his family. The protagonist ends his story with a confident reclamation of his spatial identity: "Muito obrigado japão / Por me acolher por me cuidar / Muito obrigado japão / Mas o brasil é o meu lugar" (Thank you Japan / For welcoming me and taking care of me / Thank you, Japan / But Brazil is my place). In another track, "Pedaço de Chão" (Piece of Land), the theme of homecoming and reunion is addressed metaphorically, as the protagonist returns to the piece of land where he planted his heart and let his roots grow (the first verse) and the piece of land where he had everything he wanted but hadn't realized it (the second verse); the land is, after all, a piece of himself (chorus).

Joe Hirata, *Sonho de um Brasileiro* album cover. Courtesy of Joe Hirata.

Hirata's identity search continues in his subsequent work after he terminated his business partnership with Nipomed. In his third mini-album CD, *Reencontro* (Reunion, Reconnection, or Rediscovery) (2005), homecoming, reunion, and the rediscovery of one's true self (after making some bad decisions and youthful mistakes) serve as central themes for the album's title song. The song recounts the protagonist's desire not only to return to his home and family but also to rekindle the old dreams that he once gave up and to reconnect with his true self, a self deeply rooted in his hometown. Although Hirata's narrative resonates with the typical música sertaneja storyline for the most part, here the protagonist's spatiotemporal standpoint is significantly different. In analyzing the classic música sertaneja song, "Tristeza do Jeca" (The Sadness of Armadillo Joe), the ethnomusicologist Alexander Dent identifies what he calls "the Jeca theme," variations of which prevail in many música sertaneja songs, a theme that "continues to shape the way the music fashions the split subjectivity" (2009, 57). "The Jeca theme and variations' most important attribute," argues Dent, "is that the singing, playing, and listening subject separates a debased urban present from an idealized rural past and then *uses* that rural past as a means to reprimand the present" (2009, 29). Typical música sertaneja songs provide a means of catharsis in which the protagonist musically grieves for the quandary of his split self as he bemoans his inability to return to the idyllic past "not only because the past is closed to him, but because to return to [the past] would mean relinquishing the present" (Dent 2009, 30–31). Hirata's protagonists, however, are decidedly homebound, if not already back home, and their redemptive narrative more positively embraces both the past and the present in their stories, exalting the regained completeness as a result of homecoming, instead of grieving for the self split between the "debased urban present" and the "idealized rural past."

It is important to note that, in Hirata's Nikkey música sertaneja, the context of transnational dekassegui migration adds another layer of meaning to the narrative of homecoming and rediscovery of one's spatial identity, since the search for identity in them is inseparable from migrants' recent experiences of alienation and marginalization in their ancestral homeland in Japan (Ishi 2008; Linger 2001, 2003; Lorenz 2007; Oba 2012; Roth 2005; Tsuda 2003). In his book *Strangers in the Ethnic Homeland: Japanese Brazilian Return Migration in Transnational Perspective,* Takeyuki Tsuda delineates the specific conditions of dekassegui migration and their impact on the formation of a distinctive diasporic national consciousness:

> As migrants go abroad and become new ethnic minorities in the host society, they sometimes develop a much stronger sense of belonging and allegiance toward their home country than they had *before* migration, leading to a type of "deterritorialized nationalism," where national loyalties are solidified outside the territorial boundaries of the nation-state. In this manner, migration reveals one of the ironies of nationalism: it is precisely physical absence from the nation-state that enables national sentiments to be intensified, enhanced, and articulated. (2003, 156)

In this phase of his career, Hirata engaged in the issue of spatial identity in more consciously nationalized terms. As indicated in the title of his second album, *Sonho de um Brasileiro,* Hirata began to enact his identity as *um brasileiro* more performatively by adopting the quintessential Brazilianness that música sertaneja had fashioned and popularized. While, in Hirata's narrative, the deterritorialized protagonist's strong urge to go home and reunite with his Brazilian homeland facilitates a reconciliation of the subjectivity spatially split between two countries by dekassegui, the heightened national consciousness also highlights Nikkey Brazilians' not-easily-reconcilable dual identity—a conflict between the external ethnic Japaneseness and the internal cultural Brazilianness—in more consciously nationalized terms.

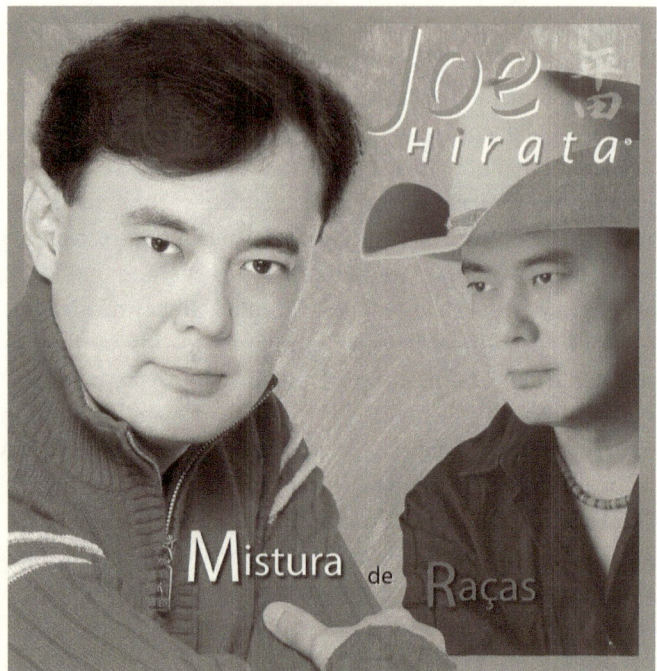

Joe Hirata, Mistura de Raças album cover. Courtesy of Joe Hirata.

Hirata most defiantly addressed the unsettling dual identity issue in his third album, *Reencontro*, and his fifth album, *Mistura de Raças* (2007). In good contrast to the image of brasileiro that he enacted in *Sonho de um Brasileiro*, for *Reencontro* Hirata adopted an album design that evokes his outer Japaneseness, with signifiers such as the red and white of the Japanese national flag, his family name written in Japanese *kanji* characters and set vertically in the center of the design, and a close-up shot of a set of black eyes. The music, though, embraces his inner Brazilian self, and, completely betrays the outer appearance. The design shares an underlying idea with the metaphor of the "banana," applied to westernized Asians with white substance under yellow skin. For *Mistura de Raças* (Mixing of Races), the upcoming centennial celebration of Japanese immigration to Brazil in 2008 provided Hirata with a new framework to negotiate Nikkey Brazilians' place in greater Brazilian history and culture. "Raça e Ginga Misturou" (Race and Groove Mixed), a song on this album that was performed over and over as a "theme song" of the centennial celebration in Nikkey community events, carried a particularly important political message.[11] In this piece Hirata not only addresses the duality of Nikkey Brazilian identity with provocative lyrics and performative visuals, as in his earlier works, but also sonically claims its space in the performance of brasilidade by incorporating the Japanese *taiko* drumming into the typical música sertaneja instrumentation. Instead of simply adding exotic flair to music of colonial origin, the taiko drumming challenges the way brasilidade is manifested in the distinctive rhythmic groove, *ginga*—a musical feature that has been used to mark Nikkey Brazilians as perpetual outsiders in the mainstream Brazilian discourse due to their perceived inability to understand or feel its quintessentially Brazilian essence (Lorenz 2007, 2011). But what is brasilidade anyway? And which Brazilians define it for whom? In the one hundred years of Nikkey Brazilian history, the taiko drumming that had originated in Japan took roots in its new home in Brazil and became an important cultural expression of the Nikkey Brazilian community. While a different beat of taiko drumming in Brazil marks its ethnic and cultural difference, after a hundred years, should it not deserve recognition as a beat of Brazil, a beat different yet as Brazilian as ginga? What Hirata demands in juxtaposing two different embodied grooves in "Raça e Ginga Misturou" is not necessarily a mixing or blending of the two races and cultures; it is rather a recognition of their coexistence in Brazilian society and history and the need of a more inclusive brasilidade narrative that would better represent its diversity.

DUPLAS

In addition to the taiko drumming, Hirata's solo singing style also sets him apart from the mainstream música sertaneja tradition. As earlier noted, the large majority of música sertaneja songs are performed by male duos called *duplas*. Although there are some exceptional cases of father-son and female-voice duos, it is traditionally two "brothers" (if not biological male siblings, two men of similar age) that perform duplas. Unlike many other genres of Brazilian popular music, which are identified by distinctive rhythmic patterns, it is the vocal harmony the two singers create at the interval of the third (or the sixth in inversion) that sonically constitutes música sertaneja as a distinctive genre of music. In analyzing the importance of this particular mode of performance, Dent distinguishes the "unified voices" of male siblings in the dupla from other types of musical harmony, which "calls attention to a multiplicity of voices singing together" (Dent 2009, 76) and expands on their different implications:

> To elaborate on the importance of melded voices, good duplas stay in tune with each other no matter what happens musically.... [I]n marked contrast with most other musical genres involving harmony, practitioners deem the togetherness of the two voices more significant than whether the overall effect remains in tune with the key of the piece as started in the song's opening—though hopefully being out of tune should not occur too often. (Dent 2009, 75–76)

Dent argues that such strong preference for unified voices in traditional música sertaneja indicates that the dupla is a sonic reminder of what was "actually sung and heard as one" before rural-urban migration significantly transformed rural subjectivity (Dent 2009, 64). The sustained popularity of duplas and the sonic enactment of "brotherhood" in them, whether the two singers are real brothers or not, is a manifestation of the fetishized longing for what was lost in this process. It "promises to underscore the continued efficacy for kinship for understanding social relations and cultural production ... [that goes beyond] conventional anthropological associations" (Dent 2009, 60). The performance of brotherhood provides a means to reconcile, if only temporarily, the various fragmentations resulting from the transition to modern urban life. Hence "the singing 'voice' is Brazilian rural music's most important attribute" (Dent 2009, 75).

Hirata's solo singing style well suits the "self-made man" narrative that he enacted in his personal story and the corporate image for Nipomed, but Hirata's music thus lacks the smooth two-voice harmony of dupla, which, Dent argues (and many Brazilians would concur), is an essential attribute of música sertaneja. Despite its questionable musical authenticity, Hirata pursues his música sertaneja singer persona seriously, and the music's nationwide popularity and cosmopolitan appeal across socioeconomic as well as regional boundaries is a reason behind his persistence. Hirata's agenda is dual-purpose: "I would like to break the stereotypical image of Nikkey [typically defined solely by their ethnic/cultural/racial otherness]," said Hirata. "I want to show we too are Brazilians; we like things that all other Brazilians like" (Hirata, personal conversation after his lecture-performance, 2005). It is important to note that in Hirata's perspective, música sertaneja is deemed not so much a portal to the brasilidade associated with the irretrievable past and the remote back country but rather an ongoing nationwide phenomenon. The recent industry trend, which features superstar solo male singers such as Michel Teló and Gusttavo Lima,[12] especially in the sub-genre of música sertaneja called *sertanejo universitario*, is a coincidence that works in Hirata's favor.

Other Nikkey música sertaneja singers do not seem to find male-sibling duplas particularly attractive or a suitable mode of presentation for their own performances either. Although they regularly listen to and enjoy dancing to the music of different duplas like Chitãozinho e Xororó, Zezé Di Camargo e Luciano, and Munhos e Mariano, the distinctive dupla style does not seem to have the kind of strong emotional appeal to them that Dent (2009) suggests. The reasons why they did not opt for the authentic male-voice duplas vary and are practical rather than ideological, though. Marcos Hatano, like Hirata, became a singer after winning a grand championship in the *Latino Nodojiman*. As he entered and moved up in the hierarchical structure of nodojiman as an individual contestant, it was a natural choice for him to continue performing solo.[13] Luciano Alvez eventually formed a dupla with a male friend, but the duo was short-lived due to scheduling difficulties for the two singers and some management problems. Alvez now performs solo with his band (Alvez interview, 2016). Although they are back in Brazil, Marcia e João Victor, also known as Novo Tempo, was a very popular dupla during their time in Japan. Although their musical backgrounds back home in Brazil were rather different, they decided to perform as an atypical wife-husband dupla rather than having João seek a male musical partner. For Marcia and Joaõ, it was only a natural choice, as they were already a married couple (Kawashima, Skype interview, 2011).

These Nikkey música sertaneja singers also tend to perform current and recent popular songs using the instrumentations typical of contemporary, more commercialized versions of música sertaneja, including electric guitar, bass, and synthesizer. Interestingly, the only dupla that devotedly performs traditional música sertaneja features two Japanese (not Nikkey) musicians, Nakanuma Hiroshi (Armando) on *viola caipira* (a traditional Brazilian folk instrument of colonial origin associated with *música caipira*, an earlier form of "country music") and Okuyama Kaori (Marina) on guitar. Unlike Marcia e João Victor, Nakanuma and Okuyama are not a married couple. Their relationship is "professional," as they work independently with other musical groups in their respective networks; they present themselves as Armando e Marina only when they perform as a dupla. Nakanuma, who is an accomplished multi-instrumentalist, learned to play the *viola caipira* by watching YouTube videos (Okuyama and Nakanuma, personal interview, 2014). Nakanuma is probably the only Japanese who professionally plays this instrument, whose preservation is considered to be of national interest by the Brazilian Ministry of Culture.[14] Interestingly, however, Nakanuma's rare talent has never been in high demand in the Brazilian community away from home. Nakanuma and Okuyama switch their instruments to steel guitar and *sanfona* (accordion), respectively, when they perform as members of Luciano Alvez's band for Brazilian community events; they almost never appear as a dupla in this context.

The absence of traditional duplas in Nikkey Brazilian música sertaneja, however, does not necessarily mean that the music this population performs and listens to is not meant or able to provide the experience of unity in performance, or to provide opportunities to manage their split subjectivity, torn between two homes in Japan and Brazil. In the last section of this essay, I will discuss distinctive ways that música sertaneja facilitates the bonding needed for this particular community.

MÚSICA SERTANEJA IN THE BRAZILIAN COMMUNITY IN JAPAN

Although so far I have discussed música sertaneja mostly as a narrative vocal music genre, contemporary música sertaneja repertoires include a significant number of dance tunes, or danceable tunes, which incorporate influences from various regional dance music styles and rhythms, especially *forró*, an accordion-driven joyful dance music from the Northeast. These *forró*-inspired tunes, in fact, are extremely popular among Nikkey Brazilians living in Japan, as public couples dancing is a cultural practice deeply engrained in their social life. Sueli Gushi, a Nikkey Brazilian samba singer who also occasionally includes música sertaneja songs in her concert programs, makes note of the different reactions of her Japanese and Nikkey Brazilian audiences and the importance of participatory dancing at the events attended predominantly by the latter audience: "I like singing for [a] Japanese audience. They listen to the music [even though they don't understand Portuguese lyrics]. Brazilians enjoy the music, but mostly, they come to dance" (personal conversation, 2014, translated from Japanese by the author).[15]

During my fieldwork in Japan, I occasionally came across scenes that impressed me how deeply engrained in the culture of Nikkey Brazilians the practice of public couples dancing is. For example, in a mini-concert featuring Sueli Gushi's solo singing, two of the singer's Nikkey Brazilian friends in the audience left their seats in the middle of the show and started dancing in a narrow passage between tables in the very crowded restaurant. Two weeks after his lecture-performance at Musashi University, I also observed Joe Hirata's performance as part of a summer festival event organized by the Brazilian community in Ōizumi, in Gunma Prefecture. The program showcased different Brazilian music styles and community talents: Hirata showed up in the middle of it and sang a few songs on the little stage set up in the storefront of a Brazilian grocery. The audience's response to the frivolous *forró*-inspired song recorded as the "B-side" of the aforementioned "Reencontro" was especially phenomenal. The music really turned them on, and soon the small festival ground in a back alley was filled and overflowing with people dancing both in pairs and solo, moving around with light and easy steps and movements. Because of the enthusiastic response, the organizers had to extend Hirata's performance by fifteen minutes. A Japanese friend also shared with me her "culture shock" experience—couples dancing that she had observed during halftime of a FIFA World Cup soccer match in a sports bar in a Brazilian community in Japan. When the first half of the game came to a close, the small venue was filled with the music that the DJ blasted and people started couples dancing. "I was really impressed that these folks never sit idle during the intermission," she said. "And I was completely alienated as I watch[ed] everyone socialize as they dance[d] around in the small crowded venue" (personal email conversation, 2007). Despite our shared "Japanese" identity, the way Nikkey Brazilians engage in social dance, especially couples dancing, pointedly differentiates Nikkey Brazilian culture from the culture of mainstream Japanese society. Like my friend in the Brazilian sports bar, I found myself completely out of my element in such an environment (Oba 2012).

For the Nikkey Brazilians who feel alienated in their ancestral homeland of Japan and marginalized from mainstream Japanese society, dancing undoubtedly plays a very important role in their ongoing emplacement and the construction of their identity narrative in the displacement. First of all, dancing turns passive spectators into active participants and cocreators of the *comunidade*. Secondly, dancing facilitates a public display of embodied diasporic history through distinctive ways Nikkey Brazilians mark their space, and thereby demarcates their unique cultural identity from their ethnic kin in Japan. Thirdly, public couples dancing enables Nikkey Brazilians to subvert the power dynamic between them and the host society, if only temporarily, by turning Japanese people into clueless outsiders in their own country. Furthermore, a closer look at community events involving public couples dancing reveals another important thread of the Nikkey Brazilian identity narrative: *família* (family).

As in most other communities, couples dancing provides the Nikkey Brazilian community with opportunities for courtship and socialization. In this community, however, public couples dancing associated with música sertaneja also strongly projects the importance of family, especially the wife-husband relationship as its foundation. Public display of familial love occurs in both insular community events and big public events, as if there were no difference between the two. At the end of his performance in the Festival Brasil 2014, an annual mega-festival held at Yoyogi Park in the center of Tokyo,[16] the música sertaneja singer Marcos Hatano took the time to invite and introduce his family on stage, acknowledging their support for his successful career as a singer. This loving gesture was somewhat odd in front of thousands of anonymous people in the crowd in the center of Tokyo (many of them fashionable Japanese youths), yet made a strong impression as to what matters to the singer and his community. In 2016, on the same stage of Festival Brasil, the featured música sertaneja singer, Luciano Alvez, was surrounded by happily dancing middle-aged couples, many of whom were his friends, fans, supporters from his community, as he shared his original song "Minha Deusa" (My Goddess).[17] I recognized husband-wife pairs I had seen in many other insular community events. The presence of a father-daughter pair among these "regulars" further confirmed the familial nature of the couples dancing. Although the lyrics of Alvez's song do not specify the identity of his *deusa*, the scene on stage enhanced the impression that the simple love song is a direct expression of love for one's life partner and family. As indicated in Hirata's life story discussed earlier, the separation of family is one of the most difficult issues that confront people in transnational dekassegui migration. A large majority of dekassegui migrants are in their thirties, forties, and sometimes fifties, and many of them left their families in Brazil when they came to Japan. It took years for many families to reunite in either Brazil or Japan. A number of others couldn't outlast the challenge of split living to see a happy ending. Although musically "Minha Deusa" is in a pop modern *sertaneja universitario* arrangement, Alvez's lyrics—especially its metaphors of olfactory and tactile sensations (scent, warmth, etc.)—provide a different narrative of love, a love that is *inteira* (eternal and whole), as opposed to either the love lost forever in typical música sertaneja songs or the impetuous passion involved in courtship, and the intimate couples dancing that spontaneously broke out embodied the story.

As noted by Nikkey Brazilian community leader Isamu Paulo Hirano, the specific conditions that resulted from dekassegui could have created a unique niche in which wife and husband duplas like Marcia e João Victor could have enjoyed a modest professional success, if the impact of global market crash in 2008 did not force them to return to Brazil with their two young children (personal conversation, 2015).[18]

CONCLUSION

Until recently it was a familiar scene in the entertainment establishments in Brazilian communities in Japan to have videos of current música sertaneja hits—excerpts of superstars' concert videos in particular—projected onto the screen as a background to the performance that was happening in real time on stage. Although the volume of the video was turned off, the audience saw two unrelated performances of Brazilian music simultaneously. The moment the performance on stage ended, the DJ would rev up the volume of the video, and the sound of música sertaneja blasting from large speakers would quite literally fill the venue during the intermission, which was as long as the performance itself. Watching on the screen the concert happening halfway around the globe, I often wondered which of the two was the main act here.

Música sertaneja spoke and continues to speak for people's shared experiences of displacement and alienation and nostalgic longing for what they left behind, both in their real lives and in their romantic imaginings. In the context of recent transnational dekassegui migration, the formulaic stories of fragmentation and split subjectivity have been integrated and reworked to meet the unique emotional needs of Nikkey Brazilians who are torn between two places called "home." A destabilized sense of belonging and experiences of alienation in their ancestral homeland prompted in them pro-Brazil reactions and a heightened sense of Brazilianness. However, Nikkey Brazilians' desire to make their connection with Brazil current negates nostalgic return to the narrative past, which failed to warrant them a space. The eye-dazzling presentation of two unrelated performances that perplexed me in the darkness of the Brazilian disco is in a way a manifestation of their reality. Through the "co-constitution of time and space in [such] activity" (Munn 1992, 97), Nikkey Brazilians not only engage in the cocreation of a split subjectivity from afar, but also belatedly yet progressively claim their space in the brasilidade narrative, at least in their imagination.

ACKNOWLEDGMENTS

I would like to express my sincere gratitude to the musicians who generously took the time to speak with me and share their knowledge and stories in person and via Skype and email: Joe Hirata, Marcia Kawashima and João Victor, Sueli Gushi, Luciano Alvez, Hiroshi Nakanuma, and Kaori Okuyama. Joe Hirata kindly granted me permission to use his official promotional materials and provided me with high-resolution images. My special thanks also go to members of Nikkey Brazilian communities in Japan: Professor Angelo Ishi, Isamu Paulo Hirano, Rafael Kinoshita, Tomio Kinoshita, Melissa Sanada, and many others; Miharu Matsuhashi and members of the community volunteer group Kimobig Brasil; Hampshire College, for funding my follow-up research in Japan; and Mintaro Oba, for his research and editorial assistance.

BIBLIOGRAPHY

Becker, Cezar de A. 2010. "Ivan Miyazato—O Japonês que renovou o sertanejo." May 24, 2010. http://www.asmelhoressertanejas.com.br/2010/05/ivan-miyazato-o-japones-que-renovou-o.html. Accessed June 18, 2016.

Dent, Alexander. 2009. *River of Tears: Country Music, Memory, and Modernity in Brazil*. Durham, NC: Duke University Press.

Hirata, Joe. Joe Hirata website. http://joehirata.com.br/. Accessed April 2, 2018.

Hosokawa, Shuhei. 2000. "Singing Contests in the Ethnic Enclosure of the Post-War Japanese-Brazilian Community." *British Journal of Ethnomusicology* 9 (1): 95–118.

Ishi, Angelo. 2003. "Transnational Strategies by Japanese-Brazilian Migrants in the Age of IT." In *Global Japan: The Experience of Japan's New Immigrant and Overseas Communities*, edited by Roger Goodman, et al., 209–21. London and New York: RoutledgeCurzon.

Linger, Daniel. 2001. *No One Home: Brazilian Selves Remade in Japan*. Stanford, CA: Stanford University Press.

Linger, Daniel. 2003. "Do Japanese Brazilians Exist?" In *Searching for Home Abroad: Japanese Brazilians and Transnationalism*, edited by Jeffrey Lesser, 201–14. Durham, NC: Duke University Press.

López-Calvo, Ignacio. 2019. *Japanese-Brazilian Saudades: Diasporic Identities and Cultural Production*. George and Sakaye Aratani Nikkei in the Americas Series. Louisville: University Press of Colorado.

Lorenz, Shanna. 2007. "'Japanese in the Samba': Japanese Brazilian Musical Citizenship, Racial Consciousness, and Transnational Migration." PhD diss., University of Pittsburgh.

Lorenz, Shanna. 2011. "Zhen Brasil's Japanese Brazilian Groove." In *Brazilian Popular Music and Citizenship*, edited by Idelber Avelar and Christopher Dunn, 155–71. Durham, NC: Duke University Press.

Munn, Nancy D. 1992. "The Cultural Anthropology of Time: A Critical Essay." *Annual Review of Anthropology* 21: 93–123.

Murphy, John P. 2006. *Music in Brazil: Experiencing Music, Expressing Culture*. Oxford and New York: Oxford University Press.

Oba, Junko. 2012. "Performing 'Japaneseness' in a Time of Post-National Transition." PhD diss., Wesleyan University.

Riley, Suzel Ana. 1992. "Música sertaneja and Migrant Identity: The Stylistic Development of a Brazilian Genre." *Popular Music* 11 (3): 337–58.

Roth, Joshua Hotaka. 2005. "Political and Cultural Perspectives on 'Insider' Minorities." In *A Companion to the Anthropology of Japan*, edited by Jennifer Robertson, 73–88. Malden, MA, and Oxford: Blackwell.

Tsuda, Takeyuki. 2003. *Strangers in the Ethnic Homeland: Japanese Brazilian Return Migration in Transnational Perspective*. New York: Columbia University Press.

DISCOGRAPHY

Joe Hirata. 1998. *Lembranças*. Nipo Music.
Joe Hirata. 1999. *Sonho de um Brasileiro*. Nipo Music.
Joe Hirata. 2005. *Reencontro*. Independent release by Joe Hirata.
Joe Hirata. 2007. *Mistura de Raças*. Independent release by Joe Hirata.
Lourenço e Lourival. 1998. *Os três Boiaderos Japoneses*. RGE.

NOTES

1. Although *Nikkei* is the spelling more commonly seen in English-language literature, I use *Nikkey* in this essay as it is how the word is spelled in Brazil. It also can mean Brazilians of Japanese ancestry descended from Japanese Americans. Despite many similar diasporic experiences, the histories of and situations surrounding these two groups are significantly different. "Nikkei" primarily refers to the latter, especially in North American English-language discourse. When *Nikkei* is used in the works cited, I follow the original authors' choice.

2. Joe Hirata lecture-performance, Musashi University, Tokyo, July 21, 2005. Hirata's biographical information appearing in this essay are from this lecture, a conversation I had with Hirata after this lecture, and stories posted on Hirata's official website, http://joehirata.com.br.

3. Official website of NHK *Nodojiman*: http://www.nhk.or.jp/nodojiman/ (Japanese only). Accessed August 23, 2016.

4. Official blog site of NHK *Nodojiman*, which introduces regional cultures of the places it travels to each week: http://www.nhk.or.jp/nodojiman-blog/ (Japanese only). Accessed August 23, 2016.

5. A video recording of "Concurso Latino Nodojiman 2009" on *agenda+*, a variety information program on IPCTV Globo Internacional, was posted on YouTube on August 6, 2009. Available at https://youtu.be/YmOo5Q2QiI4. Accessed September 5, 2012.

6. The Skype interview with Marcia Kawashima and João Victor on July 27, 2011, was conducted in a mix of Portuguese and Japanese. Special thanks to the couple and Marcia's mother, who helped me communicate with Marcia and João as an interpreter.

7. Japan's annual year-end songfest, also hosted by NHK, features popular professional singers. The show has been widely broadcast in Japanese diasporas via satellite TV.

8. The video clip is available on Hirata's official website, http://joehirata.com.br/videos/. Accessed August 23, 2016.

9. All of Hirata's recordings are available for streaming on his official website, together with the images of the CD jackets, at http://joehirata.com.br/discografia/. Accessed August 23, 2016.

10. The names of Japanese artists appear in the order of family name, then given name, according to the Japanese convention.

11. Video clips of Hirata's appearances on Brazilian talk shows hosted by Jô Soares and Hebe Camargo respectively are available on Hirata's official website, http://joehirata.com.br/videos/.

12. It is interesting that the mastermind behind this solo trend in contemporary música sertaneja is the Nikkey Brazilian producer Ivan Miyazato.

13. 「名古屋ブラジルフェスタ」出演アーティスト紹介：マルコス・トシオ・ハタノ (Marcos Toshio Hatano artist profile, Nagoya Brazil Festa). Posted June 3, 2014. http://megabrasil.jp/20140603_9844/. Accessed August 23, 2016.

14. For more information about the preservation of the *viola caipira* tradition in Brazil, see the website of Associaçaõ Naciocal dos Violeiros do Brasil, founded in 2004, https://anvbrasil.wordpress.com/.

15. For more information about Sueli Gushi, see her music blog site, *Eu Canto Samba*, http://cantorasueligushi.blogspot.com. Accessed August 23, 2016.

16. The annual summer festival sponsored by Câmara de Comercío Brasileira no Japão (Brazilian Chamber of Commerce in Japan) celebrated its eleventh year in 2016. The show, featuring different Brazilian musics, is a main attraction of the two-day outdoor festival. The program usually includes a few "big name" headliners invited from Brazil as well as musicians and groups based in Japan. The event is supported by the Brazilian government and corporate sponsors, and all activities are free and open to the public. Every year thousands of visitors enjoy different Brazilian musics and Brazilian foods. Festival Brasil official website: http://www.festivalbrasil.jp/. Accessed August 23, 2016.

17. The lyrics of "Minha Deusa" are available at https://www.letras.mus.br/luciano-alves/minha-deusa/. The music is available at https://youtu.be/g1t8L5hjXhw. Accessed August 23, 2016.

18. Marcia e Joaõ Victor (Novo Tempo) were among the featured local artists in Festival Brasil 2009. Since their return to Brazil at the end of that year, they have visited Japan for short tours at the invitation of Nikkey Brazilian promotors and sponsors in 2016 and 2018.

10

LA MÚSICA RANCHERA IN THE RECONFIGURATION OF HISPANISMO AND MEXICANIDAD IN MUSICAL EXCHANGES BETWEEN SPAIN AND MEXICO

MARTHA I. CHEW SÁNCHEZ

In this chapter, I explore notions of *hispanidad* in transatlantic imaginaries, specifically the case of *música ranchera* in *hispanismo*, emerging out of musical exchanges between Spain and Mexico. I examine the continuous negotiations and dialogues happening within the expressive form of *música ranchera*.

One of my objectives is to treat exemplary expressions of música ranchera in case studies. In what follows, I place special emphasis on: (1) the construction of hispanismo during *la época de oro del cine mexicano* (the "golden age of Mexican cinema," 1936–59);[1] (2) musical and filmic transatlantic exchanges between Spain and Latin American during *franquismo* (1939–75) and up to to Spain's membership in the European Union (1984); (3) the construction of *mexicanidad* in the performance of Chavela Vargas, the appropriation of Lucha Reyes's *estilo bravío* from the period of the Mexican Revolution, and the forgotten legacy of Cuco Sánchez in Chavela Vargas; and (4) the new transatlantic cultural dialogues embodied in Joaquin Sabina. The last two parts highlight the reconfiguration of *mexicanidad* and *hispanidad* during the last two decades within the transatlantic musical exchanges of the música ranchera genre.

FLUID AND NOT SO FLUID IDENTITIES OF HISPANISMO

Hispanismo is similar to "whiteness" in so far as what constitutes whiteness has changed over time in concert with changes in wider political-economic structures and social formations. At the same time, the core racism of whiteness as the normative umbrella concept of the global economic, social, and political order remains unchanged. For example, in the 1860s, Irish and Italian immigrants to the United States served as the constitutive outside to whiteness, only to become absorbed into its center when the discourse of whiteness set itself in opposition to a new migration of Eastern Europeans in the early twentieth century, or in opposition to the Great Migration of African Americans after the Civil War, or Jews after World War II. Hispanismo, like whiteness, is constructed mainly as a response to fear of others, and as an ideology that supports colonialism, imperialism and anti-indigenous sentiment, and promotes a narrow agenda of "purity" of blood and/or culture. Similar fluctuations in who and what counts as hispanismo can be tracked. Despite its historical variability, its core ideology remains unchanged: namely, a strong Spanish, chauvinistic supremacism designed to rationalize colonialism.

Hispanismo has been wrought in Spanish imperial projects during colonization, particularly in Latin America, where Spain imposed its language, religion, colonial government, culture, and customs. Some of the main realignments of hispanismo occurred in periods of economic and political change—often during crises. While officially, and for the most part in Spain, hispanismo is regarded as a historiographic discipline that focuses on the study of culture, language, and literature, in truth hispanismo has been semantically associated with Spanish ancestral purity, Spanish culture and customs, and, geographically with Spain—more precisely, Madrid. The Spanish state has been crucial to the institutional dissemination of *hispanismo* as a core element of Spanish national identity, with *El Día de la Hispanidad* The Day of Hispanidad) and the Instituto Cervantes functioning as the most emblematic day and institution, respectively.[2]

In 1940, in a conscious and explicit effort to shore up a revived *hispanismo* that longed for the days before Spain lost its empire in the previous century, General Francisco Franco founded El Consejo de la Hispanidad, which later became El Instituto de Cultura Hispánica. Franco carried out his campaign for a nostalgic hispanismo through Spanish-language media, particularly the film and musical industries, as the Spanish-language media had blossomed in the 1930s, evolving into important media monopolies. Across the Atlantic, it is during this era that the Mexican XEW radio station was founded, which remains the most powerful AM radio station in North America; Mexican XEW is also the forerunner to the Mexican monopoly Televisa, which for decades, has dominated Spanish-speaking countries and audiences. In fact, Televisa is the most profitable producer, exporter, and distributor of Spanish-language broadcasting, film, publishing, and music recording in the world. Important for understanding why Franco turned to the film and musical industries to reconsolidate hispanismo is the fact that XEW was the springboard for virtually all singers in the Spanish-speaking world as well as the route to Hollywood during the peak of *la época de oro del cine mexicano*. The specific musical genre promoted by XEW, and defining Mexican cinema, was música ranchera.

SPANISH POLITICAL AND ECONOMIC CONDITIONS AND THEIR EFFECTS ON ITS CULTURAL INDUSTRIES' EXCHANGES DURING AND AFTER WORLD WAR II

The world economic and political landscape changes after World War II, of course; the United States became a hegemonic power and its relationships with Latin America in general, and Mexico in particular, took on new forms of domination. Spain turned to Latin American markets mainly because of Spain's peripheral status in Europe. In Spain, the defeat of the Axis powers meant a gradual period of economic decline and the closing of western European markets. The study of how new forms of hispanismo emerged in transatlantic relationships between Spain and Mexico during both the first period of franquismo (1939–59) and the second (1959–75)[3] is warranted because, despite the absence of official diplomatic relations between Mexico and Spain, cultural, religious, and even economic relationships between the two countries never fully ceased. Hence, Franco attempted to restore Spain's hegemony—and new forms of hispanismo—among its former colonies (and globally) after World War II using these extra-political ties. The medium of his imperial project was the cultural imaginary of folkloric traditions mainly from Andalucia, Spain, and Jalisco, Mexico—such as música ranchera. Essentially, regional folkloric traditions were elevated and exoticized to represent the whole of both Spain and Mexico's national cultural identities.

To appropriate and shape the popular genre of música ranchera for imperial ends, despite Mexico's official policy wherein they broke all diplomatic ties with Spain in their rejection of franquismo and their support of Spanish Republicans, Franco exploited persisting relationships between Spain and Mexico that were unintentionally bolstered by US investments in Mexican cinema. The Mexican president, Lázaro Cárdenas (1934–40), was openly socialist, and supported the Second Spanish Republic. Cárdenas had a policy of welcoming to Mexico political and European war refugees who were in opposition to franquismo, fascism, and Nazism (Minster 2017).[4]

During both phases of franquismo and through these cultural, media, and economic relationships, hispanismo was reinvented as a bastion of Christian-Western civilization strongly based on an imperial past. The "tenor and tone" of this ideological dominance—its cultural imaginary—is best characterized as strong Catholicism, anti-Communism, and Spanish ethnic supremacism (Resina 2005). During franquismo, the military dictatorships of Latin American European elites, such as in Argentina, Paraguay, Uruguay, Cuba, and the Dominican Republic, strongly incorporated the dominant ideologies that Spain was experiencing. However, Spain did not have the economic power to build such a hegemonic cultural and social imaginary project. Despite the fact that Spain did not participate in World War II, it endured two economic boycotts, known as *El cerco*, imposed by the West because of its alliances with Germany and Italy. The lack of economic stability forced Spain to strengthen its economic and cultural bonds with Latin America. The production, distribution, and consumption of Spanish cultural industries, including film, were virtually nonexistent due to the economic blockades in 1941 and 1943. US export of oil to Spain and other Axis powers was terminated during these blockades and because celluloid, the main ingredient of film, is produced from oil, Spanish filmmakers did not have the raw materials to make film. Moreover, they had no markets in which to sell their films. Spain's full recovery in the film industry was stalled until such blockades ended.

Although Spain was not part of the Marshall Plan, the 1953 pact between the United States and Spain (*Los acuerdos de defensa mutua y ayuda económica*) ended Spanish economic isolation. This pact, regrettably, ensured Franco's rule for the rest of his life, the suppression of any hint of socialism in Spain, and therefore prolonged for decades after World War II his imperial project via the appropriation of Latin America's cultural industries. Spanish filmmakers were forced to look toward Latin American markets to sell and finance films as well as to secure the raw materials. Part of this strategy required Spanish filmmakers to consciously adopt iconic folkloric themes popular in both Spanish and Latin American cinema and to attempt to weave these folkloric traditions into transatlantic films. For example, Spanish-language films began to combine culturally expressive and specific Andalucian forms, such as flamenco dances, with the *charro mexicano* singing música ranchera. The weaving together of these iconic, regional folkloric forms—a project that involved complex negotiations over how to represent these cultural expressions, how to render the symbolic functions of public spaces such as the *plazas*, how to portray the role of Catholicism and expressions of it—thus constructed a new cultural imaginary. Because the commercial success of film and music relies on appealing to what are deeply affective and familiar responses in the audience—what essentially drives the consumer to go to the cinema or to turn on the radio—this new transatlantic media collaboration needed to produce new, powerful images and figures that appealed to a broad Spanish-speaking audience around the globe (Minster 2017).

Franco's internal hegemonic language policy is quite significant in that Castilian was proclaimed not only the official language of Spain but also the sole language variety of the Spanish nation that could be used in public settings.[5] One of the consequences of such a policy for the Spanish cultural industries was an increase in transnational partnership among media producers, because all films in Spain had to be produced only in Spanish, and foreign films had to be dubbed in Spanish (Domke 2011). Despite not achieving much cultural or economic success in the film and music industries, the Franco regime predictably had complete control over the news and the supply of information, and thus solidified public opinion in favor of the dictatorial regime (Ministerio de Educación, Cultura y Deporte n.d.).[6] The quality of Spanish cinema during franquismo was affected by extensive censorship, such as of political stances contrary to the regime, or unsuitable sexual content. This conservative position on Spanish cinema was rooted in Catholicism and a moral tradition that was quite emblematic of franquismo (Paz Rebollo 2005). One of the turning points in the Mexican and Spanish cultural industries was the Second Cinematographic Congress in Madrid in 1948 (Tuñón 2001).[7] The Franco regime created El Consejo de la Hispanidad, later the Instituto de Cultura Hispánica (ICH), which mainly functioned as a spearhead for disseminating Franco's hispanismo, with its strong imperial overtones, in Latin America (Resina 2005).[8]

MEXICO'S ECONOMIC AND POLITICAL POSITION DURING AND AFTER WORLD WAR II AND ITS EFFECTS ON THE CULTURAL INDUSTRIES

A few years after World War II, the golden age of Mexican cinema ended, owing partly to the United States' decision to focus more on its own film industry, thereby no longer granting Mexico special privileges regarding the production and distribution of films. In addition, technological changes privileged television over films, although in Mexico radio was still the primary form of media consumption. The Mexican film industry was the second largest source of income for the country after oil; it employed 32,000 workers and had seventy-two producer companies (Tuñón 2001, 123). Although the film industry was private, the Mexican state heavily invested in it and supported the industry with tax exemptions and other presidential decrees that allowed its remarkable growth.

During the Spanish Civil War, the official rhetoric of the Mexican state had been socialism, a secular state, and international social justice and solidarity (Lida 2001).[9] Twenty years after the Mexican Revolution (1910–22), the official discourse was centered on sovereign control of the economy, with special emphasis on its vibrant culture and promising political process.[10] According to Guillermoprieto (2009), "*La época de oro del cine mexicano* coincided with a rare moment, perhaps akin to the first decade of the Cuban or Chinese Revolution, in which a poor and often victimized country believed in itself."

As noted earlier, President Lázaro Cárdenas offered political asylum to Spanish republicans at the end of the Spanish Civil War.[11] Most Mexican presidents after him had an ambiguous relationship with Spain, but official diplomatic relationships were renewed only after the death of General Franco (Tuñón 2001). Alongside political relationships, ambiguous or not, firm relationships in religious, cultural, and business spheres emerged. For instance, there was an intensive exchange between Mexican and Spanish publishing houses in that period (Lago Carballo 2006).

Diplomatic and economic relationships were resumed with strength when Luis Alemán Valdés was the Mexican president.[12] Julia Tuñón (2001) affirms that after World War II, films and show business provided the main materials and sources for the Spanish imaginary construction of Mexican identity. The Mexican film industry imitated Hollywood's star system, based on developing the "cult of the actor," by glamorizing and creating personas for them, often inventing new names and life stories. In most cases it was really a "cult of singers"—that is, música ranchera singers rather than actors (Tuñón 2001). Those films tended to be centered on celebrations of Mexican nationalism based on rural traditions, with *el charro* figure as its center. In this regard, Nájera Ramírez (1994) states: "[p]roducing films with Mexican themes proved an easy task. Since *el charro* already had a history of representing *lo mexicano*, *el charro* became a major figure in these nationalistic films" (8). Mexican movies of the época de oro "defined a nation, and an era, in a way that mattered deeply not only to Mexicans: throughout Latin America, the weepy musicals and glamorous dramas held tens of millions of viewers captive in their silvery light" (Guillermoprieto 2009).

The hallmark of nationalistic films was the performance and the narrative of música ranchera. Most of the plots were clean, naïve, and romantic, with

Mexican traditions, including serenades and dances, and where the heroes (normally iconic singers of música ranchera) were honorable, handsome, proud, and romantic *caballeros* (gentlemen). The hero often had a loyal companion who, although he was almost physically the opposite of the leading character, was quite innocent and generous. The leading female characters were, for the most part, exceptionally beautiful, but, more importantly, modest, sensible, noble, and self-sacrificing. Normally these actresses did not sing música ranchera. If the film was a Spanish-Mexican production, the leading actress tended to be Spanish and would sing Spanish songs. Many were feisty, high-spirited characters who ultimately succumbed to the charms of the dominant male (Nájera Ramírez 1994).[13] About 300 actors and actresses were part of the época de oro. The two leading male singers were Jorge Negrete and Pedro Infante. The most iconic female actresses (who were not singers) were Maria Félix and Dolores Del Rio.

Jorge Negrete, *el charro cantor* (the singing charro), was the quintessential singing charro, and he is still one of the icons of Mexican, Spanish, and Latin American cinema more than fifty years after his death. The songs performed by Negrete and popularized by the movies he starred in are Mexico's unofficial anthems, songs such as "México lindo y querido" (Beautiful and beloved Mexico).[14] In films Negrete embodied the Mexican persona at its best: the good-natured, clever, and tastefully courteous male from *la provincia* (the rural province) who bears himself with virile charro elegance, a mellow smile, and a strong sense of justice and honor. Jorge Negrete was European-looking (namely, light-skinned) with the right lineage, well-educated and traveled, and most of the time he played the role of the *hacendado* (landlord).

"México lindo y querido" is probably the most emblematic Mexican song in the Spanish-speaking world because of the convergence of its great performance by Jorge Negrete, the boom of the Mexican film industry, and the nationalistic theme that was reinforced during World War II. This song is still commonly performed when Mexicans die outside Mexico and are buried in Mexico, as was the case for Jorge Negrete himself, the Mexican ambassador of hispanophile culture.[15] It is seen by many as the unofficial national anthem of Mexican popular culture in part because of its love and nostalgia for Mexico; not surprisingly, it is also sung in most important international events or competitions when Mexicans win awards or earn other achievements.

Negrete performs "México lindo y querido" in the film *Siempre tuya* (*Yours always*), released in 1952, in front of a theater audience, accompanied by a large mariachi band. They contribute the conventional *gritos* (shouts) of mariachi in the introduction, a rousing fast-paced interlude led by the violins after the first two refrains, and join Negrete in singing the last two refrains: "México lindo y querido / si muero lejos de ti / que digan que estoy dormido / y que me traigan aquí" (Beautiful and beloved Mexico / if I die far from you / say that I am asleep / and bring me here).[16] A particularly striking moment in the lyrics is that when Negrete first sings the refrain, he inserts a long pause in the third line: "*que digan que estoy . . . dormido*" ("say that I am . . . asleep"), as if giving the audience pictured on screen a moment to guess what he is going to sing—and giving audiences of the song ever since a tantalizing sense of anticipation for the word they know comes next.

Jorge Negrete studied in El Colegio Alemán in Mexico City and graduated from El Colegio Militar (Mexico's military academy), where his fascination for music developed. He was an opera singer who studied under the director of José Pierson at La Academia Nacional de Canto and sang in the most important opera venues in Europe and the United States. However, it was not until Negrete performed mariachi music on the radio and in cinema and began to dress almost exclusively in the charro national suit that he became famous throughout Latin America and Spain. His death at the peak of his artistic career when he was only forty-one years old probably made him the quintessential male icon of música ranchera. Jorge Negrete and Carmen Sevilla (a Spanish singer and actress) were the main actors of the first Spanish-Mexican film, released in 1949, *Jalisco canta en Sevilla* (*Jalisco Sings in Sevilla*). This film was directed by Fernando De Fuentes and produced as a direct result of binational agreements between Spanish and Mexican producers that came out of the Second Cinematographic Hispano-American Congress, and furthered Franco's objective of reversing Spain's marginalized status. Marina Díaz López's study on Negrete and Sevilla shows the rise to transnational stardom of these two actors: Carmen Sevilla as Spanish actress-dancer-singer and Jorge Negrete as singer personified an exceptional version of transnational musical expressions that are very much part of the cultural memory of Spanish-speaking people in the way it was envisioned by such film coproductions. The film *Jalisco canta en Sevilla* was intended to connect Latin America with Spain by intersecting the transnational careers of Negrete and Sevilla, having a coproduction between countries without formal diplomatic relationships, opening a market, and thereby reinforcing their sphere of influence in heterogeneous Spanish speaking communities throughout the world.[17] Although both actors radiated and performed national and gender stereotypes, they managed, with considerable success, to give new life to old stereotypes and participated in what was a new reconfiguration of local/global cultural exchanges between Latin America and Spain. Since the public was quite diverse and transnational, it was important to create ambiguities in the roles of El Charro and La Sevillana. Most of the plots were about transnational cultural encounters, with abundant linguistic and cultural misunderstandings that were normally resolved through increasing awareness and understanding of each other's humanity (López 2009).[18]

In Spain, the films of the época de oro, with música ranchera as a core element, were regarded by Spanish audiences as representative of hispanismo. Ernesto Giménez Caballero, a Spanish politician and pioneer of falangism,[19] stated:

> Mexico is Spain in a straight line. Mexico is a branch of the west and has incorporated to its psychology, the Spanish psychology; that is why they (Mexicans) know how to create films with Spanish themes, and we Spaniards, understand and feel Mexican films. . . . In Spain, we do not see New Spain (*La Nueva España*, the name of México before it became independent) in the films; what we see is the best of Spain: the imperial Spain that we (Spaniards) thought was forever lost. . . . We see the old use of the language, the morals and the sense of honor, our customs, songs, serenades and the use of horses. (Tuñón 2001, 128–29)

IN BETWEEN: TRANSATLANTIC MUSICAL DIALOGUES TO CONTEST DICTATORSHIPS IN LATIN AMERICA AND SPAIN

The 1950s marked the end of the economic blockade known as *El cerco*.[20] At the end of the blockade, Spain experienced profound economic changes based on economic liberalization and state intervention in the labor market through the suspension of labor rights and political freedom. Paradoxically, franquismo combined repressive measures in the labor market with a paternalistic discourse of "social justice" and well-being for working families. Throughout the Franco dictatorship, the 1939 *Ley de Responsabilidades Políticas* (Law of Political Responsibilities) was the main legal framework to carry out the *limpieza* (cleansing) of society. The main victims of such White Terror included Basque and Catalan separatists, free thinkers, liberals, socialists, communists, protestant Christians, and loyalists to the Second Spanish Republic. Importantly enough, the political violence against civilians was ideologically legitimized by the Roman Catholic Church as a mechanism to defend Christendom. This oppression gave way to multiple political contestations, many of them expressed in music, many of them underground.

In the 1950s, 1960s, and 1970s Spain participated in numerous coproductions with France and Italy (particularly in the numerous spaghetti westerns and sword-and-sandal films), and Spain was the location for many US super-productions. By the beginning of the sixties, Mexican revolutionary nationalism—the core of the Mexican film industry—had collapsed under the weight of its own broken promises. A thorough analysis of musical expressions in the sixties and seventies in Spain and Latin America is beyond this essay's scope. However, it is important to put in context that the social tensions of the sixties and seventies—around students' movements, women's rights, civil rights, and decolonization movements—were counterbalanced by conservative films that were almost always musicals, featuring stories of romance and religion, centered on strict Catholicism and traditions. Spain, Mexico, and Argentina were the main producers of such conservative musical films.[21] At the same time, the Spanish objective of using the cinema to legitimize the franquista regime faded over time. The surge of *las canciones de protesta* (protest songs) in Spain coincided with Franco's "second period," allegedly less violent than the initial fifteen years.[22] In Spain, the canciones de protesta were closer to Latin American and French songs in style and content than to US songs.[23] After Franco's death, Spanish cinema went through a period of transition where its agenda was centered not on an imperial and hispanist agenda but rather on consciously breaking with the repression of franquista censorship (Elena 2005). In fact, there was a burst of social and cultural liberation and experimentation. "*El rock de la transición*" was made by the first generation of urban rockers; the lyrics of their songs were "critical of the timid and disappointing democratic achievements of the transition" (Carlos 2014). Some important cultural manifestations were responding to global processes expressed through local manifestations. Many of these films typify what has come to be known as *la movida Madrileña*, which started as a hedonistic pop music movement, with mottos like "Madrid nunca duerme" (Madrid never sleeps) or "¡Esta noche todo el mundo a la calle!" (Everybody in the street tonight!).[24] "La movida" influenced and extended across other fields, including film, television, photography, fashion, and comics. Some of the main subjects (such as open critique of Catholicism and political conservatism, or open talk about homosexuality, sex, and drugs) were taboo and sometimes even legally prohibited during the franquista regime.

In the late seventies and early eighties, "el canto nuevo" (new chant) and la canción de protesta denounced the repressive conditions of the working class and ethnic minorities during Franco's military dictatorship.[25] The songs also represented a cultural vindication and recovery of poets, texts, and songs in languages that were prohibited.[26]

Meanwhile, Latin America was experiencing a political repression carried out by US-backed Latin American military right-wing dictatorships in the sixties, seventies, and eighties. These repressions led to the peak of canciones de protesta.[27] During the seventies and eighties, canciones de protesta from Latin America and Spain were popular on both sides of the Atlantic.[28] In Mexico this musical genre became part of the urban musical environment through artists and intellectuals who were political refugees and had influence over the radicalized youth of the time. In the eighties, *la nueva trova cubana*[29] was also widely known and consumed in Spain and Latin America. The appeal of *la música de protesta* was its anti-imperialist stand: its emphasis on anti-colonialism, Latin American indigenous identity, and empowerment. Juan Manuel Serrat, Joaquín Sabina, and other Spanish singers who faced censorship and persecution during the Spanish franquismo were quite popular in Latin America, and some lived in exile in Latin America, where they sang about self-determination and set many poems of the martyrs of franquismo to music.

SPAIN'S MEMBERSHIP IN THE EUROPEAN UNION AND SOME EFFECTS ON TRANSATLANTIC MUSICAL EXCHANGES

As Lawrence Grossberg (1997) states, globalization erases differences but at the same time reorders hierarchies linked to the markets. Like a chameleon, the "new world order" has historically changed its color in order to reorganize competing political aggregations of interests. In the case of hispanismo as a hegemonic process, it is far from linear and homogenous, due in part to international asymmetric interdependency, complex circular relationships between the local, national, and global, and the reinvention and reconnection of cultural industries to different markets. This section explores some of these changes in the cultural realm between Spain and Latin America.

Despite the fact that Spain's unemployment rate has for the most part hovered around double the average of developed countries, after the country joined the European Union in 1986 a large sector of the Spanish population not surprisingly started to enjoy a standard of living that was comparable to that of other developed European economies.[30] The content of the music of oppositional singers changed dramatically after such economic and cultural conditions changed. Specifically, Spain created "el pacto de silencio"[31] after the death of Franco in 1975, when the transition to the restoration of democracy led to a race for economic, cultural, and political modernization.[32] The progressive institutionalization of European citizenship meant that new generations identified more strongly with the European community partly because they wanted to be officially recognized as "fully European" through EU membership.[33]

Spain became a spearhead of the European Union's economic and political interests in Latin America. Economic penetration of Latin American markets and exertion of political influence were often masked as cultural and linguistic "sisterhood," taking advantage of the belief that *mi lengua es mi patria* (my language is my country), and thus capitalizing on similarities to construct a pan-ethnic consumer identity that might erase the complexity of the twenty Latin American countries with their significant regional and historical differences.[34] Spain's new status as a member of the European Union, in conjunction with neoliberal reforms that have taken place in Latin America over the last twenty years, has led to extraordinary growth in Spain's foreign investment in Latin America.[35]

Spain's membership in the European Union has affected the colonial gazes, partnerships, and topics of some genres of Spanish music in respect to Latin America (Medina Bañón 2001). According to Pérez Herrero (Morenilla 2016), the relationships between Spain and Latin America are fragmented and very little has been done toward building a true "brotherhood."[36]

The reconfiguration of economic hierarchies was reflected in the cultural industries. Regarding musical expressions, Medina Bañón (2001) states that there are three main clusters of themes drawing on Latin American regions that are emerging in Spain's musical realm: (1) the sexualization of the exotic "other" and feminization of the Cuban landscape;[37] (2) the recycling of "excesses" of mariachi, música ranchera, and the Mexican border as a bizarre place; and (3) the production of *rock en español* mainly by Argentinian and Chilean musicians.[38] In what follows I focus on the música ranchera through case studies of Chavela Vargas and Joaquín Sabina.

MIMICRY AND TOKENISM IN THE PERFORMANCE OF *MEXICANIDAD* THROUGH *MÚSICA* RANCHERA

Chavela Vargas, a música ranchera singer, was one of the most influential artists of the Spanish transition. Although born in Costa Rica, she has been known in the Spanish-speaking world for her performance of mexicanidad through mariachi music.³⁹ Spanish film director Pedro Almodóvar has included songs either performed by Vargas or in a style associated with her in many of his films.⁴⁰ Vargas also participated in the movies *Frida* (2002), directed by Julie Taymor, and *Babel* (2006), directed by Alejandro González Iñárritu. On August 5, 2012, Chavela Vargas died at the age of ninety-three, and most obituaries of the major English-language newspapers around the globe referred to her as a legend in the Spanish-speaking world, who transformed mariachi and música ranchera performance by singing mainly with one guitar, and lauding her both for being one of the few women who sang mariachi music and for being openly lesbian and having an affair with Mexican painter Frida Kahlo.

Vargas built her persona upon a complex worldwide *fridomania* and firmly attached herself to the Western construction of Frida Kahlo as a colorful, naïve, surreal artist who supposedly embodies mexicanidad, mainly because she seems to mime and decontextualize the attire and experiences of the Tehuanas (whose regional dress style Kahlo made part of her distinctive artistic identity).⁴¹ Indeed, mexicanidad as most recently constructed in the West has had a strong element of fridomania. Fridomania has been a successful commodity at least partly because Frida Kahlo herself was a Mexican of European descent who could be an ethnic "transvestite" and "crossed over" to be indigenous, a privilege that is not granted the other way around for indigenous Tehuanas. Chavela Vargas's distinctive trademark was her use of a red *jorongo* (poncho)⁴² and huaraches,⁴³ normally used by indigenous male campesinos. As transgressive as it may look, fridomania has a core element of ethnic consumerism based on denial and hedonism. It is almost playful to portray temporarily the "exotic" other without experiencing daily ethnic oppression and without paying the social cost of being a racialized minority that most indigenous people from Mexico face in Mexico and, also, in the United States.

Frida Kahlo identified herself as European-Mexican. She was the daughter of a German photographer in Mexico and a *mestiza* mother. She wore indigenous clothes as a statement of differentiation from the very indigenous people, as a way to affirm her authority, distance, and difference in a process of exoticization and marginalization—not necessarily to be in communion or solidarity with indigenous people. This is a facile act that can be and has been performed by white women all over the world—to be close to others by consumption but not by communion. At times Kahlo's liberal and communist position concealed her distant relation with indigenous Mexicans.

The "crossovers" of Chavela Vargas, with her red jorongo and huaraches, and Frida Kahlo, with her Tehuana dresses, are fraught with inequalities.⁴⁴

Vargas's campesino attire serves to rearticulate, delegitimize, and annihilate the racial and cultural struggles between Mexican indigenous communities and the West. The colonial desire, narcissistic demand of colonial authority, and re-creation of one's own image at the expense of the other makes it impossible to have a space for dialogue or communion among Westerners and indigenous Mexicans. In a way it seems that Almodóvar's intervention in Vargas's career not only "revived" her interpretation of mexicanidad through her performance of música ranchera but also reinvented a "new" Vargas strongly linked to the new, paternalistic relationship between Vargas and Spanish artists in which both have profited.

Chavela Vargas's most famous period was after she was "discovered" by Pedro Almodóvar in 1991 in Mexico City. Alcoholism sent Vargas into partial retirement for almost two decades. Almodóvar states that in the nineties while he was in Mexico City he went out for a drink at a place where Chavela Vargas was singing. Vargas's comeback to the mainstream musical stage in her late seventies was very much under Almodóvar's wing. Almodóvar takes credit for Chavela Vargas's performance at the Olympia Theatre in Paris, which allowed her from then on to be presented by him in world-class theaters in the West. Almodóvar stated that he could acknowledge and give what "Mexico could not," contrary to the *mezquinidad* (unkindness), he continued, "del país de cuya cultura Chavela era la embajadora más ardiente" (of the country of which Chavela was the most fervent ambassador) (Almodóvar 2002). Almodóvar also made possible Vargas's performance in the Palacio de Bellas Artes, the most important stage and cultural center in Mexico. This palace is known as the "cathedral of art in Mexico."[45] When Almodóvar presented Vargas at the Palacio de Bellas Artes he stated that "al fin" (at last) Vargas got the recognition that Mexican cultural officials had earlier denied her. Almodóvar presented Vargas as a pioneer in singing música ranchera without a mariachi band, and in subduing the "festive" character of the national music to make it almost like the Portuguese *fado*—the singer's tone is quite melancholic, and sounds very close to reciting a poem, with poetic lyrics mostly related to the darkest dimensions of love, death, and sadness, accompanied by stringed instruments.[46]

The remaking of mexicanidad goes hand in hand with the remaking of hispanismo. The "new" hispanismo is multicultural, tolerant, and paternalistic; it has found its way into musical expressions, in particular in the work of Joaquin Sabina, an iconic Spanish singer, songwriter, and poet known for his opposition to franquismo. Sabina lived in political exile in London for over seven years and was part of the Spanish counterculture during Franco's dictatorship. After Spain became a member of the European Union, Sabina collaborated with a number of Latin American singers. He wrote "Por el bulevar de los sueños rotos" (On the Boulevard of Broken Dreams) in 1994 as homage to Chavela Vargas. He introduces her, without naming her, in the opening lines of the song: she is a "mestiza ardiente de lengua libre" (a passionate mestiza of free speech), a "gata valiente de piel de tigre" (a brave cat with tiger skin). The lyrics function as a kind of guessing game until the last lines of the chorus, when he finally names her: "¡Quien supiera reír / como llora Chavela!" (Who knew how to laugh / as Chavela cries!).

This song acts as a repository of essentialist notions of mexicanidad. The lyrics are short, exotic vignettes that refuse a close dialogue between Sabina and the physical or cultural landscape of Mexico. He provides a snapshot of the Mexican identity Chavela Vargas supposedly embodies. The European central character of the lyrics positions himself in such a detached and yet familiar way with what allegedly represents Mexico, and at the same time denies communion and dialogue between the "bizarre" Mexican cultural landscape and himself. Joaquín Sabina's lyrics seem to construct mexicanidad in a very stable and monolithic way. The superficial insertion of highly respected Mexican artists and intellectuals in this song—Agustín Lara, Diego Rivera, and Frida Kahlo in the second verse, José Alfredo Jiménez later on— takes away their relevance and authority by placing them as "stamps" and adornments in this visual collage. The qualities attributed to mexicanidad are those of overdetermination, the devaluation of Mexican iconic artists living and creating in a context of fantasy, illogical, irrational, and excessive. Sabina seems to reenact this commodification of mexicanidad through a spectacle that caters to the notion of hispanidad and multiculturalism. The work of Homi Bhabha on the colonial discourse is useful in the sense that hispanismo is dependent on the concept of "fixity" in the ideological construction of otherness—fixity embodied in a stereotype of mexicanidad, as the sign of "cultural/historical/racial difference in the discourse of colonialism" (Bhabha 1994, 66). This use of stereotype as the major discursive strategy relies on a knowledge and identification that fluctuates between what is always chartered, ready, and at the same time something that must be anxiously repeated to be believed. In this framework the "Mexican" excesses represented in different musical expressions in Spain do not need to be proven, since repeatability produces active marginalization and predictability, and disciplines the "other." According to Edward Said (1978), the Western world's flexible, positional superiority seems to determine all possible relationships with the colonized world to such an extent that the stereotypes produced about the "other" become fixed once and for all in colonial discourse (7). These colonizing and essentialist representations of the colonial subjects are an important discursive strategy of colonialism intended to perpetuate the status quo of the colonial system. This exoticization has been replicated through Foucault's (1980) explanation of regimes of knowledge/power where knowledge is inseparable from relationships of power (4). The "knowledge" of mexicanidad as constructed by the West and exemplified in these lyrics has been so engrained in this colonial discourse that such representations of Mexican artistic sensibility and expressions are taken for granted. This "accumulation" of knowledge, in Foucauldian terms, has facilitated the progress of such representations as a cultural zeitgeist. Such imaginary and opportunistic constructions of this "bizarre" cultural identity are core to the concept of the "new" hispanismo, because such representations supposedly embrace all Spanish-speaking people and cultures and at the same time reinforce a racial and cultural hierarchy. These complex, continuous, hierarchical, and self-serving arrangements of the "self" and "other" are part and parcel of hispanismo. The "new" discourses of mexicanidad are historically situated and thus inseparable from the relationship of power between Spain and Mexico. Sabina's and Vargas's artistic practices are built on each other's appropriation and creation of a marketing product to sell a cultural identity of the "other." This song's country-style music and lyrics are both a playful and "innocent" homage to Vargas and Mexico and an "otherization" of Mexican cultural expressions that creates a market for Western consumption on Western terms.

As is often the case with cultural appropriation, the context of such expressions are often misapplied to situations that do not quite fit and often alienate those from whom cultural expressions are being taken. The performance of música ranchera by Vargas, and the tribute to Vargas by Sabina, seem to erase the social and political context of música ranchera, and to reduce it to being simply "exotic." Although cultural exchanges and cross-fertilization are part and parcel of contact and are complex and multifaceted, still it is pertinent to bring to this discussion the context and development of the "*estilo bravío*" that has been the base for female singers of música ranchera.

THOSE WHO WERE LOST IN THE TRANSFORMATION OF MEXICANIDAD AND HISPANISMO: LUCHA REYES, CUCO SÁNCHEZ, AND THE IMPORTANCE OF THE ESTILO BRAVÍO IN MÚSICA RANCHERA

Although Vargas and Sabina have incorporated to the "center" (Spain) elements of the música ranchera from Mexico, there is some denial of the peripheral, the marginal, the "uncanonized" música ranchera (from Mexico) political and social context in which it has evolved. Vargas seemed to be almost an unquestionably canonical música ranchera singer in Spain, and, therefore, inevitably privileging the supposed center by bringing back the imperial status of Spain over Latin America through reconstructing a "truth" and "reality" of what is música ranchera, both in discourse and in the material conditions of production. In various interviews, Chavela Vargas oscillates between appropriating and performing mexicanidad by singing ranchera music and decontextualizing the estilo bravío of the música ranchera sung by women.

The estilo bravío has been the main reference and foundation for Mexican female singers of música ranchera and more importantly for the *soldaderas* (soldier women)[47] of the Mexican Revolution. To sing *al estilo bravío* is to sing with bravery, courage, heroism. The most iconic singer of *la música bravía* is Lucha Reyes, a singer born ten years earlier than Chavela Vargas in 1906. She witnessed the Mexican Revolution. Her mother was a soldadera, and she started to sing as a child in a *carpa* (tent) while the revolution was still underway. Lucha Reyes was one of the first, and certainly the best-known, singer to defy patriarchy through her estilo bravío performance. In her musical performances, she celebrated women's sexuality and talked openly about intergenerational problems between mothers and daughters regarding sexuality. Lucha Reyes was the first bravío singer to weave in sexual innuendos and play on pronouns to create ambiguity regarding the gender positionality of the singer. She dignified the soldaderas in that her repertoire included songs about revolutionary heroes and battles, historical events related to the socialist revolution, love for Mexico's landscapes, and the ways of life of working-class young women, their sexualities, their love affairs, and their disappointments. Reyes's songs embodied nostalgia and an idealization of rural Mexico as well as an awareness of the new conditions and ways of life of urban Mexico. Her most iconic songs include "Los Tarzanes," "La tequilera," "La panchita," "Yo me muero donde quiera," and "Traigo un amor." Lucha Reyes also adopted the mannerisms perceived as typical of soldaderas: she introduced a very original, dramatic vocalization overflowing with expressions of grief, happiness, pride, and anger. At times she was defiant about injustices, while at other times her lyrics were quite celebratory. Her repertoire was mainly about love and heartbreak. Mexican audiences tend to venerate música ranchera singers who continue singing until they are quite hoarse, because it is a sign of devotion to their public. Lucha Reyes is known to have started this tradition of self-sacrifice to her audiences.

In her autobiography, Chavela Vargas (2002) asserts that when she was settling in Mexico and trying to find an artistic niche, she studied thoroughly the roots of the música ranchera and "understood through the Mexican style that the mannerisms and gestures of the soldaderas were an important legacy of the Mexican revolution" (50). Vargas knew the importance of the soldaderas' cultural heritage in the national imaginary and decided to mimic soldaderas: "I thought that what I saw in them was going to take me to fame. ... I always admired Mexican revolutionary women, Valentinas, soldaderas, Marietas, and I thought it was necessary to record songs that were about the experiences of those women." She continues, "in the '40s it was common to think that there *were no other ways for singing música ranchera except Lucha Reyes's style*" (Vargas 2002, 128; my emphasis). In so far as Pedro Almodóvar claimed that Chavela Vargas had been the first and only person who sung without mariachi, and in a deeply melancholic, lugubrious, disconsolate manner, he, with his colonial, outsider gaze, undermined a long tradition of ranchera songs, mainly embodied by but not limited to the strong legacy of the Mexican singer and composer Cuco Sánchez, who was also part of the época de oro. According to Granados (2014b):

> Chavela Vargas owes a lot to Cuco Sánchez, at least at the beginning [of her career]. Those who went to visit him in the nights throughout different venues of the city, in the Colonia Roma, la Zona Rosa know this. Cuco Sánchez was introspective, with a repertoire in which the mariachi was the witness of the interpreter's sinking sadness; sadness as the swirl that opens in the center of oneself through which one descends and one knows tragedy. . . . In [Sánchez's repertoire] was almost nihilism, contempt for suffering, although sometimes to the point of desperation, as if one was on the edge of an abysm, contemplates it, realizes that he does not have words, he retracts, a repertoire full of suspensive periods. (Granados 2014b)

Cuco Sánchez was born during the Mexican Revolution; his father was a paymaster of Venustiano Carranza (one of the main leaders of the Mexican Revolution) and his mother a soldadera. Pável Granados states that Cuco

Sánchez always carried with him the loneliness of the period of the Mexican Revolution:

> of the singing around a wood fireplace, a campsite night. His lyrics are impregnated with the idea that the world is only conceivable in this context: the oral tradition, the idea that life is a path without a direction, the proverbs as the great truths, dispossession as the only certainty . . . the voice that talks through Cuco Sánchez songs is that of the troubadour who goes through the paths, who extracts his convictions of his journeys . . . he had a spectacular turning point that is "Fallaste, corazón" ("You Failed, My Heart"), where he talks about himself addressing his heart, this would give material for a chapter about tearing of oneself. . . . He had a great capacity of synthesis and attachment to tradition. . . . The ends of the *canciones rancheras* have that particular intensity, that contempt for life, as theatrical as affective. (Granados 2014b)[48]

Sánchez sang canciones rancheras with a guitar only. His songs are so famous that some of his song titles and phrases have become everyday Mexican expressions.[49] He transformed the Mexican Revolution style, described Mexican landscapes, and, above all, elicited intense feelings of love, abandonment, desolation, and festivity (Granados 2014b). At times, his singing sounded like a *cante*, at others like the blues or Portuguese fado. His performances made use of strong of vocal signals that reinforced the lyrics of the songs, signals that were close to crying, sobbing, or screams of happiness.

According to Vázquez Santana (1931), música ranchera can expresses the sadness and disappointment of the rural poor: "suffering, hope, passion, disappointment, evasive happiness condemned to hardship and indifference of the leading class" have been the main topics of this genre (26). La música ranchera is perceived as a festive style to audiences outside Mexico, in good part due to the época de oro, where most films were saturated with songs, to the point that they were almost musicals of love stories and fiestas. But most of the themes and tones of música ranchera tend to be quite melancholic; these are songs about sorrow, despair, and grief.

Ironically, the Mexican soldaderas have been glorified in textbooks and by elite artists; however, in real life they experienced discrimination of all sorts. Even Cuco Sánchez and Lucha Reyes, who were children of soldaderas, with great artistic talent, are not very well known or acknowledged outside Mexico; they are not as recognized in most música ranchera musical exchanges between Mexico and Spain as they are in the Mexican working-class collective memory. Their indigenous features and social class were not palatable enough to Spanish and international audiences to build their work around their personas. Although Lucha Reyes performed for the Mexican socialist intellectual postrevolutionary elite, most notably Diego Rivera and Frida Kahlo and President Lázaro Cárdenas, she was never really treated as an equal but rather as a paid musician who offered entertainment services to them in their gatherings.

La música ranchera itself embodies some latent tensions regarding Mexican national identity: el charro as *hacendado* (landlord) and therefore, with strong Spanish ancestry; the campesino, el charro's loyal servants, as indigenous farm workers; *la china poblana*, who was not only el charro's female counterpart, but also his opposite in terms of race and class. The symbolic hierarchical order and classificatory systems of hispanismo and mexicanidad identities are based on marking difference through a racialized regime of representation. This order is also based on an irrational imaginary hierarchy with binary oppositions that are mutually exclusive. However, as much as both identities have been constructed as separate, the relationship between hispanismo and mexicanidad are interlocked and as relational as are their economies and histories. As Molk (2016) states:

> The making of Europe ... is the demarcation from the non-Europe, which is continental in scale. The core is distinguished from the periphery primarily by the axial division of labor of the capitalist world-economy, which entails core-like and periphery-like processes relational and therefore susceptible to change to the extent of substituting one another.... The core/periphery spatial dimensions, which are relational in substance and processual in manifestation, are overlooked and subsumed under conventional spaces of either the state or the market variant.

This work attempts to expose some of the unravelling imaginaries, subjectivities, and everyday expressions and negotiations that take place in the performance of hispanismo and mexicanidad through música ranchera and different states' and cultural industries' interventions. Hispanismo and mexicanidad are marked out through processes of identity formation that are inseparable from one another.

BIBLIOGRAPHY

"Group 'Latin America and the Caribbean—National Accounts': Gross Domestic Product Based on Purchasing-Power-Parity (PPP) Valuation of Country GDP (Current International Dollar." 2015. *Knoema.* https://knoema.com/IMFWEO2015Apr/imf-world-economic-outlook-weo-april-2015?tsId=1072360. Accessed August 8, 2016.
Alonso Bolaños, Marina. 2008. *La invención de la música indígena de México.* Buenos Aires: Sb Editorial.
Bhabha, Homi. 1994. *The Location of Culture.* London: Routledge.
Broyles-González, Yolanda. 2001. "Lydia Mendoza's Songworld: The Canción Ranchera." In *Re-Emerging Native Women of the Americas,* 39–60. 2nd ed. Dubuque, IA: Kendall/Hunt Publishing.
Cantú, Norma E., and Olga Nájera-Ramírez, eds. 2002. *Chicana Traditions: Continuity and Change.* Urbana: University of Illinois Press.
Carlos, Marcos. 2014. "17 canciones de rock protesta críticas con la Transición." *El Pais,* March 29. https://elpais.com/elpais/2014/03/28/planeta_futuro/1396018190_253833.html. Accessed July 29, 2017.
Chew Sánchez, Martha I. 2014. "Paramilitarism and State-Terrorism in Mexico as a Case Study of Shrinking Functions of the Neoliberal State." *Perspectives on Global Development and Technology* 13 (1–2): 176–96.
Domínguez Chávez, Humberto. 2011. *La música popular de 1940 a 1970.* http://portalacademico.cch.unam.mx/materiales/prof/matdidac/sitpro/hist/mex/mex2/HM2-3CultPortal/Musica1940.pdf. Accessed October 14, 2016.
Domke, Joan Cicero. 2011. *Education, Fascism, and the Catholic Church in Franco's Spain.* PhD diss., Loyola University Chicago.
Elena, Alberto. 2005. "Cruce de destinos: Intercambios cinematograficos entre España y América Latina." Madrid: Liceus.
Feith, Seth. 1994. "Hollywood, U.S.-Mexican Relations, and the Devolution of the 'Golden Age' of Mexican Cinema." *Film-Historia* 4 (2): 103–35.
Gabriel y Galán, Jose Antonio. 1988. "El Pacto de Silencio." *El Pais,* February 20. https://elpais.com/diario/1988/02/20/opinion/572310009_850215.html. Accessed November 4, 2016.
Granados, Pável. 2014a. *De Altamira, Tamaulipas, traigo esta alegre canción.* Ciudad Victoria, Tamaulipas, Mexico: El Instituto Tamaulipeco para la Cultura y las Artes.
Granados, Pável. 2014b. *Elogio (de Cuco Sánchez) y desprecio (de la vida).* October 23. http://www.letraslibres.com/mexico-espana/elogio-cuco-sanchez-y-desprecio-la-vida. Accessed August 23, 2017.
"Mexico Media Scandal: Televisa's Alleged Collusion with Peña Nieto." 2012. *The Guardian,* August 8. http://www.theguardian.com/world/interactive/2012/jun/08/mexico-media-scandal-televisa-pena-nieto-claims. Accessed June 15, 2016.
Guillermoprieto, Alma. 2009. "Golden-Epoch Cinema in Mexico: Creating National Myths on the Silver Screen." *ReVista.* http://revista.drclas.harvard.edu/book/golden-epoch-cinema-mexico. Accessed June 24, 2016.

Hernanz, Carlos. 2014. "Cuba, la colonia hotelera de España." *El Confidencial*, December 20. http://www.elconfidencial.com/empresas/2014-12-20/cuba-la-colonia-hotelera-de-espana_598662/. Accessed July 20, 2016.

Jones, Benjamin. 2016. "Spanish Chains Welcome U.S. Competitors in Cuba." *Hotel News Now*, February 3. http://www.hotelnewsnow.com/Articles/29592/Spanish-chains-welcome-US-competitors-in-Cuba. Accessed July 21, 2016.

Junquera, Natalia. 2014. "'El Valle de los Caídos me resultó dantesco. Nunca he visto nada igual': El secretario de derechos humanos de Argentina lamenta 'el retroceso' de España." *El Pais*, July 27: 15–21.

Lida, Clara, E., ed. 2001. *México y España en el primer franquismo, 1939–1950: Rupturas formales, relaciones oficiosas*. Mexico, D.F.: El Colegio de Mexico.

López, Marina Diaz. 2009. "Connecting Spain and the Americas in the Cold War: The Transnational Careeers of Jorge Negrete and Carmen Sevilla." *Studies in Hispanic Cinema* 5: 25–42.

Medina Bañón, Raquel. 2001. "El reencuentro de la música española con la Latinoamérica poscolonial." *Castilla: Estudios de literatura* 26: 67–82.

Menéndez-Alarcón, Antonio. 2000. "Spain in the European Union: A Qualitative Study of National Identity." *International Journal of Cultural Studies* 3 (3): 331–50.

Ministerio de Educación, Cultura y Deporte. n.d. "Archivo histórico de NO-DO." http://www.mecd.gob.es/cultura-mecd/areas-cultura/cine/mc/fe/fondos-filmicos/colecciones-especiales/archivo-historico-de-no-do.html. Accessed June 18, 2016.

Minster, Christopher. 2017. "Mexican Involvement in World War II: Mexico Helped Push the Allied Powers Over the Top." July 17. https://www.thoughtco.com/mexican-involvement-in-world-war-two-2136644. Accessed August 23, 2017.

Molk, Florence. 2016. *The Space of Policing in the Modern World-System: The Making of the European Identity in the Core*. PhD diss., Binghamton University.

Monsiváis, Carlos. 2010. "Yo soy un humilde cancionero." In *La música en México: Panorama del signo XX*, by Aurelio Tello, 180–252. México, D.F.: Fondo de Cultural Economica/Consejo Nacional para la Cultura y las Artes.

Morenilla, Juan. 2016. "El español tiene un estereotipo negativo del latinoamericano." *El Pais*, May 26.

Nájera Ramírez, Olga. 1994. "Engendering Nationalism: Identity, Discourse, and the Mexican Charro." *Anthropological Quarterly* 67 (1): 1–14.

Notimex. 2015. "Spain, Third Investment Source for Mexico Worldwide." June 29.

Paz Rebollo, Maria Antonia, and Carlota Coronado Ruiz. 2005. "Mujer y formacion profesional durante el franquismo. NO-DO 1943–1975." *Pandora: Revue d'etudes hispaniques* 5: 133–45.

Paz, Octavio. 1979. "Reflections: Mexico and the United States." *The New Yorker*, September 17: 135–56.

Poniatowska, Elena. 2000. *Las Soldaderas: Women of the Mexican Revolution*. Mexico, D.F.: Era.

Quintanilla, Susana. n.d. "La educación en México durante el periodo de Lázaro Cardenas 1934–1940." http://biblioweb.tic.unam.mx/diccionario/htm/articulos/sec_31.htm. Accessed November 26, 2016.

Resina, Juan Ramon. 2005. "Whose Hispanism? Cultural Trauma, Discipline and Symbolic Dominance." In *Ideologies of Hispanism*, edited by Mabel Morona, 160–88. Nashville, TN: Vanderbilt University Press.

Rojo, José Andrés. 2005. "Una deuda pendiente: Lázaro Cárdenas, el amigo de la República. Una semana de homenajes celebra al presidente mexicano que acogió a los perdedores de la guerra." *El País*, October 2. https://elpais.com/diario/2005/10/02/cultura/1128204001_850215 .html. Accessed August 2, 2019.

Sánchez-Alarcón, Inmaculada. 2010. "Las películas folclóricas como principales manifestaciones más características del cine musical en España." *Fotocinema: Revista Científica de cine y fotografía* 10: 23–28.

Said, Edward W. 1978. *Orientalism*. New York: Pantheon.

UNESCO Intangible Cultural Heritage. 2011. "Mariachi, String Music, Song and Trumpet." http://www.unesco.org/culture/ich/en/RL/mariachi-string-music-song-and-trumpet-00575. Accessed November 27, 2016.

Tortajada Quiroz, Margarita. 2004. "Bailar la patria y la Revolución." *Casa del Tiempo* 6 (3): 66–67.

Tucker, Joshua. 2014. "Sounding the Latin Transatlantic: Music, Integration, and Ambivalent Ethnogensis in Spain." *Comparative Studies in Society and History* 56 (4): 902–33.

Tuñón, Julia. 2001. "Relaciones de celuloide: El Primer Certamen Cinematografico Hispano-americano, Madrid, 1948." In *México y España en el primer franquismo, 1939–1950: Rupturas formales, relaciones oficiosas*, edited by Clara E. Lida. México, D.F.: El Colegio de Mexico.

Vázquez Santana, Higinio. 1931. *Historia de la canción mexicana*. México, D.F.: Talleres Gráficos de la Nación.

Vargas, Chavela. 2002. *Y si quieres saber de mi pasado*. México, D.F.: Aguilar.

Vega, Héctor. 2010. "La música tradicional mexicana, entre el folclore, la tradición y la world music." *Historia Actual* 23: 155–69. http://historia-actual.org/Publicaciones/index.php/haol/article/viewFile/506/433.

Walter, Mignolo. 2012. *Local Histories/Global Designs: Coloniality, Subaltern Knowledges, and Border Thinking*. Princeton, NJ: Princeton University Press.

Weiner, Lawrence. 2013. "How Mexico Became So Corrupt." *The Atlantic*, June 25. http://www.theatlantic.com/international/archive/2013/06/how-mexico-became-so-corrupt/277219/. Accessed June 15, 2016.

FILMOGRAPHY

Almodóvar, Pedro. 1991. *Tacones lejanos/High Heels*. Canal+/CiBy 2000/El Deseo/TF1 Films Production.

Almodóvar, Pedro. 1993. *Kika*. El Deseo/CiBy 2000.

Almodóvar, Pedro. 1995. *La flor de mi secreto/The Flower of My Secret*. CiBy 2000/El Deseo.

Fuentes, Fernando de. 1949. *Jalisco canta en Sevilla*. Chamartín Producciones y Distribuciones/Producciones Diana.

Iñarritú, Alejandro González. 2006. *Babel*. Paramount Pictures/Paramount Vantage/Anonymous Content/Zeta Film/Central Films/Media Rights Capital.

Taymor, Julie. 2002. *Frida*. Handprint Entertainment/Lions Gate Films/Miramax/Ventanarosa Productions.

NOTES

1. The "golden age of Mexican cinema" is a period between 1936 and 1959 in which the cinema of Mexico reached its artistic and commercial peak. A principal cause of this golden age was the beginning of World War II in 1939. The film industries in Europe and the United States were severely affected due to the conflict, which led to a scarcity of film-related materials such as celluloid due to rationing. Mexican movie producers were less affected, however. Mexico eventually joined the Allied cause in 1942, thus gaining an advantageous position in the film markets of those countries. During the war, the French, Italian, Spanish, and American film industries became focused on war-related films, while the Mexican film industry continued to focus on more traditional movie themes. This focus allowed for greater success for Mexican films with Mexican and other Spanish-speaking audiences.

2. All translations from the Spanish in this chapter are my own.

3. The *primer franquismo* was more authoritarian and extended from right after the Civil War up to 1959. In the *segundo franquismo*, from 1959 to 1975, Spain opened its markets, made more liberal reforms, and allowed for more oppositional movements. The United States also lifted its embargo on Spain.

4. According to Rojo (2005), Cárdenas accepted 25,000 Spanish war refugees and "adopted" 400 Spanish orphans from the Spanish Civil War.

5. Franquismo made illegal the use of Catalan, Basque, and Galician in the media, in educational settings, and in religious ceremonies. Under Franco, all Spaniards had to have a Christian name and had to be baptized as Catholics in order to be a legal Spanish citizen and have a civic identity, get married, buy property, and have access to education, health, and employment (Domke 2011). These strict language and religious policies were rooted in the concept of establishing a homogenous Spanish national identity.

6. The most notorious case of such strict control of content and dissemination of state ideology was the NODO (acronym for *Noticiarios y Documentales*), a state-produced series of films compulsorily shown before every movie Spain projected from 1943 to 1981 (Ministerio de Educación, Cultura y Deporte n.d.).

7. The Sindicato Nacional del Espectáculo de España (Spanish National Union of Spectacle) organized this important congress and the main countries in attendance were Mexico, Cuba, and Argentina, to which Franco maintained special economic and ideological ties, given that Argentina, Cuba, and Spain all had right-wing military dictatorships (Tuñón 2001).

8. In essence, the Instituto de Cultura Hispánica and El Sindicato Nacional del Espectáculo were franquismo's main propaganda vehicles at the national level but also were meant to expand Spain's influence over Latin America. These projects are exemplary of Spain's need for Latin America to build its own imaginary and relevance vis-à-vis Europe and the world. These two institutions organized a key transatlantic meeting called the Second Cinematographic Hispano-American Congress (Resina 2005).

9. Several policies enacted during the presidency of Lázaro Cárdenas had significant social and political consequences. These included the nationalization of oil in 1938 as well as land reform and the nationalization of railways. An important factor that helped sustain growth in the period 1940–70 was the reduction of political turmoil.

10. Mexico benefited from an inward-looking development strategy that produced sustained economic growth of 3 to 4 percent and modest 3 percent inflation annually from the 1940s until the 1970s. Mexico was moving from over a decade of social revolution into a process of significant social and political changes that would create some economic stability.

11. Cárdenas also gave asylum to persecuted dissidents mainly from France, Germany, and Austria. He was followed by a right-wing conservative president, Manuel Avila Camacho, who was anticommunist and Catholic. Camacho implemented an industrialization program that benefited mainly the elites, joined the US position against the Axis during WWII, and supported the US war industry by providing Mexican raw materials for war efforts.

12. Valdés's presidency was known for a high level of corruption and fraud, which enabled him to achieve personal enrichment mostly in media monopolies. The Alemán family is quite influential in the PRI ranks and has shares in Televisa, airplanes, and tourist projects. Televisa's early vertical integration made it possible to target Spanish-speaking audiences internationally.

13. This is particularly the case of Maria Felix. Felix was known to be strong-minded and play mostly the roles of women with tempestuous personalities, such as roles as a rural teacher, soldier, cabaret singer, and others.

14. Some of the most famous songs performed by Negrete were "Dulce patria" (Sweet motherland), "Ay Jalisco no te rajes" (Ay, Jalisco, do not back down), "Juan Charrasqueado," "El charro mexicano" (The Mexican charro), "Amor con amor se paga" (Love is paid with love), "La Adelita," "Jalisco canta en Sevilla" (Jalisco sings in Sevilla), and "El hijo del pueblo" (The son of the people).

15. On the other hand, Pérez Herrero invites us to take a step back and be critical of some aspects of the Mexican nationalistic ideology that constructs Spaniards as merciless conquerors. Notwithstanding, in Mexico *hispanophobia* is not really homogenous insofar as Mexican elites tend to feel closer to Spain than to Mexican indigenous populations (Morenilla 2016).

16. Each time the refrain repeats, the order is changed, with lines one and two being switched with lines three and four.

17. Negrete and Sevilla came together as the romantic leads of the film. Negrete was at the height of a professional trajectory which would end shortly with his untimely death, while Sevilla was making her acting debut after a modest career as a member of a dance troupe. Negrete was living an exceptional moment in his professional life, both on-screen and off, as he showed off the charisma and bravado that would make him an enduring star. These are features that had been the essentials of his political career as president of Mexico's National Association of Actors (ANDA). His arrival in Spain was an historic event occasioning the first popular mass demonstration that challenged the Francoist government's efforts at crowd control. His arrival at the Norte train station in Madrid was greeted by thousands of people, mostly women, who awaited the appearance of the star who represented for Spanish audiences the heroic construction of Hispanic masculinity lived as a "utopian ethnotype" (Giménez Caballero 1948, 49–58).

18. This is an empathetic eulogy from a Mexican to the fabled city, which represents a historical bridge between Spain and America song in "La Giralda." Among Negrete's most melodic repertory and evidence of his lyrical range and skills at evoking the masculine sentimentality of a very robust personality, this song's staging at the film's beginning seems to respond to a very pronounced calculation of producing a conciliatory effect for the Spanish spectator. Another

important song is "El arriero," a song by the Mexican composer Manuel Esperón and Esperón's regular lyricist Ernesto Cortázar, part of the creole song tradition, which Negrete sings at night while the cattle rest. These verses end with a characteristic falsetto. This particular effect of the Mexican musical repertory, especially of the Veracruz style, had already become part of the mariachi soloists' style, which had achieved its brilliance in Negrete's accomplished tenor voice. This song is performed in the middle of the film and is shot with a series of close-ups of Negrete in which the singer's head is topped by a charro hat that literally fills the screen.

19. Falangism was Spain's fascist movement. The Falange ("Phalanx") was founded in 1933 by José Antonio Primo de Rivera, but many of its members were absorbed into the military dictatorship of Francisco Franco. Falangism was the political ideology of the Falange Espanola de las JONS, and afterward of the Falange Española Tradicionalistas y de las Juntas de Ofensiva Nacional Sindicalista. Falangism emphasized the need for authority, hierarchy, and order. It was also crucial in the revival of the idea of the Spanish empire and Catholicism. Falangism had affiliations in Hispanic countries across the world with Hispanism at the center. Falangism evolved with the Franco military regime and adapted to global conditions.

20. In 1953 the United States and Spain signed the Madrid Agreements. Under this agreement the United States could build four military bases in Spain in exchange for economic and military help. These binational agreements marked the end of the Spanish economic blockade.

21. The Spanish producer Cesáreo González exploited an innovative way of producing films through Spanish-language transnational networks between Spain and Latin America. Despite the fact that there were some co-productions, with directors mainly from Mexico and Argentina directing in Spain and actors from the three countries with leading roles across the three countries, the operationalization of a "common market" in film between Spain and Latin America did not really happen.

22. In Spain about 100,000 disappeared during the Franco regime and about 50,000 were executed (Junquera 2014).

23. In this genre, it was common to write music to accompany poems from dissident artists, or to sing in Euskera, Valenciano, Catalan, or Gallego. There were even collective regional movement such as Els Setze Jutges in Cataluna, Ez Dok Amaru in the Basque country, and the Manifieso Cancion del Sur in Andalucia. Singers such as Victor Manuel, Anabel, Luis Lalo, Paco Ibáñez, Joan Manuel Serrat, and Luis Eduardo Aute were emblematic of their opposition to the excesses of Franco's dictatorship.

24. Some of the most iconic film directors of *la movida* are Pedro Almodóvar, Fernando Trueba, and Iván Zulueta.

25. All trade unions and political opponents across a vast political spectrum, from communists to Basque separatists, were either suppressed, outlawed, or tightly controlled.

26. Franco forbade the use of Catalan, Galician and Basque, to the extent of making illegal, null, and void all government, notarial, legal, and commercial documents that were not drawn up exclusively in Castilian.

27. To mention some: in Argentina, Mercedes Sosa, Nacha Guevara, Facundo Cabral, Jose Larralde; in Uruguay, Alfredo Zitarrosa, Anibal Sampayo, Los Zucara. In Bolivia the main representatives of this genre were Benjo Cruz, Luis Rico, Jenny Cárdebas, Nilo Soruco, Manuel Monroy Chazarreta (El Papirri), Savia Nueva, Canton Popular, and more recently the duo Negro

y Blanco, Entre 2 Aguas, Raul Ybarnegaray, and Quimbando. In Colombia the artists Ana y Jaime, Pablus Gallinazus, and Norman y Dario were the most representative. In Chile Quilapayún's music was based on Andean folkloric music. At first they were supported by President Salvador Allende; during the dictatorship of Augusto Pinochet, they were clandestine and later lived in exile in France. Their major works include *Santa María de Iquique* (1970), an album of spoken history, songs, and instrumentals about a notorious massacre in the city of Iquique, and the song "El pueblo unido jamás será vencido" ("The people, united, will never be defeated"), with lyrics by Quilapayún and music by famed Chilean songwriter and playwright Sergio Ortega.

28. Even though *La Música Folklórica Latinoamericana* was played in various South American countries, it was in Chile that Quilapayún and Inti Illimani, probably the longest-lasting and most influential musical group representative of the Nueva Canción in Latin America, were founded.

29. The movement of *La Nueva Trova Cubana* is one of the most important within the Nueva Canción Latinoamericano (New Latin American song) in terms of continental influence and musical quality. It emerged in the late 1960s and included the central figure Carlos Puebla, who was a musical chronicler of the Cuban Revolution. The most iconic singers and composers of La Nueva Trova Cubana are Silvio Rodríguez, Pablo Milanes, Vicente Feliu, Leo Brauer, and Noel Nicola. Some of their compositions were inspired by Bob Dylan and Joan Baez, as well as revivalists such as the Chilean composer and singer Violeta Parra and the Uruguayan Daniel Viglietti.

30. Spain's international trade experienced important growth after the country joined the European Union. As of 2002, the EU accounted for around 70 percent of Spain's international trade. The standard of living for most Spaniards has improved in the past thirty years; using all traditional measures such as life expectancy, literacy, and educational enrollments, as well as per capita income, Spain enjoys a relatively high standard of living.

31. El Pacto de Silencio ("The Silence Pact") was a pact created in 1976. This pact of the transition prevented national reconciliation from the explicit condemnation of the dictatorship and the political and moral recognition of the victims and reprisals of franquismo. According to Gabriel y Galán (1988), this pact is one of the most "subtle and paradoxical agreements in the history of Spain because nobody was charged with human rights violations. The core of the pact was of positive revisionism toward the dictatorship and a general erasure of important components of the history of the civil war and the dictatorship that took place. The pact silenced the massacres and extensively used euphemisms for the terrors of franquismo. Collaborators of this pact in the Spanish transition benefited from a blanket of silence. We were told that national interests were above all. But that cannot hide the reality... the lack of checks and balances would lead to a twisting of the historical interpretation of dire consequences."

32. The transition refers to the restoration of democracy in Spain after the death of Francisco Franco in 1975, through the Spanish Constitution of 1978, to the first democratically elected Spanish prime minister on October 28, 1982. Although Spain was experiencing a political and economic crisis, the transition to democracy allowed Spain to join the European Economic Community and NATO.

33. After Spain was isolated for nearly fifty years, most Spaniards saw membership in the European Union as becoming part of a select club of developed and democratic nations.

For two consecutive years after it became part of the European Union, Spain became the world's main recipient of foreign investment, with the highest rate of economic growth in the EU—above 5 percent. Between 1986 and 1995, the EU transferred funds to improve Spanish infrastructure, such as roads, bridges, and agricultural works, to enhance the economic structure, and to enable the creation of significant wealth. Importantly for Spain, within Europe it was no longer viewed as a backward, rural, conservative society, but was seen as a modern, secularized, liberal democracy. The Spaniards themselves valued this change of perception from the outside. All these circumstances reinforced their satisfaction with membership in the EU, as reflected in various surveys conducted in the late 1980s (Eurobarometer 1988, 1989, 1990; Menéndez-Alarcón 2000).

34. According to the IMF, Latin American purchasing power was US$12 trillion in 2015 (Knoema 2015).

35. Spain is the third largest investment source for Mexico worldwide. With more than 49 billion (Notimex 2015), Santander Bank and Spanish BBVA are two of the most active banks in Latin America (Abril 2015).

36. For instance, the Cumbre Iberoamericana that King Juan Carlos organized every year had the Spanish crown as the head of this event. Spanish businessmen have not done their job: there has not been much interaction with the Spanish people who formed the Spanish colony in Mexico during the Civil War. Spanish businessmen do not build upon the great and strong social and cultural network that those children of refugees have built (Morenilla 2016).

37. The Cuban hotel industry is almost a Spanish monopoly. Thirteen out of seventeen hotel companies in Cuba are Spanish. The main two are Melia and Iberostar, which are mainly in Havana, Cayo Cocom, and Varadero (Hernanz 2014). Melia is the biggest foreign hotel operator in Cuba (Jones 2016).

38. Tucker (2014) also explains some internal demographic changes that took place in Spain; after its integration into the European Union, in a short span of two decades Spain became the host country for what are now multigenerational communities from Eastern Europe, North Africa, Latin America, China, and the Indian subcontinent, even after the global economic crisis of 2008 literally stopped such migration to Spain. Such migration waves had some effects on dialogues about deterritorialized citizenship, long-distance belonging, self-reference, and in particular generic citizenship and notions of Latino unity, driven by the market and seeking to control the dislocations of identity. The notions of a uniform Latin American market have been challenged by distinct Latin American communities in their creation and performance of music in Spain.

39. Chavela Vargas was born in Costa Rica in 1917, three years before the end of the Mexican revolution. She was from a very poor rural background and was rejected by her family very early in life due to her sexual orientation. She lived in Cuba for two years as an artist and then went to Mexico. It was not until her late fifties when she became part of the mainstream. She was known for performing with jorongo, huaraches, and calzones blancos. She was close friends with the Mexican revolutionary intelligentsia, such as Diego Rivera and Frida Kahlo, as well as with most Latin American and Spanish intellectuals and politicians.

40. Vargas songs in Almodóvar films include "Piensa en mi" in *Tacones lejanos* (*High Heels*, 1991); "Luz de luna" in *Kika* (1993); "En el último trago" appeared in *La flor de mi secreto* (*The Flower of My Secret*, 1995); and "*Somos*" in *Carne trémula* (*Live Flesh*, 1998).

41. Tehuanas are women from Tehuantepec, Oaxaca, México. The city is the center of the Zapotec culture in the isthmus of Tehuantepec. The city is known for having a matriarchal culture where women make up nearly all of the buyers and sellers of the market, and, until fifty years ago, men were completed banned from the markets. The gala dress of the Tehuanas consists of a *huipil* (a straight rectangular top) made from either satin or velvet and embroidered with ornate floral or geometric borders that frame the neckline and chest.

42. The jorongo is a very large, coat-like woven poncho with a single slit in it for the head.

43. These are Mexican sandals that are made of all leather; later designs included woven string soles and occasionally thin wooden soles.

44. At the same time, Vargas (in her autobiography) and Frida (in her paintings) seem to have carefully cultivated self-images of the "heroic sufferer woman."

45. This cultural palace is administered by the Instituto Nacional de Bellas Artes, which belongs to the Mexican federal government.

46. Most of Almodóvar's work with Chavela Vargas relies on what the Mexican writer Carlos Monsiváis calls the "excesses" of Mexican working-class cultural expressions.

47. Las soldaderas participated in the Mexican Revolution (1910–1920) in almost every role in both the federal and the revolutionary armies. For the most part, las soldaderas carried out support work such as espionage, smuggling, and homemaking; they were sexual partners, mail carriers, medical aides, and in many cases they had their own battalions made up of only women. According to Poniatowska, General Emiliano Zapata was one of the few revolutionaries who acknowledged, respected, and gave leading roles to the soldaderas. The most famous soldaderas Zapatistas are Rosa Bodadilla, Maria Esperanza Chavira, Catalina Zapata Muñoz, Carmen Amelia Robles, Rosa Bobadilla Viudad de Casas (a Zapatista colonel), Juana Ramona Viudad de Flores (la Tigresa), Carmen Parra de Alanis, and Angela Gómez Saldaña (Poniatowska 2000, 16). Petra Herrera had a leading role in the Torreon battle, helping the Villistas troops, and at times passed as a man in order to be part of the revolution (Poniatowska 2000, 16).

48. Sánchez composed over 400 songs (some of the most famous are "Anoche estuve llorando," "Qué manera de perder," "El mil amores," "Grítenme piedras del campo," "Fallaste corazón," "No soy monedita de oro," "Corazoncito tirano," "La cama de piedra," "El compadre más padre," "Guitarras, lloren guitarras," and "Arrieros somos") and most iconic female and male ranchera singers performed these famous songs (Jorge Negrete, Pedro Infante, Lucha Villa, Lucha Reyes, Lola Beltrán, Lola Flores, Vicki Carr, Miguel Aceves Mejia, Antonio Aguilar, Pepe Aguilar, Vicente Fernández, Pedro Fernández, Amalia Mendoza, Amalia Rodríguez, Rosenda Bernal, Aída Cuevas, Selena, and others, including Chavela Vargas).

49. For example: "De piedra ha de ser la cama" (The bed must be made of stone), "No soy monedita de oro para caerles bien a todos" (I am not a golden coin to be liked by everybody), "El mundo, ese gran puerto donde unos llegan y otros se van" (The world, which is a great port where some come and some leave), and "Arriero somos y en el camino andamos" (We are muleteers and we follow the same path).

11

BRITISH ASIAN CULTURE AND ITS MARGINS IN EAST LONDON

NILANJANA BHATTACHARJYA

By the summer of 1999, the collective emergence of British popular musicians of South Asian heritage—along with writers, actors, and visual artists from that background—into the mainstream was celebrated as a breakthrough, both within the British Asian community and throughout wider British culture. (Within Britain, the term "Asian" is understood to refer to people of South Asian heritage.) Ironically, this new articulation of British Asian identity, and its celebration in the press, presumed a type of cohesive British Asian "community" that did not actually exist across varied linguistic, regional, religious, national, and ethnic identities and socioeconomic circumstances. It created a largely fictional fraternity among groups of people who, culturally, may not have had much in common but within Britain found their music and art thrust into and often conflated within a single collective discourse. One such group is the immigrant population from Bangladesh and their descendants, who attempted to maintain and articulate a separate identity, in the face of being absorbed within a generic British Asian identity.

When British Asian identity became recognized as a meaningful category, it created a marketable term that was both commercially and politically convenient. However, that singular construction threatened the preservation of specific British Asian identities that more truthfully reflected the reality of diverse British Asian subcultures. That tension between British Asian identity and the articulation of more particular British Asian subcultures may be traced in two celebrations of British Asian and British Bangladeshi identity, both occurring in July 1999 in East London, specifically the ward of Spitalfields and Banglatown, where many British Bangladeshis live. During my fieldwork in East London, I visited several events associated with these two celebrations and struggled to map both the intentional and unintentional connections between these two celebrations. While Arts Worldwide's Bangladesh Festival sought to celebrate the culture of Bangladesh, as well as the culture associated with the large Bangladeshi population in East London, the Whitechapel exhibition *Gallery's ooo: British Asian Cultural Provocation* showcased the work of British Asian avant-garde visual artists in their twenties and thirties. Both events explicitly incorporated British Asian popular musicians into their activities, taking full advantage of their newfound popularity with the general British public; and the terms of these musicians' participation brought this tension into greater focus.

BENGAL, BRITAIN, AND BANGLADESH

To understand the role of music in Bangladeshi identity in the late 1990s, it is necessary to consider the geopolitical history of the linguistic and cultural region called Bengal and the formation of the nation-state Bangladesh. The name Bangladesh literally translates as "Bengal(i) country" in the Bengali language, where "Bengal" refers to a region that today encompasses the country of Bangladesh as well as the state of West Bengal in eastern India. Bengal had been unified for centuries until 1905, when the British colonial administration divided it into two—leading to a Muslim-majority province in Eastern Bengal and Assam. Bengal was reunited in 1911, but the recent migration of Muslims from the west to the east had already begun to distinguish each half of the province (Metcalf and Metcalf 2001, 154). Following the independence of India in 1947, the ensuing partition of British India into largely Muslim Pakistan and largely Hindu India once again divided eastern and western Bengal. The Partition ceded West Bengal to India and East Bengal to East Pakistan, physically separated from West Pakistan by several Indian states. From 1947 onward, the Bengali speakers in East Pakistan—over 50 percent of Pakistan's population—resented what they felt to be their systematic exploitation by their richer compatriots in West Pakistan, where the central government was positioned. During the 1960s, the people of East Pakistan began to mobilize for an autonomous Bengali state. With the aid of the Indian army, the Mukti Bahini (Liberation Army) defeated the Pakistani army in December 1971 to form the present-day country of Bangladesh.

Bangladesh's tumultuous political history of coups, assassinations, and military rule since 1971 has challenged its attempts to define a cultural history distinct from that of Indian and Pakistani culture. Language, music, and art were employed to establish independent cultural legitimacy and political sovereignty in the new country of Bangladesh, even if the new government lacked resources to provide and develop much more than basic social and economic institutions. The crucial role of nationalist and patriotic songs in the classical music traditions of Bangladesh is linked to that nation's efforts to establish its political sovereignty. The patriotic and nationalist songs associated with composers like Kazi Nazrul Islam contributed a major part of the new music composed in East Bengal. During the 1930s Nazrul set many of his poems, many with anti-colonial themes, to music. Along with helping promote the Bengali language, the performance of his songs (*Nazrulgeeti* or *Nazrulsangeet*) and other patriotic Bengali songs during the 1950s and 1960s served to articulate Bengali identity and thus resist West Pakistan's attempts to dominate East Pakistan's culture, history, and economy. The performance of these songs in Bengali, as opposed to Urdu, played an especially significant role.

BENGALI MIGRATION AND SETTLEMENT IN EAST LONDON

Only after India's independence and Partition in 1947 did Bengalis from East Pakistan migrate to Britain in large numbers. By the mid-1960s, many Bengalis had settled around Brick Lane in East London, where they worked in sweatshops, and by the 1970s—during which time East Pakistan gained independence from Pakistan to become Bangladesh—Brick Lane had become mostly Bangladeshi, and had witnessed a large number of violent attacks on their community by skinheads and members of the National Front (Sandhu 2003). In April 1978 a young Bangladeshi factor worker, Altab Ali, was murdered. A park that bears his name lies almost directly across from the Whitechapel Gallery. Several anti-racist protests followed, which resulted in the increasing politicization of the Bengali population.

Many British Bangladeshi musicians came of age in the late 1970s and early 1980s, amid the population's politicization against racism. In the early 1990s, two more young Bangladeshi men from the area were killed, after which Bengalis began to feel increasingly distant from a "British Asian" identity, which they associated more with Hindus and Sikhs—that is, "success stories and model minorities." Frustrated with their parents' passivity, a younger generation of British Bangladeshis joined gangs, and others joined Islamic groups. Many second-generation British Bangladeshis still maintain ties to Bangladesh, and the younger generation often refers to their parents' native land as "home" even if they are alienated from their parents' and other older people's mostly secular politics, which had partly motivated Bangladesh's independence (Sandhu 2003). For some younger generations, the idealism surrounding Bengali nationalism and its possibilities for a newly independent nation has faded away.

British Bangladeshi musicians from the older generation used community activism to affirm their identities. One of the most significant of these activist groups was the League of Joi Bangla. Formed in East London in the early 1980s to foster a positive vision of Bengali identity, the league generated the Joi Bangla sound system, whose members later formed the Joi band, as well as State of Bengal and Asian Dub Foundation. The older musicians associated with Joi still identify strongly with this form of Bengali identity, which is linked both to the Bangladeshi struggle for independence and to the mobilization of the Bengali community during the late 1970s against racism (Gardner and Shukur 1994, 161). The original league had 150 members and organized activities for younger people, including traditional cultural shows, to connect the second generation to their parents' generation and promote Bengali culture (Mohaiemen 1999). Members of the sound system performed in a variety of venues, such as for morning television news shows as well as for different cultural celebrations, including *melas* (fairs and festivals) organized by the South Asian immigrant population. In an interview, Sam Zaman, an original member of the Joi Bangla sound system who later performed under the moniker State of Bengal, noted that many of their songs dealt with political issues and affirmed Bangladeshi/Bengali identity (Zaman 1999).

The British Bangladeshi population in East London—specifically within the borough of Tower Hamlets—is still relatively impoverished. In 1993 the British Bangladeshi population was recognized as the fastest rising youth population in Europe. Their rapid growth has loomed, though, as a threat, wherein Bangladeshi young men are figured as prone to committing physical violence, joining gangs, and selling drugs, or to becoming extremist Muslims and refusing to integrate into British (that is, English) norms. In 2002 British Bangladeshis numbered an estimated 300,000, of which 86,000 lived in the city of London, and 50,000 within the East London borough of Tower Hamlets, where they comprised 28 percent of the total population (Tower Hamlets Council 2001). The British Bangladeshi population in Tower Hamlets in the late 1990s was challenged by a rising number of street gangs and associated violent incidents, a high rate of drug addiction, scarce housing for large families, and widespread unemployment. The relative lack of opportunities for this population has discouraged many younger British Bangladeshis from pursuing community work organized around British Bangladeshi identity, a category that for them appears to have little if any political or practical use.

THE BANGLADESH FESTIVAL

In 1999 the charity organization Arts Worldwide directed their efforts toward the Tower Hamlets population and organized the Bangladesh Festival ("Arts Worldwide" 2004). The Bangladesh Festival's celebration of Bangladeshi nationalism and traditional cultures tried to remedy the fact that British Bangladeshi young people could not afford the time off or expense to visit Bangladesh and risked being distanced from their Bengali heritage. Held July 7–25, 1999, across different venues in London, the festival featured a photography exhibition, musical performances, poetry readings, plays, crafts exhibitions, storytelling, and a food fair. Founded in 1982, Arts Worldwide had previously organized other events celebrating cultures from different parts of the world. The Bangladesh Festival was the second of two internationally focused festivals organized by Arts Worldwide, the first being a Yemen Festival in 1997. Why Bangladesh was chosen as a focal point has as much if not more to do with potential funding as with the richness of Bangladeshi culture. The sources of funding for the Bangladesh Festival determined the nature of the events featured in the festivals, including those associated with British Asian popular musicians. Billed as "the largest ever celebration of Bangladeshi arts and culture in Europe," the festival had a high profile and was covered extensively in all of London's major newspapers, as well as in some other European publications.

Building the festival's relationship with "the Bangladeshi community" was a key component of the festival's original conception. The project's proposed focus on involving and empowering the "community" made it particularly attractive to public funding organizations and policymakers (Fremeaux 2000, 46). The festival patrons, as identified on publicity materials, notably included Prime Minister Sheikh Hasina of Bangladesh and Prime Minister Tony Blair, both of whom addressed audiences in person at the festival's opening ceremony in London. Private sponsors included the primary sponsor Beximco, as well as Shell, the British firm Cairn Energy, and Duncan Brothers (Fremeaux 2000, 46). As part of its mission, Arts Worldwide attempts to work with different immigrant communities in Britain to feature their respective cultures in festivals, and to involve them within those festivals as "advisors, artists and audiences" ("Arts Worldwide" 2004). Within the context of the Bangladesh Festival, the empowerment project took the form of involving local youth and other community members in the administration of the festival, and through that participation, strengthening their self-confidence as individuals and as a community. The Bangladesh Festival also encouraged outsiders to recognize the existence of Bangladeshi culture in the East End via its physical locations, which required visitors from other parts of London to visit the East End for the festival.

The Bangladesh Festival sought to present an exuberant and vital portrayal of Bangladeshi culture, whose existence is only seldom acknowledged outside Bangladesh. As a young British Bangladeshi staff member at the Festival, Kazi Ruksana Begum, pointed out, "The first thing that comes to most people's minds when you mention Bangladesh is floods" (Dhingra 1999). Amid news reports of natural disasters, political unrest, and profound poverty, Bangladesh's distinct musical and artistic traditions are often unrecognized. The relative invisibility of Bangladeshi music outside the country suggests that Bangladesh lacks any noteworthy musical traditions and thus potentially challenges British Bangladeshis' attempts to assert their cultural legitimacy, as well as their claim to more recognizably "modern" British identities.

Performances and appearances by British Asian popular musicians comprised only part of the many musical events associated with the Festival, much of which focused on classical and folk music traditions and featured guest artists who had traveled from Bangladesh. The variety of classical and folk traditions within Bangladesh was evident through the broad range of performances, which included *Dhabi's Story: A Tale from the Time of Truth*, a musical based on a traditional Bengali story and folk music and performed by local schoolchildren, and *The Heart of Bangladesh*, a performance featuring several different types of folk music and comprised of over thirty visiting folk musicians from Bangladesh, including Bauls (devotional singers and mystics), the Chittagong Drummers from southern Bangladesh, the Manipuri Dancers (performing a classical tradition from northeastern India and Bangladesh), and the Murong dancers and musicians (an indigenous group from the forest, distinguished by its use of bamboo pipes) (*Arts Worldwide Bangladesh Festival* 1999, 6).

The Bangladesh Festival also included an evening of poetry, readings, and performances in tribute to the Bengali poet Rabindranath Tagore, as well as a concert of Nazrul songs, which featured the leading performer of Nazrul songs in Bangladesh, Nilufer Yasmin (*Arts Worldwide Bangladesh Festival* 1999, 7). *Nazrulsangeet* is perhaps the only form of Bangladeshi classical music more strongly associated with Bangladesh than with India. Another concert of Baul music featured songs based on the nineteenth-century mystical poetry of Lalon (also known as Lalon Shah or Lalon Fakir) and the *zamindar* (landlord) Hasan Raja, "who renounced a life of tyrannical womanizing to become a devout philosopher and a writer of simple and moving

[Sufi] devotional songs." Bidit Lal Das, a leading exponent of Bengali folk song in Bangladesh, performed Hasan Raja's songs, and Farida Parveen, the most well-known performer of Lalon songs in Bangladesh, performed Lalon Shah's songs (*Arts Worldwide Bangladesh Festival* 1999, 9).

Baul songs are typically performed by Bauls themselves, members of a religious sect found in both West Bengal in India and in Bangladesh. For most of the nineteenth century, the Bauls' rejection of the caste system and practice of esoteric sexual and scatological tantric rituals designated them as social outcasts, morally repugnant to urban middle- and upper-class Bengali culture. In 1883, however, a young Rabindranath Tagore published a review of collected Baul poems in which he charged other Bengali writers to emulate the Baul texts' direct and natural style, as well as their longing for freedom from conventions (Capwell 1986, 22). Tagore's regard for the Bauls continues to elevate their status within middle- and upper-class Bengali culture, and the singing of Baul songs and their poetic texts, even outside their original context, serves to perform a significant role in affirming a sense of Bengali identity.

The performance of Lalon, Tagore, and Nazrul songs in the late 1960s had constituted a significant expression of Bangladeshi nationalism and resistance against the Pakistani government. Thus, while the performance of these classical and folk songs in the context of the Bangladesh Festival established, for cultural outsiders, Bangladesh's claim to a rich cultural heritage, it also served to reinforce the initial optimism associated with a relatively recent nationalist struggle for the Bangladeshi population, and to let British Bangladeshis share and affirm those patriotic feelings in a foreign space.

While the Bangladesh Festival's frequent focus on established traditions relied mostly on musicians from Bangladesh, as opposed to British Asian popular musicians, the latter still served a crucial role in the community empowerment project, particularly in the DJ and song competition called "Banglatown Sounds." In this competition, described as "the chance to find out why the East End is currently the most popular place to be in London" (*Arts Worldwide Bangladesh Festival* 1999, 9), local youth submitted recordings of their own music to a panel of prominent, commercially successful British Asian musicians and DJs, described as "key music industry figures," including Deedar Zaman and Dr. Das, the MC and bassist, respectively, for the popular band Asian Dub Foundation; Mo Magic, a DJ and music producer associated with the British Asian club and record label Outcaste; Ansar Ullah Ahmed, a community activist and original member of the British East London–based Joi Bangla band in the 1980s; Sam Zaman, a producer and

DJ known as State of Bengal, also associated with Joi Bangla; and DJ Ritu, the host of a weekly bhangra show on BBC Radio 1 and one of the first and most prominent British Asian DJs. (Deedar Zaman is of Bangladeshi heritage and the younger brother of Sam Zaman; Dr. Das [Aniruddha Das] is of West Bengali [Indian] heritage; Ansar Ullah Ahmed is and State of Bengal [Sam Zaman] was of Bangladeshi heritage; and DJ Ritu is of Punjabi heritage.)

The Bangladesh Festival's club night, the Festival Club, took place at 333, a popular club on Old Street in Shoreditch, East London, and brought together performances by the competition's winners and other established British Asian popular musicians that were to include Outcaste DJs Badmarsh, Ges-E, and Mo Magic, along with Joi and Asian Dub Foundation (*ooo zerozerozero* 1999, 9). One of Joi's two members, Haroon Shamsher, died suddenly on July 8, 1999—three days before the Banglatown Sounds and Festival Club night was scheduled—so Joi did not actually appear. The involvement of these recognized figures offered East London youth an opportunity to "break into the industry," through which the organizers of the festival intended to involve younger people from a range of socioeconomic backgrounds. Kazi Ruksana Begum, the assistant community program director for the Bangladesh Festival, explained to a reporter from the *Guardian* that her group of festival organizers had helped those youths who submitted demo tapes by working with them in a real studio (Dhingra 1999).

A separate event, a collaboration between Asian Dub Foundation and the Chittagong Drummers at the Barbican, was another of the Festival's high points and brought together Asian Dub Foundation and the "fishermen by day" from Chittagong performing "complex and dramatic music from their 3 ft-long shoulder drums at night" (*Arts Worldwide Bangladesh Festival* 1999, 17). Music critics reviewing the concert were more prepared to discuss the British dub- and jungle-influenced music of Asian Dub Foundation than the Chittagong Drummers, especially because the performance was Asian Dub Foundation's first London appearance that year. The concert was divided into three major sections: a performance by the Chittagong Drummers, then a performance by the Asian Dub Foundation with the Chittagong Drummers, and finally a performance by Asian Dub Foundation on their own, joined by the drummers during the final song. When the concert was publicized in mainstream publications, the concert was strategically billed as an Asian Dub Foundation concert. The publicity brochure framed Asian Dub Foundation as "self-proclaimed" "twenty-first-century electronic troubadours," and more specifically, as a band that specifically engaged with (South Asian) traditional music:

ADF have long been on the record as gleaning traditional folk sounds from their parents' record collections, mutating them technologically for their own musical performances. Now they get to mix live on stage with Bauls and drummers from Bangladesh. (*Arts Worldwide Bangladesh Festival* 1999, 8)

However, the brochure also took care to establish Asian Dub Foundation's then-trendy status, as it proclaimed, "ADF are one of the reasons that all things Asian are deemed definitively 'cool'" (*Arts Worldwide Bangladesh Festival* 1999, 8).

While the Chittagong Drummers' drums involve no electric or electronic production, Asian Dub Foundation's five members include an MC, a bass guitarist, an electric guitarist, and two other members on turntables and synthesizers. As Caroline Sullivan of the *Guardian* noted, the presence of Asian Dub Foundation attracted "a ravey crowd set on turning the place into a club." Sullivan remarks on how the crowd sat still through the Chittagong Drummers, whose "mad swaying was as mesmerising as their drumming." Asian Dub Foundation then returned to play on its own for the second set, "instantly bringing the crowd to their feet," as the "guitarists flung themselves across the stage, the DJs alternated between jungle breakbeats and classical Indian scales" (1999).

BANGLADESHI AND/OR BRITISH ASIAN? THE OOO EXHIBITION AT WHITECHAPEL GALLERY

The presence of British Asian musicians at the exhibition testified to their commercial success as well as their role in creating a stylish, forward-looking version of British Asian identity. *ooo* was timed to coincide with the Bangladesh Festival: it ran July 9–31 at the Whitechapel Art Gallery, which is located next to Brick Lane, the heart of the Bangladeshi community in Tower Hamlets. Curated by the British Asian artist Gavin Fernandes and curator Ilze Strazdina, *ooo* showcased work by British Asian artists, filmmakers, photographers, musicians, and writers. As a prestigious contemporary gallery, the Whitechapel Art Gallery could not, as one writer put it, "get away with a fest that simply turns Bangla for three weeks" (White 1999). The exhibition was thus intended not to present "traditional or modern Bangladesh exclusively, but panoramic images of British Asian identity as conceived by today's second generation" (White 1999). During weekdays, the exhibition space conformed to Whitechapel Art Gallery's identity as an established gallery that focuses on work by new artists, but on weekend evenings, the main exhibition space transformed into a nightclub featuring some of the British Asian popular artists involved in the Bangladesh Festival: State of Bengal, members of Asian Dub Foundation's ADFED music workshop, Black Star Liner, Kingsuk Biswas, Earthtribe, Juttla, Charged, Ges-E, Usman Project, Nitin Sawhney, Badmarsh, Mo Magic, and Joi. The transformation of the gallery is described in *2nd Generation* magazine, which promoted the exhibition (the allusion to "Brown is the New Black" will be discussed later in this chapter):

> Bhangra Beats pumping out of the reception will be the first signal that something's up in the state of Art. Sounding more like Sangeeta Music on Brick Lane than a cold white space, the ground floor has been handed over to . . . live acts . . . [who] will let us headbang maniacally and remind us how the media's Brown is the New Black was born. (White 1999)

The brochure from the exhibition related another version of the musical events:

> British-Asian music has come a long way from the full-on Bhangra experience and Bollywood babes in bulging saris, with influential protagonists immersed in most contemporary genres. The ooo zerozerozero stage will host four live club nights with lead performances from Joi, State of Bengal, Nitin Sawhney and Indian Ropeman, supported by groups and resident DJs from the nation's hottest venues. (*ooo zerozerozero* 1999)

The magazine *2nd Generation*, which debuted in 1996, spoke to a young, urban, multicultural audience; a blurb in the first issue claimed to "set a new agenda, one that transcends colour, one that celebrates the eclectic nature of your culture" (Datar 1996). The magazine incorporated the artsy, street-inspired interface of then-established style magazines such as *The Face* (now defunct) and *i-D*. Founding editor Imran Khan recognized something new in this newest generation of British Asians, and his statement is echoed by countless media reporters writing on the trendiness of Asian-influenced style during the mid- to late 1990s:

> If you consider the whole concept of an Asian culture as such, it hasn't really existed. There is no generic Asian culture. In Britain it's been manipulated by traditionalists—fat 40-year-olds in sequin suits playing bhangra.

> But now something's happening. The second generation are more united and kids are taking elements from everywhere. You can see it when kids switch from cockney to patois to Punjabi in one sentence. (White 1999)

While artists such as Nitin Sawhney and Black Star Liner corresponded to a more marketable version of British Asian identity that had little to do with East London Bangladeshi culture, artists such as Joi and State of Bengal, who had been well established in the area since the 1980s as active participants in the League of Joi Bangla, were not as seamlessly integrated into this affluent new conception of British Asian identity.

While Joi's actual performance was cancelled due to the sudden death of band member Haroon Shamsher, the fact that they, along with State of Bengal, were originally included in the *ooo zerozerozero* music performances substantiated the exhibition's attempts to include and engage with the East London Bangladeshi community. The two bands, Joi and State of Bengal, both released albums in 1999. Even if Joi, unlike State of Bengal, had no formal connections to the Anokha club and its associated "Asian Underground" compilation recording,[1] they were an established act. Originating from the Joi Bangla movement and then branching out on separate projects as the Joi Bangla Sound System, brothers Haroon and Farook Shamsher mixed bhangra and traditional Bengal folk music with James Brown, hip hop, and acid house. The Shamshers acknowledged their father, a traditional "Bangoli" flutist, as a formative influence. Their father was the owner of the first Bengali tape shop in Brick Lane, the Reena Sari & Music Center, and played music with other traditional musicians as they were growing up. As part of the Joi Bangla League Sound System, they mixed the music from their father's traditional Bengali music cassette tapes with more contemporary Western popular music:

> Back then, it was really racist, so people didn't mix. We really wanted to use the band to bring people together.... So we would be playing James Brown, Michael Jackson, and they would be dancing away—and we would slip in a little bit of Amiruddin on top, and before they knew it, they would be dancing away. Amiruddin wasn't a dance beat, but technically it does have a tempo that you can match with the dance tempo, and the chants, so you can get it to match. (Mohaiemen 1999)[2]

After Joi broke away from the League of Joi Bangla, they moved away from an exclusive focus on British Bengali identity and released sporadic recordings through the mid-1990s. They released an acid house single called "Taj Mahouse" under the name Joi in 1988 and began an "Asian night" at the Bass Clef club in London. In 1993 they released another single, "Desert Storm"—named the *NME* Single of the Week, which *NME* described as "one of the most inventive dance records ever made" (n.d.). Their "big break" arrived when they were signed to Peter Gabriel's Real World label in the late 1990s and asked to produce a full-length album for the first time.

The DJ and producer State of Bengal (Sam Zaman) was well known for his DJ sets as well as his song "Flight IC 408," a staple at the club Anokha in the mid-1990s, which also appears on the Anokha compilation. The song opens with an airline announcement announcing the departure of an Indian Airlines flight to Calcutta that leads into a swinging, irregularly metered folk instrument sample from what sounds like the *ektara*, a single-stringed instrument associated with Baul music. The song later features the *mandira*, finger cymbals, as well as a syncopated, lower-pitched, highly resonant frame drum, most likely the *duf*. While the duf is associated Middle Eastern traditional music, Sam Zaman maintained an extensive personal collection of instruments; having grown up partly in Jordan, he was exposed to music from that area and regularly incorporated its instruments and rhythmic patterns (along with traditional Bengali instruments and musical influences) into his music (Zaman 1999). The song incorporates the sound of these instruments associated with South Asian folk traditions alongside digital drum'n'bass dance beats, a relaxed surf guitar, and retro jazz/soul guitar riffs. Joi and State of Bengal's songs thus simultaneously expressed local East London Bangladeshi culture and British Asian music's commercial success and mainstream popularity.

The evening performances at the Whitechapel Gallery attracted a mixture of audience members, including typically younger museumgoers, middle- to upper-class British Asians, and a few young people from the area. The Whitechapel Gallery is not a space where most British Bangladeshis who live around Brick Lane feel comfortable. Mo White of *2nd Generation*, the magazine that sponsored the exhibition, noted: "As a gallery, the Whitechapel was originally designed to serve the community. And with the local kids growing up fast these days, it's certainly time that Bangla got a look in" (1999).

COMMUNITIES, LOCATION, AND EXPERIENCE

As I visited the *ooo zerozerozero* exhibition one day, I noticed a flyer announcing that people could convene to be taken on a tour of the area by local Bangladeshi youth. When I later mentioned this announcement to two younger British Bangladeshi friends, also from the area, they started to laugh. One of them explained, "What are they going to show you? 'My friend pushes dope on this corner, this is where I got knifed, this is where you can get cheap drugs . . . ?'" As they pointed out, the Whitechapel's tour limited itself to a sanitized, and therefore celebratory version of Brick Lane. Instead, I walked around with them to learn what they thought was worth visiting. We visited the Spitalfields Market, which was hosting the Spitalfields Community Festival that weekend. We walked into the giant market shed (since torn down) and found an older group of people in folding chairs watching a performance of traditional Bengali music on a makeshift stage. The colorful banner behind them was bilingual in English and Bengali, and women at nearby tables sold traditional crafts and clothing from Bangladesh. We then stopped at the Sweet 'n' Spicy, one of the oldest informal Indian/Bangladeshi restaurants in the area. The small, cramped space in the heart of Brick Lane featured brightly colored poster paintings of half-naked Indian wrestlers. Next we walked by the former Truman Brewery at the other end of Brick Lane, which had by then been converted into the popular Vibe Bar and some other upscale shops, including a new furniture design store which one could only enter by stooping down and crawling through a lighted tunnel. Once we entered the store, we heard cricket noises as we discovered furniture made out of the thinnest paper imaginable. What we saw was more an avant-garde installation than a furniture design shop, which pointed to the recent development of the area into an upscale, trendy area catering to wealthier Londoners.

On the days I would walk through Brick Lane on my own during that time, I was often the only Asian woman on the street. Small shops, including grocery stores, religious stores featuring Islamic materials, music stores, and clothing stores, as well as clothing manufacturers and import/export outfits, lined the streets. Walking near the Brick Lane Mosque, formerly a synagogue, I would see bearded men in the traditional white *thobe* and *taqiyah* (long robe and cap). At night, the scene would change, and young, white Londoners filled the streets as they walked from one club and restaurant to another. Hawkers in front of each Indian/Bangladeshi restaurant would call out to those passing by to come into their restaurant. While some outsiders were familiar with Brick Lane as a nightspot, most people at this time would not have visited Brick Lane during the day, an entirely different cultural space.

MEDIA COVERAGE OF THE *000 ZEROZEROZERO* EXHIBITION AND THE BANGLADESH FESTIVAL

The exhibition's physical proximity and temporal overlap with the Bangladesh Festival made it difficult to distinguish between the exhibition and the festival's respective events and performances, and the presence of the same musicians at both of the events also forged a connection between the *000 zerozerozero* exhibition and the Bangladesh Festival. The connections intentionally forged by the organizers of the respective events often encouraged others to make their own connections, most of which conflated Bangladeshi and British Asian identity.

This conflation appears in an article by Tim Marsh, a reporter with the *Times*. Marsh extolls the scale of the Bangladeshi Festival about to unfold but adds, "amid the traditional music and costumes is art that isn't afraid to shock and artists who won't be pigeonholed" (Marsh 1999). Marsh interprets these events' overlapping schedules and proximity to one another as a means through which the area was attempting to revitalize its "Asian Pride" after Brick Lane was targeted by a white supremacist with a nail bomb attack a few months earlier. In his article, he alternates between writing about the Bangladesh Festival and the *000* exhibition as if they were interchangeable, and as if they were a single collective event. In doing so, he unintentionally brings the tensions between British Asian and Bangladeshi identity to the fore. Marsh notes that the organizers of the *000 zerozerozero* exhibition had to "overcome initial skepticism from . . . the British Asian artists involved." Immediately afterward, he quotes Deedar Zaman, who was scheduled to appear at Asian Dub Foundation's performance at the Barbican (with the Bauls and the Chittagong Drummers). Zaman comments, "We've done these things all our lives and they've just been flops" (Marsh 1999)—but this relates to their participation in the Bangladesh Festival, not the *000 zerozerozero* exhibition.

Zaman's cynicism is not entirely unrelated to that of the exhibition's participants, but Marsh's conflation denies that the Bangladesh Festival and the exhibition may have had different respective aims. The Bangladesh Festival of course sought to celebrate Bangladeshi culture and, in doing so, empower the Bangladeshi population in London. Asian Dub Foundation members consider themselves activists as much as or more than they consider themselves musicians, and their lyrics take an explicit stand against racism and social injustice in Britain. In the quotation above, Zaman does not protest against being associated with Bangladeshi or Asian culture as much as he protests the fleeting and superficial celebration of Bangladeshi culture that provides little to no lasting benefit to the poorer Bangladeshi populations in London.

Marsh conflates Zaman's reluctance to participate with that of Simon Tegala, a conceptual artist featured in the *ooo zerozerozero* exhibition:

> When the Whitechapel [Gallery] first approached me I thought, "Hello, this is dodgy territory"—mainly because the reason for being invited was not specifically down to my work but because of my cultural background. ... I don't really address issues of identity ... in my work. I don't want to be labelled as an Asian artist, I want to be labelled as an artist who happens to be Asian. I think there is quite a difference." (Tegala, quoted in Marsh 1999)

Mo White in *2nd Generation* acknowledged the organizers' sensitivity to Tegala and other artists' concerns:

> Aware of the negative reception and pigeon-holing that a directly Asian tag may cause, zerozerozero has taken the abstract zero as its emblem. The title's subtext informs us that as a concept, zero originated in the Indian sub-continent. And more importantly, like the second generation itself, not to mention the artists involved, zero is an integral part of the year 2000. (White 1999)

Evoking the name of the exhibition, White's explanation bases itself in the concept of zero's origin in the Indian sub-continent, and attributing zero to South Asia helps define India and South Asia as places that were advanced enough to produce mathematical concepts that were crucial to the development of Western science and technology. At the end, however, White's comment sounds somewhat glib and suggests that very little unifies the artists and musicians who were featured in the exhibition.

The Whitechapel's decision to hold the *ooo* exhibition and thus engage the local Bangladeshi population was somewhat expected as part of its obligations to feature more culturally diverse programming and engage in community outreach:

> The decision, obviously fuelled by the Brown is the new Black school of thought, is suspect but has also been taken in the nick of time. Black Arts may be a dated concept which many artists dislike being associated with but exhibitions need themes, and artists need exposure. (White 1999)

In the quotation above, White ironically links the "Brown is the new Black" concept of marketing with the more politicized notion of Black Arts. Led by curators and artists including Keith Piper, Rasheed Araeen, Shaheen Merali, and Eddie Chambers, the Black British Arts Movement developed in the early 1980s and signaled a political alliance between both Afro-Caribbean and British Asian artists, including Keith Piper, Chila Kumari Burman, and Shaheen Merali (Beauchamp-Byrd and Sirmans 1997). Given that both Afro-Caribbeans and South Asians had been similarly discriminated against by racially defined legislation, an alliance between the two—that is, a "Black" identity—was a logical development and potent form of resistance during the 1970s and 1980s. The term "Black" accomplished many goals simultaneously, but one of the most important things it did was to question the primacy of class over race in political critiques (Brah 1996, 97). It was intended to displace the categories "immigrant" and "ethnic minority," both of which were associated with racially defined notions of cultural and political belonging and had thus worked against the unified mobilization of Afro-Caribbeans and South Asians in Britain (Brah 1996, 97). As the concept "Black" entered official state discourse, instead of building solidarity between Afro-Caribbeans and South Asians, it began to pit them against one another as they competed for jobs in the state sector, as well as for state-allocated grants, services, and other resources (Brah 1996, 98). By the 1990s many younger British Asians, many of whom were too young to remember the struggles against racism during the 1970s and 1980s, were unlikely to identify with being "Black."

CONCLUSION

When the marketing slogan "Brown is the new Black" emerged at the end of the 1990s, it did not refer to this earlier politicized history discussed above. Rather, it pointed to the fact that British Asian identity was now fashionable and conveniently marketable. While the Bangladesh Festival and *ooo zerozerozero* exhibition could in practice only represent a limited vision of Bangladeshi and British Asian culture, these events ultimately came to represent and recreate the entirety of those cultures for audiences mostly unfamiliar with them. The Bangladesh Festival was quite explicit about its attempts to recreate a virtual Bangladesh thousands of miles away from its original source, a project that in the context of Britain's colonial history recalls the extensive history of colonial exhibitions that affirmed the power of the British Empire by showcasing the riches of its subjects' cultures. The

Whitechapel Gallery's *ooo zerozerozero* exhibition was, however, attempting to represent a concept so nebulous that the Whitechapel Gallery ended up presenting definitions of British Asian culture that, in a manner similar to idealized colonial representations of colonized cultures, the gallery had itself come up with.

British Asian musicians performed a crucial function in both the Bangladesh Festival and the *ooo zerozerozero* exhibition at the Whitechapel Gallery. The identities conflated within the convenient term "British Asian" encompassed those who were more economically and socially successful, and to a substantially lesser degree, those who were not. Those who were successful were celebrated in the mainstream press as the bright future of the British Asians, and those who did not readily conform to this conception of British Asian identity were at most times ignored. The *ooo zerozerozero* exhibition served as a platform to project a more positive and optimistic formulation of British Asian identity, while the Bangladesh Festival sought to introduce a wider audience to the cultures of Bangladesh and the Bangladeshi immigrant population in London. These respective goals differed so much from the outset that any attempt to connect them would be fraught, but distancing British Bangladeshi populations from this more optimistic conception of British Asian identity would have only emphasized those populations' significant socioeconomic challenges.

British Asian musicians, and British Bangladeshi musicians in particular, were intended to form links between the two events, but more accurately, were enlisted to address the events' most profound shortcomings. The Bangladesh Festival, in its efforts to legitimize Bangladeshi culture, often ended up excluding the very population of East London British Bangladeshis the Festival was intended to engage. In a similar manner, the presence of British Bengali musicians at the Whitechapel Gallery highlighted the tension between the gallery's location in the heart of the Bangladeshi community and its inaccessibility to most of its neighbors. The presence of British Bangladeshi musicians at the Bangladesh Festival was intended to link a more ethnologically oriented Bangladeshi folk festival to contemporary East London street culture. In a similar manner, the commercial success and recognition afforded to musicians such as Joi and State of Bengal seemed to place them in the same category as the visual artists and authors featured in the *ooo zerozerozero* exhibition. While the exhibition succeeded in commodifying both British Asian artists and musicians, by including British Bengali musicians who had grown up in the area, the gallery also performed a public service toward the "community." Each of the musical events that featured British

Bengali musicians posed countless contradictions between highly artificial constructions of Bangladeshi and British Asian identity on one side and lived experience on the other. While the events incorporated British Bengali musicians' performances in an attempt to resolve those contradictions, in the end these musicians' performances instead tended to highlight the tensions and contradictions inherent in each event.

The tensions that emerged between the Bangladesh Festival and the *ooo zerozerozero* exhibition serve to articulate the complex networks in which music and identity may be understood—across news media, memory, and lived experience. The idea of Bangladesh as a referent proved as inconstant as the particular discourse around British Asian identity emerging at that moment. The physical location the Whitechapel Gallery shared with British Bangladeshi populations in London proved the only real point of continuity, and within this confined space, respective attempts to define British Asian identity and Bangladeshi identity relentlessly contested each other at each possible point of contact. In many cases, the presence of music and musicians has contributed to the resolution of cultural conflicts, and musicians have in this respect come to act as significant cultural ambassadors who promote more understanding between opposing points of view—based on the widely circulated concept of music as a "universal language." In this case, the disjunction between conceptions of British Asian and British Bangladeshi identity and experience were so profound that even that most reliable of cultural ambassadors could not resolve these tensions and, on the contrary, served to accentuate them.

BIBLIOGRAPHY

Anokha: Soundz of the Asian Underground. 1997. Quango/Island Records/Omni.

ooo zerozerozero: British Asian Cultural Provocation. 1999a. Exhibition brochure. London: Whitechapel Art Gallery.

Arts Worldwide Bangladesh Festival. 1999b. Publicity pamphlet. London: Arts Worldwide.

Census Key Statistics for Spitalfields & Banglatown Ward. 2001. Tower Hamlets Council. Cited January 9, 2005. http://www.towerhamlets.gov.uk/data/discover/downloads/censusward-SpitalfieldsBanglatown.pdf.

"Arts Worldwide: About Us." 2004. Arts Worldwide. http://www.artsworldwide.org.uk/about_us.html. Accessed August 26, 2016.

"Nation Records: Artists: Joi." [n.d.]. Nation Records. http://www.nationrecs.demon.co.uk/artistshtm/joi.htm. Accessed July 10, 2016.

Bakrania, Falu Pravin. 2013. *Bhangra and Asian Underground: South Asian Music and the Politics of Belonging in Britain*. Durham, NC: Duke University Press.

Beauchamp-Byrd, Mora J., and M. Franklin Sirmans, eds. 1997. *Transforming the Crown: African, Asian and Caribbean Artists in Britain, 1966–1996*. New York: Franklin H. Williams Caribbean Cultural Center/African Diaspora Institute.

Brah, Avtar. 1996. *Cartographies of Diaspora: Contesting Identities, Gender, Racism, Ethnicity*. London and New York: Routledge.

Capwell, Charles. 1986. *The Music of the Bauls of Bengal*. Kent, OH: Kent State University Press.

Datar, Rajan. 1996. "Breaking Away from Bhangra." *The Guardian*, October 14: 14.

Dhingra, Dolly. 1999. "The Bangladesh Beat: Organising a Cultural Festival Requires a Court Jester's Skills, Finds Dolly Dhingra." *The Guardian*, July 12: 55.

Fremeaux, Isabelle. 2000. "Community and Cultural Policy: The Arts Worldwide Bangladesh Festival." *Rising East* 3 (3): 46–68.

Gardner, Katy, and Abdus Shukur. 1994. "'I'm Bengali, I'm Asian, and I'm Living Here': The Changing Identity of British Bengalis." In *Desh Pardesh: The South Asian Presence in Britain*, edited by Roger Ballard, 142–64. London: Hurst & Company.

Marsh, Tim. 1999. "When Cultures Collide: Celebration of Bangladeshi Culture." *The Times*, July 10: 24.

Metcalf, Barbara D., and Thomas R. Metcalf. 2001. *A Concise History of India*. Cambridge: Cambridge University Press.

Mohaiemen, Naeem. 1999. "Joi: Bengali Boys from East London [JOI talks to Naeem: March 15, 1999]." *Shobak*, last modified March 15, 1999. http://www.shobak.org/joi/interview.html.

Sandhu, Sukhdev. 2003. "Come Hungry, Leave Edgy." *London Review of Books*, last modified October 9, 2003. http://www.lrb.co.uk/v25/n19/print/sand01_.html.

Sherwood, James. 1997. "Sari, Sari Nights: The New Asian Cool." *The Independent*, May 11: 3.

Sullivan, Caroline. 1999. "Pop: Asian Dub Foundation: Bangla Beat Sizzles: Barbican, London." *The Guardian*, July 20: 21.

White, Mo. 1999. "zero zero zero: never take nothing for granted." *2nd Generation* 14: 68–69.

Zaman, Sam. 1999. Interview. July 10.

NOTES

1. Talvin Singh, well-known producer and musician, founded the Anokha club night in 1995 with promoter Sweety Kapoor, and released *Anokha: Soundz of the Asian Underground* two years later. See Bakrania 2013 and Sherwood 1997.

2. The brothers are likely referring to the Sylheti Baul singer Kari Amir Uddin Ahmed.

ABOUT THE AUTHORS

NILANJANA BHATTACHARJYA is a Principal Lecturer and Honors Faculty Fellow at Barrett, the Honors College at Arizona State University. Her research interests span popular music and cinema and include popular music in South Asian diasporic communities, music sequences in popular Hindi films, and popular Hindi films and Bollywood.

BENJAMIN BURKHART studied musicology at the University of Würzburg and the University of Music FRANZ LISZT Weimar, where he received his PhD in 2019. Since 2018 he has been a research fellow at the Center for Popular Culture and Music at the University of Freiburg. His research interests are the history, sociology, and technologies of auditory cultures, the analysis and aesthetics of popular music and jazz, and qualitative empirical methodologies in music research.

IVY CHEVERS is assistant professor of creative arts at Frederick Community College in Maryland. She holds a graduate degree from the Ohio State University in Art Education with a minor in African and African American studies. Ivy served as a Peace Corps volunteer in Kingston, Jamaica, for five years. She remained in Jamaica for an additional thirteen years, where she taught art and craft at a high school in rural St. Ann. Ivy's research interests include the study of Rastafarian culture, reggae music, and multicultural and African-centered pedagogies.

MARTHA I. CHEW SÁNCHEZ is associate professor and chair of the Caribbean, Latino and Latin American Studies Program at St. Lawrence University. She is author of the book *Corridos in Migrant Memory* (2006), published by the University of New Mexico Press and translated into Spanish in 2008. Her research and teaching interests are focused on Latino studies, cultural studies, musicology, border studies, ethnic studies, and cultural ecology.

ATHENA ELAFROS is assistant professor of sociology at the University of Lethbridge. She is a qualitative cultural sociologist who studies culture and inequality. Her current projects include collaborations with Dr. Christopher Churchill on the role of different forms of labor within musical and literary cultural fields; with Dr. Amandine Pras, Grace Brooks, and Monica Lockett on sound engineers' and producers' experiences of microaggressions in the recording studio; and with Tif Semach and Wednesday Culley on collecting and preserving the oral histories of GSA (Gay Straight Alliance) and QSA (Queer Straight Alliance) members and facilitators in Alberta, Canada.

WILLIAM GARCÍA-MEDINA is a PhD student in the department of American Studies at the University of Kansas. His research currently focuses on Black ethnics and the construction and social reproduction of Black American racial identity discourse in the public humanities. In 2016 he earned an MA in curriculum and instruction from Teachers College, Columbia University, with a focus on historical literacies in elementary schools. García-Medina also has an MA in history from the University of Puerto Rico, Recinto de Río Piedras.

SARA S. GOEK is program manager at the Association of College and Research Libraries, where she also served as Mellon/ACLS Public Fellow from 2017 to 2019. She holds a PhD in History/Digital Arts and Humanities and an MA in Historical Research from University College Cork, and a BA in History and Irish Studies from Boston College. Her work has appeared in *Choice*, *Éire-Ireland*, the *Dublin Review of Books*, and the *Irish Times*. She plays Irish traditional music in her free time.

DAVID HENDERSON teaches music, film, and Asian studies at St. Lawrence University, where he is chair of the Department of Music. His work has been published in *Ethnomusicology*, *Asian Music*, and *Popular Music and Society*, and he is coeditor, with Ron Emoff, of *Mementos, Artifacts, and Hallucinations from the Ethnographer's Tent* (Routledge, 2002).

EYVIND KANG teaches at California Institute of the Arts, where he currently holds the Mel Powell Chair in music. As a composer and violist he has released more than twenty albums on labels such as I Dischi de Anglica, Abduction, Ipecac, and Tzadik.

JUNKO OBA is associate professor of music at Hampshire College. She holds a BA from International Christian University, Tokyo, Japan, and an MA and a PhD from Wesleyan University, where she was trained as an ethnomusicologist and sound recordings archivist. Her research interests include traditional and contemporary Japanese music cultures; national and nationalized identity performances in the trans- and post-national world; music and collective memory construction; and performative identity politics in Asian diasporas, especially in Brazilian expatriate communities in Japan.

JUAN DAVID RUBIO RESTREPO is a Colombian artist/scholar. As a drummer/percussionist, improviser, composer, conductor, and multimedia artist, his work goes from the acoustic to the electronic in traditional, nontraditional, and multisite-telematic collaborative settings. His current academic research deals with issues of alterity, mediation, and technology in the context of Latin American popular musics. He holds a BM in Drum Performance/Jazz Studies from the Pontificia Universidad Javeriana (Bogotá, Colombia), an MFA in Music in Integrated Composition, Improvisation and Technology from the University of California, Irvine, and a PhD in Music, Integrative Studies from the University of California, San Diego. Juan David is assistant professor of music and Chicano Studies at the University of Texas, El Paso.

GARETH DYLAN SMITH is assistant professor of music at Boston University. His research interests lie at the intersections of music making and music learning in practice and in theory. He is a member of the Music Learning Profiles Project research team. Recent publications include *The Music Learning Profiles Project* (2018), *The Oxford Handbook of Music Making and Leisure* (2016), and *Eudaimonia: Perspectives for Music Learning* (2020). Gareth is a founding editor of the *Journal of Popular Music Education*, and a drummer.

INDEX

Illustrations are in **bold**.

Africa, 95, 98, 102, 103, 140
Africa Unite, 104–5
A full, 69
Aguilar, Antonio, 40–41
Ahmed, Ansar Ullah, 224–25
Akete, 96
Alborosie, xi, 131, 133, 141–44
alcohol, 7, 106, 157, 158, 202
"Aldito el Guzanito," 59
Aldo, 58, 65
Ali, Altab, 220
alienation, 168, 172, 177, 183, 185, 204, 220
Alkaline, 139
Alkana, 60, 67, 71
Allen, Lillian, 120–21
All-Ireland Fleadh Cheoil, 6
All Seasons Reggae group, 105
All Star Jammerz, 93, 99
Almodóvar, Pedro, 201–2, 206
Alto Voltaje, 67
Alvarez, J, 67
Alvez, Luciano, 181–82, 184
Amerindians, 35–36, 49
Anokha club, 228–29
Anthem: Social Movements and the Sound of Solidarity in the African Diaspora, xiii
Anthias, Floya, 163
appropriation. *See* cultural appropriation
Araeen, Rasheed, 233
Arboleda, Blanco, 36
Ardoyne Fleadh, 157
Argentina, 50, 198, 200
Ark Band, 93, 100–102, 105
Armando e Marina, 181
Artesanías Colombia, 45–46, **46**
Arts Worldwide, xii, 218, 222
Asian Dub Foundation, xii, 221, 224–27, 231
"Asian Underground," 228–29

Athens, Greece, 112
aurality, x, 25, 34–43, 45, 47–51
authenticity, 97, 112, 132, 137–38, 180
Avinash, 73, 80, 87

Babel, 201
Baby Lores, 67
Badmarsh, 225, 227
Bah, Modou, 98
Bahini, Mukti, 219
"Bailando," 57
Baker, Geoffrey, 58–59, 61, 66, 69
Baldwin, James, 65
Bangladesh, vii, viii, 218–35
Bangladesh Festival, xii, 218, 222–27, 231–35
Banglatown Sounds, 224–25
Bañón, Medina, 200
Banton, Buju, 105, 139
Banton, Pato, 105
Barbican, 225, 231
Barrett, Leonard, 92
Barros, José, 47–48
Bass Clef Club, 229
Bayen, Maleku, 95
Beat Factory, 120, 122
Beatles, 16, 155
Beat Magazine, 100
Beenie Man, 140
Begum, Kazi Ruksana, 223, 225
Belfast, Ireland, 157, 163
Bengal, 219–21, 223–24, 228; East Bengal, 219–20; West Bengal, 219, 224–25
Benitez-Rojo, Antonio, 63, 65–66, 70
Bennett, Louise (Miss Lou), 121
Berry, Ivan, 120–21
Beximco, 222
Bhabha, Homi, 203
Bigenho, Michelle, xiii
Billboard, 57
Binomio de Oro de América, 48

Biswas, Kingsuk, 227
Black Arts, 232–33
Black August, 59
Black Experience Project (BEP), 114
Black Star Liner, 227–28
Black Uhuru, 91, 139
Blackwell, Chris, 131–32
Blair, Tony, 222
Blanco Arboleda, Darío, 24
Blondie, vii
"Blood on the Streets," 160
"Blue Skies Over Nenagh," 153–54
Blumer, Herbert, 110
Bobb, Eustace, 101
Bobb, Terry, 100–102, 103
Bob Marley and the Wailers, 93. *See also* Marley, Bob; Wailers
Bob Marley Day, 93
Boogie, Mel, 118
Boogie Down Productions (BDP), 120–21
Boston, MA, ix, 14–15, 18, 151; dance halls, 7, 8–9, 15–16; Irish music, 4, 10, 14; Roxbury, 7, 16
Bottero, Wendy, 111
Bounty Killer, 139, 141
Bourdieu, Pierre, 109–11, 125–26
Bowie, David, 157
Bradley, Deborah, 151
Brazil, xii, 168–72, 174–75, 177–85
Brazilian Ministry of Culture, 181
Breeze, Jean, 91
Bresnahan, Johnny, **15**
Brick Lane Mosque, 230
Brooks, Cedric, 96–97, 100
Brown, Dennis, 137, 139
Brown, James, 228
Browne, Packie, 10
Buchholz, Larissa, 111, 120
Buck, Andrew, 103–4
Buena Vista in the Club, 58–59
Burke, Kevin, 3
Burman, Chila Kumari, 233
Busy Signal, 137

Cabrera, Donna, 99
Cabrera, Hugo, 98–99
Cabrera, Jennifer, 99
Cairn Energy, 222
Campbell, Mark V., 119, 121
Campbell, Sean, 150
Canada, x, 111–26
"Canada Large," 123
Canadian Immigration Act, 114
Canadian Recording Industry Association (CRIA), 115
Canary Islands, 137
Candyman, 67
capital: Black cultural, 109, 124, 126; cultural, 109–10, 124–26; financial, 30, 33–34, 109–10, 120, 124–26; social, 109–10, 124; symbolic, 109–10; transnational, 64
capitalism, x, 35, 37, 57–60, 65–66, 208
Capleton, 105
Cárdenos, Lázaro, 191, 194, 208
Caribbean, x–xi, 34, 60–65, 67–68, 70–71, 93, 95, 101–2, 112–15, 119–20, 124, 132, 136, 138, 233; Colombian, 24, 37, 40, 45, 48–49; creolizations, 60–65, 71; culture, 62–63, 70, 111, 119–20, 122, 132; diasporas, 67, 109, 112–15, 119–26, 145; Hispanic, x, 70; migration, 109, 113–14, 124, 131; musical styles, 57–59, 61, 67–68, 71, 120, 126; popular culture, 111, 120, 122; Spanish, 61
Carlos Jones and the Plus Band, 93
Carozzi, María Julia, 24
Carpentier, Alejo, 65
Carranza, Venustiano, 206
Carroll, Tom. *See* SeefarI
Cartagena de Indias, 40
Carvajal, Luis de, 35
caste system, 74–75, 224
Castro, Fidel, 66, 68
Catholicism, 155, 157, 192–93, 197–98
Celso Piña y su Ronda Bogotá, 42
censorship, 193, 198–99
Cepeda, María Elena, xiii
Chamberland, Roger, 116, 119

Chambers, Eddie, 233
chants, 92, 97, 106–7, 198, 228
Charged, 227
Chávez, Alex E., xiii
Chieftains, 155
Chitãozinho e Xororó, 181
Choclair, 125
Cholombianos, 43
Christian, Mark, 94
Christianity, 101, 103, 143, 154, 157, 192, 197
Chronixx, 139
"Chupi Chupi," 66–67
Cincinnati, OH, 91, 93, 94, 99, 104, 105–6
Clancy, Liam, 4, 17
Clancy's, 155
Cleveland, OH, 93, 94, 104, 106
Cleveland Advocate, 94
Cliff, Jimmy, 105, 137
clothing and fashion, 41, 43, 64, 69, 104, 123, 125–26, 157, **157**, 166, 172, 201–2, 230
Coen, Jack, 13
Coleman, Ornette, viii, x, 74, 76–82, 84, 86–87
collective memory, xiii, 16, 96, 208
Colombia, 24, 26–28, 30, 32, 34, 37, 39–42, 45–51
colonialism, x, 25, 27, 34–35, 37, 40, 64, 70, 94, 96, 112–13, 132, 137, 140, 142, 168, 179, 181, 190, 198–99, 202–4, 206, 219–20, 233–34
coloniality, 34–37
Columbus, OH, x, 90, 92–101, 103–4, 106–7
Comhaltas Ceoltóirí Éireann, 6
commercialism, 3, 7–10, 12–13, 15–16, 24, 51, 59, 66, 70, 117–18, 132, 139, 145, 181, 192–93, 218, 224, 226, 229, 234
communism, 57, 192, 197, 201
communities, xiii, 33, 50, 170, 229–30, 232, 234; Afro-Caribbean, 115, 124, 233; Afrocentric, 105; Bangladeshi, 220, 222–23, 226, 228–29, 234; Bengali, 220–21, 224; Black, 93, 97, 105, 233; Brazilian, xii, 166–68, 181–85; British Asian, 218–19, 222–23, 224–29, 231, 233–34; British Bangladeshi, xii, 221, 222–24, 229, 234–35;
British Bengali, 220, 234–35; Caribbean, 114, 132; diasporic, xi, xiii, 63, 96, 112, 125–26, 156, 160; ethnic, 63, 174; imagined, 96; immigrant, 93, 222; Irish, ix, 3, 7, 9, 14–18, 150, 152, 155, 160; Japanese, 168; Latino, 66; marginalized, 32, 34, 37, 69, 71; Nikkey Brazilian, xi–xii, 166–71, 174–75, 177–85; racial, 63; RastafarI, 105; regional, 63; Spanish speaking, 196; subcultural, 136; transnational, 63
Concurso Latino Nodojiman, 170
Conjunto Típico Contreras, 39
"Con la ropa puesta," 69
Connolly, Mickey, 16
Conroy, Jack, 14–15
Conzen, Kathleen Neils, 16
Cooper, Carolyn, 141–42
"Corporate Transnationalism: The U.S. Hispanic and Latin American Television Industries," 64
Council for Mutual Economic Assistance (COMECON), 57–58
Cowie, Del, 120–21
Crane, Diana, 135–36
Crehan, Junior, 5
"Creolite in the Hood," 63
"Creolization in Havana," 65
creolizations, 60–71, 119
Crespo, Francisco, 41
Crichlow, Michaeline, 62
"Crisis de Fe," 59
Cruce de Caminos Ayaguara, Kooperativa Rayenari, 44
Cuba, x, 57–61, 64–71, 192, 200; Revolution, 58–59, 194
cubanidad, 60, 64–71
Cuban Rap Agency, 66
cultural appropriation, 27, 100, 131–33, 136–37, 140, 144, 189, 191–92, 204–5
culture, x, xiii, 3, 18, 32, 34, 40, 42, 47, 62–63, 74–76, 92–93, 106, 109, 114, 133–34, 143, 145, 151, 190, 222, 227, 233–34; Bangladeshi, 218, 222–23, 228–29, 231–34;

INDEX 243

Bengali, 221, 224; Black, 111, 119–20, 122, 124; British, 160, 218; British Asian, xii, 233–34; Caribbean, 62–63, 70, 111, 119–20, 122, 132; Colombian, 26–27, 40; creole, 61, 65, 70–71; cultural capital, 109–10, 124–26; cultural exchange, 133–34, 196, 204; cultural politics, 58–59, 62; cultural production, 60, 65, 67, 109–12, 120–22, 125–26, 180; cultural representation, 121–26; culture shock, 17, 142, 183; cumbia, 25; dancehall, 123, 139, 144; domains, 76, 135; ethnic, 9; hip hop, 66, 109, 112, 115, 117–19, 121, 126; Indian, 219; industry, 31; Irish, 3–4, 9, 155, 158; Jamaican, 122, 136–38, 140–42; Japanese, 183; *la colombia*, ix, 26–27, 29, 31, 40, 45, 51; mainstream, 34; media cultures, 136; Mexican, 194; Nikkey Brazilian, 170, 178–79, 182–83; Pakistani, 219–20; popular, 11, 111, 119–20, 122, 124; Rastafarian, 90–92, 96–97, 100, 106–7; sound-system, 29; Spanish, 190, 202, 204; subcultures, 134–36, 140, 145, 218; transculturality, viii, 24, 131–45; youth, 43

Cumbia! Scenes of a Migrant Latin American Music Genre, 38

Cush, 98

dance halls, viii, ix, 4, 6, 8–18; City Center Ballroom, 13; as commercial ventures, 3, 7–10, 16; as community centers, 3, 7; decline, 15–17; Dudley Street Opera House, 15; Galtymore, 10–12, **11**, 16; Hibernian Hall, 14–15, **15**; Intercolonial, 16; Jaeger House, 13; as liminal spaces, ix, 7, 16, 18; New State Ballroom, 15; O'Byrne DeWitt House of Irish Music, 14; Red Mill, 89; Rose Croix, 15; Winslow Hall, 15

dancing, 4–9, 12, 15–16, 18, 46, 65, 68, 73, 75, 107, 195; céilí dances, 6, 8, 12; couples, 182–84; cumbia, 45; flamenco, 192; jive, 11; Manipuri, 223; modern, 12; Murong, 223; Nyabinghi, 92; sexually explicit, 57

Dando Pro, 68
Das, Aniruddha, 224–25
Das, Bidit Lal, 224
Dávila, Arlene, 61
Dayton Daily News, 105
Dayton Reggae Festival, 105–6
D'Boys, Alexis, 66
de Castro, Eduardo Viveiros, 83
decolonialization, x, 24–25, 34, 37, 51, 198
De Fuentes, Fernando, 196
Delay, Jan, 139, 144
Deleuze, Gilles, 80–82
Delgado, Alexander, 68–69
Del Rio, Dolores, 195
Dent, Alexander, 176, 179–81
Dernesch, Noël, 141
Derrane, Joe, 16
Derrida, Jacques, 77
Descartes, René, 82
"Desert Storm," 229
Dhabi's Story, 223
"Diaspora," 152–53
diasporas, vii, ix, xi–xiii, 162–63, 168, 170, 177, 183; African, viii, 91, 93–96, 106–7; Afro-Caribbean, 119, 145; Black, 121, 123, 125; Black Canadian, 119, 125; Caribbean, 67, 109, 112–15, 119–26, 145; Irish, viii, xi, 4, 149–52, 158–60, 162
Diawara, Manthia, 61
Díaz, Diomedez, 48
displacement, vii, xii, 167–68, 183, 185
DJ Grouch, 117
DJ Power, 119
DJ Ritu, 225
domains, 79, 135; core, 135; cultural, 76, 135; formal, 79; natural, 76; partial, 84; peripheral, 135; urban, 135
Dooley, John P., 151
Drake, 115
Dr. Das, 224–25
Dropkick Murphys, 155
drugs, 43–45, 49, 198, 221

drumming, xi, 97, 105–6, 150, 156–58, 160, 225–26; Burru, 92; Chittagong, 223, 225–26, 231; Nyabinghi, 92; steel, vii; taiko, 179
Duarte, Mario, 45–46, **46**
Dub Inc, 137
Dublin, Ireland, 152, 153–54
Dubliners, 155
Dudley Square, 7, 8–9, 14–16
Dueñez, Gabriel, ix–x, 25–33, **28**, **31**, 36–37, 47–48
Dueñez, Juanita, 26, 28, 29–32, **31**, 48
Dutta, Jyoti Prakash, 76

Earthtribe, 227
Easton, George, 90
economic issues, x, xii, 10, 27, 32–38, 60, 62, 66, 73, 109, 112, 115, 118, 124, 190–97, 199–200, 208, 219–20, 223, 234
Ecuador, 24, 33
Edouard Glissant, 61
El Cata, 69
El Chacal, 67
El Consejo de la Hispanidad, 190, 193
El Día de la Hispanidad, 190
"Elements of Style," 120
Elijah, 138
El Instituto de Cultura Hispánica (ICH), 190, 193
El Micha, 60, 68, 71
"El Mochuelo," 46
"El Sonidero," 32
Emcee Motion, 119
"Emperifollarse," 67
emplacement, xi–xii, 183
Empress Menen Educational Center, 105
England, 10, 90, 150–51, 156–57, 159. *See also* Great Britain
Enlightenment Promotions, 93, 104–5
estilo bravío, 189, 204–8
"Estoy pa'Dartela," 67
Ethiopia, viii, 91, 94–96, 107, 141; battle of Adwa, 94

"Ethiopian, The," 94
Ethiopian World Federation (EWF), 95
Ethnic Diversity Survey, 114
European Union, 189, 199, 200, 203, 215, 216
"Everybody's Welcome to the Hooley," 160
"Every Day's St. Patrick's Day," 158
Eyerman, Ron, 106

Face, The, 227
Fahey, Paddy, 11
Fakir, Lalon, 223–24
"Fallaste corazón," 207
Farruko, 67
Félix, Maria, 195
Fernandes, Gavin, 226
Fernandes, Sujatha, 57–58
Fernandez L'Hoeste, Héctor, 38
Ferrer, Buenaventura, 65
Festival Brasil, 184
Festival Club, 225
"Fields of Athenry, The," 161
film industry, 39, 40–41, 58, 135, 189–98, 201, 207, 226. *See also* Mexican cinema
Finbar, 155
First Priority/Atlantic Records, 119, 122
Flex Crew, 93
"Flight IC 408," 229
Fligstein, Neil, 112
Flogging Molly, 155
Flores, Juan, 63
Flynn, Karen, 112
folklore, 67, 121, 191–92
Foodland Ontario, 122
Forever, Jacob, 68
Foucault, Michel, 204
Four Music, 143
France, 132, 198
Franco, Francisco, 190–94, 196–98, 200, 202–3
Frida, 201
Furey, Eddie, 155

Gabriel, Peter, 229
Gaelic League, 6

Gallagher, Bridie, 11
Gallagher, Liam, 155
Gallagher, Noel, 155
Gámez Torres, Nora, 58–60
gandha, 83–84
gangsterism, 43–44, 221
García, Osmani "La Voz," 60, 66–67
Garratt, Dean, 159
Garvey, Marcus, 94–95, 98, 103, 104, 105, 107
Gayle, Rupert, 120
Gebrekidan, Fikru Negash, 94
gender, 7, 37, 60, 63–64, 67, 69–70, 110, 112–13, 124, 198, 200, 204–6
Gente de Zona, 57, 64, 67–69
Gentleman, xi, 100, 131, 133, 139, 141–44
Germaican Records, 139
Germany, viii, x, xi, 131–45, 192
Ges-E, 225, 227
Ghandarva, Kumar, 74
Ghosh, Pannalal, 74
Gilly, Sam, 137
Gilroy, Paul, 119, 156
Giménez Caballero, Ernesto, 197
Glissant, Edouard, 61–63, 68, 71
Globalisation and the Post-Creole Imagination, 62
globalization, 62–64, 73, 75, 97, 131, 134, 199
Go, Julian, 111
Gonzales, Mileidys, 60, 67, 71
Granados, Pável, 206–7
Great Britain, viii, 4, 7, 10, 18, 137, 149–50, 154–57, 159–63, 219–20, 222, 227, 231; dance halls, 8, 9, 17; dances, 7–8; housing shortage, 10, 221; music, 7–8, 10, 131, 218
Grisey, Gerard, 81–82, 84
Grossberg, Lawrence, 199
Guardian, 225–26
Guattari, Félix, 80–82
Guillén, Nicolás, 65
Guillermoprieto, Alma, 194
Gupta, Gautam, 73–87
Gushi, Sueli, 182
Gutiérrez, Alfredo, ix, 32, 40, 48

Hafez, 87
Haggard, Merle, vii
Half Pint, 91, 105
Halifax, Nova Scotia, 113
Hall, Reg, 12
Hall, Stuart, 44, 109–10, 135
Hamill, Robert, 160
Hammond, Beres, 105
Hara, Minoru, 83
Harmolodics, viii, x, 74–81, 83–87
harmony, 74–75, 78–79, 81, 84, 168, 179–80
Harris, Roxy, 151
Harrison, George, 155
Hasina, Sheikh, 222
Hatano, Marcos, 181, 184
Hatch, Amos, 96
Havana, Cuba, 59, 65, 69–70
Havana Club, 67
Havana Cultura, 67–69
Heart of Bangladesh, The, 223
Helbig, Adriana, xiii
Henke, James, 105
Henry, Frances, 114
Henry, Kevin, 6
Herder, Johann Gottfried, 133
Here's Mud in Yer Eye!, 154
Heritage, Morgan, 105
Hernández Salgar, Oscar, 41
"Heroes," 157
Herrero, Pérez, 200
Hinduism, 219
Hip Hop Ukraine, xiii
Hirano, Isamu Paulo, 184
Hirata, Joe Akio, viii, xi–xii, 166–67, **167**, 169–84, **173**, **176**, **178**
hispanidad, 189–90, 193, 203
hispanismo, xii, 189–93, 197, 199, 202–8
Hollywood, CA, 41, 191, 194
home, viii, xiii, 3, 17–18, 119, 151, 167, 176–77, 183, 185, 220
homophobia, 132, 140, 144. *See also* sexual orientation
Horslips, 155

246 INDEX

Hotel Capri, 69
House of Riddim, 137
Husserl, Edmund, 85

i-D, 227
identity, x, xi, xii–xiii, 8–9, 17–18, 24, 33–34, 37, 43–45, 50, 110, 120, 126, 140, 152, 156–57, 163, 167, 172–76, 178, 232, 234–35; artistic, 201; Bangladeshi, xii, 219, 221, 231, 235; Bengali, 220–22, 224; Black, xii, 114; British, ix, xii, 223; British Asian, xii, 218, 220, 224, 226–29, 231, 233, 235; British Bangladeshi, xii, 218, 235; British Bengali, 221, 228; Canadian, 109, 121–25; collective, 58, 106–7, 110, 125; Cuban, 65, 70; cultural, 109–12, 115, 121–22, 124, 125–26, 183, 191, 204; diasporic, 109, 111, 121, 125; ethnic, 16, 18, 126, 151, 160, 200, 218; formation, 38, 61, 208; hybrid, 123, 125; indigenous, 199; individual, 106; Irish, ix, 4, 9, 12, 16–18, 149, 151–54, 156–63; Irish American, ix, 160; Jamaican, 123–24; Japanese, 183; linguistic, 218; Mexican, 191, 194, 203, 208; narrative, 38, 183; national, 50, 208, 218; negotiation, 168; Nikkey Brazilian, 178; reflexive, 111; regional, 50, 218; religious, 218; Spanish, 190–91; spatial, 175; theories, 110; transnational, 64
Identity, Race and Protest in Jamaica, 92
Iglesias, Enrique, 57
immigrants and immigration, ix, 24, 27, 37, 42, 50, 64, 93, 119, 153, 157, 222, 233; Afro-Trini, 114; Bangladeshi, 218, 234; to Canada, 112–15, 124; Caribbean, 114, 124, 131; Irish, viii, 4, 6, 7–10, 12, 14–18, 152, 160, 190; Italian, 190; Jamaican, 124; Japanese Brazilian, 168–70, 178; Latin American, 28, 36; laws, 171; points system, 113–14; South Asian, 221, 233; West Indian, 132; young, 145. *See also* migrants and migration
Immigration Control and Refugee Recognition Act, 171

In All Languages, 79
Iñarritú, Alejandro González, 201
India, 219–20, 223–25, 232; Partition, 73, 219–20
Indian Ropeman, 227
indigenous populations, 35–37, 40, 49, 83, 190, 199, 201–2, 208. *See also specific populations*
Infante, Pedro, 195
Instituto Cervantes, 190
instruments, 5–6, 8, 65, 96, 106, 155–57, 168, 181–82, 202, 223, 229. *See also* drumming
Insurrecto, 67
International Federation of the Phonographic Industry, 115
International Press, 166
Internet, 33, 70, 76, 181
Invisible Children, 103
Ireland, ix, xi, 3–18; Carrigan Committee, 6; cultural traditions, 3–6, 9, 15–18; economy, 4; football, 161; house dances, 4–6, 10, 13; identity, 4; Irish Free State, 5; Irish Republican political party, 159; migrants, 3–4, 7, 9, 16; potato famine, 160–61; Provisional IRA, 159–60; Tipperary, 153; Tramore, 153–54; Troubles, 159–60; unification, 159
"Ireland's Call," 162–63
Ishi, Angelo, 166–67, 172–74
Islam, 98, 104, 219, 221
Israel, Haile, 101–2
Italy, 94–96, 131, 137, 141–42, 192, 198

Jackson, Michael, 228
Jah9, 139
Jah Sun, 138
Jalisco canta en Sevilla, 196
Jamaica, viii, x, 90–100, 102, 103, 105–7, 113, 120–23, 131–32, 135–45; cultural codes, 90; patois, 120–23, 125, 138, 141
"Jamaican Funk—Canadian Style," 120, 122–23
Jamaica Observer, 97

Jamison, Andrew, 106
Janssen, Susan, 112
Japan, xii, 166–68, 170–75, 177–79, 181–85
Jiménez, José Alfredo, 203
Johnson, Elmer, 91
Johnson, Linton Kwesi, 91
Joi Bangla, 221, 224–25, 227–29, 234
Jones, Puma, 91
Journey to Jah (album), 131, 143
Journey to Jah (film), xi, 133, 141–43
"Journey to Jah," 143
Judaism, 190
Juttla, 227

Kabaka Pyramid, 139
Kahlo, Frida, 201, 203, 208
karaoke, 169–71
Kardinal Offishall, 125
Karnik, Olaf, 143
Kawashima, Marcia, 170
Kebede, Alem, 106
Kelley, Robin D. G., 66
Kemist, Kris, 137
Kennedy, John F., 102
Kenny, Kevin, 159–60, 162
Kent, Mary Mederios, 93
Khan, Imran, 227
Kheshti, Roshanak, 45
King Arts Complex, 104
Kingston, Jamaica, 90–92, 114, 119, 121, 142
Knottnerus, David, 106
Koffie, Hattie, 95–96
Kōhaku Utagassen, 171
Köhlings, Ellen, 132, 144
Kola Loka, 67
K-os, 119, 121
KRS-One, 120
Kuipers, Giselinde, 111–12

"La gozadera," 64
Lalon, 223–24
L.A. Luv, 120, 123
Lamarque, Libertad, 40–41

Landero, Andrés, 40, 42, 48
"La Niña Robot," 59
"La número uno," vii
"La panchita," 205
"La Piragua," 47–49
"La Puteri," 67
Lara, Agustín, 40, 203
Laruelle, Francois, 79
"Last Call," 174
"La tequilera," 205
Latin America, 24, 33–36, 38–39, 41, 47, 50, 57, 60, 66, 189–200, 203, 205
Latino Nodojiman, 181
La Tropa Colombiana, 42
Laure, Mike, 41–42
Lawrence, Stephen, 160
Legacy Recordings, 67
Leibniz, Gottfried Wilhelm, 77–79
Lembranças, 174
"Lembranças," 174–75
Lennon, John, 155
Levy, Barrington, 105
Ley de Responsabilidades Políticas, 197
Light of Saba, 96
Lilly, Pete, 132, 139–40, 144
Lima, Gusttavo, 180
Lo major que suena ahora, 69
London, England, ix, xi, 10–12, 17–18, 151–53, 155, 157, 158, 221–25, 229, 231–32, 234–35; bombings, 159–60, 231; Brick Lane, 220, 226–31; dance halls, 7, 16; East London, 218, 220–25, 228–29, 234; Irish bar circuit, 161; Irish community, 3, 6, 12, 156; Irish music, 4, 6, 10, 12–13, 149; Metropolitan Police, 160; Tower Hamlets, 221–22, 226
"Looking for the Real Nigga," 66
López, Cristóbal, 44
López, Marina Díaz, 196
L'Oqenz, 117
"Lo que te mereces," 58
Los Aldeanos, 58–60, 64
Los Confidenciales, 67
Los Corraleros de Majagual, 39–40, 42, 48

Los Cuatro, 67
Los Panchos, 40
"Los Tarzanes," 205
Los Vallenatos de La Cumbia, 42
"Loud and Proud and Bold," 153–54
Lourenço e Lourival, 168
Luciano, 105
Lydon, John "Johnny Rotten," 155
Lynch, Jerry, 8–9
Lynn, Terry, 141

MacGowan, Shane, 149, 153–55
Madden, Joe, 13–14
Madrid, Spain, 190, 193, 198
magazines, 135–36, 138. *See also specific magazines*
Maldonado-Torre, Nelson, 34
Malone, Mary E., 151
Maloney, J., **15**
Mannix, Craig "Big C," 118
Manuel Villanueva, 39
Marc, Isabelle, 134
Marcia e João Victor, 181, 184
marginalization, x, 4, 24–27, 32–35, 37–38, 40, 42–44, 50–51, 69, 71, 109, 115–19, 124–25, 177, 183, 196, 201, 203, 205
Marley, Bob, 97, 98, 100–102, 103–5, 107, 132, 137–39. *See also* Bob Marley and the Wailers
Marley, Damian, 137, 141
Marley, Ziggy, 105
Marley Legend, 105
Marsh, Tim, 231–32
Martín, Eloísa, 24
Masouri, John, 137
"May the Road Rise with You/Go N-éiri an bóthair leat," 161–62
McAdam, Doug, 112
McCartney, Paul, 155
McDermott, Kevin, 11
MC Lyte, 121
McMahon, Martin, 17
McMahon, Teresa, 17

Mead, George Herbert, 110
media industry, xii, 63, 118; Cuban, 59; Latin American, 64; Mexican, 39–42, 49; Spanish-language, 190–91, 193; United States, 64
Meditations, 105
Mellow Mood, 138
melody, 74–75, 78, 81, 84–86
Memorial Hall, 93–94
Menen, Empress, 107
Menilek II, 94
Merali, Shaheen, 233
Mertz, Kathryn, 33
Meuleman, Roza, 112
Mexican cinema, 189, 191, 193–98; campesinos, 201; el charro figure, 194–95, 197, 208; época de oro, 189, 191, 194–95, 197, 206–7
mexicanidad, xii, 189, 200–208
Mexico, viii, xii, 189, 191, 193–208; Revolution, 189, 194, 198, 205–7
"México lindo y querido," 195–96
Meza, Lisandro, 40, 48
Miami, FL, 66–67
Micha, 67
Michael, Ras, 101
Michelob, 106
Michie Mee, xi, 109, 112, 114–16, 119–26
Mignolo, Walter, 35, 51
migrants and migration, vii–viii, xii–xiii, 39, 42–43, 63, 71, 95, 109, 113, 134, 159, 162, 190; Bengali, 220–21; Brazilian, 167–68; Caribbean, 109, 113–14, 124, 131; coerced, 159, 161; dekassegui, xi, 166–68, 170–75, 177, 184–85; Irish, 3–4, 7, 9, 16; Muslim, 219; urban, 167–68, 180. *See also* immigrants and immigration
Mike Laure y sus Cometas, 39
"Minha Deusa," 184
Miranda, Michael Sierra, 60, 68, 71
Miss Ena's Caribbean Kitchen, 95
Mistura de Raças, 178, **178**
Miyazato, Ivan, 169

Mokonnen, Tafari. *See* Selassie, Haile
Molino, Aniceto, 40
Molk, Florence, 208
Mo Magic, 224–25, 227
Montemayor, Diego de, 35
Monterrey, Mexico, viii, ix, 24–31, 33–46, 49–51; industrialization phase, 36–37; *la colombia*, 25–26, 28, 30, 31, 32–34, 40, 42, 45–46, 50; La Independencia, 25, 30; Loma Larga, ix, 25–27, **26**, 29–31, 43, 49; mining, 35, 37; Puente del Papa bridge, viii, 25, **26**, 30; San Pedro Garza García zone, 25
More or Les, 18
Moving Hearts, 155
Mumbai, India, 73–74
Munhos e Mariano, 181
Murphy, Delia, 11
Musashi University, 166, **173**, 182
music: acid house, 228–29; Baul, 223–24, 226, 229, 231; Bengali, 230; bhangra, 225, 227–28; British Asian, 224, 226–27, 229, 234; canciones de protesta, 198–99; canciones rancheras, 207; céilí bands, 6, 8, 10–13; Colombian, 28, 30, 32, 34, 39–40, 42, 45, 48–50; country, 168, 204; Cuban, 57, 61–62, 67; cubatón, viii, x, 57–71; cumbia, viii, ix, 24–28, 30, 32–34, 37–42, 44–45, 47–51; cumbia rebajada, ix, 24–25, 27, 29–32, 34–35, 38–49, 51; dance, 182; dancehall, viii, x, xi, 68, 91, 99, 111, 119, 121–23, 131–34, 136–40, 144–45; duplas, 168, 179–82; forró, 182–83; hip hop, x, xi, 57–61, 64, 66–71, 109, 112, 115, 117–26, 228; Indian classical, 75–76; industry, 57, 59, 109, 124, 131, 190–93; Irish, xi, 3–18, 149–63; jazz, viii, 5, 7–8, 144; J-pop, 172, 174–75, 198; *la colombia*, 25–26, 28, 30, 31, 32–34, 40, 42, 45–46, 50; Latin, 57; mariachi, vii, 48, 195–96, 200–202, 206; Murong, 223; música ranchera, viii, xii, 189, 191–92, 194–97, 200–208; música sertaneja, viii, xi–xii, 166–69, 172, 174–77, 179–85; música tropical, 27, 39, 42; Nazrulsangeet, 220, 223, 227; popular, x, 8, 11, 13–14, 34, 59, 74, 115–21, 125–26, 131–42, 145, 150, 175, 179, 218–19, 224; psychoceilídh, viii, xi, 149–50, 153; punk, xi, 149, 153, 156, 158; rap, viii, x, xi, 59, 66–67, 69, 71, 109, 115–26, 144–45; reggae, viii, x, xi, 90–93, 96–107, 119–20, 122–23, 125, 131–34, 136, 138–45; reggaetón, 57–59, 61, 66–71; Rock and Roll, 11, 115–19, 158, 200; timba, 57, 59; urban, 116, 118; vallenato, 42, 44–46
Music and Social Movements, 106
musicking, 38, 41
Mutaburuka, 91

Nagel, Joane, 18
Nagoya, Japan, 170
Nakanishi, Yasushi, 174
Nakanuma, Hiroshi, 181–82
Nanny, 96
Nazrul Islam, Kazi, 220, 223–24
Neck, xi, 149–63
Negrete, Jorge, 195–96
Negril Jamaica Records, 99
Nelson, Ron, 116
Nelson, Rosemary, 160
Nettleford, Rex, 92
Newman, Carl, 93, 98–99
New York City, NY, ix, 12–14, 17–18, 121, 152, 157; Bronx, 13, 17, 120–21; dance halls, 7, 9, 13, 16; immigration to, 12, 16; Irish music, 4, 9, 10, 12, 13
NHK, 169–71
Nipomed Sistema de Saúde, 173–74, 176, 180
NME, 229
nodojiman, 169–74
Northern Ireland, 159, 162
"Note on Sanskrit Ghanda, A," 83
Novo Tempo, 181
Now Generation Band, 105
Now magazine, 124
Nuevo Reino de León, 35

Oasis, 155
O'Brien, Jimmy, 13
O'Byrne DeWitt, Ellen, 14
O'Byrne DeWitt, Justus, 14
Ó Ceannabháin, Jimmy, 10
Ochoa, Kelvis, 70
O'Connell, Connie, 5
O'Donoghue's Pub, 161
O'Flynn, John, 155, 162
Of Universal Synthesis and Analysis, 77
Ohio, viii, x, 90–93, 96, 105–6. See also individual cities
Ohio State Monitor, 94
Ohio State University, 95, 99, 100, 103
O'Keefe, Leeson, viii, xi, 149–63
Okuyama, Kaori, 181–82
Olvera Gudiño, José Juan, 24–25, 28–29, 39
Olympia Theatre, 202
O'Neill, Diarmuid, 160
"On this Mic," 122
oral histories, ix, 4, 96, 102, 121, 207
Orishas, 69
"Os três Boiaderos Japoneses," 168
"Ourselves Alone," 159
Outcaste, 224–25
Outlines of Pyrrhonism, 82
Owens, Joseph, 92

Pacheco, Adolfo, 46
Pakistan, 219–20, 224; East Pakistan, 220; West Pakistan, 220
Palacio de Bellas Artes, 202
Pará, José María, 35
Parveen, Farida, 224
Patrice, 139
Peace Corps, 91, 97, 103, 237
"Pedaço de Chão," 175
People Existing in All Colors Eternally, 79
Pepillo, Goza, 70
Pérez Prado, Dámazo, 40
Perry, Lee "Scratch," 139
Perry, Marc, 58, 60, 66
Personal Reflections of Rastafari in West Kingston in the Early 1950s, 90

Peru, xiii, 24, 33, 50
Pfleiderer, Martin, 144
Phenomenology of Internal Time Consciousness, The, 85
Philipps, Helmut, 137, 143
Pierson, José, 196
Piña, Celso, 48
Piñón, Juan, 64
Piper, Heather, 159
Piper, Keith, 233
piracy, 27, 32–34, 50
Pitbull, 69
place, vii–x, xiii, 45, 156
Planxty, 155
"Plastic and Proud," 156
"Plastic Paddy," 156
Pogues, 153, 155
politics, x, xii, 34–38, 42, 51, 59–60, 66, 68, 136, 190, 199–200, 204–5, 218–24, 233; Irish, 6; Mexican, 193–97; Spanish, 191–93, 197
Popcaan, 139
Popes, 153–54
"Por el bulevar de los sueños rotos," 203
poverty, 73, 136, 142, 223
Power, Vince, 153
Pressure Busspipe, 138
Priest, Maxi, 137
Prieto, Abel, 66
Prieto, Nydia, 44
Public Dance Halls Act of 1935, 6
Puerto Rico, 66, 68, 70

Queen, Sister, 104
¡Qué pasó raza! magazine, 44
Quijano, Aníbal, 34
Quinn, Louis, 14

"Raça e Ginga Misturou," 178–79
race, 24–25, 27, 33–38, 40–42, 45, 49–51, 60–61, 63–65, 67, 70–71, 74, 77, 93, 95–97, 109–12, 114, 116–18, 124, 126, 132, 137, 142, 145, 151, 156, 160, 179–80, 197–98,

201, 203–4, 208; African Americans, 16, 94–96, 107, 190; racial tensions, 16; white, 112–13, 140–42, 189–90
racism, 43, 109, 113–15, 118–19, 124–25, 160, 189, 220–21, 228, 231, 233
radio, 7, 115, 117–18, 190–91, 193, 196, 225
Rafferty, Mike, 12–13
Raja, Hasan, 223–24
Rajam, N., 73
Ramayana, Valmiki, 83
Ramírez, Nájera, 194
Rampton, Ben, 151
Ranks, Danny, 140
"Rap is War," 59
Ras Michael & the Sons of Negus, 101, 104
Rastafarian movement, x, 90–107, 132, 140–42, 144
Rastafarians of Jamaica, The, 92
Rastafarians: Sounds of Cultural Dissonance, The, 92
Ratts, Alex, 91
Real World label, 229
Rebel, Tony, 105
Recado, Ziggi, 138
Reckford, Verona, 92
recording industry, 12, 65, 115–16
recording media: cassette tapes, 31–33, 42, 45, 50, 228; CDs, 58, 74, 80, 98, 174–75, **176**, **178**; records, vii, ix, 7, 27–30, **28**, 32–33, 37, 40, 42, 50, 91; USB flash drives, 50, 58
record labels, 12, 27, 67, 116, 118, 139, 172, 224. *See also individual record labels*
Redmond, Shana, xiii
Reena Sari & Music Center, 228
Reencontro, 166, 176, 178, 183
Reid, Junior, 91
religion, 6, 83, 102, 151, 190, 191, 194, 198, 218, 224. *See also specific religions*
Reyes, Lucha, 189, 205–8
Reynolds, Larry, 8–9, 18
Riddim magazine, xi, 132–33, 135–42
Ring Ding, 121
Rivera, Diego, 203, 208

Rivera, Raquel, 61
Rivera-Rideau, Petra, 61
Robinson, John, 95
Rock and Roll Hall of Fame, 93
Rodríguez Magda, Rosa Maria, 75
Rojas, Nydia, vii
Rolling Stone magazine, 138
Romero, Raúl, 24
Roosevelt, Franklin D., 96
Rootdown Records, 139
Roots Records, 93, 98–99
"Run for Cover," 122

Sabina, Joaquin, 189, 199, 200, 202–5
Sadu, Itah, 120–21
Saho, Leah, 104–5
Said, Edward, 203
"Saigo no Iiwake," 174
Salon Rojo, 69
Samkhya system, 80–81, 83
Sánchez, Cuco, 189, 206–8
Santiago, Chile, 69–70
Saucedo, Leticia, 43
saudade, 168
Savage, Mike, 112
Sawhney, Nitin, 227–28
Scobie, Niel, 122–23
Scott La Rock, 120–21
Second Cinematographic Congress, 193, 196
2nd Generation magazine, 229, 232
Seeed, 139, 144
SeefarI, 93, 102, 103
Selassie, Haile, 91, 93, 95, 97, 98, 102, 103, 104, 105, 107
Semán, Pablo, 24
Serrat, Juan Manuel, 199
Sevilla, Carmen, 196
Sex Pistols, 155
Sextus Empiricus, 82
sexualization, 57, 66, 140, 193, 198, 200, 205, 224
sexual orientation, 40, 70, 110, 112, 140, 201, 205. *See also* homophobia

Shabba Ranks, 139
Shah, Lalon, 223–24
Shamsher, Farook, 228
Shamsher, Haroon, 225, 228
Sharpe, Sam, 96
Shelemay, Kay Kaufman, xiii
Shell, 222
Shriver, Thomas, 106
"Siege of Ennis," 6
Siempre tuya, 195–96
Silva, Elizabeth B., 112
Silverman, Carol, xiii
Sizzla, 98, 105, 139–40
Skankland, 99
Skatalites, 96
slavery, 35, 40, 62, 70, 77, 96, 113, 137, 142
Small, Christopher, 38
Small, Millie, 132
social class, 12, 14, 24–25, 33–38, 42–43, 45, 49–51, 63, 69–70, 74, 110, 138, 198, 205, 207–8, 224, 229
socialism, 60, 191–92, 194, 197, 205, 208
soldaderas, 205–7
Sol Guy, 119
Solitair, 116, 118
Sonho de um Brasileiro, 175, **176**, 177–78
"Sonho de um Brasileiro," 175
Sonido Dueñez Hermanos, 26, 29, 31
sonidos and sonideros, ix, 26–33, **28**, 37, 39, 50
Sony Music, 64, 67
sound, vii, ix–x, 9, 14, 18, 29–31, 38, 45, 47–48, 50, 57–58, 70, 74–76, 78, 80–82, 85, 100, 106, 122, 134, 138, 142–45, 150, 154–56, 166, 168, 185, 202, 207, 226–27, 229
Sounds of Crossing, xiii
sound systems, 28–30, 32, 50, 90, 221
South Africa, 90, 159
South Asia, 218, 221, 225, 229, 232–33
Southerly, Ben, 105
Soviet Union, 57–58
spaces, viii–x, xii–xiii, 6, 10, 45, 49, 59, 62–63, 66, 71, 110, 168, 171, 183, 185, 192, 202; aural, 45, 179; cultural, 45, 230; liminal, ix, 7, 16, 18; Rasta, 92; reggae, 91, 98; urban, 59
Spain, xii, 189–208; blockades, 192, 197; Civil War, 194; el pacto de silencio, 199–200; EU membership, 189, 199–200, 203; franquismo, 189, 191–93, 197–99, 202
Spencer, William, 91–92
spirituality, 101, 140–44
Spitalfields Community Festival, 230
Spitalfields Market, 230
Springer, Moritz, 141
sruti, 82, 84, 86
State of Bengal, xii, 221, 225, 227–29, 234
Statistics Canada, 114, 116
Steffens, Roger, 99, 100
Stephens, Richie, 141–42
stereotypes, 160, 203–4; ethnic, 12, 180; gender, 196; Irish, 158; mexicanidad, 203; national, 196; racialized, 49, 180
Stewart, Addi "Mindbender," 117
Stinson, Matt, 103
St. Lucia, 100–101
Stone-Davis, Férdia, 150
St. Patrick's Day, 158
Strangers in the Ethnic Homeland, 177
Strazdina, Ilze, 226
Strickland, Will, 116
Sturm, Sebastian, 138
Sugarman, Jane, xiii
Sullivan, Caroline, 226
Summerjam Festival, 143
Sunshine Sound Crew, 121
Super Grupo Colombia, 48
Swami, Ashish, 73, 76, 80, 86–87
Sweet 'n' Spicy, 230

Tagore, Rabindranath, 223–24
"Taj Mahouse," 229
Taymor, Julie, 201
technology, 30–31, 33, 47, 49, 63, 69–70, 193, 226

Tegala, Simon, 232
Tehuanas, 201
Televisa, 190
television, 39, 41, 49, 64–65, 102, 112, 135, 193, 198, 221
Teló, Michel, 180
Thakur, Omkarnath, 74
Thatcher, Margaret, 159
Thin Lizzy, 155
Third World, 91, 105
333, 225
"Tide Is High, The," vii
Tokunaga, Hideaki, 174–75
Tokyo, Japan, 166, 170–71, 184
Tone Dialing, 74, 80–81, 83–84
Toronto, Ontario, viii, xi, 109, 112–26; Greater Toronto Area (GTA), 114, 123; Toronto Census Metropolitan Area, 116
Torres, Flores, 36
Tosh, Peter, 93, 139
tourism, 58–59, 65–66
Tovar, Rigo, 39, 41–42
"Traigo un amor," 205
transduction, viii, 79, 83
translation, viii, 75–76
transmodern totality, viii, 73, 75
transnationalism, viii, xi, 24, 27, 39, 60–71, 111–12, 120–21, 124, 126, 134, 168, 174, 177, 184–85, 193, 196–97
transposition, viii, 75–79, 82
Treaty of Guadalupe Hidalgo, 36
Trespeso's Silega y Joe, 69–70
"Tristeza do Jeca," 176
Truman Brewery, 230
Tsuda, Takeyuki, 177
Tuñón, Julia, 194
Turino, Tom, xiii
Turner, Victor, ix

Uganda, 103
United States, vii, x, 4, 7, 18, 120, 137, 155, 159, 163, 190, 191–93, 198–99, 201; Cuban diaspora, 66; dance halls, ix, 8, 9, 17; dances, 8; music, 8; racial discourses, 71; reggaetón artists, 66
Universal Negro Improvement Association (UNIA), 94
urbanization, 41, 71
Urban Music Association of Canada, 116
Usman Project, 227

Vacaciones, 69
Valdés, Luis Alemán, 194
"Vampiros," 59
van Gennep, Arnold, ix
Varèse, Edgard, 75
Vargas, Chavela, 189, 200–206
Vázquez Santana, Higinio, 207
Verboord, Marc, 112
Vibe bar, 230
Vice magazine, 120
Victor, João, 181
"Victory Is Calling," 122
Vila, Pablo, 24, 38
violence, 37, 43, 57, 140, 142, 144, 159–60, 197–98, 220–21, 231
Vistelas, Orlando, 66
Visualizate, 69
Vybz Kartel, 139

Wade, Peter, 41
Wailer, Bunny Livingston, 93
Wailers, 105. *See also* Bob Marley and the Wailers
Walcott, Rinaldo, 109, 111, 119–20, 124, 125
Walters, Basil, 97, 100
Warner, Oswald S., 114
Warner, Remi, 119
Watkins, Amanda, 43–44
Weeknd, The, 115
Welsch, Wolfgang, 132–33
West Indian Domestic Scheme, 113
White, Mo, 229, 232–33
White, Mrs. J. E., 94
Whitechapel Art Gallery, xii, 219, 220, 226–30, 232, 234–35

Williams, Oswald "Count Ossie," 92
Wisniewski, Richard, 96
Wong, Ketty, 24, 33
Wunder, Gee, 115

X-Alfonso, 70

Yared, 102
Yasmin, Nilufer, 223
Yeats, William Butler, 161
Yeiko, 68
"Yo me muero donde quiera," 205
youths: Black ghetto, 145; British Bangladeshi, 221–22, 224–25, 230; *colombia*, 42–46, 49, 51; Cuban, 58–59, 69, 71; European, 132; Japanese, 184; radicalized, 199

Zaddach, Wolf-Georg, 144
Zaman, Deedar, 224, 231–32
Zaman, Sam, 221, 224–25, 229
Zarazúa, José Carlos, 44
000: British Asian Cultural Provocation, xii, 219, 226–29, 231–35
Zezé Di Camargo e Luciano, 181
Zinc Fence, 91
Zumba fitness, 64, 67
Zurbano, Robert, 70

www.ingramcontent.com/pod-product-compliance
Lightning Source LLC
Chambersburg PA
CBHW030616230426
43661CB00053B/2009